THE LONGING FOR
TOTAL REVOLUTION

THE LONGING FOR
TOTAL REVOLUTION

Philosophic Sources
of Social Discontent
from Rousseau to Marx
and Nietzsche

Bernard Yack

UNIVERSITY OF CALIFORNIA PRESS
BERKELEY · LOS ANGELES · OXFORD

University of California Press
Berkeley and Los Angeles, California

University of California Press, Ltd.
Oxford, England

Library of Congress Cataloging-in-Publication Data

Yack, Bernard, 1952-
    The longing for total revolution : philosophic sources of social
discontent from Rousseau to Marx and Nietzsche / Bernard Yack.
        p.   cm.
    Originally published: Princeton, N.J. : Princeton University Press,
1986, in series: Studies in moral, political, and legal philosophy.
    Includes bibliographical references and index.
    ISBN 0-520-07852-7 (alk. paper)
    1. Revolutions.   I. Title.
JC491.Y33 1992
321.09'4—dc20   91-37848

For my mother and father

CONTENTS

PREFACE TO THE PAPERBACK EDITION   xi

PREFACE   xvii

ACKNOWLEDGMENTS   xxiii

INTRODUCTION   3

Longing and Social Discontent   3
Misleading Religious Analogies to Modern Discontent   10
The Philosophic Sources of the Longing for Total
Revolution   18
An Outline of the Argument   27

Part One

ONE. MONTESQUIEU'S AND ROUSSEAU'S APPEALS TO
CLASSICAL REPUBLICANISM   35

The Appeal to Antiquity   36
Montesquieu's Appeal to Classical Republicanism   40
Rousseau's Longing for Ancient Virtue   49

TWO. THE NOVELTY OF ROUSSEAU'S DISSATISFACTION
WITH MODERN MEN AND INSTITUTIONS   61

The Novelty of Rousseau's Demand for Community   62
Rousseau and the Historicity of Modern Institutions   72
Rousseau and Revolution   81

Part Two

THREE. THE SOCIAL DISCONTENT OF THE KANTIAN LEFT   89

From Rousseau to Kant   90
The Kantian Left   98

CONTENTS

The French Revolution and the Kantian Left 107
Total Revolution and the Spirit of Modernity 118
The Three Waves of Left Kantian Speculation 125

FOUR. SCHILLER AND THE "AESTHETIC WAY" TO FREEDOM 133
Schiller's Social Discontent before Kant and the
   Revolution 134
Schiller's Critique of the Spirit of Modern Society 147
Aesthetic Education and Political Community 164
To Become Whole Again 177

FIVE. HEGEL: THE LONGING TAMED 185
The Young Hegel's Social Discontent 188
Hegel's Resignation to the Limitations of Human
   Freedom 209

Part Three

SIX. THE SOCIAL DISCONTENT OF THE HEGELIAN LEFT 227
Hegel and the Hegelian Left 230
Cieszkowski and the Third Epoch of "Praxis" 234
Left Kantian Echoes in Left Hegelian Social
   Criticism 238
Feuerbach and the Return to Nature 247

SEVEN. MARX AND SOCIAL REVOLUTION 251
Marx's Categorical Imperative 255
New Answers to Old Questions 261
Communism 264
The Capitalist Mode of Production 269
Proletarian Revolution 280
Contradictions Underlying Marx's Concept of
   Communism 290

EIGHT. NIETZSCHE AND CULTURAL REVOLUTION 310
Human Dignity and the "Bildungsphilister" 314
The Historical Sense and the Spirit of Modern Culture 322

CONTENTS

Nietzsche's Longing for Tragic Culture and Hegel's
    Acceptance of the "Death of Art"   329
"The Most Interesting Animal": Nietzsche's Later
    Understanding of Man's Humanity   341
Nietzsche's Longing for Great Politics: The
    "Spiritualization of Cruelty" and the Cruelty of the
    Spirit   356

CONCLUSION   365

BIBLIOGRAPHY   370

INDEX   387

PREFACE TO THE PAPERBACK
EDITION

IN THE YEARS since the original publication of *The Longing for Total Revolution* an epoch in political history has come to an end with the collapse of communism in Eastern Europe and the former Soviet Union. In coming years, the cooling of cold-war passions may create a better environment for understanding the especially intense and violent forms of social discontent that have characterized this epoch. But the demise of communism seems so far to have produced only a revival of simplistic and misleading theories about the nature of modern revolutionary sentiments, the most popular of which locates the origins of totalitarianism in the wild and wilful visions of modern philosophers such as Rousseau, Marx, and Nietzsche.

The Longing for Total Revolution attempts to replace these theories with a subtler and more accurate account of the connection between philosophic ideas and modern revolutionary sentiments. Although I reject theories about the philosophic origins of totalitarianism, I still believe that philosophers make an important contribution to the peculiar breadth and intensity of modern forms of social discontent. But I locate this contribution more in their new ways of thinking about what is wrong with our lives than in their new visions of a healthy social order.

The identification of the deeper reasons for our dissatisfaction with the world is one of the most influential activities undertaken by intellectuals. Everyone can find cause for dissatisfaction with the way things are. But it is primarily intellectuals—from priests and philosophers to journalists and political organizers—who devote special efforts to explaining why the world contains these sources of dissatisfaction. Their efforts inspire new longings for social change by focussing our discontent on the deeper obstacles to human satisfaction that they uncover. Moreover, different understandings of these obstacles will inspire very different kinds of social discontent. The mystic who treats the world's impermanence as the primary reason for our dissatisfaction will not share the indignation against individuals and social institutions of those who long for a world without sin or exploitation. The Marxist who locates the obstacle to human satisfaction in a historically specific mode of social interaction will embrace worldly remedies to human suffering far more enthusiastically than will the Christian or Platonist who longs to transcend the human condition itself.

European philosophers such as Rousseau, Marx, and Nietzsche introduce and popularize a new perspective on the limitations of individuals and institutions, a perspective that tends to turn even relatively minor complaints into systematic problems that can be corrected only by a "total revolution" against the spirit of modern society. For, from this perspective, it is the "spirit" of modern individuals and institutions—the dehumanizing social ethos that shapes modern society as a whole—that accounts for our dissatisfaction with ourselves and the world. In *The Longing for Total Revolution* I try both to identify the philosophic innovations that ground this new understanding of the obstacles to human satisfaction and to show that, despite their many differences, a wide range of European philosophers and social critics share this understanding and the longings for social transformation that it inspires.

My genealogical arguments also support a critique of the call for total revolution issued by Marx and Nietzsche. They support such a critique by uncovering the unstated assumptions about freedom, nature, and history that lead Marx and Nietzsche to focus their discontent on the spirit of modern society. Once we identify and reflect upon these assumptions we must acknowledge, I argue, that the spirit of modern society, as they conceive of it, is an immovable obstacle to our satisfaction and that their goal of total revolution is a logical and practical impossibility.

In the wake of the collapse of communism one has to wonder, however, whether there remain any social theorists or revolutionaries against whom one might direct this critique. The last place one would look for traces of the longing for total revolution is among the highly conservative and defensive apparatchiks who cling to the communist legacy. And among radicals it has become fashionable, following the lead of French intellectuals, to scorn dreams of human emancipation. Many radical intellectuals, echoing Nietzsche and Foucault, now treat the attachment to morally elevated ideas of "humanity"—the purported "emancipatory subject" of world history—as a major source of mental and physical cruelty in the modern world.

But the Nietzschean echoes in the rhetoric of contemporary radicals make me wonder whether we really have turned the page on this chapter in intellectual history. In the final sections of *The Longing for Total Revolution* I try to show that Nietzsche's boasts about having overcome German philosophy and its discontents are premature and misleading. I argue there that while Nietzsche does rebel against the vision of humanity and historical progress he finds in the German philosophic tradition, he never abandons its obsession with the dehumanization of modern individuals and institutions. Nietzsche merely inverts the values bequeathed to him by his philosophic predecessors. In the end, he persists in their efforts to correct the decline of humanity in the modern world, despite his violent rejection of their more "humanistic" understanding of the truly human form of life.

Of course, the Nietzsche celebrated by contemporary radicals cuts a very different figure from the philosopher described in *The Longing for Total Revolution*. Theirs is the playful, anti-essentialist Nietzsche who gleefully informs us that there are no facts, only interpretations—the Nietzsche whom one invokes in achingly cute titles such as *Exceedingly Nietzsche* or "Reading Derrida Reading Heidegger Reading Nietzsche"—rather than the deeply discontented philosopher who strives so hard to confront and overcome the burdens of two thousand years of Christian culture. For them Nietzsche is the joyful founder of the postmodern age, rather than the desperate and self-defeating promoter of a cultural revolution against the spirit of modernity. Hence even if I am correct in my interpretation and critique of Nietzsche, it seems that postmodernist radicals have cheerfully abandoned the very elements of his thought upon which I focus my attention. For this reason, they may seem unlikely to share his longings for total revolution.

Nevertheless, there remains at least one element in the rhetoric of postmodernist radicals that makes me suspect that they have not entirely abandoned the philosophic sources of Nietzsche's social discontent. In spite of the postmodernists' repeated attacks on essentialism and foundationalism, in spite of all their scorn for historical "meta-narratives," there is one meta-narrative that serves as a philosophical foundation for all postmodernist thinking: that something called "modernity" exists and has shaped modern individuals and institutions, even if it is now beginning to lose its grip on us. Postmodernist radicals may have abandoned Marx's "fetishism of commodities," but they still cling to a *fetishism of modernities*. That the obsession with modernity is, to a certain extent, a fetish, is something that I try to demonstrate in *The Longing for Total Revolution*. It is a fetish, I argue, because it treats historical epochs such as "modernity" as if they were real dividers and shapers of human behaviour, rather than as intellectual constructs. Historical epochs, such as modernity or classical antiquity, are constructs that we design in order to highlight, through historical comparison, distinctive elements of any set of practices and institutions. With the "fetishism of modernities" these conceptual constructs come back to haunt us as the real-world obstacles to our goals. In this regard postmodernists differ from Nietzsche and the other social critics I study only in their belief that we have somehow leapt—quietly, without any revolutionary upheavals—to the other side of the real-world barrier created by modernity.

But little has changed in the world to justify claims about the advent of a "postmodern condition"—except for the ways in which postmodernists have changed their minds about the universalistic goals that once inspired them. While we may be able to escape "modernity"—i.e., the intellectual construct—by changing our minds, we cannot so easily escape the new social practices and institutions that led earlier social critics to construct the concept of modernity in the first place. When postmodernists wake up to this fact, they will have to confront all over again the distinctive social conditions that the concept of modernity was developed to highlight. At that time, some postmodernists may discover that postmodernism stands, ironically, for reconciliation with modernity, for the abandonment of the intense dissatisfaction with the spirit of modern society that characterizes the works of so many "modernist" artists and intellectuals. Others, however, may discover that they continue to be just as dissatisfied with modern individuals and institutions as Rousseau, Marx, and Nietzsche. When they make this discovery, we may witness—along with the predictable calls for a "new realism" or a "new materialism"—a new wave of the longing for total revolution. For this reason, among others, my study may continue to provide critical as well as genealogical arguments about distinctively modern forms of social discontent.

PREFACE

THE INCREASING preoccupation of historians of political thought with meta-historical and meta-theoretical issues puts some pressure on an author to make a declaration of first principles before he or she embarks on a new study in the field. I shall resist this pressure for two reasons. First, I do not present my study as an illustration of a meta-historical position. Of course, I have brought to it all kinds of intellectual baggage, which sometimes furthers, sometimes impedes my work. And by working at my materials over the years I have gained some understanding of the advantages and disadvantages of different approaches to the study of political thought. But in historical research, it seems to me, the proof is still in the pudding. We take up historical research because something interests us in the words and actions of the past. Likewise, an approach to the study of a historical phenomenon is valuable to the extent that it allows us to learn something we otherwise would not have learned, whether about the phenomenon itself and its relation to us or about ourselves and our problems. From this pragmatic point of view, the adherence to a strict and pre-defined methodology is valuable only for its ability to yield new insights.

Second, the resolution of one's meta-historical first principles prior to historical research not only is unnecessary for studies in the history of political thought, but also can be, and often has been, an obstacle to the development of insights into the phenomena that interest us. The current preoccupation with meta-historical and meta-theoretical questions has developed, in part, out of the increased sophistication with which twentieth-century philosphers have addressed problems of language and meaning. But it also bespeaks an exhaustion of interesting and provocative historical theses. The debates that rage around the recent historical works by

Quentin Skinner, John Dunn, and J. G. A. Pocock focus almost exclusively on the meta-historical questions they raise.

But while I do not offer this study as an example of the application of predetermined meta-historical principles, I do think it necessary to say something, at least, in defence of the legitimacy of my approach. Since the approach I use does not correspond to any of those most frequently defended in recent scholarly debates, I fear that suspicions of illegitimacy may cloud the minds of many of my readers.

The materials I examine in this study are a series of writings by philosophers, including Rousseau, Schiller, Hegel, Marx, and Nietzsche, whose works have already received an enormous amount of attention. These writings are commonly recognized to have played a great role in the development, or at least in the expression, of the discontent with the modern world that figures so prominently in the social and political thought of nineteenth and twentieth century European intellectuals. I try to identify and account for a particular state of mind, a form of social discontent, which these philosophers all share. I use their writings to try to show how the inadequacies of the world appear when viewed from the perspective of a particular philosophical position, a position that comprises a new understanding of human freedom and a belief in the internal coherence of historical epochs. In this way I use philosophic concepts as the context within which to identify and explain a shared uneasiness about the modern world.

Since my study enters a realm where historians of political thought have overreached themselves in the past, my approach might at first appear to exemplify the kind of flaws in postwar scholarship that have partly inspired the current preoccupation with meta-historical questions. A glance at the title and Table of Contents of this book might bring to mind Jacob Talmon and the debate about the philosophic origins of totalitarianism which his books initiated shortly after World War II. Most scholars today have little interest in that debate. They judge, correctly in my opinion, that it taught us very little about either philosophy or totalitarianism. The interesting questions, whether and how philosophic concepts have contributed to the discontent of modern European intellectuals, were lost in the flurry of accusations against and defences of philosophers alleged to have totalitarian affinities.

I do not seek in this study to reopen the debate about the philosophic origins of totalitarianism. The major problems with Talmon's studies, apart from implausible interpretations of some of his material, develop out of his attempt to find explanations in eighteenth- and nineteenth-century concepts for the horrifying cruelty of certain twentieth-century regimes. Talmon never explains how philosophic concepts might represent the "origins" of totalitarian democracy. Instead, he offers analogies between twentieth-century events and institutions and the writings of earlier philosophers and intellectuals as if they represented explanations. Talmon's failure was, I believe, inevitable, for however helpful the identification of new concepts and philosophic perspectives may be in explaining new attitudes and states of mind, I do not think they can provide the key to the explanation of later events, let alone institutions.

In this study I offer no explanations of totalitarianism, of any revolution, or even of any individual political action. Instead, I try to identify and account for a particular state of mind—a new form of social discontent shared by many European philosophers and intellectuals since the beginning of the nineteenth century—which I call the longing for total revolution. The philosophic concepts that I try to bring to light will allow us to identify and account for the character of that state of mind, not for the character of any twentieth-century political institutions.

Many students of the history of political thought might still wonder, however, whether I share with Talmon an exaggerated sense of the importance of philosophic concepts, even if I deny that they can be used as the explanatory context of political actions and institutions. Using philosophic concepts as an explanatory context even for a shared state of mind still will appear hopelessly abstract and idealistic to many scholars. However, as I argue in the introductory chapter, most of the best-known studies of revolutionary, utopian, and Messianic discontent have misconstrued the role of new concepts in generating social discontent, because they focused on the way these concepts define alternatives to present social limitations rather than on the way they shape our understanding of those limitations. My account will, I hope, make conceptual explanations of new forms of social discontent somewhat more plausible. Nevertheless, given the way contextual interpretation is commonly understood, my approach may still seem like an implausible, idealistic flight from the "real" context of political thought.

Contemporary historians of political thought, however, often show insufficient awareness of the nature and limitations of the different kinds of contextual interpretation. There are two broad categories of contextual interpretation, which between them encompass all approaches to the interpretation of historical texts. The first aims at situating the interpreted material within the totality of its possible meanings and associations. When one tries to "put something in context" in this way, one seeks, as far as possible, to avoid abstraction from the web of associations within which any act of expression takes place. The other form of contextual interpretation does the opposite. By abstracting from the complex web of associations that surrounds any individual act of expression, it constructs contexts, be they linguistic, economic, religious, or textual, which allow us to interpret individual acts of expression in terms of meanings they share with other such acts.

My study, like the majority of works in the history of political thought, falls into the second broad category of contextual interpretation. Other species of this genus include most of the currently popular approaches to the interpretation of political thought, from the Marxist's to Quentin Skinner's to the strictest textualist's. The partisans of these approaches might reject my classification. But Marxists do not usually realize that they abstract from the complex and often self-contradictory motivations behind individual acts of expression to focus on the shared interests of classes. Likewise, students of Skinner abstract from the "uncommon" usage of words by the writers they study in order to treat common usage as the reliable guide to an author's meaning. And textualists abstract from other forms of expression than the text itself in their effort to take the internal coherence of the text as their only guide to its meaning. Marxists construct class interest, Skinnerians common usage, and textualists the covers of a text as contexts for the explanation of the acts of expression that interest them. All of these approaches to the study of political thought, like mine, abstract from *the* context of political expression. None is more or less abstract than another.

But all too often the various species of this genus of contextualism, all of which involve abstraction from the "real" context of expression, claim for themselves the virtues of the other genus. A context of explanation, like class interest or common linguistic usage, presents itself as *the* context of those acts of expression and treats all attempts to construct alternative explanatory contexts as illegitimate attempts to rip that act of expression "out of context." It is only in the light of this illegitimate claim of one context to represent the context of discourse that the use of philosophical concepts as an explanatory context appears more "abstract" than the use of shared economic interest or common usage of language as explanatory contexts. Collective interest and common usage can be portrayed much more plausibly than philosophic concepts as the concrete context of political discourse. But that portrayal is a masquerade. They are no less constructions, abstractions from the context of acts of expression, than a shared set of concepts.

The context of a political discourse is, of course, something which non-omniscient creatures can only approximate. We can learn a great deal from efforts to reconstruct in the imagination the full context of an individual's or even an epoch's characteristic acts of expression. But even such imaginative reconstructions depend on the previous construction of explanatory contexts for the meanings that they attempt to integrate into the full portrait of an individual or age.

In short, the demand for an exclusive definition of the context of political discourse stems from conceptual confusion. It leads only to inflated explanatory claims and acrimonious, repetitive meta-historical debates that add little to our understanding of the past or of ourselves. Historians of political thought, like all intellectual historians, seek to identify interesting explanatory contexts for the acts of expression which they study. The value of their work rests, to a great extent, on their ability to identify *which* context will yield the greatest insights into the material studied. The selection of appropriate contexts is an art which every historian of political thought must learn, and one which, willy-nilly, they all practise.

But this art is best practised in the midst of, rather than prior to, historical research. Only familiarity with our material will help us determine which context will yield the most interesting results.

Princeton, New Jersey
October 1985

ACKNOWLEDGMENTS

I WOULD like to thank the Canada Council, the Mellon Foundation, and Princeton University for financial support that allowed me to begin and complete this study. I am very grateful to the friends and colleagues who put so much time and thought into discussing my work and locating my errors. I benefited immensely from the insights of the following scholars, all of whom made their way through the entire manuscript in one of its many incarnations: Rüdiger Bittner, Marshall Cohen, Don Herzog, Stephen Holmes, Rogers Smith, Tracy Strong, Charles Taylor, and Dennis Thompson. Discussions with Samuel Assefa, Allan Bloom, Harvey C. Mansfield, Jr., Zbigniew Pelczynski, Pat Riley, Jerry Seigel, Paul Sigmund, Adam Sloane, Peter Stillman, Robert Tucker, and Michael Walzer about portions of the work and the authors examined therein were also very helpful and encouraging. I note, with special pleasure, my debt to Judith Shklar. No one could ask for a more responsive adviser or a more stimulating friend. Finally, I express my deep gratitude to Marion Smiley. Her insights have improved each chapter and forced me to think through problems I would have otherwise ignored. Her unending patience, interest, and encouragement have made difficult work a pleasure.

THE LONGING FOR
TOTAL REVOLUTION

INTRODUCTION

Longing and Social Discontent

THERE are moments in our lives when we cannot help but be filled with disgust at the dangerous, vulgar, and unruly aspects of human society. At these moments, we long to escape the limitations of our social existence. Since such sentiments are probably coeval with civilized life, it is not surprising to discover that there has been a longing for social transformation in every culture and every historical epoch. On the other hand, the intensity, direction, and impact of this longing vary enormously from one epoch and culture to another. The longing for social transformation can manifest itself as a gentle nostalgia for a distant past or as a violent yearning for the Apocalypse; it can focus on particular objects and institutions or make us uneasy with all of our social relationships; it can provide an individual with a pleasant diversion or inspire mass movements.

This study seeks to define and account for a specifically modern form of the universal longing for social transformation, a form of longing that takes shape in the minds of European philosophers and intellectuals at the end of the eighteenth century. There is little doubt that since the French Revolution, European intellectuals have been prone to especially intense and violent longings for social transformation; their discontent has been the subject of much study. This discontent clearly takes many forms and has many, often conflicting sources; I do not attempt here to examine them all. Instead, I try to define and account for one particular form of discontent, a state of mind shared by a group of extremely influential European philosophers and social critics, including Rousseau, Marx, and Nietzsche. In particular, I attempt to show how the development of a set of new concepts in the last half of the eighteenth century makes possible an especially intense form of social discontent which I call the longing for total revolution.

3

The horrifying acts committed by the twentieth century regimes that claim some of these social critics as their prophets have imparted to the study of their social discontent a special significance and urgency. Many scholars have set out to discover the "origins" of totalitarianism in the ideas and attitudes of eighteenth- and nineteenth-century European philosophers.[1] I do not try in this study to follow in their footsteps. As I have suggested in the Preface, the hopes of finding the key to twentieth-century institutions in the ideas of eighteenth- and nineteenth-century philosophers have encouraged an emphasis on analogies between the ideas and the institutions that distorts our understanding of both. Robespierre once warned students of the French Revolution against being misled by analogies between the revolutionary regime and the institutions advocated by political philosophers. "The theory of revolutionary government is as new as the revolution that leads to it. You should not search for it in the books of the political writers."[2] I take Robespierre's warning about misunderstanding revolutionary institutions to be as relevant for us as it was for his contemporaries.

Totalitarian regimes have developed out of events and circumstances that their founders, let alone their purported forefathers, could not foresee. At best, a reconstruction of the state of mind of the latter can contribute to an understanding of totalitarian actions and institutions only indirectly, by shedding some light on the attitudes brought to them by some of the participants in those events. Whether my study makes such a contribution, I leave to others to determine. Although it would be unrealistic to expect any late twentieth-century scholar to be deaf to totalitarian

[1] The first and most influential of these attempts is Jacob Talmon's *The Origins of Totalitarian Democracy*. Talmon's book, along with other works published shortly after World War II, sparked a debate about the alleged totalitarian affinities of great political philosophers, a debate that influenced most scholarly treatments of their ideas throughout the 1950s. Although this debate no longer dominates Anglo-American discussions of the history of political thought, it has surfaced again in France with the rediscovery of totalitarianism by the generation of 1968. See, for example, A. Glucksmann, *The Master Thinkers*, B. H. Levy, *Barbarism with a Human Face*, and J. Mareijko, *Jean Jacques Rousseau et la dérive totalitaire*, for recent French attempts to discover the origins of totalitarianism in the ideas and attitudes of the philosophers.

[2] M. Robespierre, *Oeuvres*, 10:274.

4

resonances in the texts with which I shall deal, I still think it best, in reconstructing the attitudes and ideas expressed in these texts, to abstract from such resonances as much as possible, especially if one is interested in how the social discontent of these philosophers has contributed to later developments. For without a clear picture of those ideas and attitudes apart from the needs and goals of later generations, it will be impossible to understand how and to what extent later generations of intellectuals, on whom any study of the intellectual background of the establishment of totalitarian institutions should focus,[3] appropriate those ideas and attitudes.

To identify and account for the particular state of mind that I call the longing for total revolution, we first need to look at the phenomenon of "longing" in general; for longing itself is a peculiar and rarely examined state of mind. Kant, in his *Anthropology*, provides a useful definition of it. Longing, he suggests, is "the empty wish to overcome the time between the desire and the acquisition of the desired object"; an "empty wish" he defines as a wish "directed toward objects for whose production the subject himself feels incapable."[4] The subjective awareness of the inability to produce a desired object distinguishes a longing from a desire and allows us to account for the different attitudes which we associate with these two states of mind. In both longing and desire we feel the uneasiness created by the lack of a desired object. But while in desire our uneasiness focuses on the desired object, thus promoting attempts at its acquisition, in longing the awareness of our present incapacity to acquire the object diffuses our uneasiness. The energy produced by that uneasiness has no obvious outlet—thus the vague, generalized feeling of uneasiness which most of us associate with longing.

---

[3] Like Zeev Sternhell I welcome the recent studies that turn away from the search for intellectual "ancestors" of fascism and totalitarianism in the writings of philosophers "from Plato to Fichte" and concentrate instead on the more immediate intellectual environment out of which these movements grow. See Z. Sternhell, "Fascist Ideology," 315-77, 360-61. See also K. D. Bracher, "Turn of the Century and Totalitarian Ideology," 70-80. Some of the best of these studies include F. Stern, *The Politics of Cultural Despair;* H. S. Hughes, *Consciousness and Society: The Reorientation of European Social Thought;* and Z. Sternhell, *La droite révolutionnaire 1885-1914,* and *Ni droite, ni gauche: L'idéologie fasciste en France.*

[4] I. Kant, *Anthropology: From a Pragmatic Point of View,* 155.

But the general sense of uneasiness associated with longing is not as aimless and unproductive as is commonly thought. Indeed, I suspect that it is one of the most important prods to intellectual inquiry. The awareness of our present inability to satisfy desires tends to refocus our uneasiness on the obstacles to achieving this satisfaction. We tend to wonder about what prevents the satisfaction of our desires; and our present uneasiness increases the urgency of such reflections. When we discover the obstacle to our satisfaction we generate a new object of desire: a world without that obstacle to our satisfaction. And if we find ourselves incapable of removing this obstacle, our desire becomes a longing which, in turn, generates the definition of new objects of desire. In this way longing tends to generate, at higher levels of reflection, new desires and longings. I want my lover when she is by my side; I long for her when we are separated; I desire the destruction of stratified societies when I discover that it is class difference that keeps us apart; I long for a classless society when I become aware of obstacles to the overcoming of social stratification.

One of the most characteristic activities of the intellectual, whether as priest, philosopher, or ideologist, is the definition of obstacles to our satisfaction. Intellectuals search out the connections between seemingly unrelated phenomena and thus provide us with deeper explanations of our dissatisfaction with the world. In this way the concepts which they develop redefine objects of desire and longing.

One aim of this study is to demonstrate that the discovery of new objects of hatred can, as much as the discovery of new ideals of a good life, generate new forms of the longing for social transformation. Most attempts to characterize and account for the social discontent of modern philosophers and the intellectuals they have influenced have focused on new ideals, rather than on new obstacles. This approach has proven somewhat problematic with regard to the figures studied here, especially Marx and Nietzsche, since they have so little to say about the content of a good life. How could such a weak and undeveloped image of the good life inspire such intense longing? To answer this question, those who study these philosophers in this way usually try to tie their discontent to other traditions of social criticism, the most important of which are messianism and utopianism, which have more fully developed visions of the good life. In the following section of the Introduction, I shall argue that the evidence usually cited to justify appeals to the Messianic tradition is inadequate. In this section I try to show that such appeals are unnecessary. They only appear necessary because insufficient attention has been paid to the way that new understandings of what we should hate generate new objects of desire and longing.

Let us begin with the presumably unobjectionable assumption that in every age individuals experience dissatisfaction. Longing would then be as universal a phenomenon as desire. We should further expect that a second level of desire and longing, for a world without obstacles to our satisfaction, also would be a universal phenomenon.

We reach historically specific expressions of the longing for world transformation with reflections on why we cannot satisfy our desire for a world without obstacles to our satisfaction. The way the obstacle to such a world is defined shapes the character of new desires and longings. The Platonist who sees the impermanence of the world as the major obstacle to satisfaction will not share the indignation against individuals and institutions of those who long for a world without sin or exploitation. The Marxist who sees a particular form of social interaction as the obstacle to satisfaction will not reject the world in the same way as the Christian or Platonist who sees the ontological condition of man as the source of our dissatisfaction. Uncovering new definitions of the obstacle to a world without sources of dissatisfaction is thus one way to identify new forms of social discontent.

The longing for total revolution develops out of a redefinition of that obstacle first suggested in the second half of the eighteenth century: the "dehumanizing" spirit of modern society. For the last two centuries, the greatest source of indignation among European intellectuals educated in the German philosophic tradition has been the "spirit" of modern social relations. The conditions of modern life, it is said, deform and dehumanize individuals. Modern men, then, are somehow less than human. They are not real men; they are bourgeois, philistines, last men—nothings. One of the greatest

7

indignities that modern society imposes on us is that it teaches us to think that human beings can be nothing more than the small-minded and slavish creatures we see around us. We should not judge humanity, it is said, by the characteristics of individuals living under modern conditions. They do not represent the full measure of humanity. Only if we escape the iron cage of modern society, only if we get beyond the spirit in which modern man thinks, lives, and relates to others, will we know men who are fully human.

This complaint is one of the most frequently repeated refrains in the discourse of modern intellectuals. We can hear it both on the radical left and right, among those who measure humanity by egalitarian and inegalitarian standards, among those who long for the overcoming of social injustice, of cultural philistinism, or of human weakness. It is raised by, among others, Marx and Nietzsche, is echoed by their philosophic heirs from Marcuse to Heidegger, and resonates, less clearly, among the countless intellectuals and artists they have influenced. There is great disagreement about the specifically human characteristic that modern society dehumanizes—labour, the capacity for self-overcoming, our closeness to Being—as there is about what defines the spirit of modern society—the mode of production, moral values, culture, race. But all who make this complaint express at least two basic attitudes which define their shared state of mind: modern man is not fully human, and to become human man must get beyond the debilitating spirit of modern social interaction. Despite the bitter disagreements among them, this state of mind, I suggest, is something that is shared by Rousseau, Schiller, the young Hegel, Marx, Nietzsche, and most of their twentieth-century disciples.

I shall try to identify and account for the characteristics of this new form of social discontent in terms of its philosophic sources, that is, the concepts that make possible the designation of the dehumanizing spirit of modern society as the obstacle to a world without social sources of dissatisfaction. I shall then show how this redefinition of the obstacles to our satisfaction generates a new and more intense form of social discontent which I call the longing for total revolution.

The longing for total revolution develops out of reflection on the obstacles to overcoming the dehumanizing spirit of modern society. Such reflections begin among German Kantians, such as Schiller, Schelling, and the young Hegel, in reaction to the events of the French Revolution. In 1793, Schiller asks himself why the revolution against irrational privilege and authority failed to free the French. He answers that a political revolution will never succeed, by itself, in ending the dehumanization of man.[5] Marx later echoes Schiller's argument when he states that "political" emancipation tends to blind us to the need for real, "human" emancipation. Political transformation simply does not reach the real sources of our dehumanization.[6] What is needed, Schiller writes, is "a total revolution in his [man's] whole way of feeling."[7] The term "total revolution" is introduced here by Schiller, and used later by Marx, among others, as a contrast to the partial, "political" revolution that took place in France.[8] The Communist revolution, Marx argues, will be a "total revolution," aimed at the "mode of activity" which degrades man. "In all revolutions up to now the mode of activity remained unchanged, and it was only a question of a different distribution of this activity."[9] The obstacle to the overcoming of the dehumanizing spirit of modern society is located by these social critics in some fundamental, sub-political sphere of social interaction which shapes human character. The removal of this obstacle requires a total revolution: a revolution which transforms the whole of human character by attacking the fundamental sub-political roots of social interaction.

[5] F. Schiller, *On the Aesthetic Education of Man*, Letter 3.

[6] K. Marx, "On the Jewish Question," in Marx & Engels, *Werke* (hereafter *MEW*), 1:369ff.; translated in Marx & Engels, *Collected Works*, (hereafter *CW*), 3:167ff. (Except where otherwise noted, citations of the works of Rousseau, Schiller, Hegel, Marx, and Nietzsche refer first to editions in the original language and then, after a semicolon, to translations of these works. All editions used are listed in the bibliography.)

[7] F. Schiller, *Aesthetic Education*, Letter 27, 204.

[8] The concept of "total revolution" seems to have been first introduced by Friedrich Gentz, Edmund Burke's German translator and popularizer. He used it as a way of distinguishing and negatively characterizing the French Revolution. See K. Griewank, *Der Neuzeitliche Revolutionsbegriff*, 201.

[9] K. Marx, *The German Ideology*, in *MEW*, 3:38-39; *CW*, 5:54.

Total revolution thus designates in this study a revolution in what is perceived as the definitive sub-political sphere of social interaction, rather than a comprehensive and simultaneous attack on all social institutions. All who long for total revolution recognize that political institutions are secondary obstacles to human satisfaction. Some go so far as to deny that political revolution is a necessary part or means of such a transformation. Schiller, for example, looks to "aesthetic education" to bring about the "total revolution in man's whole way of feeling" that is necessary to human emancipation. Marx, however, joins the need for total revolution conceived by the German philosophic tradition to the French tradition of political revolution. I shall argue in Chapter 7 that he thus redirects the aim of revolutionary politics toward a philosophically defined target, the "mode" of social production. With Marx, the discontent generated by the longing for total revolution becomes, for the first time, an important element in the discontent of modern revolutionaries.

Misleading Religious Analogies to Modern Discontent

Before proceeding to my own account of the conceptual sources of the longing for total revolution, I must discuss the often-noted analogies between the social discontent expressed by modern intellectuals and that expressed by earlier Christian thinkers and rebels. For these analogies have suggested the most influential and, I shall argue, misleading contextual explanations for the discontent of modern intellectuals: the attempts to explain their discontent in terms of religious concepts such as religious faith, messianism, and world redemption.

Modern intellectuals, it is repeatedly said, never completely overcome the religious sentiments that they attack so violently. They may attack the content of Christian faith in the name of critical rationalism, but they keep its spirit. They may not believe in the divine perfection of heaven, but they do believe in the possibility of such perfection on earth. They have "secularized" faith, not overcome it. According to this view, *faith* in the possibility of a perfect secular order is the source of modern intellectuals' intense dissatisfaction with social institutions. The passion they express is old and familiar: the longing for the divine perfection of heaven or for the Messianic end of days. The specifically modern element of this attitude is the secular character of the object of their faith.

The persistence of the spirit of Christian faith among professedly anti-Christian philosophers and revolutionaries has been asserted so often and in so many ways that the relevance of religious concepts to the explanation of modern social discontent is rarely questioned today, even by those who are suspicious of the broad claims that usually accompany "secularization" arguments. When Carl Becker proposed his argument about the persistence of religious faith among the *philosophes,* he sought to turn conventional opinion on its head.[10] That atheistic intellectuals may express "secularized" religious ideas and sentiments is hardly a shocking claim today. Indeed, it seems almost a commonplace. Concepts such as "political messianism," "revolutionary faith," and "religion of revolution" crop up in most studies of modern discontent. They are so familiar that they no longer need an argument to explain or justify their use. For example, James Billington subtitles his recent history of revolutionary movements since the French Revolution, *Origins of the Revolutionary Faith.* "Modern revolutionaries," he suggests, "are believers no less committed and intense than were Christians and Muslims of an earlier era. What is new is the belief that a perfect secular order will emerge from the possible overthrow of traditional authority."[11]

One would expect such a claim to be followed either by an analysis that demonstrates that religious and revolutionary attitudes represent two species of the genus "faith" or by a genealogy that brings to light the historical roots of the latter in the set of attitudes inherent in the former. But Billington provides us with neither. Repeated reference to these analogies has made their explanation unnecessary. The author can count on the reader's familiarity with the arguments suggested by the analogies. Billington's remarks indicate that he leans toward the first argument, that religious and

[10] C. Becker, *The Heavenly City of the 18th Century Philosophers.*
[11] J. Billington, *Fire in the Minds of Men: Origins of the Revolutionary Faith,* 3.

revolutionary discontent are species of the same genus. More often, however, casual references to these analogies imply the historical argument about the origins of the discontent of modern intellectuals in religious attitudes. Such an argument points to the "secularization" of the substance of a religious concept or attitude such that it can appear in an unexpected nonreligious form. Typical of this argument is the statement, "Millenarianism did not disappear, only its Christian content; . . . a revolutionary chiliasm *sprang* from faith in absolute power."[12] (Emphasis added.)

It is not surprising that historians, philosophers, and sociologists have been attracted to the religious analogy. Religious fanaticism is one of the only precedents we have to help us make sense of the intense passions for social change expressed in the last two hundred years. The first uses of the religious analogy, by anti-Jacobins and early students of the French Revolution, were designed to impress upon readers the intensity of revolutionary passions. They also used it to embarrass the partisans of revolutionary enthusiasm by proclaiming that their passions derived from the attitudes of their enemies. Volney, for example, complains even in the 1790s about what he calls the "Hebrew fanaticism" of the revolutionaries. He blames Rousseau, among others, for giving religious fanaticism a new outlet.[13]

But what can the reference to religious sentiments and concepts actually tell us about modern forms of discontent? As a means of impressing upon us the intensity of modern feelings of discontent, the religious analogy certainly has its value. But the very power of the metaphor has, I believe, misled many scholars who try to explain the social discontent of modern European intellectuals. Instead of asking why modern, secular expressions of discontent *resemble* the passions of religious fanaticism in their breadth and intensity, they have tried to use earlier religious sentiments to explain the form and/or origin of modern discontent.

It is the intensity of revolutionary discontent that suggests the analogy to religious forms of discontent. For example, Billington,

[12] R. Nisbet, *The Sociological Tradition,* 11.
[13] C. F. de Volney, *Leçons d'histoire,* in Volney, *Oeuvres,* 592. Toqueville also uses the religious analogy in his description of revolutionary passions in the opening pages of *The Old Régime and the French Revolution,* 10-13.

as already noted, insists that "modern revolutionaries are believers no less committed and intense than were Christians and Muslims of an earlier era."[14] But instead of asking what in modern attitudes leads to such intense forms of dissatisfaction, many historians, like Billington, ask themselves what it is that promotes the *religious believer's* rejection of social institutions, and then they look for traces of a similar attitude among modern intellectuals. For the religious believer, faith in the divine perfection of a heavenly or Messianic kingdom promotes the total rejection of contemporary society. For the modern unbeliever, it must be faith in a perfect human order which produces a longing for total revolution. In this way the degree of intensity characteristic of both religious and revolutionary discontent generates the assumption that they also have the same structure.

The late Jacob Talmon's indictment of modern European philosophy in *The Origins of Totalitarian Democracy* and *Political Messianism* is the best-known and most influential attempt to explain the discontent of modern European intellectuals in terms of religious analogies. His works provide abundant examples of the fallacies that plague most such attempts. Yet although contemporary historians of political thought show little respect for his arguments, they still make frequent use of some of the concepts he popularized, such as "political messianism" or "revolutionary religion."

Talmon attempts to define one "religion of revolution" that includes philosophers like Rousseau, Hegel, and Marx; nineteenth-century revolutionaries of every stripe; and the founders of twentieth-century totalitarian institutions. He describes the philosophers as the "high priests" of the revolutionary religion. And the passion which drives them all is called "political messianism," the faith in the immanence of a perfect secular order.[15] Like Volney and other anti-Jacobins, he clearly expects to embarrass the supporters of revolution by unearthing the religious sources of their enthusiasm.

But even Talmon, the most relentless proponent of the relevance of religious categories to the explanation of the discontent of mod-

[14] J. Billington, *Fire in the Minds of Men*, 3.
[15] J. L. Talmon, *Political Messianism: The Romantic Phase*, 17-18; idem, *The Origins of Totalitarian Democracy*, 2, 8-11, 17-18.

ern intellectuals, never goes beyond the exploitation of suggestive analogies.[16] His use of these analogies suggests a secularization argument. For example, by castigating the political messianism of the right as "bastard messianism," Talmon implies that left-wing messianism is somehow a legitimate offspring of religion.[17] Yet Talmon never recites the story of its conception. He provides no genealogy to establish paternity. Thus he never makes clear whether political messianism owes its origin to religious messianism or merely expresses itself in similar ways, even though his concepts provide a plausible explanatory context for modern discontent only if the former is true. Talmon assumes that the analogies he has uncovered provide sufficient evidence of a fundamental continuity in the expression of social discontent to justify the use of religious concepts to explain secular discontent.

Like far too many historians who suspect unexpected continuities over traditionally recognized historical dividing lines, Talmon proceeds as if the discovery of similarities between phenomena on either side of the division is, in itself, a demonstration of structural continuity. Like them, he commits the fallacy of turning analogies into explanations. And like Billington, he asks what the similarities he has discovered explain, rather than what explains these similarities. His "explanations" of modern discontent are merely extensions of the original analogies. If modern intellectuals' behaviour shows some similarity to that of religious fanatics, then, he concludes, they must share motivations—they must have a religion of revolution, a political messianism, and a secular faith in redemption.

Despite the continued use of many of Talmon's concepts, there have been few serious attempts to supply the missing argument that would justify this use. Most secularization arguments are advanced in a casual and uncritical way.[18] To be worthy of serious consideration, a secularization hypothesis must provide more than

---

[16] See J. L. Talmon, *Totalitarian Democracy*, 8-11, 63, 253, and idem, *Political Messianism*, 25, 80-81.

[17] J. L. Talmon, *Political Messianism*, 514.

[18] For examples and a brilliant critique of the most familiar types of secularization explanations, see H. Blumenberg, *The Legitimacy of the Modern Age*, 3-120.

an elaboration of analogies between religious and secular phenomena. These analogies only suggest to us the possibility of a process of secularization. An advocate of a secularization hypothesis must, at least, point to evidence of a process by which religious attitudes gain a place in self-consciously secular forms of discourse and then generate the same kind of sentiments among unbelievers that they inspired in their religious context among believers.

Very few of the attempts to explain the social discontent of modern intellectuals by means of a secularization argument provide this kind of evidence.[19] Most such explanations, like Norman Cohn's well-known study of mediaeval millenarianism, usually offer much detail about one end of the supposed process of secularization, be it the religious roots or the modern growth, but little about the process itself.[20] On the rare occasions when scholars attempt to trace the process of secularization, they are often compelled to exaggerate the importance of marginal, transitional figures in their genealogies of modern attitudes. For example, the *Testament* of Jean Meslier, a renegade eighteenth-century priest, is the key link in Charles Rihs's secularization argument, since it provides the most striking expression of a historical conjunction between religious messianism and atheistic revolutionary sentiments. But even Rihs has to admit that Meslier had little influence on French revolutionaries and socialists.[21]

Yet the social discontent of modern intellectuals is one of the most frequent targets of secularization hypotheses. What makes

---

[19] The most serious and persuasive examples of such studies, such as E. L. Tuveson's study of the origins of the idea of progress among seventeenth-century English writers, *Millenium and Utopia*, have too narrow a focus to demonstrate that the longing for social transformation discussed here represents a secularized form of a religious state of mind. One might say that Melvin Lasky tries, in *Utopia and Revolution*, to extend Tuveson's argument by suggesting a connection between the discontent of nineteenth- and twentieth-century European intellectuals and the utopianism of seventeenth- and eighteenth-century English writers. But Lasky does not trace out the course by which eighteenth century ideas and sentiments were transferred to their later forms. He merely adds remarks about analogies to contemporary states of mind to the great amount of detail on English utopianism that he presents in his study.

[20] N. Cohn, *The Pursuit of the Millenium.*

[21] C. Rihs, *Les philosophes utopistes,* 143ff. See also G. Niemeyer, *Between Nothingness and Paradise.*

secularization explanations seem so plausible, apart from suggestive analogies, is a general expectation of continuity in historical development. If there is any similarity between earlier and later attitudes, we expect that our knowledge of the past will help explain
what follows. Secularization arguments thus often tend to rely on
what Peter Gay aptly calls "spurious persistences."[22] But, in fact,
secularization arguments themselves often offend expectations of
continuity. The expectation of continuity in historical development
should work against arguments that focus on the secularization of
Jewish and Christian ideas and attitudes, for "to speak of secularization . . . only shift[s] the difficulty to the question of when the
historically constant quantity was originally 'desecularized.' "[23]
Secularization arguments assume that the "de-secularization" introduced by Christianity is the fundamental discontinuity in Western history. They are thus, despite their appearance, arguments
about where to locate the most important discontinuities in Western history. But since they object to a location of discontinuity in
the more recent past in favor of a much older discontinuity, the
prejudice in favour of historical continuity still lends them plausibility.

In the end, as Hans Blumenberg points out, most secularization
explanations can be reduced to the convincing but uninformative
thesis that modern developments are unthinkable without earlier
religious developments, as in the claim that "the modern age is unthinkable without Christianity." Such a claim is, of course, undeniable. "Much in the modern age is 'unthinkable without' the
Christianity which went before it. So much one would expect in advance of any deep inquiry. But what does it mean in the particular
case of concrete characteristics?"[24] This formula only points towards preconditions of modern developments, preconditions that
only a fool would forget. It does not provide explanations of any
"concrete characteristics."

The most serious attempt to trace the discontent of modern philosophers back to religious sources, and the attempt that touches

[22] P. Gay, "Carl Becker's Heavenly City," 27-51.
[23] H. Blumenberg, The Legitimacy of the Modern Age, 29.
[24] Ibid., 30.

most directly on the state of mind I shall be examining, is Karl Löw-ith's *Meaning in History*.[25] But Löwith makes this mistake of iden-tifying the preconditions of modern attitudes with their explana-tion. He presents a powerful and mostly persuasive argument that the triumph of Christian over Greek views of history is a necessary precondition of modern conceptions of human and historical devel-opment.[26] But this argument only amounts to showing that mod-ern philosophies of history are "unthinkable without" Christian at-titudes toward history. No modern attitude or institution would be quite the same without the preceding fifteen hundred years of Christianity, but there is a vast array of possible developments that would be compatible with Christian preconditions. Each would gen-erate very different intellectual, social, and political consequences. An examination of Christian preconditions of modernity can only show us the limits within which future developments will take place. It can neither account for which path of development is taken within these limits, nor help us very much in understanding the consequences of taking that path.

In short, although many historians and philosophers have been intrigued by the religious analogies to the discontent expressed by modern intellectuals, they have offered little evidence to justify the explanation of modern forms of social discontent in terms of reli-gious categories. Instead, they merely point to religious precondi-tions of modern developments or extend and elaborate the original analogies. In the following section I suggest that we can explain these analogies, without reference to religious categories, by turn-ing to the questions and desires generated by philosophic perspec-tives introduced in the second half of the eighteenth century.[27] The

[25] K. Löwith, *Meaning in History*, 1-19, 191-203.

[26] Similar problems plague Eric Voegelin's attempts to trace modern social discon-tent back to Gnostic sources. See E. Voegelin, *The New Science of Politics*, 124-28, and *Science, Politics, and Gnosticism*. See also L. Kolakowski, *Main Currents of Marxism*, 1:11-80; cf. especially 1:23-24 to *The New Science of Politics*, 128.

[27] Blumenberg, on the contrary, suggests that analogies to religious attitudes among modern secular philosophies arise because old questions, associated with re-ligious inquiry, continue to be asked and addressed to the new secular philosophies. Analogies arise through the "reoccupation" of old "question positions," rather than through the secularization of the content of religious faith. See H. Blumenberg, *The Legitimacy of the Modern Age*, 47-52. However enlightening this approach may be

search, inspired by these analogies, for religious sources of modern discontent is, in the present case, unnecessary.

The Philosophic Sources of the Longing for Total Revolution

I have suggested that conceptual innovations can generate new desires and longings by identifying the obstacles to our satisfaction, obstacles which we become aware of in longing for a desired object. By reconceptualizing our situation in the world, we alter the perspective from which we reflect on our dissatisfactions. The discovery of a new understanding of the obstacles to our satisfaction makes possible a new desire, a desire for the removal or overcoming of those obstacles.

This is the sense in which I speak of new ways of conceptualizing human freedom and history as the "philosophic sources" of the longing for total revolution. These philosophic concepts provide a perspective that suggests the possibility that the obstacle to a world without sources of dissatisfaction is the dehumanizing spirit of modern society. I do not mean to suggest that the longing for total revolution is a necessary consequence of the new concepts I examine. Every new conceptual perspective opens up far more lines of inquiry than can possibly be actualized. That some possibilities rather than others are actualized often depends on factors external to the concepts themselves. And possibilities actualized, in turn, direct old questions along narrower paths, while opening up a new range of possible paths of inquiry. Thus one can never deduce a later intellectual development from its conceptual sources; even the most obvious corollaries of new concepts are sometimes left undeveloped. But one can show how a conceptual innovation opens up particular lines of inquiry that make possible later intellectual developments, even when they stray very far from the context in which the original innovation was presented.

Of course, by focusing on the lines of inquiry made possible by

---

with regard to the issues and thinkers Blumenberg examines, to follow him in the cases studied here would grant too much to the secularization thesis. I shall try to show that the questions examined here, as well as the answers, are generated by new philosophic perspectives.

particular conceptual innovations to the exclusion of lines of inquiry opened by other innovations, conceptual or non-conceptual, I abstract, to a certain extent, from the context within which the authors whom I study express themselves. But as I suggested in the Preface, some abstraction from the context of acts of expression is a necessary, if unacknowledged, feature of almost all studies in the history of political thought. I cannot, and do not wish to, demonstrate that this context is the only context in which to study the social discontent of modern intellectuals. Other perspectives will bring to light and account for interesting phenomena which mine leaves untouched.

That one can profitably look at acts of expression from more than one perspective does not imply, however, that all contexts are equally appropriate as explanations of all acts of expression. Different explanatory contexts must still meet standards of evidence before they can be considered appropriate to a given subject matter. In particular, two kinds of evidence are required before one should consider the use of conceptual innovations as a context for the explanation of later intellectual developments. First, one needs to show that the later thinkers did in some way encounter and become familiar with the new conceptual perspective. Second, one needs to show that this perspective in some important way structures their inquiries. The great majority of the attempts to explain the discontent of modern intellectuals in terms of religious categories provide neither kind of evidence and thus never justify themselves. My discussions of Rousseau, Schiller, Hegel, Marx, and Nietzsche present the historical and analytic evidence that supports my use of new concepts as an explanatory context for the discontent shared by these philosophers. But before turning to these individual philosophers, let me outline how the new concepts I discuss make possible the redefinition of the obstacle to a world without sources of dissatisfaction and suggest how they might help explain commonly noted analogies between religious states of mind and the discontent expressed by these figures.

The longing for total revolution, I have suggested, develops out of reflection on the failure of the French Revolution to achieve what some German Kantians perceived as its goal: the overcoming of the

dehumanization imposed on modern man by the spirit of his institutions. But how does the "dehumanization" imposed by peculiarly modern forms of social interaction come to be seen as the
obstacle to our satisfaction with our social world? Complaints about
"inhuman" or "inhumane" institutions, institutions that subject
human beings to unnecessary and unjustified cruelty, are probably
universal. But complaints about dehumanization, the uprooting of
one's humanity by social institutions, are not. They develop only
at the end of the eighteenth century in Western Europe.

To see the dehumanizing spirit of modern society as the obstacle
to our satisfaction, one must believe at least two things about human life. First, one must think of the "human" as a term of distinction among individual human beings, not just as what distinguishes man from animal. Man can be, and usually is from this
perspective, less than human. The humanity of man is thus an
achievement, not a species characteristic. The second belief is that
there is a general spirit of interaction that informs all social phenomena in a given epoch. The underlying unity of all social phenomena makes the achievement of a "human" life through individual effort or excellence impossible. When institutions do not in
some way create or embody our humanity, they dehumanize us.
The spirit that informs these institutions can then be seen as the
means of dehumanization. New ways of thinking about freedom
and history spread these two beliefs, especially among German intellectuals, at the end of the eighteenth century.

First, let us examine the new way of thinking about freedom. The
use of "human" as a term of distinction among men develops out
of the new understanding of freedom introduced by Rousseau and
Kant. For them, freedom gives us our "human" character in that it
allows us to oppose our own ends to those imposed on us by nature
and society. To follow the impulses of our nature, no matter how
satisfying, is not "human" behaviour.[28]

Such an understanding of man's humanity would have made lit-

---

[28] Rousseau, of course, values the satisfactions of the natural life, even if they do
not meet the standards of human dignity, far more than does Kant. See Chapter 1
for a discussion of Rousseau's ambivalence toward both natural inclination and
moral freedom.

tle sense to philosophers before Rousseau and Kant. Traditionally, the humanity of man was associated with the species difference that defines human nature. To respect human dignity was to respect man's distinctive natural capacities. But Rousseau and Kant perceived a threat to that understanding of human dignity in eighteenth century philosophizing about human nature. And, as Jean Ehrard has shown in his study of the idea of nature in eighteenth century French thought, their perception was accurate.[29] The same eighteenth century thinkers who used the concept of human nature as a weapon against the tyranny of irrational and conventional privilege were rendering that concept meaningless through their empiricist analyses of human behaviour. What is human nature if nature itself, let alone human convention, produces infinite variations in the life and character of men? The studies of the variations in behaviour produced by climate and *moeurs,* so popular among the *philosophes,* brought into question the concept of a single, unified human nature that entitles man to special respect. Nevertheless, most of them continued to rely on that concept in their battles against conventional hierarchies.[30]

Rousseau and, even more decisively, Kant challenge this ambiguous understanding of man's humanity. Rousseau questions the identification of man's distinctive humanity with his nature. The natural condition, however desirable, is for him a *pre-human* condition. The socialization of man, notwithstanding the misery it has created, has changed the human creature "from a stupid, limited animal into an intelligent being and a man." Purely natural inclinations, however much Rousseau longs for them, provide no guide to man's humanity, "for the impulse of appetite alone is slavery."[31] The citizen gains his dignity by opposing natural inclination. Political education is a process of "denaturing."[32] Rousseau thus opens up a dichotomy between humanity and nature which Kant refor-

[29] J. Ehrard, *L'idée de la nature en France dans la première moitié du XVIIIème siècle,* 1:252ff.

[30] Ibid.

[31] J.-J. Rousseau, *On the Social Contract,* in Rousseau, *Oeuvres Complètes,* 3:364-65; 56.

[32] J.-J. Rousseau, *Emile,* in *Oeuvres Complètes,* 4:250; 40.

21

mulates and popularizes as a dichotomy between human freedom and natural necessity. By distinguishing between man's humanity and his natural inclinations in this way Kant can defend human dignity against sceptical attacks. And with the *Critique of Pure Reason* Kant believes he can demonstrate that no external or internal conditioning can rule out the possibility of a freely willed act.

Kant's critical philosophy rescued the twin aims of Enlightenment philosophy: the advancement of scientific knowledge and the emancipation of man from arbitrary, conventional authority. At least so it seemed to his German heirs, which accounts for the tremendous influence of his arguments. His dichotomy between human freedom and natural necessity, I shall argue, forms the conceptual foundation upon which all of the most influential nineteenth century German moral philosophers and social critics, even those like Marx and Nietzsche who explicitly reject it, erect their positions. As a result, the new understanding of man's humanity is an important part of their perspective on modern individuals and institutions.

Let me now turn to the new way of thinking about history, the second conceptual innovation that makes possible the identification of the spirit of modern society as the obstacle to a world without sources of dissatisfaction. It represents one form of the set of attitudes toward social development that has come to be called *historicism*. Historicism is another philosophic perspective, with roots in the eighteenth century, that comes to dominate nineteenth century German social thought. In general, it can be defined as the belief that "the adequate understanding and assessment of the value of a phenomenon depends on the place it occupies in the overall process of development."[33] All versions of historicism demand explanation and evaluation of individual phenomena in terms of the historical context of their development. But the different species locate that context in different ways. Herder, for example, looks to the origins of a people in order to bring to light the underlying character of its institutions. This version of historicism was especially important to

[33] M. Mandelbaum, *History, Man, and Reason*, 42.

Humboldt, Ranke, and the German "historical school."[34] Another common approach locates the context of individual phenomena by relating them to perceived general laws of historical development. This is the form of historicism that most scholars attribute to St. Simon, Comte, and Marx.[35]

However, it is another, less well-defined form of historicist approach that interests us here. Rather than uncovering origins or general laws of development, it uses historical comparison of epochs to identify the specific character, or spirit, of social interaction that informs individual phenomena. Employing, in particular, ancient/modern comparisons, it is commonly used to articulate the peculiar character of contemporary society by comparing it to the spirit of past epochs.

Montesquieu is the father of this form of historicism, Hegel its greatest master. Montesquieu's concept of the "general spirit" of the laws had a great influence on the development of historicism in general. As Hegel writes, "Montesquieu proclaimed the true historical view, the genuinely philosophic position, namely that legislation both in general and in its particular provisions is to be treated not as something isolated and abstract but rather as a subordinate moment in a whole, interconnected with all the other features which make up the character of a nation and an epoch."[36] The application of Montesquieu's concept of the general spirit of the laws to the comparison between ancient and modern institutions had a tremendous impact on those social critics like Rousseau, Schiller, and the young Hegel, who were already accustomed to locating the flaws of modern institutions in terms of the strengths of the ancients. Montesquieu's concept of the general spirit provided the conceptual tool required for more powerful social explanations of the frequently noted contrasts between ancient and modern societies. It thus reinforced the tendency to use ancient/modern contrasts to bring out the failings of modern institutions.

Two important influences on philosophically educated intellectuals at the end of the eighteenth century strengthened their incli-

[34] See Humboldt's formulation in his essay "On the Historian's Task."
[35] M. Mandelbaum, *History, Man, and Reason*, 47.
[36] G. W. F. Hegel, *Philosophy of Right*, paragraph 3.

nation to analyze social institutions in terms of epochal breaks and comparisons. The partisans of the Enlightenment had taught intellectuals to think of themselves as the promoters and defenders of a new epoch in the history of man. To break through the darkness of the past age into the light of the new era—that was the vocation of the *philosophe* and the *Aufklärer*.[37] Moreover, reflection on the Revolution in France inclined intellectuals, especially in Germany, to look toward a new epoch break as the means of overcoming what dissatisfied them in modern society. As Enlightenment intellectuals had defined themselves as the harbingers of a new age, so these thinkers defined themselves as the harbingers of a new post-Enlightenment, post-revolutionary epoch, which would leave behind the limitations of the present epoch, introduced, in part, by the Enlightenment and the French Revolution. Comparison of modern institutions with the institutions of earlier epochs pointed to the limitations of the new epoch ushered in by the Enlightenment. The Copernican revolution that introduced the Enlightenment had to be repeated. The critical intellectual must reverse and thus transcend the perspective of the modern epoch.[38]

These new attitudes toward human freedom and historical context make possible the new interpretation of the obstacles to a world without sources of dissatisfaction that I have outlined above. The Rousseauian-Kantian understanding of human freedom introduces a new way of viewing the failings of social institutions: institutions that do not in some way embody our freedom to define our own ends strip us of our humanity. And the failure of social institutions to recognize and embody our humanity is seen as *the* obstacle to a human life only when all social phenomena are viewed as part of an interdependent whole. If the same spirit of social interaction informs all institutions and individual actions, there will be no "human" sphere of society into which we can escape to develop our humanity. Given this perspective on the world, we must choose between accepting the inevitability of dehumanization or searching

[37] K. Griewank, *Der Neuzeitliche Revolutionsbegriff*, 195.

[38] For an interesting discussion of the repeated demand for "Copernican" reversals, see H. Blumenberg, *The Legitimacy of the Modern Age*, 445ff., and *Die Genesis der Kopernikanischen Welt*, 99ff.

for a means to hasten the end of our epoch. Those who choose the latter express the desire to overcome the spirit of modern society, and it is out of this desire that the longing for total revolution develops.

The discontent generated by this redefinition of the obstacle to a world without sources of dissatisfaction has a breadth and intensity comparable to that of the Christian fanatic. The discontent of Messianic radicals, for example, is so intense partly because they believe that the redemption of the world hastens their own redemption. The fate of the institutions they hate determines the success of their pursuit of psychic health. The destruction of the old order redeems *their* souls as it cleanses the world. The end of the old world ends their dissatisfaction with themselves.

In a similar way, psychic health also rides on the fate of social institutions for Rousseau, the young Hegel, Marx, and Nietzsche. Social criticism is for them also self-criticism, for the limitations of modern society are the limitations of modern man. This is one reason why their discontent is personal and intense. When Voltaire cries *écrasez l'infame* or Diderot demands that the last king be strangled with the guts of the last priest, they leave no doubt that the enemy is without, not within. Rousseau, on the other hand, writes that "all institutions which put man into contradiction with himself are worth nothing."[39] For Rousseau, the defects of society are within us, not just around us. The inhumanity of our social relations is our inhumanity, no matter what role we play in society. Most individuals are unaware of this, but Rousseau, like many later social critics, knows his own inhumanity since he understands both what freedom demands and the interdependence of all social phenomena. He may hate the prevailing spirit of social interaction, but he also knows that he cannot escape it within the boundaries of contemporary society.

Pointing to the underlying spirit of social interaction as the obstacle to our satisfaction tends to broaden feelings of discontent with contemporary society. It focuses particular sources of dissatisfaction, be they political, social, cultural, psychological, or aes-

---

[39] J.-J. Rousseau, *Social Contract*, 3:464; 128.

thetic, on the underlying spirit which informs all social interaction. Since one cannot adequately understand particular problems in abstraction from the spirit of the whole, dissatisfaction with a particular feature of modern society easily grows into total rejection. When one views the world from this perspective, dissatisfaction with the world can easily reach a level of intensity similar to that reached by the religious fanatic who rejects the world and longs for world redemption.

But while this understanding of the obstacle to our satisfaction may promote total rejection of modern institutions, should it not also lead to resignation, since only an unprecedented *total* revolution can produce any significant change in our lives? Not necessarily, since it also tells us that the sources of all our fundamental problems are historical and, therefore, changeable. A comparison between epochs both brings to light the inherent limitations of our society and teaches us that these limitations are not necessary conditions of human existence. Thus Rousseau suggests that without our knowledge of the Spartans, we might think man could be nothing more than he is today.[40] And Marx argues that without our knowledge of earlier modes of productive activity, capitalism and the bourgeois forms of individual freedom and social interaction would remain mysteries to us, immutable, eternal truths.[41] If the obstacle to our satisfaction is a particular historical form of social interaction, then our limitations are not inescapable.

The most profound and influential social critics of the nineteenth and twentieth centuries, philosophers like Marx and Nietzsche, profess disdain for speculative visions and a determination to ignore all abstractions. Yet their social criticism combines expressions of unlimited longing with claims of uncompromising realism. Does this prove that two souls, one visionary, the other scientific, war within their breasts? I think not. Their understanding of the obstacle to a world without sources of dissatisfaction promotes a total rejection of modern institutions that can present itself in good conscience as realistic, anti-utopian, and even scientific. For it is their

[40] See J.-J. Rousseau, *Oeuvres Complètes*, 3:83.
[41] K. Marx, *Capital*, in *MEW*, 23:90; 87.

analyses of present and past societies, not their visions of the future, which inspire their discontent. Marx and Nietzsche devote almost all of their intellectual energy to uncovering the nature and causes of the specific limitations of modern man and society. Genealogical studies and cross-epochal comparisons constantly bring to light the specific limitations of modern life. At the same time, by emphasizing the historicity of our limitations, their studies reinforce hope that these limitations can be overcome. Their hopes for the future are thus defined by the negation of the limitations of the present, not by utopian blueprints or secularized remnants of religious visions. Although one may indeed call it utopian to plunge forward into a future defined only by the negation of the obstacles to satisfaction, such utopianism is inspired by hatred of present obstacles, not by an infatuation with kingdoms of the imagination.

An Outline of the Argument

Although the larger part of this study deals with German thinkers, I begin in Chapter 1 with an exploration of Rousseau's dissatisfaction with modern individuals and institutions. Rousseau's social criticism provides a suitable beginning for the study of almost any European intellectual development of the last two centuries, for there are few new states of mind which he did not in some way anticipate. His expressions of discontent are especially relevant to the study of modern German philosophy and culture. No foreign or even native writer had a greater influence on the extraordinary group of philosophers and poets who produced, between 1770 and 1830, some of the greatest works of German culture. Indeed, some of the most characteristic "German" attitudes—uncompromising moral idealism and uncompromising self-indulgence, the glorification of self-sacrifice and the exaltation of independence, the worship of nature, the longing for classical antiquity, the faith in pure feeling—are, in all their contradictoriness, Rousseauian attitudes.[42]

---

[42] Nietzsche, for one, was deeply disturbed by the Rousseauian tinge of German culture. Nevertheless, he chided his countrymen for the characteristic self-absorption which led them to forget their debt to Rousseau. See F. Nietzsche, *Human-all-too-Human*, in Nietzsche, *Sämtlichte Werke*, 2:651-52.

But I have a more specific reason for beginning with Rousseau and his appeal to the classical republics. My analysis of Rousseau's critique of modern society shows that he sees the dehumanizing spirit of modern society as the obstacle to our satisfaction with the social world. By comparing his appeal to classical republicanism with Montesquieu's, which is in many ways its source, I try to show that this new understanding of the obstacle to human satisfaction gives Rousseau's dissatisfaction with modern individuals and institutions its novel character. I then further illustrate and defend my claims about the novelty of his social discontent in the second chapter, where, among other arguments, I make an effort to distinguish Rousseau's communitarianism from that advocated by the classical political philosophers with whom he often identified himself.

In the second part of the study I turn from Rousseau to a group of Kant's most creative and influential followers, a group which I call the "Kantian left." In the third chapter I suggest that these individuals—Fichte, Schiller, Schelling, and the young Hegel, among others—come to share something very similar to Rousseau's novel conceptual perspective on modern man and society and, as a result, also come to share Rousseau's longing to get beyond the dehumanizing spirit of modern individuals and institutions. The greater part of the chapter is devoted to showing how these individuals appropriate Kant's philosophy of freedom in a way that promotes among them a concern about dehumanization that Kant himself does not share. In particular, I suggest that they develop a longing for the realization of man's humanity, a longing which Kant himself never expresses. It is this longing for the realization of Kantian freedom that defines the Kantian left in this study.

In the fourth chapter, I focus on one of the first left Kantian social critics, the poet-philosopher, Schiller. I analyze his social criticism at length in order to illustrate and defend the suggestions made in the preceding chapter. Although Schiller is not the first "left" Kantian, he is the first of Kant's disciples to identify the spirit of modern society as the obstacle to the realization of man's freedom, as well as the first to search for means of bringing about a "total revolution" to take us beyond the spirit of modern society. Thus a careful analysis of the nature and sources of Schiller's social discontent is especially significant for this study, for it sheds a great deal of light on the discontent of the social critics, such as Marx and Nietzsche, examined in later chapters. I am not suggesting that these later social critics are Schiller's disciples. Instead, I suggest that there are important parallels between the sources of Schiller's and Marx's and Nietzsche's discontent, parallels obscured by the later thinkers' anti-philosophic rhetoric. A familiarity with the conceptual sources of Schiller's social discontent will help us clear away that rhetoric.

The discussion of Hegel's social thought, which follows in Chapter 5, has two aims. First, it attempts to add to our understanding of Hegel's dissatisfaction and eventual reconciliation with the spirit of modern institutions by situating the development of his social thought in the context of left Kantian social criticism, the context constructed in the preceding two chapters. The young Hegel, I suggest, develops a diagnosis of modern society's ills very similar to that of Schiller, and he searches for means of bringing about the total revolution in individual character and perception that will fully realize our humanity in the world. But he eventually comes to believe that the obstacle to fully "humanized" institutions is insurmountable. I suggest that underlying Hegel's famous (or infamous, depending on one's point of view) reconciliation with the spirit of modernity is the recognition that the *complete* "humanization" of our social world could be achieved only if we were not "human." What makes us "human," from the perspective of those seeking to realize man's humanity, is our ability to oppose our ends to those given by nature; the *complete* externalization of our humanity in our institutions would either require us to stop acting in a "human" fashion or require nature to stop behaving in a "natural," that is, contingent and purposeless, fashion. This argument is implicit in most of Hegel's later writings and lectures. I try to make it explicit, since I believe it helps identify fundamental ambiguities and contradictions in Marx's and Nietzsche's social criticism. The second purpose of this chapter is thus to lay the foundations of a Hegelian critique of Marx and Nietzsche.

The final part of my study focuses on Marx's and Nietzsche's longing for total revolution and the reformulations of the critique of modern society out of which their longing grows. It begins, however, with a brief discussion of the social discontent expressed by left Hegelians. In Chapter 6 I suggest that much of left Hegelian social criticism represents a resurgence and reformulation of left Kantian demands and longings. In particular, I suggest that the characteristic left Hegelian demand for the "realization of philosophy" represents a reformulation of the left Kantian demand for the realization of freedom. This brief examination of the left Kantian foundations of left Hegelian social criticism serves to tie my account of Marx's longing for total revolution to the conceptual innovations discussed in the first two parts of the book. For Marx's innovations, I shall argue, represent, at least in part, new answers to left Hegelian questions—questions which themselves grow out of a resurgent left Kantian perspective on the world.

Chapters 7 and 8 deal with Marx and Nietzsche respectively. Both Marx and Nietzsche seem certain that the conceptual contradictions that Schiller struggled with and Hegel declared insoluble pose no serious obstacle to the satisfaction of the longing for total revolution. Each is confident that these conceptual problems are merely remnants of the idealist's disdain for reality. This confidence that the longing for total revolution can be satisfied removes all self-restraint from their criticism of modern institutions. But I shall argue that Marx's and Nietzsche's claims to transcend the freedom/nature dichotomy, which they scorn as the idealistic limitation of their predecessors, are unfounded. Their claims represent, I suggest, little more than the expression of a need for an argument that has been remarkably successful at masquerading as that argument itself. I try to show that the freedom/nature dichotomy represents both the indispensable foundation of their critiques of modern institutions and the obstacle that, they claim, their theories of social transformation have overcome. The dependence of their social criticism on the freedom/nature dichotomy popularized by Kant has been masked by their violently anti-idealist and anti-philosophic rhetoric. A large part of both Chapters 7 and 8 is devoted to cutting through that rhetoric to the conceptual foundations of their arguments. Stripped of their rhetorical masks, Marx and Nietzsche are, in a very important sense, left Kantians.

The story I tell thus serves a critical as well as an explanatory end. My attempt to bring to light the conceptual sources of the longing for total revolution also suggests the futility of searching for a means of satisfying that longing. By pursuing such means, I argue, Marx and Nietzsche end up at odds with themselves. On the one hand, the dichotomy between human freedom and natural necessity proves to be a key, but unacknowledged, assumption that allows them to identify the spirit of modern society as the obstacle to human satisfaction. On the other hand, they must deny that same assumption in order to conceive of the possibility of overcoming the obstacle to human satisfaction posed by the spirit of modern society. I conclude, then, that dehumanization, as Marx and Nietzsche understand it, is an immovable obstacle to satisfaction with our institutions and that the total revolution they long for is a self-contradictory goal.

PART ONE

ONE

MONTESQUIEU'S AND ROUSSEAU'S APPEALS TO CLASSICAL REPUBLICANISM

ROUSSEAU's appeal to the spirit of classical republicanism expresses a new kind of social discontent. The feeling that things were somehow better in the past is, of course, a universal sentiment. And many earlier writers appeal to the ancients as a means of criticizing their own contemporaries. But despite the many unflattering comparisons to the ancients that precede Rousseau's, his is the first to suggest that the spirit of modern social interaction is the obstacle to human satisfaction and completeness.

We have difficulty discerning the novelty of Rousseau's dissatisfaction with modern men and institutions because he borrows much of his rhetoric from earlier philosophers, such as Machiavelli, Montaigne, and Montesquieu, who also appeal to classical republicanism as a means of criticizing modern institutions. In this chapter I shall try to bring to light the novelty of Rousseau's dissatisfaction with modern institutions by comparing his appeal to classical republicanism with that of Montesquieu. For of all the earlier appeals to ancient political life, Rousseau owes the most to Montesquieu's. Montesquieu provides the account of classical republicanism that inflames Rousseau's imagination: an analysis of republican virtue as an all-embracing passion that rechannels our self-preferring inclinations toward the common good. Indeed, the famous fighting words of the *Discourse on the Arts and Sciences*, "Ancient politicians spoke incessantly about morals and virtue, ours speak only of business and money,"[1] paraphrase Montesquieu's words in *The Spirit of the Laws*: "Greek politicians . . . knew no other force but virtue to sustain them. Those of today speak to us only of manufactures, commerce, finance, wealth, and even luxury."[2]

Montesquieu, however, can recognize the force of the appeal to ancient virtue and still live with and even encourage the incessant talk of business and money. Rousseau cannot. By probing for the motives beneath the rhetoric of their respective appeals to classical republicanism, I seek to uncover the conceptual sources of their opposing evaluations of the spirit of modern institutions. My comparison of the two thinkers' use of contrasts between ancient and modern institutions thus provides the means by which I identify the conceptual sources of Rousseau's discontent with modern men and institutions.

The Appeal to Antiquity

The appeal to antiquity, an influence on almost every area of modern Western thought and culture, plays an especially important role in the development of modern political thought. Some of the most original conceptions of modern political philosophers have been introduced with appeals to ancient theory and practise—one need only think of Machiavelli, Rousseau, and Nietzsche. If we take into account the authors whose works, at least in part, were written to counter that appeal, including Hobbes (writing against the influence of Renaissance and Scholastic humanism), the Federalist (writing against the identification of popular government with the small republics of antiquity), Benjamin Constant (writing against Rousseau and Jacobinism), and Hegel (writing against the Graecophilia of his youth), we could treat a large part of the tradition of modern political thought as a controversy about the value and relevance of ancient institutions.

Indeed, the persistence of the appeal to classical republicanism in

[1] J.-J. Rousseau, *First Discourse*, in *Oeuvres Complètes*, 3:19. Hereafter, except where otherwise noted, citations of works by Rousseau will include only the title of the work and the appropriate volume and page number(s) of *Oeuvres Complètes*.
[2] C. S. de Montesquieu, *The Spirit of the Laws* (hereafter *Spirit*), bk. 3, chap. 3, in Montesquieu, *Oeuvres Complètes*, 2:252.

modern political thought has suggested to some that we should think of it as the foundation of an alternative tradition of discourse among modern thinkers, rivaling liberalism in the depth and extent of its influence. For example, in an influential recent work, J. G. A. Pocock argues that among modern republicans there is a continuous tradition of discourse, extending from fifteenth-century Florence to seventeenth-century England and eighteenth-century France and America, that relies on this appeal. The general identification of early modern political thought with the tradition of liberal discourse has, he argues, hidden this counter-tradition of "civic humanism" from view.[3]

But the variety of perspectives held by the thinkers Pocock assigns to this tradition of discourse should make us wonder whether it represents anything more than a common fund of rhetoric that can be used in the pursuit of a wide range of different and often contradictory ends. The substantive continuity of this tradition seems especially doubtful when we consider political thinkers, like Montaigne and Montesquieu, who use the appeal to antiquity to further ends favoured by early liberal thinkers.

To make sense of modern appeals to classical republicanism, we must probe beneath their rhetoric. Rather than identify the shared rhetoric of these appeals as the context that explains the social discontent of their authors, we should view the authors' discontent with contemporary institutions as the context in which to understand their rhetorical appeals to classical republicanism. Modern thinkers with very different understandings of the relationship between human needs and political institutions have found the contrast with the virtues of the ancients an attractive means of highlighting and criticizing the flaws they see in modern institutions. The grandeur of a familiar and much-admired past adds weight to their arguments. But the meaning of that past, of ancient virtue itself, changes according to what they find lacking among the moderns. Classical antiquity is not a concrete object, a collection of artistic treasures, inspirational writings, and political institutions that excite our imagination. Classical antiquity and the virtues associated with it are concepts we develop through comparing our own

[3] J. G. A. Pocock, *The Machiavellian Moment.*

art, lives, and institutions with those of the ancients. As we change the perspective in which we see our needs and institutions, so we change our understanding of the ancients. Montesquieu and Rousseau, let alone the more widely separated participants in the tradition of "civic humanism," have very different understandings of human needs and, therefore, very different reasons for appealing to republican virtue.

Rousseau appeals to Sparta and republican Rome as examples of the successful socialization of individuals. According to Rousseau, social dependence does not impose on the Spartan or Roman the painful contradictions that are the source of the modern individual's misery. His appeal to the ancients is clearly anti-liberal. The removal of constraints on the social individual's inclinations, he argues, only increases his or her misery and self-contradiction. Since Rousseau's time, many social critics have used the polis as the model from which to build homes for alienated intellectuals. But Rousseau was the first to view the polis in this way; he was the first to identify the spirit of modern social interaction as the obstacle to individual wholeness and satisfaction. Indeed, the persistent power of his rhetoric and the influence of his concepts distort our perspective on earlier appeals to classical republicanism. We tend to see the Rousseauian enthusiasm for ancient virtue where it does not exist. We have to be reminded that there are other, very different reasons for appealing to the classical republic as a model.

The most direct and obvious reason for the appeal to classical republicanism is, as noted above, to add weight to republican arguments. For early modern republicans, the records of classical antiquity were a treasure house of republican models and arguments whose age commanded respect, even in a world whose view of politics was shaped by the experience of monarchic government. While the modern Italian republics could be and were used as models against monarchic regimes, arguments for mixed regimes gained a luster from association with Roman examples and with the authority of Aristotle and Polybius that contemporary models, like the Venetian republic, could not provide.[4]

---

[4] See Z. Fink, *The Classical Republicans*, 55ff., for a discussion of this use of the appeal to classical republicanism by English republicans.

A less obvious, but even more important motivation behind early modern writers' appeal to ancient politics is opposition to the influence of the Church on modern political life. Classical politics were pagan as well as republican. The public-spiritedness of the ancient republics was achieved without a Christian education directed by an organized, hierarchical Church. The appeal to ancient virtues established, in an indirect way—often the only way it could safely be established—that a healthy political regime could dispense with the Church's moral guidance. By appealing to ancient virtues, one could safely dwell on the virtues of a secular political order while living in a Christian regime. "Our philosophers," writes Benjamin Constant, an heir of the Enlightenment and a critic of Rousseauian enthusiasm for the polis, "impelled by the desire to undermine European institutions . . . found it safe and convenient to attack them by drawing indirect comparisons. In order to render these comparisons more striking and conclusive, they searched in remote places for subjects to praise."[5] Praise for the ancient republics by Enlightenment thinkers is often, like praise of China, Persia, or the inhabitants of the New World, an indirect means of political and religious criticism. An appeal to the classical tradition, however, is for them a more powerful subversive tool than the celebration of exotic lands to the east and west. For the Church, while attacking ancient paganism, had adopted and adapted classical ideas and examples to its own purposes. Christian education spread and legitimized an interest in classical antiquity. By uncovering the true, or secular, character of ancient virtues, *philosophes* like Montesquieu could use that interest in classical antiquity to challenge the Church's claim that a healthy regime needs its moral guidance. This is the purpose of Montesquieu appeal's to classical republicanism in both *The Spirit of the Laws* and the *Considerations on the Causes of the Grandeur and Decline of the Romans*. Montesquieu's work demonstrates how the appeal to classical republicanism can serve a liberal end— the separation of politics from the demands for moral unanimity and religious guidance made by the Christian churches.

Rousseau's approach is very different. He appeals to ancient vir-

---

[5] B. Constant, *Commentaire sur l'ouvrage de Filangierie*, 2:31-32.

tue not so much to voice opposition to religious interference in politics—although a conflict between Christianity and true republicanism is inevitable for Rousseau—as to voice opposition to the kind of
individual produced by the secular society emerging from the Enlightenment's attack on the Church. Rousseau turns to the classical
republics to find a solution to the personal problems of that very individual whose interests Montesquieu seeks to liberate and secure
from the moral claims of the Church. The real novelty of Rousseau's discontent with modern institutions comes to light when we
see how differently he and Montesquieu use the appeal to classical
republicanism.

Montesquieu's Appeal to Classical Republicanism

More than any other writer, Montesquieu is responsible for the revival in the eighteenth century of interest in classical republican
politics.[6] Classical republicanism must have seemed especially irrelevant at the end of the seventeenth century in the nation dominated by the court of Louis XIV. Even the partisans of the ancients
in the celebrated "quarrel of the ancients and moderns" did not appeal to the republican institutions of antiquity. The infrequent references to Sparta by poets and philosophers in early eighteenth-
century French writing were usually adverse or frivolous. Sparta
was the butt of crude jokes and even the setting for a pornographic
novel.[7] But Montesquieu's great work, *The Spirit of the Laws*, altered the general attitude toward Sparta through its reinterpretation of the nature of civic virtue. It thus laid the foundation of the
cult of Spartan virtue celebrated by Rousseau, Mably, and their Jacobin disciples.

But unlike his followers, Montesquieu is ambivalent about the
value of the conception of political virtue that he draws from clas-

[6] D. Leduc-Fayette, *Rousseau et le mythe de l'antiquité*, 27. E. Rawson, *The Spartan Tradition in European Thought*, 227-30.

[7] E. Rawson, *Spartan Tradition*, 223. See also L. Guerci, *Libertà degli antichi e
libertà dei moderni: Sparta, Atene e i "philosophes" nella Francia del Settecento*,
11-45, for early eighteenth-century references to Sparta.

sical examples.[8] Ancient virtue seems to fascinate and repel him at the same time. He draws the contrasts between ancient public-spiritedness and modern selfishness that inspire Rousseau's enthusiasm for the polis, yet he makes his preference for the commercial spirit of the modern English regime quite clear. This combination of an appeal to ancient public-spiritedness and a defence of modern commercialism suggests to many of Montesquieu's readers that he is confused or ambivalent about the ends of government.

The confusion lies, however, in the minds of his readers, who tend to think of the appeal to classical republicanism as a homogenous tradition with one object, the encouragement of public-spiritedness among one's contemporaries. If Montesquieu means to flay his contemporaries for their lack of public spiritedness, then there is indeed an essential inconsistency in *The Spirit of the Laws*. The praise of the republican regime in the earlier Books (II-VIII would contradict his preference for the English regime in the rest of the Books (especially in Books XI-XII). Some scholars argue that the tension between Montesquieu's two models reflects a change of mind that occurred only after his long stay in England. Both his earlier and more mature preferences, they suggest, appear in the work.[9] Others argue that Montesquieu's English ideal is a synthesis of classical and modern commercial republicanism, in which public spiritedness is united with the protection of individual liberty.[10] Still others argue that the tension between the two models represents an implicit contest between Montesquieu's two contenders for the best regime, a contest decided in favour of modern England.[11]

[8] Franco Venturi's warning not to be fooled by the "classical luminescence" of Montesquieu's view of republican politics (*Utopia and Reform in the Enlightenment*, 44), is misplaced. Although not meant simply as a historical analysis of the classical republics, Montesquieu's image of republican virtue is clearly drawn from ancient models. For an exhaustive, if somewhat pedantic, description of Montesquieu's classical sources, see L. M. Levin, *The Political Doctrine of Montesquieu's Spirit of the Laws: Its Classical Background*.

[9] See R. Shackleton, *Montesquieu: A Critical Biography*, for a detailed study of the genesis of *The Spirit of the Laws*. See also R. Derathé, "Rousseau et Montesquieu," 383.

[10] M. Hulliung, *Montesquieu and the Old Regime*, ix, 2, 148, 218. D. J. Fletcher, "Montesquieu's Concept of Patriotism."

[11] T. Pangle, *Montesquieu's Philosophy of Liberalism*, chap. 4.

There is, however, a contradiction to explain only if one assumes, as most readers do, that the identification of political virtue with republican institutions represents for Montesquieu a reason for preferring the republican regime. This assumption, fostered by the connotations of the word *virtue* and our familiarity with Rousseauian rhetoric, is mistaken. Montesquieu is, indeed, an admirer of ancient virtue and its achievements. But he does not think that we should necessarily imitate that which inspires our admiration. "The heroism which morality approves touches few. It is the heroism that destroys that strikes us and causes our admiration."[12] It is the very destructiveness of the great acts of republican virtue that strikes our imagination. The grandeur of the ancients' virtues was an effect produced by the risks to which they exposed themselves. But they could only create this grandeur by imposing death and danger on others. Thus the ancients "conquered without reason, without utility. They ravaged the earth in order to exercise their virtue and demonstrate their excellence."[13]

And the civic virtue of the ancients was no less cruel to its practitioners than it was to its victims. Ancient love of country reminds Montesquieu of the perverse passion monks sometimes develop for self-laceration. Like monkish self-discipline, republican virtue deprives citizens "of all the things the ordinary passions feed on; thus there remains only the passion for the very rule that afflicts them."[14] For Montesquieu, few insults could be more damning than the suggestion of an inclination toward the morality of monks.[15] Unlike Rousseau, he never develops the taste for self-affliction that allows one to ignore or justify the afflictions imposed on others by the grand acts of ancient and monkish virtue. We should take Montesquieu at his word when he distinguishes political from moral virtue.

> It is not a moral virtue, nor a Christian virtue, it is *political* virtue; and it is the spring that sets republican govern-

[12] C. S. de Montesquieu, *Pensées*, in *Oeuvres Complètes*, 1:1305.

[13] Montesquieu, *Oeuvres Complètes*, 2:210.

[14] *Spirit*, bk. 5, chap. 2, 2:274.

[15] Nevertheless, some readers see in this description of republican virtue a sign of Montesquieu's admiration. See Hulliung, *Montesquieu*, 21.

ment in motion, as honour is the spring that sets monarchy in motion. I had new ideas; I was obliged either to find new words or give new meaning to old ones. Those who do not understand this have me speaking absurdities that would be revolting in all countries of the world because all countries of the world are partial to morality.[16]

Montesquieu's analysis of republican virtue is part of a classification of political regimes according to the predominant passion that sets the regime "in motion." Every regime, be it moderate or despotic in its exercise of power, depends on some passion to encourage individuals to obey authority and accept social constraints on their behaviour. If political regimes depended for their authority on calculation of interests, individual inclinations, or self-abnegation, Montesquieu suggests, we would have long since descended into anarchy. Passion, not rational calculation of interest or duty, leads individuals to accept social constraints. Political authority persists by drawing on some passion to restrain antisocial inclinations and interests.

Each type of regime has its characteristic passion, or "principle," as Montesquieu terms it. The republican principle is love of country, which Montesquieu calls political virtue; the monarchic principle is love of individual honour; and the despotic principle is fear. Each principle works to some extent in the other regimes but is not essential to the exercise of authority within them. The principle of a regime is its "mechanical soul," the spring that sets all of its institutions in motion and gives each regime its characteristic form of social cohesion. The principle appropriate to a particular people depends upon the "general spirit" of that people, its underlying character formed by the interaction of "climate, religion, laws, past examples, morals, manners."[17]

Although made familiar to us by Rousseau's celebration of patriotism, Montesquieu's characterization of political virtue as an unreasoning passion is something new in the history of political

[16] *Spirit*, "Advertisement," 2:227-28.
[17] Ibid., bk. 3, chaps. 1-9, especially chaps. 3-4; bk. 19, chap. 4.

thought. Aristotle called virtue a habit;[18] Montesquieu's suggestion that it is really a kind of passion probably would have shocked
him. It is not hard to imagine the horror with which Aristotle and
Plutarch would have viewed the spectacle of Rousseauian rhetoric,
in which passion, "usurping the place of reason and indignantly denying her libertine past, . . . begins to pass judgment, in the severe
accents of Catonic virtue, on reason's turpitudes."[19] Plutarch, after
all, presents Cato, Rousseau's model of patriotic passion, as a Stoic,
a model of learning and calm reflection.[20]

This understanding of political virtue also would have been foreign to Machiavelli, Montesquieu's most important predecessor as
a modern interpreter of ancient virtue. Montesquieu's concept of
political virtue accounts for the behaviour of the obedient common
soldier, Machiavelli's for the behaviour of the manipulative patrician. Machiavelli distinguishes between virtue and goodness
(*bonta*). The patricians possess the former, the plebians the latter.[21]
Machiavelli's description of plebeian goodness bears a great resemblance to Montesquieu's description of political virtue. They both
refer to an unreasoning passion that redirects self-preferring inclinations toward the common good. But for Machiavelli, such passions are not the source of virtue; rather, virtue is the capacity for
clearsighted calculation and energetic pursuit of one's interests. It
is both amoral and a form of rational calculation. For Montesquieu,
virtue is also amoral, but it is an unreasoning passion.

Montesquieu's conception of virtue is, in one sense, closer to ancient models than Machiavelli's, since it returns to the earlier emphasis on public-spiritedness. But by denying that reason is the
source of virtuous behaviour, he departs from those models even

---

[18] Aristotle, *Nicomachean Ethics*, 1103a18.

[19] L. Strauss, *Natural Right and History*, 252.

[20] Plutarch, "Life of Cato the Younger," in Plutarch, *The Lives of the Noble Greeks and Romans*, 918-59.

[21] See N. Machiavelli, *Discourses*, bk. 1, chaps. 37, 53, 55. In Book 1 of the *Discourses* Machiavelli shows how the "virtue," that is, the superior skill, energy, and abilities of the patricians, maintained plebeian self-abnegation, even when it plainly served patrician interest rather than the common good. The distinction between virtue and goodness is unfortunately obscured by inconsistent translations. The Modern Library edition, for example, translates *bonta* as "virtue" in the crucial passages of Book I, Chapter 55, in which Machiavelli praises the people.

more decisively than Machiavelli does. Virtue, as he understands it, requires no special talents or background. It "is a very simple thing; it is love of the republic; it is a sentiment and not the consequence of knowledge; the last man in the state can share this sentiment in the same way as the first."[22] So understood, virtue can be practised equally well by all citizens, a claim ancient authors would deny, but one that strongly recommends Montesquieu's conception of political virtue to Rousseau.

Montesquieu seems to restore a moral element to civic virtue, since he describes virtue as a constraint on self-preferring inclinations. But political virtue remains, in his eyes, a passion, that is, a form of self-love, even if it restrains other self-preferring inclinations. According to Montesquieu, all regimes, not just republics, depend on such passions to constrain inclinations. Fear serves this function in despotisms, honour, or, not to put too fine a point on it, vanity, in monarchies. Love of country is no more a moral virtue than either fear or vanity. Its ability to constrain selfish inclinations, therefore, should not lead us to prefer, let alone imitate, the republican regime.

We have no choice but to rely on some form of self-constraining passion. Which passion to rely on depends on the social and environmental context, the general spirit, as well as on our evaluation of the different effects of each passion on social interaction and the character of individuals. And as we have already seen, Montesquieu condemns both the external and internal effects of the practise of republican virtue. Although he does not explicitly make the distinction between "the passions and the interests" elaborated by Albert Hirschman,[23] he clearly prefers the acquisitive passions encouraged by modern commercial regimes (Hirschman's "interests") to the fiercer, more destructive passions fostered by the classical republics (one example of what Hirschman calls "passions") as a means of constraining self-preferring inclinations. Rousseau, as we shall see, reverses this evaluation. Using Hirschman's terms, one could say that Rousseau wants to use the passions—especially the

[22] *Spirit*, bk. 5, chap. 2.
[23] A. Hirschman, *The Passions and the Interests*.

passion for glory—to constrain the interests, the acquisitive passions that Montesquieu encourages.

The major political aim of Montesquieu's analysis of the principles of the different regimes is to prove that moral virtues are not needed for a desirable political order. Legislators need only foster common passions—the fierce passion of patriotism or the softer vices of vanity and greed. Moderate regimes have no need of common moral virtues, and thus they have no need to support the authority of the institution that claims to define and defend the moral beliefs necessary to society's well-being, the Church. Montesquieu tries to show that when we uncover the true spirit of classical republicanism, that is, after we remove the layers of interpretation with which Christian and philosophic moralists have covered it, we will learn that passions can be used to restrain selfishness. Then we may no longer feel compelled to empower religious institutions to engage in a hopeless and destructive attempt to eliminate the influence of the passions.

Christian education has socialized modern men to identify devotion to the common good with otherworldly self-abnegation. But "the ancients did things which we no longer see today and that astonish our small souls" by harnessing, not by opposing, this-worldly passions.[24] Montesquieu's interpretation of republican virtue subverts the Church's claim that the state must impose on its citizens the moral unanimity that only the Church has the knowledge and authority to define.

The anticlerical intention of Montesquieu's appeal to classical republicanism is even clearer in his *Considerations*. This work fits into a tradition of pointedly anticlerical, even anti-Christian discussions of the Roman character and institutions, the most notable examples of such works being Machiavelli's *Discourses on Livy* and Gibbon's *Decline and Fall*.[25] As in Gibbon's work, Christianity, and especially its sectarianism, receives more than its share of criticism, while Church opponents such as Julian the Apostate are praised.

Montesquieu's overriding goal in this work is to provide a secular

[24] *Spirit*, bk. 4, chap. 2.
[25] On Montesquieu's debt to Machiavelli, see A. Levi-Malvano, *Montesquieu e Machiavelli*, and R. Shackleton, "Montesquieu and Machiavelli: A Reappraisal."

and nonmoral explanation of those Roman virtues that excite our admiration. He fears that without such an explanation "we would see events without understanding them; and not being aware of the difference of situations we might believe that in reading ancient history, we were looking at men of some other kind than our own." His account shows that the Romans made themselves into "more than men" through the severity of their physical discipline and the regularity of their exercise. As Montesquieu tells the story, the men who performed the deeds that "astonish our small souls" had superior bodies, not superior souls. But the real reason the Roman achievement seems so grand, even superhuman, to us is that we are unfamiliar with the passion for public affairs characteristic of well-ordered republics. "There is nothing as powerful as a republic in which the law is obeyed not through fear, not through reason, but through passion, as it was with Rome and Lacedaemon; for then the strength which only a faction can have is joined with the wisdom of good government."[26]

These are the foundations of Roman grandeur. But since political grandeur was never Montesquieu's goal, he does not recommend their reconstruction. In the original edition of the *Considerations*, he writes that the legislator must choose either the grandeur or the felicity of his people as his goal.[27] Montesquieu clearly prefers felicity over grandeur as the aim of modern legislation. Thus he scoffs at Frederick of Prussia's attempt to build a military system on the Roman model. And he does not consider the lack of universal military service a hindrance to English political freedom.[28] Since Montesquieu is deeply suspicious of the value of ancient grandeur, there is no need to imitate the institutions that made it possible.

Furthermore, when one reads the *Considerations* carefully, it becomes clear that, despite his concentration on republican public-spiritedness, Montesquieu does not even see Rome as a model of civic unity. Indeed, he uses Roman examples to press the case that moral and political unanimity are not necessary to a healthy polit-

---

[26] C. S. de Montesquieu, *Considerations on the Causes of the Grandeur and Decline of the Romans* (hereafter *Considerations*), in *Oeuvres Complètes*, 2:80, 85.

[27] C. S. de Montesquieu, *Oeuvres Complètes*, 2:1488.

[28] *Considerations*, 2:155; *Spirit*, bk. 11, chap. 6, 2:406.

ical order. Rome, he argues, owed her freedom to her ability to tolerate the energy of political agitation and factionalism and to re-channel it in constructive directions (destructive directions for her foreign victims). Free government, Montesquieu argues, is government subject to continual agitation. There are no surer signs of despotism than complete political tranquility and harmony of opinion.

> That which is called union in a political body is a very equivocal thing. The true sort is that harmony that makes all parties, while opposed to each other as they appear, concur in the general good of society; as in music, dissonances agree in total concord. There can be union in a state where we see nothing but disorder. . . . It is like the parts of the universe, eternally linked by the action of some and the reaction of others.[29]

The stifling conformity of Sparta inspires no enthusiasm in Montesquieu. It is a symbol of everything he opposes in modern, Church-supported despotisms. Despite what one might initially expect, given Montesquieu's understanding of republican virtue, his analysis of Roman grandeur supports rather than contradicts his famous argument in *The Spirit of the Laws* about using counteracting ambitions and interests to guarantee political and personal freedom. There is no contradiction between Montesquieu's explanation of the success of Roman political institutions and his advocacy of the English constitution. Roman love of country made her great; her toleration of political disagreement and agitation made her free. Disdaining grandeur as a political goal, Montesquieu heeds only the lessons about freedom offered by the Roman experience.

The history of Rome thus provides confirmation of the superiority of modern indirect forms of government rather than a model for imitation. Montesquieu uses the appeal to the republican virtues of the ancients only to help clear the ground of demands for religious and moral unanimity that might prove an obstacle to the development of political institutions that secure and foster the expression of opposing interests and opinions.

---

[29] *Considerations*, 2:116, 119. He uses the metaphor of cosmic unity through opposed forces once again, in *Spirit* bk. 3, chap. 7, to describe the way in which the kind of modern indirect governments which he prefers operate.

Rousseau's Longing for Ancient Virtue

Rousseau's "intoxication" with ancient virtue is well known.[30] Although he liked to style himself the *citoyen de Genève*, the true home of his republicanism is the city-state of classical antiquity. His rhetoric often dresses the Genevans in Spartan garb, and his feverish imagination often leads him to confuse rhetoric with reality. But when speaking directly to his fellow citizens rather than to the French, Rousseau expresses no illusions about his countrymen's virtues.

> You are neither Romans nor Spartans; you are not even Athenians. Leave aside these great names that ill suit you. You are merchants, artisans, bourgeois, always occupied with private interest, work, business, and gain; people for whom freedom itself is only a means of acquiring without obstacle and possessing with security.[31]

The Genevans are "subordinate sovereigns four hours a year," and "subjects for the rest of their lives."[32] They are thus no better than the English, whom Rousseau considers free only for the brief moment in which they cast their votes.[33] Despite the rhetorical flourishes and flights of imagination with which Rousseau embellishes his memories of Geneva, the republics of classical antiquity provide the models for his version of republican virtue and freedom.

And the classical republic admired by Rousseau is that described in *The Spirit of the Laws*, the regime set in motion by love of country. Rousseau seizes upon Montesquieu's unorthodox interpretation of ancient political virtue as an unreasoning passion and uses it as a stick with which to beat his contemporaries. "These two words, *patrie* and citizen should be effaced from modern languages." "The true meaning of these words has been almost entirely lost to mod-

---

[30] The term "intoxication" is Rousseau's. See Confessions, 1:416; 430. (As in the footnotes in the Introduction, a reference to the English translation follows a semicolon after the reference to the work in the original language.)

[31] *Letters from the Mountain*, 3:881.

[32] Ibid., 3:814-15.

[33] *Social Contract*, 3:430; 102.

ern men."[34] Rousseau makes explicit what was only implicit in Montesquieu's work: the distinction between the virtue that moves republics and the vanity that drives monarchies is really a distinction between the spirit of ancient and modern institutions.[35]

But Montesquieu's image of classical republican virtue inspires very different sentiments when it is viewed in the light of Rousseau's understanding of the fundamental aims of government. For Rousseau, political institutions are measured by the individuals they produce.

> I had come to see that everything was radically connected with politics, and that, however one proceeds, no people will be anything but what their government makes them. Thus this great question of the best possible government appeared to me to be reduced to this: What is the nature of the government suited to forming the most virtuous, enlightened, wisest, in short, the best people, taking the word best in its widest sense.[36]

While Montesquieu seeks to reform institutions, Rousseau seeks to use institutions to transform men. For Montesquieu, the fundamental political problem is the cruelty and arbitrariness of authority; for Rousseau, it is the quality of individual citizens. To use Montesquieu's language, Rousseau seeks grandeur of soul over felicity as the aim of legislation. He rebels against the spirit of modern institutions because it forms weak and internally divided individuals.

Yet Rousseau makes few criticisms of modern men and institutions that cannot be found in the works of Montaigne or Montesquieu, the two philosophers from whom he borrows the most.[37]

[34] *Emile*, 4:250; 40. *Social Contract*, 3:361n; 54n.

[35] Benjamin Constant makes this point as well, arguing that Montesquieu's meaning would have been much clearer if he had distinguished between the "esprits" of ancient and modern peoples rather than between the principles of republics and monarchies (*Les "Principes de Politique" de Benjamin Constant*, 2:505).

[36] *Confessions*, 1:404-5; 417-18.

[37] For Rousseau's debt to Montaigne, see C. Fleuret, *Rousseau et Montaigne*, 46-48, 57-58 passim. The famous perorations in the *First* and *Second Discourses* that reproach man with his inferiority to the ancient citizen and to the savage, respectively, come close to being paraphrases of Montaigne. Cf. especially *First Discourse*, 3:30; 64, to M. de Montaigne, *Essays*, 105.

50

Why does Rousseau rebel against the spirit of modern institutions and seek to reproduce the grandeur of Plutarch's heroes, while Montesquieu, who draws Rousseau's attention to the limitations of modern men and institutions, is content to live within and even promote that spirit? Given the great differences between them in status and character, social and psychological explanations of their different reactions to contemporary limitations quickly suggest themselves. The contrast between Montesquieu's aristocratic moderation and Rousseau's outsider's hypersensitivity is obvious and important. But Rousseau's longing to escape the spirit of modern institutions also follows from the questions his new conceptual perspective leads him to ask. His understanding of human freedom makes it extremely difficult for him to accept the limitations imposed on us by modern institutions; from Rousseau's perspective, they deprive us of our very humanity, not just of opportunities for grandeur. His new conception of human freedom completely transforms the stakes in the evaluation of modern institutions.

It is Rousseau's refusal to accept what one could describe, depending on one's point of view, as either Montesquieu's philosophic moderation or his conceptual confusion with regard to human freedom that leads him to part company with his teacher. In *The Spirit of the Laws* Montesquieu provides a purposely narrow, "political" definition of freedom, advising legislators to separate the political from the philosophic conception of freedom. They need not concern themselves with the latter. With regard to the constitution, freedom is the regular functioning of the laws; with regard to the individual subject, it is security from arbitrary attack or punishment.[38] That is all legislators need to know about the nature of freedom. But that is not all Rousseau thinks they should know about freedom. Rousseau demands a more radical approach to the discussion of political freedom. He refuses to divorce the political from the philosophic conception of freedom.[39]

[38] *Spirit*, bk. 12, chap. 2; bk. 11, chaps. 3-4.
[39] Rousseau's disclaimer in *The Social Contract* (3:365; 56), "the philosophic meaning of the word freedom is not my subject here," seems a little disingenuous. For this disclaimer closes a chapter in which Rousseau develops the distinction between human freedom and natural independence.

Rousseau complains that Montesquieu fails to unite his unsurpassable analysis of positive right with a comparable analysis of "political right," that is, with an analysis of the principles that make political authority legitimate.[40] The principles of legitimate authority are, for Rousseau, those that allow individuals to establish political authority without losing their freedom. How can Montesquieu leave unanswered the question of whether the "political" freedom he seeks is genuine or whether it is just another opinion about the nature of freedom?

From the perspective of his general, "philosophic" conception of freedom, Rousseau has to wonder about the value of the political freedom sought by Montesquieu. Montesquieu seeks to liberate our natural and self-preferring inclinations from unnecessary and destructive demands for moral and religious unanimity. Yet he, more than any other *philosophe*, with his discussion of the influence of climate, *moeurs*, and laws on the formation of the spirit of individuals, subverts the concept of a single human nature used by the *philosophes* as the measure of impositions on our freedom. Human nature cannot both vary with climate and other empirical influences and remain as the standard by which we stigmatize certain acts as unnatural and unjustified impositions on our freedom. Montesquieu, like the great majority of the *philosophes*, is content to leave this contradiction unexamined, so that he can continue to use the concept of human nature as a means of subverting cruel and arbitrary institutions, even while investigating empirical variations in human behaviour.[41] Rousseau is not. Underlying Rousseau's understanding of politics and shaping his discontent with modern institutions is a bold and original analysis of human freedom that separates what is human in man from what is natural.

Rousseau distinguishes and makes use of two mutually exclusive concepts of freedom in his criticism of social institutions. The first is freedom from dependence on other wills, or what he sometimes calls natural freedom. The Rousseauian savage enjoys this freedom to the fullest, since, in his isolation, he depends on no other indi-

[40] *Emile*, 4:836, 850-51; 458, 468.
[41] J. Ehrard, *L'idée de la nature*, 1:331-32.

viduals for his satisfaction. Free from concern with others, his inclinations rule his actions. In this he is no different from other animals. Natural freedom, or independence, is freedom from dependence on other humans and rule by nature.

Human freedom, on the other hand, replaces the rule of natural inclinations with devotion to a self-imposed end of our own making—the general will of a community of individuals. Human freedom, the special *qualité d'homme* that defines man's humanity,[42] is an achievement of our institutions that raises man above nature. To create citizens, political institutions must "denature," even "mutilate" our natural inclinations.[43] Rousseau thus severs the connection between human nature and the special dignity of the human being that goes back to Plato and Aristotle—a connection that the insights of eighteenth-century philosophers already had made questionable. Rousseau, at his most rigorous, sees *human* dignity as an assertion against nature. To be free means to be independent either of human will or of natural inclination. Although there is often a conflation of these two conceptions of freedom in his rhetoric, Rousseau is well aware that they "mutually exclude each other."[44]

Rousseau tries to demonstrate that all of the problems of modern men flow from their lack of freedom in one sense or the other. They have lost the independence of their natural state but do not possess the human freedom that would compensate them for their loss. Their dependence on others, rather than freeing them from dependence on natural inclinations, has only extended the empire of

---

[42] *Social Contract*, 3:356; 50. See P. Riley, *Will and Political Legitimacy*, 100-102.

[43] *Emile*, 4:250; 40. "Geneva" manuscript of *Social Contract*, 3:313; 180.

[44] *Letters from the Mountain*, 3:841; see also *Oeuvres Complétes*, 3:283. To some readers my emphasis here on the dichotomy between human freedom and natural inclination might appear to impose a Kantian conceptual framework on Rousseau's understanding of freedom. In Chapter 3 I compare the Rousseauian and Kantian philosophies of freedom and suggest that they represent two contrasting versions of an argument based on a dichotomy between nature and humanity. I suggest there that familiarity with Kant's philosophy of freedom not only tempts Rousseau's contemporary interpreters to illegitimately impose Kantian categories on his argument, but also often blinds us to non-Kantian formulations of the nature/humanity dichotomy, such as we can find in Rousseau.

nature over their actions. Savages are satisfied with the necessities of life; and since, in Rousseau's judgment, their powers extend as far as their needs, they are happy.[45] But the imagination of socialized individuals inflates their needs far beyond their abilities to satisfy them. Recognizing their dependence on others for the satisfaction of their needs, socialized individuals try to foresee and control events. But by searching the present for future obstacles to their satisfaction they only create new needs and add the torments of anticipation to the sources of their unhappiness. Nature's empire of pain and pleasure is thus extended across the globe by the socialization of human needs. The happiness of individuals can be crushed by actions, or even by fear of actions, in lands they have never seen.[46] Such individuals are, according to Rousseau, weak and slavish creatures; they are both ruled by nature and fearful of the whims of men.

Individuals suffer this degrading double dependence as soon as they develop social needs and obligations. They develop a "double being" that "joins the vices of the social state to the abuses of the state of nature."[47] Modern philosophers and social critics only compound their misery, since they confuse the liberation of natural self-love with political freedom. Liberal Enlightenment thinkers seem to believe that natural selfishness and political freedom can coexist, and thus, like Montesquieu, they encourage the liberation of enlightened self-interest from the chains of moral and political repression. But since the interests and inclinations they seek to liberate are already socialized, their efforts, to the extent they are successful, only deepen the contradictions within modern souls.

> He who in the civil order wants to preserve the primacy of the sentiments of nature does not know what he wants. Always in contradiction with himself, always floating between his inclinations and his duties, he will never be either man or citizen. He will be good neither for himself nor for others. He will be one of these men of our days: a Frenchman, an Englishman, a

[45] *Emile*, 4:304; 80.
[46] Ibid., 4:306-8; 81ff.
[47] "Favre" manuscript of *Emile*, 4:57.

bourgeois. He will be nothing. To be something, to be oneself and always one, a man must act as he speaks; he must always be decisive in making his choice, make it in a lofty style, and always stick to it. I am waiting to be shown this marvel so as to know whether he is a man or a citizen, or how he goes about being both at the same time.[48]

Man or citizen, natural or political freedom—we must make a choice.[49] "Give man completely to the state or leave him completely to himself if you wish to make him happy." In society, "nature's gentle voice is no longer an infallible guide."[50] Thus one must either try to protect the growth of natural inclinations from social influence or make dependence on others so complete that concern for the community will override the natural voice of self-love within the individual. The former is the goal of private education as outlined in *Emile*; the latter is the goal of public education, an art about which the moderns, Rousseau complains, know nothing.[51]

Public institutions should thus be measured in terms of the individuals they produce. "All institutions that put man into contradiction with himself are worth nothing."[52] The institutions of the classical republics produced citizens, individuals whose love of their communities freed them from the constraints of their natural self-love. Modern institutions produce only divided souls. They are, therefore, worthless. Only institutions that can restore the wholeness individuals lost in entering the social state, either by freeing them from dependence on natural inclinations or by preserving those inclinations from social influence, are not worthless in Rousseau's eyes.

It is in the light of this understanding of freedom that Rousseau considers Montesquieu's image of republican virtue. The ancient citizens' passionate devotion to their community is a reproach to our divided souls. Their existence demonstrates that we need not

[48] *Emile*, 4:249-50; 40.
[49] On this theme, see J. Shklar, *Men and Citizens: A Study of Rousseau's Social Theory*.
[50] *Oeuvres Complètes*, 3:510. "Geneva" manuscript of *Social Contract*, 3:283; 158.
[51] *Emile*, 4:249; 40.
[52] *Social Contract*, 3:464; 128.

suffer our debilitating and degrading disunity. A knowledge of their state of mind should stifle our complacency and leave us dissatisfied with our contradictory freedoms and our endless quest for security and satisfaction. There once were individuals who lived in society yet remained whole. They were something to admire; next to them, we are nothing.

Rousseau's "intoxication" with ancient virtue represents something more than the product of a childhood fixation or of an oversensitive imagination. It develops out of his original analysis of the obstacles to satisfaction and human dignity. According to Rousseau's own account in the *Confessions*, it began in the early 1750s, as he was developing his new understanding of freedom and human needs which he first presented in the *Discourse on Inequality* and in the *Encyclopedie* article on *Political Economy*. "This intoxication had commenced in my head, but had passed on into my heart."[53] It began in his head, with his new ideas, and then inspired a new passion in his heart as he looked at old experiences in the light of his new ideas. Up to that point, despite the childhood enthusiasm for Plutarch's heroes which Rousseau shared with many of the *philosophes*,[54] he managed to maintain his sobriety. What led him, unlike his Parisian colleagues, to rekindle that enthusiasm in his maturity was the same insight that separated his social criticism from theirs: his dichotomy between the demands of nature and the demands of civic virtue. It was his novel understanding of the obstacle to human satisfaction posed by the spirit of modern institutions that made the image of ancient virtue, recently analyzed with such clarity by Montesquieu, so intoxicating to his head and heart.

Like the travelers' accounts he uses in the *Discourse on Inequality*, Montesquieu's image of republican virtue provides material with which Rousseau tries to reconstruct in his imagination a state of mind that transcends the internal divisions and contradictions that plague modern minds. Montesquieu's description of ancient virtue helps him to imagine what it would be like to lose one's insistent self-preference, just as the descriptions of savage life help

[53] *Confessions*, 1:416; 431.
[54] *Confessions*, 1:9; 7. See P. Gay, *The Enlightenment: An Interpretation*, 1:46-47.

him imagine the sentiments one would experience in the complete absence of social dependence.[55] But in both cases it is his analysis of present obstacles to satisfaction that allows Rousseau to define the character of those lost states of mind. The reports of ancient virtue and savage independence help him develop his projections of what it would be like to live without the obstacles to satisfaction that he experiences. But the myths of Spartan virtue and of the noble savage do not inspire Rousseau's discontent with modern society. Rather, it is his discontent, fed by his novel understanding of human freedom, that inspires his celebrations of those myths. If we wish to explain Rousseau's enthusiasm for those myths, we need to examine not the myths themselves, but the discontent with modern society that makes Rousseau turn to them.

In his celebration of ancient virtue, Rousseau does not attempt to hide behind a nostalgic haze the destructive and self-lacerating characteristics of ancient virtue that so appalled his teacher, Montesquieu. Indeed, those very characteristics are the ones he celebrates. "Every patriot is harsh to foreigners. They are only men. They are nothing in his eyes. . . . The essential thing is to be good to the people with whom one lives." His description of the Spartan mother who runs to give thanks to the gods on hearing that her five sons were killed in a Spartan victory is short and to the point: "*Voilà la citoyenne.*"[56]

Rousseau seems to "start by drawing the most extreme conclusions that a republican can draw from Montesquieu's analysis of republics."[57] If the cultivation of virtue requires a ban on luxury, a general ignorance of the arts and sciences, continual warfare, even slavery, Rousseau proclaims himself ready to accept these conditions. He tells the Poles that they must choose between peace and freedom, for freedom demands continual warfare. Recognizing that the leisure that made Spartan virtue possible depended upon slave labour, he asks us to consider the paradox that the extreme of free-

---

[55] See J. Starobinski, *Jean-Jacques Rousseau: La transparence et l'obstacle*, 81ff., for an interesting discussion of Rousseau's ability to transport himself into different states of mind.

[56] *Emile*, 4:249; 39-40.

[57] L. Strauss, "On the Intention of Rousseau," 60.

dom might depend upon its opposite.[58] He does not doubt the truth of Montesquieu's famous maxim, *"Les connaissances rendent les hommes doux."* But since he questions the value of the softening of human passions, he is quite willing to limit acquaintance with foreigners and knowledge of the arts and sciences.[59] In general, he admonishes his contemporaries that out of fear of "the vices that attend vigour and courage you have substituted those of small souls."[60]

Why, then, does Rousseau endorse all the painful and repressive features of civic virtue that so repel Montesquieu? Because what is at stake for Rousseau is the dignity of man, not just the relative merits of different forms of political socialization. The wholeness of the natural man, based on his lack of social dependence, is not an option for us. The obstacle to our self-sufficiency and contentment, the socialization of our needs, cannot be rolled away. Like Rousseau, we can only dream of the sentiment of existence which the natural man experienced constantly.[61] But the obstacle to political freedom, to the overcoming of our self-contradictions that would evolve with the mastery of our natural inclinations, is not, by definition, immovable. Our distaste for the harshness of ancient virtue keeps us from gaining an appreciation of the sublime sentiments that Rousseau associates with patriotic self-sacrifice, sentiments that our lives lack.

In *The Social Contract* Rousseau appeals to these sentiments as the only compelling reason to prefer the social to the natural state.

> Although in this state the individual is deprived of many advantages which he derives from nature, he acquires some just as great; his sentiments are ennobled, his entire soul raised to such a degree that if the abuses of this new condition did not often degrade him below the level from which he has emerged, he ought to bless without ceasing the happy chance that re-

[58] *Government of Poland*, 3:954; *Social Contract*, 3:431; 103.
[59] *Spirit*, bk. 5, chap. 2. For Rousseau's discussion of this maxim, see *Oeuvres Complètes*, 3:72 and 4:1088-90.
[60] *Lettres morales*, 4:1089-90.
[61] See Rousseau's *Reveries*, 1:1046-47; 68-69, for a description of one such dream.

leased him from it forever and that made from a stupid and limited animal an intelligent being and a man.[62]

Without the passage to civil society, "we would never have enjoyed the soul's most delicate feeling, love of virtue."[63] The exaltation of soul experienced in self-denial is a sentiment which the savage, for all his independence, cannot experience. Our capacity to experience the sublime satisfactions provided by this noble passion compensates us for the loss of the savage's independence and pleasure in the contemplation of his existence. It alone raises us above him. Indeed, in the passage quoted above the term *man*, "that made from a stupid and limited animal an intelligent being and a man," is a term of distinction. Our "humanity" is an achievement that rests on our ability to subordinate our self-love. The modern institutions and sentiments that Rousseau opposes thus threaten our humanity. Although he never uses the expression, Rousseau could say; as have many of his followers, that the spirit of modern institutions "dehumanizes" us. The ancients' appearance as "men of some other kind than our own" is not the illusion that Montesquieu insists it is. Their political institutions gave ancient citizens a "human" character that our institutions deny us. Political institutions thus make or break our humanity. Our institutions produce a kind of individual who is something more than savage but less than human, "good neither for himself nor for others"—an individual who is, in short, a "nothing" rather than a man.[64]

The ancient grandeur to which Rousseau appeals against modern institutions is greatness of soul, not collective political achievement. Although Rousseau protests against modern politics in the name of the ancient republican institutions, he is far more interested in his reconstruction of the ancient state of mind than in the character and fate of the ancient state itself. Republican virtue, for Rousseau, is a state of mind, the sublime loss of self-reference in the experience of the passion of patriotism. We can now only imagine what that state of mind was like, but the Spartan example

[62] *Social Contract*, 3:364-65; 56.
[63] "Geneva" manuscript of *Social Contract*, 3:283.
[64] *Emile*, 4:249-50; 40.

teaches us not to become reconciled to the contradictions and weakness of our souls and it proves that our lack of political freedom and psychological unity is not the necessary and inescapable condition of mankind. "The embarrassment of my adversaries," Rousseau writes, "is visible every time they must speak of Sparta. What wouldn't they give for that fatal Sparta not to exist?"[65]

Montesquieu draws the contrasts between the spirit of ancient and modern institutions that inspire Rousseau's longing for the spirit of the polis. But they do not inspire in Montesquieu the same discontent with modern institutions because humanity is not, for him, something that can be won or lost. The idea that modern men are somehow less human than ancient citizens would have made little sense to him. Individuals can be, and usually are, treated "inhumanely" by their governments, that is, with arbitrary and unnecessary cruelty; but that does not make those individuals any less "human," however much cruel treatment leaves its mark on their bodies and their characters. The humanity that Montesquieu wants our institutions to respect is a natural quality of the species, not our own achievement. However much Montesquieu's concepts and research bring into question the concept of a universal human nature, however fascinated he is by the different characters exhibited by different peoples, he never thinks of humanity as an achievement of man. The spirit of a nation's laws may shape the character of the individuals within it; it does not bestow on them their humanity. Thus no set of institutions could become, for Montesquieu, the obstacle to the achievement of our humanity which the spirit of modern institutions becomes for Rousseau.

[65] "Last Response to M. Bordes," 3:83.

T W O

THE NOVELTY OF
ROUSSEAU'S DISSATISFACTION
WITH MODERN MEN AND
INSTITUTIONS

IN THIS chapter I try to clarify my claims about the novelty of Rousseau's social discontent by defending them against possible objections. The most important of these would raise doubts about the
novelty of Rousseau's argument for community and about the significance historical comparisons have for his social discontent.

Many scholars, for example, have found precedents for Rousseauian communitarianism in Rousseau's classical Greek sources.
In the first section of this chapter I try to show how Rousseau's understanding of political freedom sets his arguments for political
community apart from the arguments of the classical writers whom
he so admired and, as a result, leads him to develop a completely
new justification for the subordination of the individual to the community. In the following section I discuss the nature, role, and extent of historical comparison in Rousseau's thought. The purpose of
this discussion is to anticipate the objection that, by placing such
importance on the contrast between the spirit of ancient and modern institutions in my interpretation of Rousseau's discontent, I
write back into Rousseau's works historicist attitudes that develop
only after his death. In the final section I point to one of the obstacles that has made it difficult to recognize the novel aspects of Rousseau's social discontent outlined in the first chapter: the absence of
this novelty among the French revolutionaries who established
both a cult of Rousseau and a cult of classical republicanism. Here I

briefly distinguish between the revolutionaries' Rousseau and the aspects of his thought discussed in this book. I then go on to suggest that the most novel aspects of his social discontent are appreciated and developed only by German-speaking intellectuals of the post-Kantian generation.

The Novelty of Rousseau's Demand for Community

Rousseau treats his break with the political principles of his contemporaries as a return to the ancients, who, like himself, "spoke incessantly about morals and virtue."[1] He invites us to reflect on classical writers and examples if we wish to recover the true meaning of citizenship and community. Thus it seems that we would only be taking Rousseau at his word if we conclude that he returns to the classical Greek understanding of the priority of the community to the individual as part of his revolt against the "false abstraction" of modern individualism.[2]

This impression of Rousseau as the reviver of ancient communitarianism lasts only as long as we remain under the spell of his rhetoric and refrain from comparing his arguments with those of his classical sources. The spell of that rhetoric, however, reaches further than one might think. It distorts many contemporary interpretations of the polis and of classical political thought, as well our understanding of Rousseau himself. Rousseau has had many admirers who, like him, want to use the communitarianism of the polis as a stick with which to beat the individualism of liberal theory and practise, and who do not hesitate to read Rousseauian and post-Rousseauian arguments for political community back into ancient thought and practise.[3]

Thus I deem a comparison of Rousseau's argument for community with those offered by Greek political philosophers essential to a proper understanding of his social discontent. We need to clear the air of some of the anachronistic echoes of modern ideas that reso-

---

[1] *First Discourse*, 3:19; 51.

[2] C. E. Vaughan, *The Political Writings of Rousseau*, 1:55-56.

[3] I discuss below the most influential twentieth-century example of this practise, Hannah Arendt's interpretation of the polis and "political" activity.

nate about influential interpretations of ancient Greek political thought and practise in order to understand the relationship between Rousseauian and classical communitarianism. When we do so, it becomes clear that classical sources are not very helpful in identifying and accounting for the discontent with liberal theory and practise expressed by Rousseau and the heirs to his argument for community.

The traditional arguments for the subordination of the individual to the community stress the overriding importance of some collective goal, for example, social justice, political stability, or imperial power; the most common argument has always been the need to increase the military and political power of the state. The Greek philosophers, such as Plato, Aristotle, and Plutarch, from whom Rousseau draws much of his communitarian rhetoric, argue that justice and stability should take priority over the ends of individuals as those individuals conceive of them.

But these arguments are not the ones that compel Rousseau to call for the "total alienation of each associate, with all of his rights, to the whole community."[4] In demanding the alienation of the individual to the community, Rousseau seeks to legitimize and make tolerable the chains of dependence that we must bear in civil society. We can justify our loss of self-sufficiency and happiness only if we compensate the individual with the political freedom that raises him above nature, the freedom that makes him worthy of our respect in a way the independent savage never could be. Here is the great paradox of Rousseau's political thought: he demands the complete subordination of the individual *for the sake of the individual*, not to further the collectively shared goals that constitute the community. It is by pursuing the needs of the single individual that Rousseau comes to demand his total alienation to the general will of the community.

Compare first Rousseau's argument for the subordination of the individual to the community with that of Plato. Plato, the most radical social critic among the Greek political philosophers, and Plutarch are the two classical philosophers whom Rousseau most ad-

---

[4] *Social Contract*, 3:360; 53.

mires and follows.⁵ Rousseau's comment in the *Emile* about Plato's *Republic* is most revealing. He suggests that most readers mistake the *Republic* for a work on politics, when it is really a treatise on education, the greatest ever written.⁶ Plato does indeed treat education at length in the *Republic*, but the dialogue is structured around an examination of the nature and limits of justice. It asks the question, what is justice? To answer that question, Socrates and his interlocutors design from scratch a community in which one can observe the relationships among individuals within a political community. They discover that justice is the simple principle, to each his own. Justice requires that each individual—and within the individual, each part of the soul—be in the place that suits his real (that is, natural) abilities, rather than his opinions about his abilities. Complete justice thus requires a regime in which an individual, the philosopher, whose vision of natural abilities is completely free of conventional evaluations, directs the distribution of tasks and status among individuals within that regime.

However one judges Plato's concept of justice, it is clear that he demands the subordination of the individual to the community in order to establish just proportions among individuals in the distribution of goods and honours. When one of the participants in the dialogue, Adeimantus, asks whether this regime will make its citizens, or even its rulers, happy, Socrates brushes the question aside, arguing that their aim is the wholeness and happiness of the city, not of its individuals.⁷ Justice, in Plato's eyes, requires the subordination of the ends that individuals conceive for themselves to their collectively shared ends. Public education in the *Republic* is a means of discovering and perfecting the natures of individuals so that they can perform the functions in the community to which they are suited. Far from seeking to *denature* individuals, as Rousseau would have it, Platonic public education seeks to locate and

⁵ See M. J. Silverstone, "Rousseau's Plato." This study emphasizes similarities between Rousseau's and Plato's arguments, but that is because it concentrates on Rousseau's direct borrowing from Plato's *Laws*, rather than on his attempt to recreate the spirit of Plato's more radical work, *The Republic*.
⁶ *Emile*, 4:250; 40.
⁷ Plato, *Republic*, 419a-20e.

nurture the nature of individuals. The guardians need a political and religious education in order to behave both gently toward their fellow citizens and fiercely toward their city's enemies. The prospective philosopher-king needs a philosophic education in order to teach him where to find natural standards of judgment in the midst of convention and change.

It is for Rousseau, not Plato, that education represents the fundamental problem of political life. "This great question of the best government possible appeared to me to reduce itself to the following: What kind of government . . . forms the best people?"[8] Rousseau begins with the needs of the social individual, weak and internally divided as he is, and asks what kind of institutions can make him whole and respectable. The political institutions he recommends aim to satisfy the *individual's* need for internal order, rather than the shared need of individuals to establish principles of justice to order their social interactions. Politics thus becomes public education. Transform divided modern men or independent savages into citizens, and "all difficulties vanish"; "you have everything if you can form citizens."[9] Rousseau is not so naive that he believes there were no serious "difficulties" among the virtuous citizens of the classical republics. His lack of interest in the social conflicts in the ancient republics indicates that his deepest concern is the establishment of a respectable order *within* the individual, rather than among individuals.

Plato is also interested in the order within the individual. But that order need not be the gift of political institutions. In the climax of the *Republic* in Book IX, Plato describes the best political regime as a "pattern laid in heaven" for imitation within our souls.[10] Justice in the city, the proper proportion among the individuals who make up the political community, becomes the pattern for justice in the individual soul. But that is not the same thing as treating political institutions as the means of introducing order into the soul. If Plato asks us to model our souls on the proportions of a truly just

[8] *Confessions*, 1:404-5; 417-18.
[9] *Discourse on Political Economy*, 3:254, 259; 218, 222.
[10] Plato, *Republic*, 592b.

community, Rousseau asks us to model our communities according to what will produce noble and integrated souls.

Rousseau's concern for establishing the political conditions that will produce healthy souls does not resemble the concerns that led classical writers to admire Sparta, his model community. It is the individual Spartan's state of mind that most excites Rousseau's admiration and envy. That is the last thing about Sparta that inspired envy among the ancient philosophers whom Rousseau loves to cite. For them, the strength and stability of the Spartan regime, and the self-discipline and lack of personal ambition that preserved it, were its most impressive features. They regarded the limited perspective of the individual Spartan as the unfortunate, if necessary, means of preserving those virtues, but certainly not as a desirable end in itself. To glorify Spartan ignorance as a superior state of mind would be a betrayal of the intellectual life to which they were all devoted, a betrayal that, beginning with Rousseau, becomes ever more tempting to European intellectuals.

In Thucydides' comparison of the Athenian and Spartan regimes, the Spartans win many points. But Thucydides leaves no doubt that, as individuals, the Athenians surpass the Spartans. What makes Sparta superior to Athens is its domestic stability (although Thucydides has no illusions about the cost paid by the Helots for that stability). The individual Spartan's subordination to his laws and leaders gives his regime a strength and moderation that the Athenian regime cannot match. The absence of these virtues in Athens eventually leads to her defeat. But however much Thucydides, as an Athenian, may envy Spartan stability, he never expresses envy of Spartan ignorance.[11]

Aristotle treats Sparta as one of the very few existing regimes worth considering as a candidate for the title of best regime. Sparta is worthy of admiration because it actively promotes the virtues of its citizens, rather than leaving moral education to chance. But Spartan virtues fall far short of those described by Aristotle in his ethical writings as necessary for the good life. The Spartan regime

[11] The contrast between Athens and Sparta is developed throughout Thucydides' *The Peloponnesian War.* The most concise characterizations of the two regimes and its citizens occur in Book I in the speeches given at the first congress of Spartan allies.

treats military virtue as the whole of virtue. It only prepares its citizens for conquest and defence—and it does not even do that well enough. The Spartan does not have the ability to lead the good life when his country is at peace.[12] Aristotle does not envy the life, let alone the mind, of the individual Spartan.

Even Plutarch, whose "Life of Lycurgus" and collections of Spartan sayings provide Rousseau with his examples of Spartan virtue, does not emphasize the greatness of the individual Spartan. In his account of the Spartan founding, Plutarch concentrates on showing the steps Lycurgus took to ensure justice and stability in his regime. He begins by discussing Lycurgus's aristocratic reordering of political authority, proceeds to his redivision of land, and only then turns to his provisions for public education. He does defend Spartan laws against the charges of injustice made by Thucydides and Aristotle, but he makes no extravagant claims for the individual Spartan as a model of the good life.[13]

Plutarch does not celebrate the Spartan state of mind as Rousseau does because he has a very different understanding of the nature of civic virtue. Plutarch's—and Rousseau's—greatest hero, Cato the Younger, appears in Plutarch's works as a moderate and reflective man who studies philosophy. Reason, not passion, inspires his virtue. For Rousseau, on the other hand, civic virtue is the fierce and unreasoning passion of patriotism, an intoxicating state of mind. Although this is a state of mind that he associates with Plutarch's greatest heroes, Plutarch himself ridicules such passions. Rousseau's intoxication with virtue resembles nothing more in Plutarch's writings than his comic account of Cato's immoderate admirer and imitator, Marcus Favonius. Cato's virtue threw Favonius into "perfect transports and ecstasies like strong wine," but his drunken love of Catonic virtue inspired only immoderate and ridiculous actions.[14]

---

[12] Aristotle, *Politics*, 1269a-1271b20, 1333b, 1334a10ff.

[13] Plutarch, "Life of Lycurgus," in *Lives*, 52-59, 71. See also his "Sayings of the Spartans" and "Sayings of Spartan Women," in Plutarch, *Moralia*, 2:242-424, 454-72.

[14] Plutarch, "Life of Cato the Younger," in *Lives*, 921, 923, 944. Idem, "Life of Brutus," in *Lives*, 1207. One of Favonius's histrionic calls to virtue provides comic relief in Shakespeare's *Julius Caesar*, Act IV, Scene 3. Favonius is the "poet" who

Finally, despite appearances, Rousseau does not return to the Aristotelian position that the political community should make the promotion of happiness, the good life, its end. Aristotle does not define the virtues that produce the·good life in terms of the self-overcoming that Rousseau demands of the virtuous citizen; indeed, the very idea of self-overcoming is foreign to Aristotle. The Aristotelian virtues perfect our natural inclinations through habit and education; they do not raise us above our nature. No matter how much the development of our virtues may owe to our laws and institutions, virtue, as well as the good life it produces, remains for Aristotle a natural capacity, not a human creation. The majority of the Aristotelian moral virtues, let alone the intellectual virtues described in Books VI and X of the *Nicomachean Ethics*, do not depend on participation in political life. We may need the institutions of a well-ordered participatory republic to perfect and practise the full range of our capacities, but we need not be slavish and virtueless in their absence. One can and should be a good man in a bad regime. There are virtues that transcend the character of one's political institutions. In the best regime the good man is equivalent to the good citizen, but in all regimes we are likely to encounter in this world, the virtues of the good man do not coincide exactly with those of the good citizen.[15] Since virtue is not completely dependent on our regime, our institutions cannot "dehumanize" us.

Rousseau, on the other hand, identifies virtue with love of country, at least in his political writings. Virtue is impossible without the republican institutions that cultivate patriotism. To Aristotle's distinction between the good man and the good citizen, Rousseau opposes a distinction between the good and virtuous individual. Goodness and virtue are mutually exclusive.[16] Only an individual with no need of others can be good; only an individual who subordinates his needs for the sake of others can be virtuous. Bad institutions fix the individual in the unhappy condition in which he can depend neither on the goodness of his inclinations nor on the

---

rushes into Brutus's tent to separate and scold the quarreling Brutus and Cassius. It is not difficult to imagine Rousseau playing the part.

[15] Aristotle, *Politics*, 1276b15-1277b33.

[16] See especially *Dialogues*, 1:823-24.

strength of his will. Only an escape from or a transformation of such institutions offers a way out of this condition. The former is the path to goodness, the latter the path to virtue. Our socialization erects a barrier on the path to goodness, a barrier which, Rousseau admits, only dreams can take us beyond. Thus Rousseau's analysis encourages us to look to the transformation of our political institutions as the only practical means by which we can make something whole and respectable of our divided souls. We will not find a similar opinion expressed in the works of Aristotle or any other ancient writer.

In the end, Rousseau, like Hobbes and Locke, and despite his communitarianism, determines the legitimate ends of government from a consideration of the needs of the individual. But those needs are so much more demanding for Rousseau than they are for Hobbes and Locke. Political institutions must not only secure the conditions in which the individual seeks satisfaction, they must also ennoble his character and heal the wounds of his socialization. The legitimate state must produce healthy individuals as well as secure homes.

Following the social contract tradition that derives the legitimacy of the ends and powers of government from the needs that would guide enlightened individuals to bow to a common authority, Rousseau treats these distinct needs as the foundation of a right that individuals hold against their institutions. That institutions do not transform individuals into virtuous citizens makes them illegitimate. Rousseau insists that one should accept the loss of happiness and self-sufficiency that result from entering into civil society only if provided with this compensation.

That I am not a better person thus becomes for Rousseau a grievance against the political order. Modern institutions have deformed *me*. They have made me the weak and miserable creature that I am. What value do the virtues and services provided by the best of modern political institutions—peace, security, regular enforcement of the laws, the growth of the arts and sciences, the abolition of slavery, the protection of my property, the protection of my freedom of expression and religion—have for me, when I myself am deformed by them? Only institutions that will resolve my inner contradictions can have value for me. I must condemn all others as illegitimate.

Although presented as a return to the ancients' understanding of politics and virtue, Rousseau's demand for the subordination of the individual to the community represents a radicalization of the modern concern with individual freedom. Rousseau, like his contractarian predecessors, must justify the existence of political institutions. He begins by asking *why* an individual should accept the constraints imposed on his independence by government, rather than *what* order, what principles of justice, should shape the community, as Plato and Aristotle ask. An interpretation of what is required by freedom takes priority over the demands of justice in designing desirable political institutions.

We need to recognize this difference between the classical and Rousseauian demands for the primacy of the community in order to understand the discontent with liberal institutions expressed by Rousseau and those intellectuals who follow him in his demand for community. One of the great ironies of the discontent with liberal institutions expressed by Rousseau and Marx is that, while outraged over the inequality, the injustice, which those institutions must leave untouched, they offer another interpretation of freedom, not new principles of justice, as the foundation of an alternative order. Institutions that truly respect and embody our freedom and humanity, they suggest, will remove the sources of injustice from human society. Create citizens, writes Rousseau, and "all difficulties vanish."[17] The demands of justice, demands that figure so prominently in the Rousseauian critique of modern institutions, are reduced to one in the foundation of the alternative institutions Rousseau and Marx envision: render man what he is owed as a *human* being.[18]

Some of the most famous and influential modern interpreters and advocates of the Greek understanding of political community have read this demand back into Greek political thought and prac-

[17] *Discourse on Political Economy*, 3:254; 218.
[18] In the first sections of Chapter 7 I try to show that this reduction occurs in Marx's critique of modern institutions as well.

tise. Hannah Arendt, for example, interprets the Greek sense of political action this way.

> The "good life," as Aristotle called the life of the citizen, therefore was . . . "good" to the extent that by having mastered the necessities of sheer life, by being freed from labor and work, and by overcoming the innate urge of all living creatures for their own survival, it was no longer bound to the biological life process.[19]

It is hard to imagine Aristotle, with his teleological understanding of human nature, ever describing the good life as the "overcoming [of] the innate urge of all living creatures for their own survival, . . . no longer bound to the biological life process." Why does anyone as familiar with Aristotle's works as Arendt use such expressions to paraphrase his ideas? I suggest the reason is that Arendt reinterprets Aristotle's understanding of man's political nature in the light of a modern philosophy of freedom that opposes our human qualities to our natural qualities, a philosophy of freedom she has inherited from Rousseau and his German heirs. Any influence, such as poverty, that "puts men under the absolute dictates of their bodies, that is, under the absolute dictates of necessity" represents for her a "dehumanizing force."[20] For Arendt, political activity is an achievement of human freedom against natural inclination—the mastery of our "innate urge" for our "own survival." The language Arendt imposes on Aristotle's understanding of political community makes our political character something we assert *against* nature, our victory over the "biological life process." This reinterpretation of Aristotle and the Greek polis has unfortunately become the conventional wisdom on the subject for many contemporary students of political thought. "For the Greeks," it is often repeated, "the realm of politics was the realm of freedom, the truly human, in which man raised himself above the natural order."[21]

[19] H. Arendt, *The Human Condition*, 33.

[20] H. Arendt, *On Revolution*, 54.

[21] E. M. Wood, *Mind and Politics*, 174-75. For an interpretion of Aristotle's understanding of man's political nature that tries to correct this misreading of his ideas, see B. Yack, "Community and Conflict in Aristotle's Political Philosophy."

As I hope my comparisons between Rousseau and his classical sources have demonstrated, Arendt's definition of political activity expresses an appreciation of the value of political community more akin to Rousseauian ideas than to those developed by Aristotle or any other Greek philosopher. It is a sign of the strength of the Rousseauian conception of political community and of the ancient polis among contemporary critics of liberalism that a conception of political life that raises man "above the natural order" could come to be viewed as Aristotelian. Arendt's advocacy of political activity follows the basic structure of Rousseau's demand for political community. The political community is, for her, as for Rousseau, the means by which individuals raise themselves above nature. Through political activity individuals achieve the special *human* dignity that their innate urges deny them. Political institutions that do not make such activity possible deny individuals their humanity. And like Rousseau, Arendt writes her subordination of justice to the demands of human freedom back into her Greek sources.[22] By doing so, she obscures the novelty and sources of the discontent with modern institutions that she and Rousseau both express.

Rousseau demands the total alienation of the individual to the community in order to realize moral-political freedom, the individual's special human dignity. The *total* alienation he demands derives from the internal needs of the individual, not from the collective needs of his community. There is no precedent for such a demand for community in Rousseau's classical sources. It represents an original argument for community and expresses a new kind of discontent with political institutions, both of which develop, at least in part, out of Rousseau's new understanding of human freedom.

Rousseau and the Historicity of Modern Institutions

In the Introduction I suggest that the new conceptual perspective that makes possible Rousseau's longing to get beyond the dehu-

---

[22] Hanna Pitkin makes a similar complaint about the disappearance of a concern for justice in Arendt's account of Aristotle's communitarianism. See H. Pitkin, "Justice: On Relating Private and Public," 338-39.

manizing spirit of modern society has two basic elements: his understanding of human freedom and the contrast between the spirit of ancient and modern institutions that he takes from Montesquieu's *The Spirit of the Laws.*

By emphasizing the historical contrast between ancient and modern in Rousseau's work, my account of the novelty of his discontent rests on controversial ground. For Rousseau's historical sense has often been doubted. The author of one of the best studies of Rousseau's political thought does not hesitate to call him "the last of the Classical utopists, . . . the last great political theorist to be utterly disinterested in history."[23] If Rousseau is indeed "utterly disinterested in history," then he is unlikely to have thought that any historically specific set of institutions could represent the obstacle to the realization of our humanity. The historical examples he discusses then would provide means only of bolstering arguments, rather than of identifying and pointing the way beyond our historically limited characters.

There are good reasons to doubt Rousseau's interest in the historical specificity of individuals and institutions. He has little of the disinterested curiosity in historical development and individuality that Meinecke and most other scholars use to define the new sense of history that develops in late eighteenth-century Europe.[24] Thus it is not surprising that while Meinecke devotes a long chapter to Montesquieu in his study of the eighteenth-century sources of "historism," he deals with Rousseau in a single page. Rousseau shows none of Montesquieu's delight in contemplating the variety of customs and institutions that human beings have produced. When he dwells on the sentiments and institutions of some other era, as he does in his discussions of the pre-social savage and of classical republicanism, his interest always arises out of a philosophic, political, or moral argument he wishes to make, rather than out of disinterested curiosity. Moreover, unlike Montesquieu, he is not particularly interested in investigating the causes of the rise and fall of historical institutions. His rhetorical remarks about the corrup-

[23] J. Shklar, *Men and Citizens*, 1.
[24] F. Meinecke, *Historism*, lv. M. Mandelbaum, *History, Man, and Reason*, 42.

CHAPTER TWO

tion of ancient institutions by the arts and sciences do not express
the serious interest in the historical development of social institutions demonstrated in Montesquieu's *Considerations*. Rousseau
quits his projected histories of Sparta and Rome shortly after starting them.[25] If curiosity about historical development and individuality defines historical interest, then Rousseau is indeed uninterested in history.

But disinterested curiosity is not the only motive that inspires
the new feeling for the historicity of human character and institutions that develops in the eighteenth and nineteenth century. It is
the motive most emphasized by investigations of this new sentiment, since these investigations are usually written by academic
historians, for whom such curiosity is a professional obligation. But
there are other motives that have had as great an influence on modern social thought and criticism. The analysis of modern individuals and institutions undertaken by social critics like Rousseau also
produces an awareness of the historical specificity of our character
and institutions.[26] That awareness creates an interest in the spirit of
other eras as contrasts to our own. Earlier eras provide the contrasts
that allow us to define our limitations more precisely and the guides
that allow us to imagine what it would be like to live without those
historically specific limitations. Such motives are hardly disinterested, but they do represent an interest in the historical specificity
of the human institutions most important to us, our own.

Rousseau's talents as a guide to our own limitations, and his vivid
imagination of the sentiments one might experience without them,
give his writings the deep and peculiar sense of human historicity
that has impressed so many of his readers. That sense is hard to put
one's finger on. George Kelly reaches for it when he speaks of
Rousseau's ability to re-create the past as "super-nows, vibrating in
his own person in a way that no *philosophe* could imagine."[27] Höl-

25 See the fragments collected in *Oeuvres Complètes*, 3:538-551.
26 For general discussions of the novelty and originality of Rousseau's attitude toward historicity, see L. Gossman, "Time and History in Rousseau"; G. Buck,
"Selbsterhaltung und Historizität," 208-302; and C. Borghero, "Sparta tra storia e
utopia. Il significato e la funzione del mito di Sparta nel pensiero di Jean-Jacques
Rousseau."
27 G. A. Kelly, "Borrowing and Uses of History in Rousseau," 133.

derlin celebrates that sense of historicity when he writes in his ode to Rousseau:

> You've heard and understood the strangers' voice,
> Interpreted their soul! To him who yearns
> The hint sufficed, for since ancient times
> With hints have the Gods spoken.

Hölderlin hears through Rousseau's words "the strangers' voice," the voice of sentiments lost in the past and promised in the future. Rousseau seems able to reconstruct from the few "hints" of those sentiments left us in our records of antiquity the state of mind which we have lost.[28]

I do not mean to make of Rousseau some kind of superior *historien des mentalités*. His reconstructions of lost states of mind take as their premises the negation of our own limitations, not inductions from the examination of sources. The voice Rousseau hears in the state of nature is that of the man who lives without the obstacles to satisfaction we experience because of our dependence on others. The voice he hears in the polis is that of the man who lives without the painful tensions between love of self and duty to others that is such an obstacle to our spiritual satisfaction.

Nevertheless, Rousseau has an extraordinary ability to create from negative premises, with the aid of past examples, a vivid sense of lived experience. His "ego enters into a reality of which it is the author" and experiences there passions more intense than most of us experience in reality.[29] Rousseau's reconstructions are not very good guides to the historically specific sentiments felt in the past, but they do communicate a strong sense of the historicity of our own sentiments, a sense more powerful than any disinterested study of the sources could produce. We need not think of Rousseau as "the discoverer of human historicity"[30] to recognize this sense of the historicity of our needs and its influence on his discontent with modern institutions.

---

[28] F. Hölderlin, *Poems and Fragments: A Bilingual Collection*, 130-31.

[29] See J. Starobinski, *La transparence et l'obstacle*, 81, and L. Gossman, "Time and History in Rousseau," 348-49.

[30] P. Burgelin, *La philosophie de l'existence de J. J. Rousseau*, 191.

The nature and importance of that influence becomes clearer when one compares Rousseau's social criticism with that of the "Classical utopists" who are indeed "utterly disinterested in history." The great utopian thinkers, taking Plato and Thomas More as models, construct imaginary regimes that transcend the limitations that particular conditions impose on political institutions. Their utopias provide a means of bringing to light and judging the limitations of all historical regimes. Judith Shklar argues that Rousseau's construction of models of the good life serves the same purpose. She suggests that he has two competing models, the golden age of pre-political family existence, that is, by definition, a non- or prehistorical model, and Sparta, which might as well be nonhistorical given the way Rousseau reconstructs its character.[31]

Rousseau's Spartan model, like the ideal regimes constructed by the classical utopians, is meant to reproach us with the limitations of the life we lead and the institutions we accept. But the reproach it delivers has a very different character than that delivered by classical utopias. Although sharply critical of contemporary practises, Plato and More use their ideal regimes to bring to light the limitations of all societies at all times. They are tools for teaching us the nature and limits of the human condition. Rousseau's historical model, the classical republic, is, in contrast, a reproach specifically directed at modern men and the spirit of their institutions. Rousseau tells us to read about Spartans and Romans in Plutarch if we want to recognize our weaknesses. His "miracle," unlike that of the classical utopians, "takes place *in history*, not in the land of nowhere." It thus serves as a reminder of the "marvels of the possible."[32] Rousseau tells us not what men should be, but what they *were*. What they were should make us ashamed of what we are. They were *men*. They achieved the humanity we can only dream about.

Without our knowledge of Sparta we might think that the "smallness" of our souls is a universal and inescapable condition of human life rather than the imposition of our institutions. The clas-

---

[31] J. Shklar, *Men and Citizens*, 5.
[32] L. Guerci, *Libertà degli antichi e dei moderni*, 17.

sical utopians point to the obstacles to satisfaction that are rooted in the human condition. Rousseau points in the same direction when he speaks of the lost happiness and self-sufficiency of the natural man. But when he speaks of Sparta and classical republicanism he points to the obstacles to our satisfaction rooted in the particular institutions under which we live. The classical utopias thus inspire a longing to transcend the limitations of the *human* condition; Rousseau's Spartan model inspires a longing to transcend the *modern* condition. No matter then that Rousseau constructs that model from the negation of modern limitations rather than from historical sources; its historical setting is an essential element of the discontent it inspires. The memory of Sparta reminds us that our weakness and disunity is not necessarily the human condition. "Taking men as they are and laws as they could be,"[33] that is, without utopian flight from the limitations of historical existence, we could live otherwise.

Sparta is for Rousseau not so much a model for imitation as proof of his conclusion about the historicity of our limitations. In the account of classical republicanism he draws from Montesquieu and Plutarch, Rousseau finds a state of mind that corresponds to the one he associates with the transcendence of contemporary limitations. The existence of that state of mind in places like Sparta provides Rousseau with a powerful defence against critics who accuse him of demanding more than is possible of man. If they deny the historicity of our limitations and the different character of the citizens of classical republics, Rousseau can claim that their lack of awareness of their own historical limitations makes them incapable of recognizing an alternative state of mind. That is why he expects his "adversaries" to be embarrassed "every time they must speak of Sparta."[34]

Of course, some of Rousseau's most intelligent adversaries have not been embarrassed to speak of Sparta. Volney, for example, condemns Rousseau's attachment to an idealized image of the ancients as a new outbreak of the "Hebrew fanaticism" which he and his fel-

[33] *Social Contract*, 3:351; 46.
[34] "Last Response to M. Bordes," 3:83.

low *philosophes* struggled to extinguish. "Our ancestors swore by Jerusalem and the Bible; the new sect," introduced by Rousseau, "swears by Sparta, Athens, and Titus Livy." A truer account of ancient history would convince us "that the governments of the Mamelukes of Egypt and the Deys of Algiers do not differ essentially from those of Sparta and Rome; and that the Greeks and Romans, whom we venerate so much, lack only the names of Huns and Vandals to excite in us the ideas we have been taught to form of those nations."[35]

A much more serious and penetrating critique of Rousseau's appeal to classical republicanism comes from another opponent of the Jacobin cult of antiquity, Benjamin Constant. Constant does not challenge Rousseau's reconstruction of classical republicanism. Instead, he dwells on the limitations of the modern character. The experience of life under the Jacobin republic, he argues, proves the inappropriateness of classical republican virtues and freedoms for modern peoples.

> When the course of events during the French Revolution brought to the head of public life men who had adopted philosophy as a prejudice, these men thought themselves able to exercise public power as it was exercised in the free states of antiquity. They believed that everything should even today be ceded to collective authority, that private morality ought to be silent before the public interest, that all the attacks against civil freedom would be compensated by the enjoyment of political freedom in its greater reach. But the collective authority was only able to find ways of wounding individual independence, without destroying the need of it. Private morality was silent; but since the public interest does not exert over us the empire it held over the ancients, it was a hypocritical and violent egoism to which private morality was sacrificed.[36]

Constant accepts Rousseau's characterization of the historicity of our sentiments but argues against Rousseau that modern sentiments would overwhelm the very attempts to attack them. The Jacobin republic of virtue was itself the expression of the ends sought by individual wills. An attempt to denature man's self-preference under modern conditions leads only to a masked, self-deluding, and hypocritical egoism that is much more destructive than the openly acknowledged egoism that precedes it.[37]

In the nineteenth century, Fustel de Coulanges tries, with great insight and erudition, to expose the inaccuracy of Rousseau's reconstruction of Sparta. His famous study, *The Ancient City*, clearly aims to break the spell of Rousseau's image of ancient freedom. "It is a singular error . . . to believe that in the ancient city men enjoyed liberty."[38]

But Fustel de Coulanges's efforts have no more broken the spell of Rousseau's rhetoric than Volney's. Demonstrations of historical inaccuracy, however well documented, rarely have much effect on the longing to escape modern limitations that the Rousseauian perspective on classical antiquity inspires. Critics like Volney and Fustel de Coulanges assume that a false reconstruction of the past sours the Rousseauian's appreciation of the present, when it is more often the case that it is an analysis of the present that produces the need to distort the past. Historical criticism can prove that Rousseau is mistaken about the origin and function of this or that ancient institution; it cannot *prove* that the Spartans did not experience the state of mind Rousseau ascribes to them. For the Rousseauian can turn the tables on his critic and argue that the critic's ignorance of his own limitations makes it impossible for him to recognize the alternative spirit that moved the Spartans. If the critic denies the characterization of modern institutions offered by a philosopher like Rousseau, the latter can say that the critic's unawareness of historical alternatives causes him to treat the limitations of contemporary institutions as the limitations of man.

No matter how successful it has been, however, this defence against criticism is a circular one. It asserts that one cannot understand the spirit of the past unless one recognizes one's own histor-

---

[37] For a full account of Constant's fascinating reflections on the modern masks of virtue and democracy, see S. Holmes, *Benjamin Constant and the Making of Modern Liberalism*, chaps. 3-4.

[38] See N. D. Fustel de Coulanges, *The Ancient City*, 221-23.

ical limitation. But one cannot know present limitations without recognizing alternatives to present limitations in the past. If our interpretation of past alternatives indicates a fundamental continuity with the present, then we must be projecting the present into the past. And if we deny present limitations as historical limitations, it must be because we are unaware of alternatives in the past.

Constant's strategy for dealing with this defence—accepting the thesis that modern limitations are historical and concentrating on showing that they are, nevertheless, inescapable—seems more promising than attempts, like Volney's and Fustel de Coulanges's, to expose the inaccuracy of reconstructions of the past. This is the critical strategy that the mature Hegel takes up against the discontent with modern institutions expressed by post-revolutionary romantics and radicals.[39] And it is the strategy that, in the final chapters of this book, I shall borrow from Hegel to display the inconsistency of Marx's and Nietzsche's critiques of modern institutions.

But while this critical strategy avoids the circular defences I have described, it runs straight into an even more powerful barrier to criticism: the hope that we can remove the obstacles to human satisfaction—a hope that arises once one identifies those obstacles as historical. It is relatively easy to live with inescapable limitations on our aspirations when we can make God or nature responsible for them. But when we say that the actions of human beings are responsible for our woes, limitations on our aspirations become much harder to tolerate. If the actions of human beings create our problems, should not human beings be able to resolve them? The recognition of the historicity of human problems and virtues has produced in some minds a despair over the loss of unchanging standards of judgment. But in other minds it produces an exuberant sense of liberation and hope that can withstand almost all criticism. For if all obstacles to our satisfaction can be tied to our specific limitations, and those limitations are indeed historical, then we can conceive of a life *in this world* in which we escape all obstacles to our satisfaction.

[39] As I interpret it in the last section of Chapter 5 of this volume.

But with these reflections I go beyond my present concern with Rousseau and anticipate my treatment in the following chapters of nineteenth-century German social criticism. Rousseau would be the last person one would expect to subscribe to the optimistic maxim that human beings must be able to solve the problems which they have created. However much Rousseau points to the historicity of our present limitations and longs to transcend them, his view of history is overwhelmingly, depressingly, pessimistic. If history has for Rousseau any direction at all, it is down. Our natural independence is irretrievably lost, no matter how much delight we can take from dreaming about it. Human freedom is still possible but growing ever less likely with the continual deepening and expansion of our selfish needs. To argue, as I have in this section, that Rousseau's sense of the historicity of modern institutions and sentiments is an essential element of his social discontent is not to say that he has any hopes that his longing to transcend modern limitations will ever be satisfied.

Rousseau and Revolution

No matter how strong his longing to escape the dehumanizing spirit of modern institutions, Rousseau cannot conceive of a historical agent who could effect that escape, other than the godlike legislator of *The Social Contract* whose coming to the right place at the right time would be nothing short of miraculous. Rousseau foresees, with a clarity unmatched by any of his Parisian rivals, the violent social upheaval in France that will sweep away the *ancien régime*.[40] "We are approaching a state of crisis and the age of revolutions. . . . I hold it impossible that the great monarchies of Europe still have long to last." But Rousseau sees the coming of political revolution as a storm to be weathered rather than as a promise of well-being. No man, he proclaims, "has a greater aversion for revolutions and conspirators of every kind."[41]

Given Rousseau's evaluation of his contemporaries, the reasons

[40] See R. Koselleck, *Kritik und Krise*, 134-35, 208 n. 97.
[41] *Emile*, 4:468; 194. *Dialogues*, 1:935.

for his fear of political revolution are not hard to fathom. The overthrow of laws and institutions, no matter how imperfect they may
be, by individuals who have not been educated to subordinate their
inclinations to the general will only expands the opportunities for
imposing the particular ends of some individuals upon others.
Thus, in his famous letter to Mirabeau, Rousseau is willing to argue
for the "most arbitrary despotism" if we have anything less than
the most complete subordination of men to the law. "For the conflict between men and laws, that throws the state into continual civil
war, is the worst of all political conditions."[42]

Rousseau's understanding of the character of socialized needs,
which he expresses in works like *Emile* and the *Discourse on Inequality*, checks the longing to transform the spirit of modern institutions inspired by his understanding of human freedom and historicity. If social dependence extends the empire of selfishness over
our actions, he cannot conceive of the socialized men with whom he
is familiar initiating a process by which that empire would be dissolved. And unlike the German heirs to his longing to transcend the
spirit of modern institutions, Rousseau cannot conceive of any
process of historical development that could perform this service for
man. Thus, despite his desire to escape the spirit of modern institutions, he cannot see in any revolution, total or partial, a means of
satisfying that desire.

Rousseau uses the word revolution to describe the great trans-
formations of man's character that bring him into civil society, as
well as to describe political upheavals.[43] The period in which individuals began to live in huts with their mates "was the epoch of a
first revolution" in man's character. This state, Rousseau argues,
was "the least subject to [further] revolutions"; yet the discovery
of metallurgy and agriculture produced the "great revolution" that

[42] J.-J. Rousseau, Letter to Mirabeau, July 26, 1767, in Rousseau, *Lettres philosophiques*, 167-68. This statement, exaggeration though it may be, indicates that
Rousseau, for one, had not forgotten the reasons sixteenth- and seventeenth-century political thinkers inclined toward absolutism, as Koselleck claims he had in *Kritik und Krise*, and which Koselleck uses as an explanation of Rousseau's and his contemporaries' need to hold government to the standards of private morality.
[43] See K. Griewank, *Der Neuzeitliche Revolutionsbegriff*, 166ff., to which I owe
much of this discussion.

completed man's transformation into a socially dependent being. [44] But Rousseau views such revolutions with even greater horror than he views political upheavals. They represent the steps by which man becomes the miserable and divided creature he is today. Voltaire and many of the *philosophes* speak of such revolutions as the steps by which man progresses toward a richer and more humane life. The revolution they expect and promote will be a *révolution des esprits,* rather than the political upheaval Rousseau foresees. [45] But even if such a revolution does take place, Rousseau would expect only a deepening of our dependence and a further degeneration of our character as its result.

The French Revolution introduces a new understanding of revolution that combines both senses discussed above. The partisans of the Revolution see it as a political upheaval that effects a *révolution des esprits.* [46] Since Rousseau could see nothing positive in either form of revolution, the revolutionaries must distort his ideas to appropriate them for the Revolution.

We will not find the discontent I have described in this chapter among Rousseau's revolutionary disciples. Even his most loyal follower among the revolutionaries, Robespierre, never understood the philosophic perspective that gives rise to this discontent. Robespierre does not recognize the opposition of virtue and nature in Rousseau's thought. "Happily, virtue is natural to the people, despite aristocratic prejudice."[47] Rousseau is the source of his belief in the people's natural virtue, but his Rousseau is not the Rousseau whom I have been examining here. Robespierre's Rousseau is the author of *La Nouvelle Héloïse* and the *Discourse on the Arts and Sciences,* the Rousseau who attacks the *philosophes* and aristocrats as corrupters of the simple but reliable morality of less civilized peoples—in short, the Rousseau who was most familiar to Robespierre's pre-revolutionary generation. [48]

---

[44] *Discourse on Inequality,* 3:160, 170-71; 3:146, 151-52.
[45] K. Griewank, *Der Neuzeitliche Revolutionsbegriff,* 161ff.
[46] Ibid., 189ff.
[47] M. Robespierre, *Oeuvres,* 10:355.
[48] See J. McDonald, *Rousseau and the French Revolution,* 172-73, and D. Mornet, *Les origines intellectuelles de la Révolution française.*

Robespierre's Rousseau teaches that the task of government is to protect the native virtue of the people from external corruption, rather than to transform selfish individuals into patriotic citizens. For Robespierre, there is no need to denature individuals in order to turn them into citizens. Protect the people from the corrupting influence of aristocrats, foreigners, and atheistic philosophers and you will have good and virtuous citizens. Robespierre charges the National Convention "with respecting not only the rights but the character of the French people."[49] Even his measures aimed at promoting a Rousseauian civil religion attempt to protect rather than transform the character of the French people. Robespierre never tires of saying that atheism is an aristocratic imposition on the people, encouraged by the decadent and immoral sophistication of philosophers.[50] However much he hates the spirit of the *ancien régime*, Robespierre does not see it as an obstacle to his own virtue. He does not need the Revolution to overcome the contradictions of his internal life, for even without it he can still be the paragon of virtue he takes himself to be.

Nor does the revolutionary cult of antiquity to which Robespierre contributes express Rousseau's longing to escape the dehumanizing spirit of modern institutions. Though the cult of antiquity draws heavily from the image of ancient republican virtue bequeathed to the revolutionaries by Montesquieu and Rousseau,[51] there is little evidence that it expresses the same kind of "intoxication" with ancient virtue that we have seen in Rousseau. More than anything else, ancient examples provide the revolutionaries with moving and easily recognized symbols with which to express antimonarchical and anticlerical sentiments, the two most important motivations for the appeal to classical republicanism before Rousseau.[52] The celebration of antiquity, for example, the substitution

---

[49] M. Robespierre, *Oeuvres*, 9:496; 10:196, 198, 355, 453, 467, 554.

[50] Ibid., 10:196, 452, 456.

[51] H. Parker, *The Cult of Antiquity and the French Revolutionaries*, 34-35, 61-65, 120-21. See also P. Vidal-Naquet, "Le mirage grec et la Révolution française."

[52] Recent research has produced a subtle and complex picture of the Revolution's symbols and rhetoric that de-emphasizes the importance of ancient models. See especially L. Hunt, *Politics, Culture, and Class in the French Revolution*, and M. Agulhon, *Marianne into Battle*, 11-37.

of pagan for Christian first names, is a means of expressing republican sympathies and insulting the Church. One need only consider the discontent with modern institutions inspired by the spirit of antiquity in the minds of men like Schiller and Hölderlin, as I shall in the following chapters, to recognize how little the cult of antiquity represents an attempt to escape the limitations of the spirit of modernity. Even amid the corruptions of Paris, Robespierre never looks beyond the present for a home.

The revolutionaries, despite all of their Rousseauian enthusiasms, do not share the Rousseauian state of mind I have outlined in Chapters 1 and 2. Across the Rhine, however, Rousseau's new form of social discontent comes to be shared by some of the most creative and influential philosophers and social critics of the post-Kantian generation. I turn to these individuals in the following chapter.

PART TWO

THE SOCIAL DISCONTENT
OF THE KANTIAN LEFT

IN THIS chapter I try to show how Rousseau's new perspective on modern society and the discontent it inspires are re-created for a group of innovative and influential German intellectuals, whom I describe as the "Kantian left." I then go on to suggest that reflection upon the obstacles to getting beyond the spirit of modern society leads some of these thinkers, beginning with Schiller, to develop a particular understanding of the limitations of the modern world, an understanding that generates another new form of social discontent: the longing for total revolution. This chapter thus lays the foundations for the rest of the book, which studies the origins and development of the longing for total revolution.

The analysis of social phenomena in terms of the general spirit of social interaction particular to a people or an epoch is developed in a variety of ways by late eighteenth-century German intellectuals. And the widespread acceptance of Kant's philosophy of freedom disseminates among large numbers of German intellectuals one version of the new understanding of humanity introduced by Rousseau; for, as I shall suggest below, Kant's philosophy of freedom is inspired by and reformulates Rousseau's distinction between man's humanity and his nature. The simultaneous acceptance of both of these conceptual innovations by a large group of German intellectuals leads many of them, I argue, to identify the dehumanizing spirit of modern society as the obstacle to a world without social sources of dissatisfaction.

As I noted in the Introduction, a particular kind of discontent does not follow as a necessary consequence of adhering to these two conceptual innovations. By providing a new perspective on man and society these innovations open up a number of possible paths of development. In this chapter I try to show why the most influential post-Kantian philosophers take the path opened by Kant's philosophy of freedom that leads to a concern with "dehumanization"—a concern that Kant himself does not share.

In the first section of this chapter I show how Kant reformulates Rousseau's new understanding of man's humanity and, through his own philosophy of freedom, popularizes it among late eighteenth-century German intellectuals. In the second section I try to define and describe what I call the "left Kantian" position and its characteristic concerns. In the third section I suggest that the influence of revolutionary events in France encouraged this particular appropriation of Kant's conceptual innovations. In the fourth section I show how German commonplaces about the superiority of the spirit of classical Greek society are reformulated in the light of the left Kantian perspective on freedom and nature. In particular, I show how such a reformulation makes possible the historicization of the left Kantian understanding of the obstacle to a world without social sources of dissatisfaction, so that the spirit of modern society comes to be seen as the obstacle to the overcoming of dehumanization. In the final section I sketch the history of the left Kantian tradition of social criticism beyond the immediate post-Kantian period.

From Rousseau to Kant

Nowhere, not even in France, did Rousseau's life and works have a greater impact than in the German-speaking lands. Nowhere did Rousseau win more distinguished followers. The greatest figures in that extraordinary outburst of creativity in Germany at the end of the eighteenth century—Goethe, Schiller, and Hölderlin among the poets; Kant, Fichte, and Hegel among the philosophers—all considered themselves, in some way, Rousseau's disciples. "In his name," Goethe writes, "a silent community had been disseminated far and wide."[1]

[1] J. W. Goethe, *Truth and Poetry: From My Own Life*, 1:486.

To trace and account for Rousseau's impact on German intellectual life would thus be an enormous project, so enormous that no scholar has yet seen fit to undertake it.[2] Here it is only necessary to distinguish between two broad categories in speaking of Rousseau's general impact on German intellectual life: his direct and indirect influence. For it was only indirectly, as reinterpreted by Kant, that Rousseau's new understanding of man's humanity was received and developed by German philosophers. Rousseau, himself, is almost never credited by them with this conceptual innovation.

Despite the ubiquity of Rousseauian enthusiasms among late eighteenth-century German intellectuals, most of the sentiments associated with Rousseau's name in Germany—the love of nature, the disdain for convention, the reverence for antiquity, the exaggerated devotion to sincerity, the celebration of simple moral truths and the accompanying fear of philosophic sophistication—were widely shared before his works became generally known. Rousseau's rhetoric reinforced, justified, and energized these sentiments. His name provided isolated German intellectuals with a rallying cry and a sense of community. His works touched very deep sentiments in Germany, often deeper sentiments than in France; but these were, for the most part, preexisting sentiments.

Rousseauian rage against the glittering pretenses of Parisian society found a large and sophisticated audience among German intellectuals because it sent a message that they were already inclined to accept. Rousseau expressed, in a form they themselves could never express, their resentment and defensive disdain toward French culture and courtly society in general. "The *gens d'esprit*," wrote Kant, while discussing Voltaire, "are the demagogues of the *monde galant*." The French, Herder suggested, expressing a widespread sentiment, are satisfied with approximations to the truth as long as they are expressed in a provocative and polished manner; the Germans, on the other hand, sacrifice grace and fluency of

---

[2] Not until 1980 did anyone produce even a survey of the reception of Rousseau's writings among German intellectuals. See J. Mounier, *La fortune des écrits de J. J. Rousseau dans les pays de la langue allemande*. See also R. Fester, *Rousseau und die Deutsche Geschichtsphilosophie*; K. Guthke, "Zur Frühgeschichte der Rousseauismus in Deutschland"; and G. Kelly, *Idealism, Politics, and History*, 2-6.

expression to the pursuit of the truth.[3] Rousseau made the argument against French culture, which German intellectuals wanted to hear, with a grace and beauty of expression that could only come from mastery of the cultural forms they disdained. In Rousseau's works German *Gemutlichkeit* must have appeared to them to dance with French style and grace. No wonder they found his rhetoric irresistible.[4]

Moreover, German intellectuals were more inclined than their French counterparts to accept Rousseau's self-portrayal as the outsider, the simple, honest Genevan seeking for truth amid the corruption of Paris, because it corresponded to their own self-image. Rousseau's fate, that he should be forced to flee from country to country, only to die alone and unacknowledged in the very centre of French civilization, not only reinforced their feelings of resentment toward the French, but also seemed to them to mirror their own fate. They too felt they were struggling for truth in a world that seemed interested only in either raw power or false civility. "Rousseau had really touched our sympathies," Goethe recalled. "Yet we found, on considering his life and fate, that he was nevertheless compelled to find his highest reward in the fact that he was allowed to live unacknowledged and forgotten in Paris."[5]

Living "unacknowledged and forgotten" because of one's uncompromising pursuit of the truth was the fate that most German intellectuals feared and, indeed, often felt they were living. The estrangement from polite society which Rousseau chose they had forced upon them by their social situation. For in Germany there was no Paris, no centre of aristocratic social and cultural life in which young men of talent could seek advancement, to reject. With rare exceptions—such as Weimar in the last quarter of the eighteenth century—German intellectuals found their way into aristocratic society blocked, and thus they tended to take their stand

[3] I. Kant, *Anthropology*, 239; J. G. Herder, "Travel Journal 1769," in Herder, *Sämtlichte Werke*, 4:427ff.
[4] Though not completely free of the French predilection for the *faux-brillant*. See, for example, the criticisms of Rousseau's style in J. G. Herder, "Travel Journal 1769," 4:417-18, 427.
[5] J. W. Goethe, *Truth and Poetry*, 1:421.

against its standards of polite and civilized behaviour. Forced to find their way themselves, they were, not surprisingly, proud of their independence and suspicious of those who possessed the grace and charm they associated with courtly behaviour. For those intellectuals who could not escape the pettiness and irrationality of Germany's provincial courts, the worship of a martyred Rousseau provided solace, as well as an inflation of the importance of their own suffering.[6]

German intellectuals were thus predisposed to accept the martyr's crown which Rousseau placed upon his own head. Some of Germany's greatest poets and intellectual figures, including Schiller, Hölderlin, Herder, and Jacobi, celebrated his martyrdom in verse. But they rarely based such celebrations of Rousseau the man on careful examination of Rousseau's arguments. Schiller's eulogy of Rousseau (1782), for example, was inspired by H. P. Sturz's pedestrian account of Rousseau's life and conversations. There is no evidence that he was familiar with any of Rousseau's major works, apart from the *Letter to d'Alembert on the Theatre*, when he wrote it.[7]

Kant was the only major figure of the 1760s and 1770s who made a serious effort to analyze Rousseau's works rather than just exploit his image and rhetoric.[8] Not that Kant was unaffected by Rousseauian rhetoric and enthusiasm. "I must read and reread Rousseau," he noted, "until the beauty of expression no longer disturbs me; only then am I able to use my reason to judge him."[9] But very few of Rousseau's German disciples practised Kant's self-restraint when they read his works. As a result, unlike Kant, they failed to recognize and appropriate Rousseau's greatest conceptual innovations.

[6] See N. Elias, *The History of Manners*, 1:39ff., and, in general, his contrast of the conditions and character of German and French society in the eighteenth century (1:1-50).

[7] See W. Liepe, "Der Junge Schiller und Rousseau," in Liepe, *Beiträge zur Literaturgeschichte und Geistesgeschichte*.

[8] See J. Ferrari, *Les sources françaises de la philosophie de Kant*, 171; J. Mounier, *La fortune des écrits*, 47, 309; E. Cassirer, *The Question of Jean-Jacques Rousseau*, 58; and G. Kelly, *Idealism, Politics, and History*, 76.

[9] I. Kant, *Werke*, 8:618.

Rousseau's new understanding of man's humanity plays an essential role in the development of Kant's philosophy of freedom. It is no exaggeration to say that Kantian "practical philosophy is inconceivable without Rousseau."[10] The combination of the notes Kant made while reading Rousseau's major works in the 1760s and the structural similarity of many of his arguments to those developed in the *Emile* and *Social Contract* leave little doubt that it was Rousseau who opened up the conceptual path to Kant's philosophy of freedom and inspired him to set out along it.

I am not suggesting that Kant's reformulation of Rousseau's dichotomy between human freedom and natural independence represents an accurate interpretation of Rousseau's arguments. Rather, I view their philosophies of freedom as two species of a new genus of possible arguments founded on the dichotomy between humanity and human nature, a dichotomy that Rousseau first suggests and Kant introduces into general philosophic discussion. Kant's conceptualization of this dichotomy differs in many important ways from Rousseau's. Nevertheless, Kant's philosophy of freedom is founded on the dichotomy between humanity and human nature that he discovers in Rousseau.

By treating the Rousseauian and Kantian philosophies of freedom as two formulations of the same dichotomy between man's humanity and his nature it may appear that I am imposing an inappropriate Kantian conceptual framework on Rousseau's arguments. It would not be the first time that Kantian arguments and sentiments have been written into Rousseau's words. The neo-Kantian interpretation of Rousseau, popularized by Ernst Cassirer, often makes this mistake, as, for example, when Cassirer suggests that "Rousseau did not hesitate for an instant in elevating this ethical conception of personality far above the mere state of nature."[11] "Not . . . for an instant?" Clearly Kant's, not Rousseau's, state of mind is being described here.

But familiarity with Kant's philosophy of freedom may lead us not only to write Kantian concepts into Rousseau's words; it may

---

[10] J. Ferrari, *La philosophie de Kant*, 251ff.

[11] E. Cassirer, *The Question of Jean-Jacques Rousseau*, 56. See also G. Gurvitch, "Kant et Fichte, interprètes de Rousseau," 392.

also lead us to discount the importance of Rousseauian innovations that resemble Kant's. Because it is Kant's formulation of the dichotomy between man's humanity and his nature that has introduced that dichotomy into general philosophic discussion, we tend to associate it with his philosophy of freedom. Read in the light of our knowledge of the Kantian philosophy of freedom, Rousseau's arguments suggest either inadequate approximations or anachronistic echoes of Kantian arguments. A pre-Kantian formulation of this dichotomy in Rousseau's works thus appears to us as either a foreshadowing of Kantian concepts or our own imposition on the texts before us. Our knowledge of Kant's philosophy of freedom tends to close our mind to the possibility of alternative formulations of the dichotomy between man's nature and his freedom, and thus we are likely to miss Rousseau's own conceptual innovations and misunderstand the sources of Kant's.

Rousseau's new understanding of man's humanity is, I suggest, the discovery that Kant celebrates in the most famous of his notes on Rousseau.

> I am myself by inclination an inquirer. I feel an overwhelming thirst for knowledge, and either a restless desire to extend my knowledge or contentment when progress is made. There was a time when I believed that all this constituted the special honour of mankind; and I despised the rabble who knew nothing of these feelings. Rousseau set me straight. My blinding sense of superiority disappears; I learn to honour human beings and would consider myself as far more useless than the common labourer, if I did not believe that the establishment of the rights of man gave my reflections on all these subjects some value.[12]

Before reading Rousseau, Kant apparently thought of man's humanity in terms of man's most refined and, for Kant, most satisfying, natural inclination: the desire for knowledge. Rousseau "set [Kant] straight" by showing him that this attitude merely expressed his own vanity. After reading Rousseau, Kant came to see

---

[12] I. Kant, *Werke*, 8:624.

"intelligence, wit, judgment, and the other *talents* of the mind" as
mere "gifts of nature," which bestow no merit on their possessors.
"Everything good that is not based on a morally good disposition
. . . is nothing but pretense and glittering misery."[13] Kant's "pretense" was his belief that a special kind of inclination, the kind that
he possessed, establishes man's special dignity. By defining man's
humanity in terms of his most distinctive natural inclinations, he
had come to think of himself as more human than the "rabble."
Rousseau taught him, however, that the possession of distinctive
inclinations in no way raises man above the rest of nature's creatures.

Under Rousseau's influence, Kant comes to think of man's humanity in terms of self-imposed, rather than naturally conditioned,
ends and activities. Thus, like Rousseau, he contrasts man's humanity with his nature. Kant's description of the transition from a
natural to a human state echoes Rousseau's in Book I, chapter 8 of
The Social Contract. Rousseau describes this transition as that
which "changed him [man] from a stupid, limited animal into an
intelligent being and a man." For Kant, "it was the transition from
an uncultured, merely animal condition to the state of humanity,
from bondage to instinct to rational control—in a word, from the
tutelage of nature to the state of freedom."[14] But by omitting from
his paraphrase of *The Social Contract* Rousseau's qualification of
the desirability of this transformation—"if the abuses of this new
position did not often degrade him beneath the condition he left"—
Kant reminds us of his differences with Rousseau. For Rousseau,
the dichotomy between nature and humanity is a dichotomy between two kinds of freedom: freedom from dependence on other individuals, or natural independence, and freedom from dependence
on the ends imposed by natural inclinations, or moral/political freedom. For Kant, on the other hand, there is only one kind of freedom: freedom from externally conditioned objects of desire, what
Kant calls autonomy.[15]

[13] I. Kant, *Fundamental Principles of the Metaphysics of Morals*, 11. Idem, "Idea
for a Universal History," in Kant, *On History*, 21.
[14] Cf. *Social Contract*, 3:364; 46, to I. Kant, "Conjectural Beginnings of Human
History," in *On History*, 60.
[15] On this point see S. Shell, *The Right of Reason*, 29-30.

Kant reformulates Rousseau's nature/humanity dichotomy as a dichotomy between natural necessity and human freedom, between heteronomy and autonomy. Both distinguish the humanity of man from his nature and define humanity in terms of human freedom. But while for Rousseau nature versus humanity represents a sad choice between mutually exclusive and equally valuable alternatives, a choice between a happy life of independence and a sublime life of self-rule, for Kant, the choice between the two is clear and unambiguous. Goodness and virtue, independence and self-rule, which Rousseau divides between nature and humanity, are combined in Kant's concept of autonomy, so that there is nothing of value left on the natural side of his dichotomy except pleasure.

Kant could reconcile his own understanding of goodness and virtue with Rousseau's only by suggesting that Rousseau's argument about the goodness of man's natural inclinations "is not his real opinion." He suggests that Rousseau celebrates the goodness of the natural man not as something we have lost through civilization, but as something we can gain through a moral disposition. The mutually exclusive alternatives of nature versus culture are merely "preludes" to The Social Contract and Emile, in which "we find our way out of the labyrinth." Rousseau, he argues, never wanted to go back to a natural state. Rather, he wanted us to look back at a natural state to help construct the goal of moral striving.[16]

It should be clear from what I have stated here and in the preceding chapters that I do not think Kant's reading of Rousseau represents an adequate interpretation of his arguments. Kant's philosophy of freedom popularizes among German intellectuals Rousseau's new conception of humanity in a reformulation that tends to supplant and even hide Rousseau's original formulation of the dichotomy between man's nature and freedom. Kant is both Rousseau's most attentive reader among German intellectuals of his generation and one of the major contributors to their misunderstanding of Rousseau's arguments.[17]

Hegel is probably the only major post-Kantian philosopher of the 1790s who is aware of the Rousseauian roots of Kant's philosophy

[16] I. Kant, Anthropology, 243-44.
[17] J. Mounier, La fortune des écrits, 309.

of freedom. He recognizes Rousseau's distinction between natural and human freedom and suggests that the true "principle of freedom emerged in Rousseau. . . . This development furnishes the transition to the Kantian philosophy, which, theoretically considered, made this principle its foundation."[18]

But this connection between the Rousseauian and the Kantian philosophies of freedom usually passes unnoticed by Kant's disciples in the 1790s. Even the self-styled Rousseauians among them, like Fichte and Schiller, criticize Rousseau's understanding of man's humanity from the perspective of Kant's philosophy of freedom. Fichte, for example, complains that the "sentimental foundation" of Rousseau's thinking kept him from penetrating to a true understanding of man's humanity and the task of the critical intellectual. And in pointing to man's natural state as the goal of human striving, Rousseau is criticized by Schiller for celebrating the "mindless uniformity" associated with that state.[19] When they speak of the dichotomy between man's nature and his humanity, they think of Kantian rather than Rousseauian concepts. My reconstruction of the conceptual sources of the social discontent of post-Kantian philosophers must thus start with the Kantian rather than the Rousseauian formulation of this new understanding of humanity.

The Kantian Left

The widespread acceptance of Kant's conceptual innovations introduces Rousseau's new understanding of man's humanity to a large portion of the German intellectual community. Indeed, this new concept of man's humanity is one reason why Kant's innovations inspire so much enthusiasm.

The success of Kant's critiques in resolving ambiguities that surround the use of concepts like nature and freedom in Enlightenment philosophy would have attracted, in itself, a large following for his conceptual innovations. But Kant's critique of theoretical reason obviously does more. Among other things, it demonstrates conclusively for his German followers at the end of the eighteenth

[18] G. W. F. Hegel, *History of Philosophy*, in Hegel, *Werke*, 20:308; 3:401-2.
[19] J. G. Fichte, *The Vocation of the Scholar*, 1:197. F. Schiller, *On Naive and Sentimental Poetry*, in Schiller, *Werke*, 20:451; 128-29.

century that neither argument nor behaviour can disprove man's special dignity within the universe. For it demonstrates that the existence of human freedom, that special quality that raises man above the natural order of causal necessity, is irrefutable. Moreover, Kant's critiques secure human freedom and dignity from the sceptic's criticisms without undermining scientific rationality. They thus liberate his followers from a painful choice between the defence of human freedom and the pursuit of scientific rationality.

But there is a price to pay for this liberation, as Kant's followers discover when they begin to look at the world from the perspective of Kant's conceptual dichotomies. It is part of that price that Kant's philosophy of freedom isolates, as well as liberates, man's humanity from the external constraints of natural law and social convention. For if there is nothing "that can be called good without qualification, except a *good will*,"[20] then there is nothing absolutely good in the external world. From this perspective, the individual can find no reflection of himself, of his special human qualities, in the external world, not even in the actions and interactions of human beings. In the external world of nature and society, we can see no unconditioned wills; we see only the newest links in the chain of cause and effect. The cost of Kant's defence of human freedom and dignity seems to include the constriction of our humanity to a noumenal kingdom of ends and the consequent devaluation of the external world.

The "consciousness of a chasm between subject and object, of the isolation of the spirit," is part of the "fundamental experience" of the generation of the 1790s that rushes to take up the new standpoint provided by Kant's critical philosophy.[21] Kant's philosophy of freedom contributes to and, more important in the present context, helps explain that experience of alienation from the external world. For if Kant is correct in his characterization of man's humanity, then alienation from the external world follows from becoming reasonable. The liberation from the authority of conventional and natural constraints offered by Kant's philosophy of freedom renders man a solitary. Nothing we find in nature or share in our interac-

[20] I. Kant, *Fundamental Principles*, 11.
[21] P. Szondi, *Poetik und Geschichtsphilosophie I*, 221.

tions with other individuals reflects our human character—the capacity for self-determination that gives us our special and irrefutable dignity. "Would that I had never entered your [German] schools," laments Hölderlin's modern Greek hero, Hyperion. "Among you I became so truly reasonable, learned so thoroughly to distinguish myself from what surrounds me that now I am a solitary in the beautiful world, an outcast from the garden of nature."[22] Hölderlin presents the feeling of spiritual isolation from the external world as a necessary consequence of becoming "truly reasonable." There can be little doubt what kind of philosophy Hyperion learned in his German schools.

No one evaluation of the external world follows necessarily from this fundamental experience of spiritual isolation generated by a Kantian perspective on the external world. Such a perspective could lead one to a deep scepticism about all worldly claims to authority or to search for some superhuman authority to guide one's way in the world. It could lead one to withdraw from the world altogether or even to follow Kant's own complex but little-imitated responses to this perspective.

In this chapter I focus on only one particular reaction to this fundamental experience of spiritual isolation generated by Kant's conceptual dichotomies: that it is intolerable and must be overcome—that man's humanity must be realized in the external world, and that natural and social phenomena must be rescued from devaluation. From this point of view it becomes the "sole interest of reason to suspend such rigid antitheses" as those "between reason and sense, spirit and nature, subject and object." "Dichotomy [Entzweiung]" appears to be "the source of the need of philosophy." One must "recompense nature for its mishandling in Kant's and Fichte's system, and set reason itself in harmony with nature, not by having reason renounce itself or become an insipid imitation of nature, but by reason recasting itself into nature out of its own inner strength."[23]

Kant's conceptual innovations liberate his most creative and in-

[22] F. Hölderlin, Hyperion, 123.

[23] G. W. F. Hegel, The Difference between the Systems of Fichte and Schelling, in Hegel, Gesammelte Werke (hereafter GW), 4:12-13, 8; 89-90, 83.

fluential disciples, Fichte, Schiller, Schelling, and Hegel, from one set of problems, the simultaneous defence of freedom and scientific rationality, only to suggest another, even more troubling set of problems: the discovery and overcoming of the obstacles to the realization of man's humanity in the external world. His dichotomy between natural necessity and human freedom is thus both the starting point of their reflections on natural and social phenomena and the obstacle which they struggle to overcome. No sooner do Kant's most creative disciples take hold of his concepts than they seek to transcend them. Unlike Hegel, Kant lived to see his followers chop up his arguments to serve as the foundations of their own philosophic systems. Indeed, he eventually felt compelled to issue a public letter denying that his system is a "propaedeutic" to a more complete and systematic philosophy of freedom as claimed by Fichte, Schelling, and Reinhold.[24]

Philosophic innovations that answer fundamental questions without immediately suggesting new problems inspire the growth of schools of disciples and commentators. Philosophic innovations that by answering one set of questions suggest the importance of another set of problems inspire the search for further innovations. Kant's innovations are of the latter sort. It is not so surprising, then, that his attempt to limit the scope of theoretical reason should inspire a veritable "explosion" of philosophic speculation and system-building, the like of which has only been seen in post-Socratic Athens.[25]

Given the distance that his self-proclaimed disciples travel from his own arguments, Kant's consternation is understandable. But neither Kant's indignation nor the disdain his disciples sometimes express for the Kantian positions they seek to transcend should lead us to interpret their philosophic speculation as a simple rejection of Kantian principles. The young Hegel may claim that every philosophy worthy of the name seeks to overcome dichotomy and thus Kantianism is not a truly philosophic position. "Dichotomy," he

---

[24] I. Kant, *Philosophic Correspondence*, 253-54.
[25] R. Kroner, *Von Kant bis Hegel*, 1:1-2.

argues, is always "the source of the need of philosophy."[26] However, from our vantage point, it is clear that the "need of philosophy" that Hegel describes is in fact the need of the post-Kantian
philosopher, for whom the experience of spiritual isolation generated by the Kantian perspective is intolerable. The outburst of speculation about the overcoming of dichotomies that follows the dis-
semination of Kantian philosophy is best seen as an attempt to solve
problems suggested by a Kantian perspective on natural and social
phenomena.

I describe the group of philosophers who share this reaction to
Kant's conceptual innovations as the "Kantian left." And I refer to
reflections on the problem of the realization of humanity so understood as "left Kantian" speculation. Included in the Kantian left are
the most creative and influential German philosophers from Fichte
to Hegel. The two characteristic left Kantian concerns are the demand that man's humanity—defined in terms of autonomy—be realized in some way in the external world and the need to locate and
overcome the theoretical and practical obstacles to the fulfillment of
this demand. As we shall see, these concerns, inspired by Kant's
conceptual innovations, persist far beyond the philosophic ferment
of the 1790s.

I describe this group of philosophers as the Kantian *left* to emphasize their dissatisfaction with, and determination to replace, any
social condition that does not fully reflect and embody man's humanity, rather than to indicate any particular political position, especially with regard to the course of events in France. While all of
these individuals are sympathetic to what they perceive as the original goal of the French Revolution, the revolutionary regime inspires very different reactions among them. Fichte is clearly its
most enthusiastic supporter, Schiller its strongest critic. What all of
these figures share, however, is the conviction that man is justified
in rejecting all political institutions that do not embody the capacity
for autonomy that Kant's critiques had rendered irrefutable.

Like Schiller, they begin with an authentically Kantian premiss.

---

[26] G. W. F. Hegel, *The Difference between the Systems*, 4:8; 89. See also idem,
Faith and Knowledge, in *GW*, 4:322-24; 63-65.

"The work of blind forces possesses no authority before which freedom need bow; everything must yield to the highest end which reason erects in man's personality." From that premiss, however, they draw a radical conclusion, never asserted by Kant. Man has the duty to bring not only externally conditioned maxims of ethical behaviour, as Kant argues, but also the externally conditioned authority of all social and political institutions "before the tribunal of pure reason" and find them wanting. For man can settle for nothing less than "true freedom [as] the basis of political association."[27]

Such a conclusion is hardly a self-evident implication of Kantian premisses. Those familiar with Kant's political writings will recognize that Kant himself denies it. Indeed, one can even imagine the derivation of a "right Kantian"—not Kant's own—position that grounds religious and political orthodoxy in Kantian premisses. Given the dichotomy between noumenal freedom and phenomenal necessity that Kant elaborates, it would not be difficult to develop an argument that "true freedom," moral autonomy, has nothing to do with the "principles of political association." For the self-legislation that legitimates authority in the moral sphere can have no analogue in the political sphere, conditioned as it is by natural necessity. In politics we face each other as conditioned and interested individuals. And if we must rely on external conditioning in politics, one might conclude, why not rely upon its oldest and most effective form, religious authority?

The young Schelling wages war against such a "right Kantian" position, a position he discovers among his teachers at the Tübingen seminary. (The theologian, G. C. Storr, is his bête noire.) Those who take this position, he warns, modestly claim "merely to believe what the dogmatist imagined he knew." But for them, he complains, the true essence of Kant's critical philosophy "consists in leading in through the back door what was thrown out by the front."[28]

In opposition to this "right"-wing use of Kantian arguments,

---

[27] F. Schiller, *Aesthetic Education*, 12-13, 8-9, 24-25.
[28] F. Schelling, "Über Offenbarung und Volksunterricht," in Schelling, *Werke*, 1:400. See also his early (1795) essay "Philosophical Letters on Dogmatism and Criticism," in *Werke*, 1:205-266.

Schelling sounds a left Kantian call to arms: "Subject every heteronomous power to your own autonomy."[29] In this exhortation, Schelling calls for something more than Kant's demand that we make unconditioned pure reason the determining ground of the will. While Kant calls on us to overcome the heteronomy of the will, Schelling and the Kantian left in general call on us to overcome the heteronomy of the external world. They demand that we subject the external powers that govern our interaction with nature and other individuals to the control of our unconditioned reason. In other words, while Kant asks us to act autonomously, the Kantian left demands that we realize our autonomy.

What would it mean to make "true freedom the principle of political association," when Kant defines "true freedom" as autonomy? What would the realization of autonomy look like? If our present communities "dehumanize" us by not realizing our autonomy, what would a fully "human" community look like?

Kant himself describes a community that includes every rational being, and whose principle of association is moral freedom. As a morally free being, every rational creature belongs to what Kant calls a "kingdom of ends." This kingdom is a community in which every individual shares the same end: the moral law that defines our freedom. In this community "true freedom" is the basis of association, for we are associated with each other in the "kingdom of ends" only to the extent that we act freely and treat other individuals as ends in themselves. In such a community every individual is equally "member" and "sovereign," for each individual legislates the same end, freedom, for each other.[30]

But given Kant's dichotomy between freedom and nature, the freedom we share as rational beings cannot become manifest to each other. "A rational being, even if he punctually follows this maxim [the categorical imperative] himself, cannot reckon upon all others being true to the same maxim, nor expect the kingdom of nature and its orderly arrangements shall be in harmony with him as a fitting member, so as to form a kingdom of ends to which he himself

---

[29] F. Schelling, *New Deduction of Natural Right*, in *Werke*, 1:272.
[30] I. Kant, *Fundamental Principles*, 50.

contributes." We act as a member of such a kingdom of ends every time we follow the moral law. But that means we are members of this fully "human" community only to the extent that we abstract from the external conditioning of our interaction with nature and other individuals. Thus the kingdom of ends "is certainly only an ideal"; it is the idea of a human community by which we measure the limitations of the actual communities that we share with other individuals.[31]

To make "true freedom the principle of political association," we would have to realize Kant's kingdom of ends somehow in the forms of social interaction we share. Our humanity, which Kant defines by abstracting from the external conditioning that constitutes individuals as members of different communities, must itself become the condition that constitutes us as members of a community. Only then would our community deserve to be described as "human," for only in such a community does external conditioning by political authority and social interaction lose its heteronomous character. Only there does social and political influence express man's "human" character, his free, rational will. The compulsion to live in anything less than such a community could then be characterized as "dehumanizing."

Out of the left Kantian reaction to Kant's philosophy of freedom thus develops the goal of a fully human community, a form of association that is both human, in that its ordering principle is moral freedom, and a genuine "community," in that our freedom is manifest to each other and shared in our social institutions and interactions. Most left Kantians, like Rousseau, celebrate the identification of the individual and the community in a way that makes their commitment to human freedom seem questionable to most liberals. Their celebration of community seems especially strange coming from philosophers who build their arguments on the foundation of a Kantian concept of autonomy. But, like Rousseau, they argue that the individual's freedom can be realized only through an identification of the individual's will with the general will of the community. The human community for which they strive seems a para-

---

[31] Ibid., 55, 50.

doxical goal, in that it appears that the definitions of humanity and community on which it relies contradict each other. The first requires the abstraction from external conditioning, the second is itself a form of mutual conditioning among individuals. Plainly, such a community is impossible unless Kant is wrong in arguing that our freedom cannot manifest itself or act as a force in the phenomenal world. That Kant is indeed mistaken on this point is precisely what left Kantians set out to demonstrate.

The immediate legacy to the Kantian left of Kant's philosophy of freedom is thus twofold and ambiguous. On the one hand, it provides a much wanted and seemingly irrefutable defence, against scepticism and materialism, of man's special dignity in the universe. On the other hand, it provides a new understanding of the real source of our dissatisfaction with the external world of nature and society: the inability of our purposive and autonomous reason to penetrate the causal chains that seem to determine our interaction with nature and each other.

One of Kant's aims in the *Critique of Pure Reason* is to demonstrate that no knowledge of the external world or any interpretation of human behaviour can call the freedom and inherent dignity of human beings into question. When one accepts this demonstration, then man's *incapacity* to act in a free and "human" way no longer appears to be the obstacle to his satisfaction in the world. Rather, it is the dichotomy between the noumenal and phenomenal realms, the incongruity between the "kingdom of ends" and the "kingdom of nature,"[32] that proves to be the obstacle to our satisfaction in the world. By redefining in this way the obstacle to a world without sources of dissatisfaction, Kant's conceptual innovations generate a new kind of longing, the longing for the *realization* of freedom and humanity in the world, which quickly becomes a longing for a fully human community.

Why should a redefinition of the obstacle to human satisfaction generate such an outpouring of hope for the transformation of the world, when the conceptual innovations that provide its foundations seem to make that obstacle immovable? As I have suggested

[32] Ibid., 56.

in the opening pages of this book, intense longings and hopes for social transformation arise just as much out of new definitions of obstacles to satisfaction as out of discoveries of new ways around previously defined obstacles. A new definition of the obstacle to a world without sources of dissatisfaction can in itself generate intense excitement about the possibilities of world transformation simply by providing a common explanation of seemingly distinct sources of dissatisfaction. By doing so, it establishes for us a single aim, the overcoming of that obstacle, rather than a multitude of separate, often conflicting goals. And by focusing our activity on a single aim, it gives rise, at least for a time, to the hope that we can uncover and withdraw the roots of our dissatisfaction, rather than chop away endlessly at its various manifestations.

The members of the Kantian left, as I shall suggest in my discussions of Schiller and the young Hegel in the following chapters, use the dichotomy between freedom and nature to explain almost all sources of dissatisfaction in the modern world. Like Rousseau's, their social criticism draws on outrage against various aspects of modern social life, such as injustice, inequality, hypocrisy, vulgarity, and servility, but always returns to the realization of freedom as the means of correcting them. By making dehumanization appear to be the source of all our woes, and the realization of freedom the answer to all our complaints, Kant's conceptual innovations provide the dissatisfaction of his followers with a focus that deepens and intensifies their social discontent.

The French Revolution and the Kantian Left

The left Kantian position is only one of many possible reactions to a world viewed from the perspective of Kant's dichotomy between human freedom and natural necessity. Why do the most creative and influential philosophers attracted to critical philosophy in the 1790s share this reaction, while Kant does not?

The generational gap between Kant and the left Kantians certainly contributes to their different reactions to Kantian dichotomies. Kant was almost sixty when he published the *Critique of Pure Reason* in 1781; the oldest of the left Kantians, Schiller, was just over twenty at the time. The left Kantians were educated during the height of the *Sturm und Drang*. Their imaginations fired by *Sturm und Drang* tirades against positive laws and conventions, they were far less likely than Kant to tolerate external limitations on man's freedom. Moreover, simply in suggesting the need for new conceptual innovations, the left Kantian reaction to Kant's dichotomies must have been attractive. For the most creative disciples are often attracted to interpretations of their masters' teaching that suggest that it must be surpassed.

But the most important factor contributing to the left Kantians' appropriation of Kant's innovations is, I suggest, an accident of timing that brought Kant's philosophy of freedom to their attention at the same time as the Revolution was being fought in France. Although the *Critique of Pure Reason* was published in 1781, it did not become generally known to the German reading public until the end of the 1780s. All of the greatest figures associated with the philosophic ferment of the 1790s turned to Kant's philosophy after the outbreak of the French Revolution in 1789—Fichte in 1790, Schiller in 1791, Schelling, Hölderlin, and Hegel while at the Tübingen Seminary during those same years.

The elaboration of analogies between what quickly came to be known as the Kantian "revolution" in philosophy and the French Revolution in politics has since been a favorite pastime of German philosophers and historians. Heine's ironic comparison between the two revolutions, culminating in his award of the title of supreme terrorist to Kant, the "deicide," over Robespierre, the regicide, is the most famous of these discussions.[33] But Heine was only reformulating a well-worn theme, already expounded by some of the most important and influential thinkers of the 1790s.

Schelling, for example, points to the importance for his contemporaries of the coincidence of the "revolution in actuality there [France] and the ideal revolution here." In his eulogy of Kant (1804), he describes how his generation wondered at this coincidence without "recognizing that it was one and the same spirit"

[33] H. Heine, *Religion and Philosophy in Germany*, in Heine, *Works*, 5:137.

that shaped both revolutions.[34] For Fichte, the French Revolution adds form and colour to the "substance" of the image of freedom drawn by Kant, so that now its outlines must be clear even to "dull eyes." The Kantian philosophy "shatters humanity's last and strongest chains" and thus parallels the political events in France. Fichte thinks of his own philosophic system as both the completion of Kant's innovations and the theoretical "system of liberty" that corresponds to the political revolution in France. Just as "that nation delivers humanity from its material chains, my system will deliver humanity from the yoke of the thing-in-itself."[35] Similar reflections, minus Fichte's characteristically boastful rhetoric, upon the significance of analogies between the philosophic and political revolutions occur in the writings of Schiller, Hegel, and Hölderlin.[36]

This coincidence in timing and the search for analogies it encourages have certainly contributed to the often-noted tendency of German intellectuals to impose abstract metaphysical and moral meanings upon the events of the French Revolution.[37] Here, however, I suggest that it has contributed to another, and to my mind more significant, tendency in post-Kantian social criticism: an inclination toward "revolutionary" interpretations of the significance of Kantian metaphysical and moral principles—toward what I describe as left Kantian positions.

Nietzsche once suggested that "noble and enthusiastic spectators" viewed the French Revolution "according to their own indignation and enthusiasms for so long, and so passionately, that *the text* finally disappeared under the interpretation."[38] Perhaps something similar has happened to the Kantian dichotomy between human freedom and natural necessity. Kant never demands the "realization" of autonomy, and he probably would have suggested that such a demand conceals a contradiction in terms. But interpreted in

---

[34] F. Schelling, "Immanuel Kant," in *Werke*, 1:588.

[35] J. G. Fichte, *Schriften zur Revolution*, 82-83. Idem, *Briefwechsel*, 1:449.

[36] And not only among partisans of one or both revolutions. One enemy of the new French regime, Benedict Stattler, went so far as to suggest that a Latin translation of the *Critique of Pure Reason* was one of the chief causes of the French Revolution. See K. Röttgers, *Kritik und Praxis*, 55n.

[37] See J. Droz, *L'Allemagne et la Révolution française*, 27ff.

[38] F. Nietzsche, *Beyond Good and Evil*, *Sämtlichte Werke*, 5:56; 49.

the light of the overthrow of the old regime, Kant's conceptual innovations have generated a demand for the realization of autonomy that has become, for many German social critics, the main thrust of his philosophy of freedom.

The fame and influence of Kant's philosophy peak during the years in which the Revolution breaks out. The young generation of philosophers and intellectuals in Germany is thus trying to understand the significance of both philosophic and political challenges to received authority at the same time. It is only natural that they should hope that an understanding of one of these challenges would shed light on the other, especially when their almost simultaneous occurrence makes their analogies seem so striking.

I suggest here that it is the background light shed by the Revolution on their appropriation of Kant's conceptual innovations that most inclines Kant's heirs toward the left Kantian position and its demand for the realization of autonomy. The Revolution lends the left Kantian position a "metaphysical pathos" it otherwise lacks.[39] It is this pathos that inclines those who try to make sense of Kantian philosophy and the Revolution at the same time toward the left Kantian position. To them, the realization of freedom in the external world seems something more than a speculative implication of a metaphysical system. It is, rather, a drama being played out before the eyes of the world and engaging the interests of all spectators.

There is more than enough material in both the substance and form of Kant's conceptual innovations with which to construct striking analogies to the French Revolution. As Heine notes, by demonstrating the illegitimacy of all attempts to disprove man's autonomy, Kant disarms all the opponents of human freedom of their theoretical weapons, just as the revolutionaries in Paris disarm freedom's enemies of their physical weapons. "On both sides of the Rhine we see the same break with the past. All respect is denied to tradition; as in France every right, in Germany, every thought must justify itself. And as the monarchy fell here [in

[39] I borrow this expression from Arthur Lovejoy's *The Great Chain of Being*, 10-14.

France], so there fell deism, the keystone of the spiritual ancien regime."[40]

Moreover, Kant presents himself as a philosophic, if not a political, revolutionary. Kant presents his critical philosophy as the "single and sudden revolution" needed to found the science of metaphysics.[41] Philosophy needs, he argues in the Second Preface to the *Critique of Pure Reason*, a "Copernican" reversal of perspective, not a long and slow accumulation of knowledge. Thus Kant disposes of all theoretical challenges to human freedom through a philosophic revolution.

It is no wonder, then, that his followers draw analogies between critical philosophy and political revolution in France. They have before them what appear to be the two great innovations of their age, innovations that totally alter their understanding of what is possible and obligatory for mankind. Their enthusiastic identification of the two events still reverberates in later accounts of the period like Heine's or, to cite an even later example, Dilthey's.

> It was just during those years, 1788 to 1793, that there occurred the two world-historical events which at one and the same time brought the age of Enlightenment to a close and opened the gates of a new era: Kant completed the recasting of German thought, and the Revolution in France destroyed the old state and undertook the establishment of a new order of society.[42]

How does this perception of the age affect the way these thinkers appropriate Kant's philosophy of freedom? There is no direct testimony from them addressed to such a question. Schelling claims that by appearing to mirror and even prophesy the unprecedented events in France, Kantian philosophy gained an audience that went far beyond that ordinarily open to philosophic works. "The great event of the French Revolution procured him a general and public influence which his philosophy in itself would never have brought

---

[40] H. Heine, *Religion and Philosophy in Germany*, 5:130.
[41] I. Kant, *Critique of Pure Reason*, 21-22.
[42] W. Dilthey, *Die Jugendgeschichte Hegels und andere Abhandlungen*, 13.

him."[43] But he does not ask how that event has shaped his own appropriation of Kantian concepts.

Let me suggest how it may have inclined Schelling and his contemporaries toward the shared reaction to Kant's philosophy of freedom that I describe as left Kantian. The overthrow of the *ancien régime* suggested the possibility of a break in the continuity of development, an escape from the weight of the past, which would have been unthinkable only a few years before. François Furet suggests that the thought that human will and effort could introduce the "advent of a new age" was perhaps the "seminal idea of the French Revolution itself."[44] Whether the prospect inspires joy or terror in their minds, the contemplation of such a break with the past certainly preoccupies many observers of the events in France. In his Berlin lectures on world history Hegel recalls the impression this drama made on his generation.

> The thought, the concept of right now made itself felt all at once, and the old framework of injustice could offer no resistance to it. . . . [O]nly now does man come to recognize that thought ought to govern spiritual reality. Thus it was a splendid dawn. All thinking beings shared in the celebration of this epoch. A sublime emotion ruled at that time, a spiritual enthusiasm thrilled the world as if the actual reconciliation between the Divine and the world was for the first time accomplished.[45]

Turning from their contemplation of events in France with this suggestion in mind, that "thought ought to govern spiritual reality," the new generation of philosophers must have found in Kant's philosophy of freedom an explanation and justification for the unprecedented attack on conventional authority in France. Here was a philosophy that defined man's humanity as his freedom from external conditioning; a philosophy that declared any heteronomous source of moral authority illegitimate; and, most important, a phi-

[43] F. Schelling, "Immanuel Kant," 1:587-88.
[44] F. Furet, *Interpreting the French Revolution*, 13. See also K. Griewank, *Der Neuzeitliche Revolutionsbegriff*, 189-90.
[45] G. W. F. Hegel, *Vorlesungen über die Philosophie der Geschichte*, 926. See partial translation in Hegel, *Philosophy of History*, 447.

losophy that once and for all refuted the arguments that supported
despotism by bringing into question man's capacity for self-rule.
Read with the attack on conventional political and social authority
in France in mind, Kant's philosophy of freedom must have appeared to be an "ideal equivalent and theory of the French Revolution."[46] But it only appears that way—it only supports the impression that "thought ought to govern spiritual reality"—when the
dichotomy between natural necessity and human freedom is perceived as an obstacle to be overcome, rather than as an account of
our experience, as Kant perceives it. Events in France lend such a
reaction to Kant's dichotomy an emotional force that it might
otherwise lack.

Of course, there can be no conclusive proof of such a suggestion.
But I think that a comparison of the way Kant and the individuals I
have described as left Kantians interpret the Revolution makes my
suggestion seem quite plausible. For, unlike Kant, they all tend to
conceive of the Revolution as an attempt to realize man's moral
freedom in the external world.

Kant's refutation of a moral right to revolution occurs in essays
published in the 1790s.[47] It puzzled his contemporaries, since he
was generally known to be a supporter of the Revolution—which,
indeed, he remained to the end of his life—as it continues to puzzle
Kant's readers to this day. But since his explicit refutation of the
right to revolution occurs only in later works that follow both the
outbreak of the Revolution and the general reception of his conceptual innovations, it did nothing to hinder his disciples from drawing
revolutionary implications from the Kantian philosophy of freedom.

All left Kantians agree, at least in the early 1790s, with Schiller's
description of the Revolution as an attempt—in Schiller's opinion,
an unsuccessful attempt—"to set law upon the throne, to honour
man at last as an end in himself and to make true freedom the principle of the political bond." "A question that has hitherto been de-

[46] G. Kurz, *Mittelbarkeit und Vereinigung: Zum Verhältnis von Poesie, Reflexion, und Revolution bei Hölderlin*, 2.
[47] In Kant's essay on "Theory and Practice" (1792), in Kant, *Political Writings*,
and in *The Metaphysical Elements of Justice* (1797).

cided by the blind right of might is now, so it seems, being brought before the tribunal of pure reason."

> However skillfully blind caprice may have laid the foundations of her work, . . . with whatever appearance of venerability she may surround it—man may in these operations treat it all as though it had never happened. . . . In this way any attempt on the part of a people grown to maturity to transform its natural state into a moral one arises and justifies itself."[48]

Note how in this description the revolutionary interpretation of Kantian metaphysics and the metaphysical interpretation of the Revolution are fused. Describing the analogy between the Kantian and French revolutions, Heine writes, "[A]s in France, every right, in Germany every thought must justify itself." In a manner characteristic of the Kantian left, Schiller interprets Kantian philosophy as a set of thoughts that challenges all established right and the Revolution as an attempt to bring right before the tribunal that judges thought.

From this point of view, Kant had taken the first, essential, albeit inadequate step toward a moral revolution that would replace force with freedom as the basis of all social bonds. Few left Kantians carry the identification of the Kantian revolution with the revolutionary challenge to the *ancien regime* quite so far as Fichte, for whom, one can state without fear of exaggeration, "the liquidation of Louis XVI corresponded to the liquidation of the thing in itself."[49] But for all of the great philosophers whom Kant inspired in the years immediately after the Revolution, from Fichte to Schiller to Hegel, heteronomy represents an external condition of the world that the Revolution tried to abolish.

Despite his own unwavering support for the Revolution, Kant never views it as an attempt to bring political institutions "before the tribunal of pure reason" and "make true freedom the principle of political association." Indeed, as is well known, Kant condemns political revolution from the moral point of view. It is man's moral duty, he argues, to establish and maintain the common authority of

[48] F. Schiller, *Aesthetic Education*, 24-25, 8-9, 12-13.
[49] B. Willms, "Introduction" to J. G. Fichte, *Schriften zur Revolution*, 20.

the sovereign as the necessary foundation of the lawful resolution of disputes among individuals. To challenge, let alone subvert, that authority thus contradicts one's moral obligations.[50]

Kant approves of the Revolution only from an instrumental point of view, as a means toward the general establishment of the rule of law. As an event that seems to push mankind toward the rule of law, which it is man's moral obligation to promote, the Revolution evokes a disinterested sympathy in the eyes of observers.

> The revolution we have seen taking place in our own times in a nation of gifted people may succeed, or it may fail. It may be so filled with misery and atrocities that no right-thinking man would ever decide to make the same experiment again at such a price, even if he could hope to carry it out successfully at the second attempt. But I maintain that this revolution has aroused in the hearts and desires of all spectators who are not themselves caught up in it a *sympathy* that borders on enthusiasm, although the very utterance of this sympathy was fraught with danger. This sympathy cannot therefore have been caused by anything other than a moral disposition within the human race.[51]

It is the sentiment of those who observe the revolution, not of those who make it, that Kant offers as proof of man's moral disposition. It is not the Revolution itself, but rather our reaction to it, that represents a moral experience. This Revolution "may be so filled with misery and atrocities that no right-thinking man would ever decide to make the same experiment again." But Kant is "concerned only with the attitude of the onlookers," not with that of the Revolution's participants and victims. As if to emphasize this point, Kant claims elsewhere that disapproval of a revolutionary event, the execution of the king, also demonstrates man's moral disposition.

> But of all the outrages attending a revolution through rebellion, even the *murder* of the monarch is not the worst; for it is still possible to imagine that the people did it because they

[50] I. Kant, *Metaphysical Elements of Justice*, 84ff.
[51] I. Kant, "The Contest of the Faculties," in *Political Writings*, 182.

feared that if he were allowed to survive, he might recover his power and mete out to the people the punishment they deserved, in which case their behaviour would not be an act of penal justice, but simply an act of self-preservation. It is the formal *execution* of a monarch that must arouse dread in any soul imbued with ideas of human right, and this feeling will recur whenever one thinks of events like the fate of Charles I or Louis XVI. But how are we to explain this feeling? It is not aesthetic (like the sympathy that comes from imagining oneself placed in the sufferer's situation), but rather moral, being our reaction to the complete reversal of all concepts of right.[52]

Kant conceives of the moral revulsion experienced at the execution of the king as a reaction against the perversion of the rule of law. For by executing the king, the revolutionaries use the forms of the rule of law to destroy its foundation, the authority of the sovereign.

For Kant, the Revolution represents a panorama of events that alternately engage the sympathy or the disgust of our moral dispositions. While it is clear that Kant approves of the general direction of those events, it is just as clear that the Revolution does not represent for him an attempt to replace force with moral freedom as the basis of political association. In a sense, the left Kantian interpretation of the Revolution appears more "Kantian" than Kant's own. For it is only according to their interpretation that the realization of moral freedom is at stake in the fate of the Revolution.[53]

Prior to the Revolution Kant had given a few hints that he would not consider political revolution morally liberating. In his famous essay, "What is Enlightenment," he even quotes with approval Frederick the Great's advice to his subjects: "Argue as much as you will, and about what you will, only obey."[54] Kant argues that, paradoxically, greater political freedom than Frederick offered does not promote the freedom of the mind, "the escape from self-imposed tutelage" that he seeks to promote. But that conclusion could easily

---

[52] I. Kant, *Metaphysical Elements of Justice*, 87n.

[53] I leave it to other scholars to render consistent his complex reaction to the Revolution. See especially K. Röttgers, *Kritik und Praxis.*, 52ff., and L. W. Beck "Kant and the Right of Revolution," 171-87.

[54] I. Kant, "What is Enlightenment," in *On History*, 10.

be forgotten given the ringing rhetoric of the beginning of that same essay.

> Enlightenment is man's release from his self-incurred tutelage. Tutelage is man's inability to make use of his understanding without direction from another. Self-incurred is this tutelage when its cause lies not in lack of reason but in lack of resolution and courage to use it without direction from another. *Sapere Aude!* "Have the courage to use your own reason!"—That is the motto of enlightenment.
>
> Laziness and cowardice are the reasons why so great a portion of mankind, after nature has long since discharged them from external direction, nevertheless remains under lifelong tutelage, and why it is so easy for others to set themselves up as their guardians.[55]

Kant's denial that man should have any other guardian than his own reason was enthusiastically received by his followers, but it was interpreted, in the light of events in France, against what would be Kant's own opinion on the individual's obligations to the sovereign. The French, according to some of their left Kantian admirers, had simply developed the energy and courage to do away with their guardians. Fichte's defence of the Revolution, for example, echoes Kant's rhetoric against self-imposed tutelage. Laziness and cowardice, he argues, are what keep us from getting rid of our political guardians and taking our destiny into our own hands. When you deny the possibility of political self-rule, Fichte tells his opponents, "at least be honest and do not say we *cannot* realize your principles. Rather say what you really mean: we *will not* realize them." And when Schiller recalls Kant's "*sapere aude,*" it is in the context of a discussion of the Revolution and the need to realize our freedom in political institutions.[56]

Kant views his philosophy of freedom as a revolutionary way of explaining and defending moral freedom. He insists that critical philosophy offers no new moral guidelines, only new ways of for-

[55] Ibid., 3.

[56] J. G. Fichte, *Schriften zur Revolution*, 108. F. Schiller, *Aesthetic Education*, 50-51.

3

mulating and defending the moral duties already known to all.[57] But viewed in light of its analogies to the political revolution in France, Kant's Copernican revolution in philosophy comes to be seen as the beginning of a moral revolution that promises a transformation of the world. His express denial of being the founder of a new moral order notwithstanding, Kant is described as the "Moses of our nation, who leads it out of Egyptian bondage into the free solitary wilderness of speculation, bringing the life-giving law down from the sacred mountain."[58] "Soon," writes Fichte, "Jesus and Luther, ye sacred guardians of freedom, a third who has completed your work, . . . who, perhaps without knowing it, shatters humanity's last and strongest chain, will be gathered to your side."[59] Hegel only expresses a widely shared expectation when he writes to Schelling in January 1795 that "from the Kantian system and its completion I expect a revolution in Germany."[60]

The revolution that Hegel, like the other members of the Kantian left, expected to follow from the completion of the Kantian system was the realization of autonomy. The French, it seemed to them, had attempted such a revolution. The Germans, privileged with a clearer understanding of human freedom, should, they assumed, have a greater chance of successfully completing it.

Total Revolution and the Spirit of Modernity

I have suggested in the Introduction that two conceptual innovations make possible the longing to get beyond the dehumanizing spirit of modern society: the distinction of man's humanity from his nature and the analysis of social phenomena in terms of coherent and integrated wholes shaped by historically specific spirits of social interaction. The first innovation makes possible a concern for dehumanization. The second allows one to identify the spirit of modern society as the obstacle to overcoming dehumanization.

[57] I. Kant, *Critique of Practical Reason*, 8.
[58] Kant is so described by Hölderlin in a letter to his brother, January 1, 1799, quoted in R. Kroner, *Von Kant bis Hegel*, 1:3.
[59] J. G. Fichte, *Schriften zur Revolution*, 137.
[60] G. W. F. Hegel, *Briefe von und an Hegel*, 1:23-24.

Kant's dichotomy between human freedom and natural necessity introduces the first innovation to the German intellectual community. The second conceptual innovation, the new approach to the analysis of social phenomena, is even more widespread among German intellectuals at the end of the eighteenth century than is the Kantian philosophy of freedom. Unlike the Kantian philosophy of freedom, which develops out of the "single and sudden revolution" introduced by Kant's *Critique of Pure Reason*,[61] the tendency of German intellectuals to analyze epochs and societies as internally coherent and historically specific individual units, each defined by a particular spirit of social interaction, has many sources in eighteenth-century thought. It is not necessary to account for them all here.[62] No individual thinker shapes this historical approach in the same way Kant shapes German intellectuals' understanding of human freedom and dignity.[63] Thus no particular formulation of the new approach to the analysis of social phenomena has the same importance as a source of the new forms of social discontent examined here as Kant's philosophy of freedom.

This general approach to the analysis of modern society allows left Kantians to historicize their understanding of the obstacle to the overcoming of dehumanization. If a single spirit of social interaction informs all of man's external relations, then dehumanization cannot be overcome through individual effort. All external actions, no matter how well intentioned, will be caught up and shaped by the contemporary spirit of social interaction. In other words, individuals cannot realize their humanity in the world unless the spirit of social interaction is itself "humanized." Likewise, all institutions informed by a spirit of social interaction that does not realize hu-

[61] I. Kant, *Critique of Pure Reason*, 21-22.

[62] The standard reference works on the origins of German historicism are F. Meinecke, *Historism*, and E. Troeltsch, *Der Historismus und seine Probleme*. See also P. Reill, *The German Enlightenment and the Rise of Historicism*.

[63] Herder is the most promising candidate for this role. But though his numerous works were widely read, he never produced a sustained theoretical formulation and defence of his approach. There is thus little talk among German intellectuals at the end of the eighteenth century of a "Herderian" revolution in history and social science comparable to the "Kantian" revolution in philosophy which they so frequently commented on.

man freedom must be rejected as dehumanizing, no matter what other virtues they may possess.

But why assume the spirit of social interaction can be "humanized?" If the spirit of social interaction shapes the totality of external forces that condition individual actions, why not conclude that our social dependence inevitably dehumanizes us by making subordination to "heteronomous powers" necessary?

Social critics like Schiller and the young Hegel answer this question in the same way Rousseau did. The character and behavior of the ancients teach us that the spirit of social interaction has not always been dehumanizing. When we look, for example, at the Greeks, with their harmony of intellect and sensuality, we recognize that the dichotomy between nature and man's humanity is the imposition of the spirit of modern society, not the universal condition of human existence, as Kant and his less creative followers seem to believe.

What Kant treats as the inescapable condition of human life then appears, in reality, as a "matter of regional climate," as Hegel puts it.

In the form of fixed reflection, as a world of thinking and thought essence in antithesis to a world of actuality, this dichotomy falls into the northwest. As culture spreads, and the development of those outward expressions of life in which dichotomy can entwine itself becomes more manifold, its regional sanctity is more firmly established and the strivings of life to give birth once more to its harmony become more meaningless, more alien to the cultural whole.[64]

Although dichotomy is a necessary part of any human culture, modern culture makes dichotomy the organizing principle of life and knowledge. Only in this condition, in which "the might of union vanishes from the life of men and the antitheses lose their living connections and gain independence," is philosophic speculation needed to restore feeling for the higher unity between freedom

---

[64] G. W. F. Hegel, *The Difference between the Systems*, 4:14-15; 91-92.

and the external world.[65] We only think such a unity impossible because of the peculiar character of modern life. Reflection upon Greek culture will teach us, however, that what we call the limitations of human existence are, in fact, those of our own world. We may not at this moment be able to explain this "higher unity," and the Greeks themselves cannot provide us with an adequate explanation of it. But since the Greeks *lived* this unity, there must be a higher unity for philosophers to explain. We should not, they argue, let our current limitations—the fact that we seem able to explain phenomena only through dichotomy and analysis—become objectified as the limitation of the human condition.

This connection between admiration for the Greeks and post-Kantian philosophic speculation merits more attention than it has been given.[66] In one of the best attempts to examine this connection, Hans Freier argues that Schelling's and Hegel's philosophy of identity represents a new answer to the old quarrel of the ancients and the moderns. The philosophy of identity, Freier argues, provides them with the means by which modern culture can raise itself up to and beyond the level of ancient culture.[67]

I, however, would turn this explanation of the connection between German Graecophilia and post-Kantian speculation around. Rather than look for an answer to the challenge of ancient to modern culture in philosophic speculation, post-Kantian philosophers find in the superiority of ancient culture an answer, or at least the hope of an answer, to the theoretical and practical challenges laid down by Kant's dichotomies. Like Rousseau's intoxication with ancient virtue, the enthusiasm for the Greek polis expressed by Schiller, Hölderlin, Schelling, and Hegel represents more than a mere infatuation with a mythical image of the past. They celebrate

[65] Ibid., 4:14; 91.
[66] For discussion of this theme, see H. Freier, *Die Ruckkehr der Götter*, and J. Taminiaux, *La nostalgie de la Grèce à l'aube de l'idéalisme allemand*. The best known treatments of German Graecophilia are devoted primarily to its literary manifestations; see, for example, W. Rehm, *Griechentum und Goethezeit*, and M. Butler, *The Tyranny of Greece over Germany*. See also P. Szondi, "Antike und Moderne in der Aesthetik der Goethezeit," in *Poetik und Geschichtsphilosophie I*, 11-266.
[67] H. Freier, *Die Ruckkehr der Götter*, xi.

an idealized image of the polis with such enthusiasm because it suggests that the dehumanizing limitations of their own society are not inescapable.

The interpretation of the superiority of Greek culture to modern culture in light of the left Kantian understanding of man's humanity reproduces for these philosophers something very much like Rousseau's perspective on the limitations of modern individuals and society. It historicizes the left Kantian understanding of the obstacle to human satisfaction, thereby leading some left Kantians to focus their discontent on the spirit of modern society as the source of dehumanization.

As Montesquieu's understanding of ancient virtue takes on an entirely new meaning when interpreted in terms of Rousseau's understanding of human freedom, so the Winckelmannian image of the Greek state of mind, so widely accepted by eighteenth-century German intellectuals, takes on a new meaning when viewed in the light of the Kantian philosophy of freedom. Winckelmannian commonplaces are echoed in, for example, Schiller's characterization of the Greek state of mind. "It is humanity alone which to the Greek contains all the idea of beauty and perfection." "The Greeks approach quietly with a noble and measured step."[68] But these observations take on a new meaning for Schiller because they are made in the light of Kantian dichotomies. Greek behaviour defies the dichotomy between nature and humanity which Kant taught was universal and inescapable. "Never for the Greek is nature purely physical nature, and for that reason he does not blush to honour it; never is reason for him purely reason, and thus he need not tremble in submitting to its rule."[69]

From the left Kantian perspective it appears that the Greeks, with their characteristic good fortune, stumbled upon this harmony without ever realizing what they had achieved. To us, Schiller writes, "[t]hey are what we were; they are what we shall become again . . . by means of our reason and freedom."[70]

How can one *consciously* reproduce Greek harmony? How can

[68] F. Schiller, *Grace and Dignity*, in *Werke*, 20:254. Idem, *Aesthetic Education*, 212-13.
[69] F. Schiller, *Grace and Dignity*, 20:254-55.
[70] F. Schiller, *On Naive and Sentimental Poetry*, in *Werke*, 20:414; 84.

one marry freedom and natural necessity "by means of our reason," if reason tells us that freedom and natural necessity are mutually exclusive? That is the problem that left Kantian speculation must face. In my opinion, it is a problem which it cannot solve.[71]

But the historicization of the obstacle to human satisfaction posed by the Kantian dichotomy allows one to postpone a solution to this question and pour one's energy instead into analyses of the limitations of modernity. Rather than focus one's attention on a highly questionable theoretical construction of possible alternative forms of social life, one can focus on the limitations of the present, confident that the negation of present limitations will usher in a new and liberating epoch. The tremendous sense of uneasiness, the feelings of isolation from the world generated by the left Kantian perspective, can be poured into a new form of discontent: the longing to escape the dehumanizing limitations of the spirit of modern society.

This new longing naturally focuses the attention of these philosophers on the obstacles to its satisfaction. How can one transform the spirit of modern society if all social interaction is informed by that spirit? Certainly not through a change in political institutions, since the efficacy of political authority depends upon the characteristic forms of social interaction that bind individuals to each other. It follows from the new approach to the analysis of social phenomena that political institutions will always adapt themselves to the contemporary spirit of social interaction, so that the attempt to overcome the spirit of modern society directly through political change is bound to be fruitless. Such is one of the most important lessons which Schiller, among other German social critics, draws from the course of the French Revolution.[72] One can, indeed, impose a political constitution on a nation unprepared for it. But it will have little effect on individual behaviour, and without the use of force it will tend to revert to a constitution more appropriate to the spirit of social interaction at the time.[73]

Thus how can one, as it were, get hold of the spirit of social in-

[71] For the arguments that support this opinion, see the final sections of Chapters 5, 6, 7, and 8 and especially the Conclusion.
[72] F. Schiller, *Aesthetic Education*, 44-45.
[73] See G. W. F. Hegel, *Philosophy of Right*, paragraph 274.

teraction, when every action undertaken within a particular society is likely to be informed by its underlying spirit? Only if there is some special sphere of social interaction that shapes the character of interaction throughout the entire society, and which our actions can influence. If such a sphere of interaction exists, then a revolution there will effect a "total revolution," the complete transformation of the spirit of individuals and social institutions, which political revolution fails to achieve. The location of such a sphere of social interaction allows one to identify the obstacle to the overcoming of the dehumanizing spirit of modern society: the present character of that sphere, however it is defined. It leads one to focus on social relations in that sphere as the source of all forms of dissatisfaction with the world. And it leads one to long for the total revolution that would be brought about by a transformation of the character of that sphere of social interaction. Until such a total revolution has been effected, though it be "a task for more than one century," "we must regard every attempt at political change—[that is, every attempt to realize human freedom]—as untimely and every hope based upon it as chimerical."[74]

In this way the longing to overcome the dehumanizing spirit of modern society makes possible the development of the longing for total revolution. The latter longing does not necessarily follow from the former. Some of those intellectuals who begin with the left Kantian concern about dehumanization never go beyond the longing to overcome the spirit of modern society, for they are unable to locate the obstacle to such an overcoming and thus cannot conceive of the means of bringing it about. But Schiller, the first left Kantian to identify the spirit of modern society as the source of dehumanization, also suggests that the transformation of a particular sub-political sphere of social interaction could take us beyond the spirit of modern society. He thus becomes the first to express the need for a "total revolution" as I have defined it here. The following chapter examines Schiller's social discontent and its conceptual sources in detail. In later chapters I shall show that the young Hegel, Marx, and Nietzsche all follow a path of reflection similar to the

[74] F. Schiller, *Aesthetic Education*, 44-47, 204-5.

one I have just outlined, and thus that they all come to share Schiller's longing for total revolution.

The Three Waves of Left Kantian Speculation

My association of some of the most important post-Kantian philosophers with intense longings for social transformation will be no surprise to anyone familiar with the intellectual environment in Germany over the last two hundred years. What is new in my account is the attempt to use conceptual innovations to identify and account for the source and character of those longings.

That such a wide spectrum of social criticism, encompassing so many incompatible approaches, should appear to start from the same concern—the dehumanization imposed on man by the spirit of modern society—most often has been explained by intellectual historians in three ways. Some simply deny the phenomenon, arguing that the appearance of a common foundation in a shared state of mind is an illusion of perspective that does not stand up to close examination. Others suggest that the shared concern indeed reflects some aspect of life in modern societies. A third group points to some shared source of discontent that precedes and shapes the social criticism of these intellectuals, such as secularized religious passions or an infatuation with an idealized image of the past or the future.

I reject the first explanation. As I suggested in the Preface, shared states of mind are always the constructions of an observer; thus they are, to a certain extent, always abstractions from the concrete context in which acts of expression develop. There is no way of finally confirming whether there exists "out there" a shared state of mind apart from my reconstruction of it. We can only ask whether there is sufficient and appropriate evidence to justify constructing such a shared state of mind as a context that helps us to explain a variety of acts of expression. The rest of this book presents the evidence that leads me to offer an affirmative answer to this question. As I noted in the Introduction, though the construction of explanatory contexts necessarily involves some abstraction from the way ideas and sentiments are expressed, that does not make the choice of these contexts a merely subjective and arbitrary act.

I do not by any means rule out the second explanation. It is possible that some aspect of the social experience of the philosophers I discuss might also provide a context that will help us to identify and account for their shared state of mind, albeit in a different manner than I attempt here. But such an account need neither contradict nor exclude my own. Since political, socioeconomic, or linguistic contexts are no less abstractions from *the* context of the acts of expression examined here than is the conceptual context that I invoke, one need not assume that one form of contextual explanation necessarily excludes the others.[75]

As for the explanation of the social discontent of post-Kantian philosophers in terms of earlier religious ideas and attitudes, it does seem, at first glance, much more plausible than similar accounts of the discontent of the Parisian *philosophes*. The language used by German philosophers in their demands for the self-realization of humanity and the rescue of the external world from mere mechanical necessity suggests religious sentiments much more directly than that used by eighteenth-century French intellectuals. With the German philosphers—at least until one gets to Marx, Nietzsche, and the Hegelian left—one need not begin such explanations by disentangling the religious "substance" of their discontent from their violently anti-Christian rhetoric, as one must do with the French. In Protestant lands the Christian Church did not, at least in principle, represent to intellectuals an enemy of enlightenment and freedom of conscience, as it had to the *philosophes* in Paris. German intellectuals could find religious support for liberty and enlightenment in the principles of the Reformed Church that was unavailable to their French counterparts, given the Catholic Church's unashamed defence of religious and moral hierarchy. German *Aufklärer* do not hesitate to use religious concepts and rhetoric to make their points in a manner that often surprises those more accustomed to the rhetoric of the French partisans of enlightenment.

Post-Kantian philosophers thus provide plenty of material that

[75] See my Preface, xiv-xv.

supports explanations of their discontent in terms of religious concepts and experience. I have pointed out the basic problems with such explanations in the Introduction. There I concluded that they do not meet the appropriate standards of evidence that would justify invoking religious concepts and experience as an explanatory context for the discontent of the philsophers and intellectuals treated in this study, and I suggested that my use of conceptual innovations will meet these standards. To justify the use of either context one needs two kinds of evidence: evidence of historical continuity, that is, evidence that the later thinkers are indeed familiar with the state of mind that is said to explain their discontent, and evidence of logical continuity, that is, evidence that the earlier state of mind in some way suggests the fundamental questions asked and solutions sought by later thinkers. As I have shown in the Introduction, the proponents of secularization explanations almost always substitute the elaboration of analogies for this kind of evidence. The *resemblance* of the form and substance of philosophic expressions of discontent to religious expressions is taken by itself to demonstrate historical and logical continuity.

In the following chapters I shall present the evidence of historical and logical continuity that justifies my use of the conceptual innovations discussed here as an explanatory context for some of the new forms of social discontent shared by German philosophers and social critics since Kant. Rather than use what evidence there is to construct and evaluate a more adequate secularization explanation of these forms of social discontent than its advocates have offered, I shall concentrate on demonstrating that the evidence supports a very plausible alternative to these explanations. That demonstration will culminate in an attempt to refute the often-repeated assertion that Marx's advocacy of " 'human emancipation' and the 'realization of philosophy' [is] quite unintelligible" apart from "its heavy and unmistakable Judeo-Christian content."[76]

Establishing the persistence among these different philosophers of the new historical approach to the study of social phenomena and its central role in shaping their questions and needs is a relatively

[76] R. N. Berki, *Insight and Vision: The Problem of Communism in Marx's Thought*, 44.

easy matter. The evidence of the historical and logical continuity with regard to this conceptual innovation will appear in the discussions of individual thinkers in the following chapters. My contentions about the left Kantian perspective on freedom and nature are, however, more controversial, and the persistence of that perspective is much more difficult to establish. Therefore, it might be helpful to provide a brief sketch of my view of the nature, extent, and persistence of the left Kantian tradition of social criticism, before proceeding to these discussions of individual thinkers.

The importance of Kant's conceptual innovations, especially his dichotomy between human freedom and natural necessity, as a persistent source of social discontent is difficult to establish because of the nature of the reaction it inspires. A tendency to deny the Kantian sources that inspire its position is built into the left Kantian perspective. As we have seen, Kant's dichotomy is both the starting point of the left Kantians' discontent and the obstacle they seek to overcome. If they find a solution to the problem that Kant's dichotomy inspires, that is, overcoming the theoretical and practical obstacles to the realization of human freedom, they will deny that dichotomy. Their proposed solutions will conceal the original problems they address.

Thus the evidence presented in this book for the persistence of the left Kantian perspective and its role as a source of social discontent cannot always take the form of direct acknowledgments by the philosophers examined. To produce evidence of my claims, I must try to reconstruct the questions that these philosophers' arguments are meant to answer and show how these questions arise out of a left Kantian perspective. Such a reconstruction of the basic left Kantian concerns will not prove difficult for the immediate post-Kantian period. But since Marx and Nietzsche directly and violently denounce the conceptual innovations of idealist philosophy, it will take a greater effort to establish in their cases evidence of historical and logical continuity with the left Kantian perspective on human freedom.

There have been, I suggest, three great waves of left Kantian speculation. The first takes place during the period discussed in this chapter: the heady years immediately following the publication of

Kant's critiques and the outbreak of the French Revolution. This first wave peaks in Hegel's philosophic system. Its idealist synthesis puts to rest, at least temporarily, speculation about how to bridge the gap, left by Kant's philosophy, between man's humanity and the external world.

A second wave of left Kantian speculation emerges shortly after Hegel's death. The outburst of social criticism and philosophic speculation usually described as the "young" or "left" Hegelian movement focuses on the closing of the gap between human reason and reality that opens up for them when Hegel's synthesis breaks down under the pressure of political events and critical examination. The failure of the 1848 revolutions effectively puts an end to this second wave of left Kantian speculation, for it dashes the hopes raised by the Hegelian philosophy of freedom that human reason could be fully realized in the external world. But this wave of speculation does not subside before Marx discovers that one can use the categories of classical political economy to develop highly original and suggestive answers to left Hegelian questions. These answers lead him to identify the realization of humanity with the revolt of the working class.

Marx's "demystification" of the longing for the realization of humanity hides for a long time the questions his turn to political economy was meant to answer. The recovery of these questions in the twentieth century leads to an outburst of speculation about the alienation and dehumanization of modern man that deserves to be called a third wave of left Kantian speculation. A succession of European Marxists have since grappled with the problem of dehumanization as left them by the young Marx. And they frequently turn to Hegel's and Schiller's formulations of similar problems for conceptual clarification.

The "critical theory" advocated by Horkheimer and Adorno represents one of the most interesting manifestations of this third wave of left Kantian speculation in that it combines the rejection of all forms of social interaction that do not fully externalize man's true freedom and reason with a commitment to unmask as reification all attempts to demonstrate the possibility of the full realization of man's humanity.[77] As Jürgen Habermas puts it in his recent critique of the founders of the Frankfurt school, "[T]hey submitted subjective reason to an unrelenting critique from the ironically distanced perspective of an objective reason that had fallen irreparably into ruin." Their "appeal to social solidarity can merely indicate that the instrumentalization of society and its members destroys *something*; but it cannot say explicitly wherein this destruction consists."[78]

One might describe this position as "terminal left Kantianism," for it obliges critical theorists both to declare dehumanizing any constraint imposed on us by our social institutions that does not embody our humanity and to unmask as false all claims to satisfy their longing for the realization of humanity. Permanent, hopeless longing seems to be the critical theorists' obligation as well as their fate.

I agree with those German critics of critical theory who have seen in it a return to the unresolved problems of left Hegelian social criticism.[79] I suggest that it suffers from the same difficulties as the left Hegelian attempt to "realize" Hegelian philosophy.[80] Both groups of social critics try to "realize" Hegel's realization of freedom. That project is represented as a return to the concrete reality of social practise. In fact, as Rüdiger Bubner demonstrates, "praxis," the reality to which they demand we return, is itself nothing but an abstraction from an abstraction. Their concept of praxis "falls into abstract opposition to theory in that it is defined as what theory is not."[81] To determine whether the self-contradictory abstraction that follows from their demands for the realization of the Hegelian philosophy of freedom is avoidable, we need more familiarity with the premises and limitations of the first wave of left Kantian speculation. We need to know more about why Hegel and his contem-

[77] I am thinking here primarily of Adorno's *Negative Dialectics* and their joint effort, *The Dialectic of Enlightenment*.

[78] J. Habermas, *The Theory of Communicative Action*, 377, 389.

[79] See R. Bubner, "Was ist Kritische Theorie," 160-209, and M. Theunissen, *Gesellschaft und Geschichte: Zur Kritik der Kritische Theorie*, especially 14ff.

[80] See H. Stuke, *Die Philosophie der Tat: Studien zur Verwirklichung der Philosophie*, and Chapter 6 below.

[81] R. Bübner, *Theorie und Praxis: Eine Nachhegelsche Abstraktion*, 7.

poraries set out in the first place to seek the realization of humanity in the external world.

Habermas suggests that the German philosophy of freedom, which begins with Kantian criticism, "retrogresses to gesticulation" in the hands of its latest representatives, the critical theorists. They point right and left to irrationality in modern social relations while indignantly rejecting demands that they explain and justify the standard of rationality that allows them to recognize irrationality when it exists. If such empty gesticulation is the fruit of the pursuit of human emancipation undertaken by the " 'German' line" of social criticism, no wonder that Habermas wants to abandon that line.[82] Like Marx before him, he recommends that we "leap' out of the "paradigm" of German philosophy of freedom, although he would have us leap into Anglo-American philosophy of language rather than into political economy.

Habermas's call for a shift of paradigm from German philosophy of freedom to modern philosophy of language sounds like it should spell an end to the left Kantian perspective and the social discontent it generates. But I wonder. Marx too called for such a shift of paradigm. Confronted with what appeared to him as the dead end of left Hegelian criticism, Marx sought answers to left Kantian questions in the concepts and categories of political economy. Marx's leap into the study of socioeconomic reality abandoned the philosophic formulation of the demand for the realization of humanity, but he carried with him the need to answer left Kantian questions. That need was registered in the *way* he conceptualized key economic concepts.[83] As I shall try to show in Chapter 7, what Marx actually did was to write the solution to left Kantian questions, the means of the realization of freedom, into the concepts with which he characterized social production.

Does Habermas's shift in paradigm represent a break with left Kantian questions or a new answer to them? I suspect the latter, given that, implicit in the actual conditions of communication, he finds all of the characteristics of humanity that left Kantian criti-

---

[82] J. Habermas, *Theory of Communicative Action*, 385-87, 399, 366, 386.
[83] I develop this interpretation of Marx's social criticism in Chapter 7.

cism seeks to realize: autonomy, rationality, and equality, for example. Moreover, he states that the shift in paradigm is needed to pursue the goals of Horkheimer's and Adorno's critique of reification, which amounts to saying that it is a necessary means to the realization of humanity.

I thus doubt that Habermas's rush to take up Anglo-American philosophy of language frees his arguments from the goals of the post-Kantian philosophy of freedom any more than does Marx's leap into English political economy. An American philosopher, sympathetic to Habermas's suggestions for the reform of social theory, has spoken recently of the critical intellectual's role in "nurturing the type of dialogical community in which *phronesis* can be practiced and where the freedom of all human beings is concretely realized."[84] Perhaps a fourth wave of left Kantian speculation is already upon us.

[84] R. Bernstein, *Beyond Objectivism and Relativism*, 175.

F O U R

SCHILLER AND
THE "AESTHETIC WAY" TO
FREEDOM

SCHILLER is neither the first nor the most influential social critic
whose critique of modern society is shaped by left Kantian questions about the realization of man's humanity. He has a prominent
place in this study because he is the first to identify the spirit of
modern society as the obstacle to the realization of human freedom,
as well as the first to suggest that the transformation of one particular sphere of social interaction in modern society could effect a total revolution that would take us beyond its dehumanizing spirit.
Moreover, in Schiller's social criticism and his argument for aesthetic education the philosophic sources of the longing for total revolution manifest themselves most clearly. Schiller's arguments
contain none of the anti-philosophic rhetoric that obscures the philosophic sources of Marx's and Nietzsche's social discontent.

The focus of this chapter is a detailed examination of Schiller's
account of the obstacles to political freedom in the modern world,
as it is developed in his *Letters on the Aesthetic Education of Man*.
The role of Schiller's philosophic essays in the development of post-
Kantian idealism has often been noted. It has been said that "the
influence of the *Letters on the Aesthetic Education of Man* on the
development of idealism cannot easily be overestimated."[1] Hegel,
himself, suggests that "it is Schiller who must be given credit for

---

[1] R. Kroner, *Von Kant bis Hegel*, 2:45.

breaking through the Kantian subjectivity and abstraction of thinking."[2]

Without denying their importance as a transitional stage between Kantian and Hegelian philosophies of freedom or, for that
matter, their intrinsic value as attempts to deal with problems that
are still with us, I turn to Schiller's philosophic arguments more for
the questions they pose than for the answers they provide. By focusing on the questions Schiller asks, I believe I can bring to light
the philosophic sources of the new form of social discontent that he
shares with the other German social critics examined in this study.

Schiller's Social Discontent before Kant and the Revolution

In arguing that Kant's philosophy of freedom is the most important
source of the mature Schiller's social discontent I do not mean to
suggest that Kant's philosophy is responsible for his being dissatisfied with the spirit of modern society. Given the repeated and
often violent criticism of modern society in Schiller's early works,
that would be an absurd claim.

Indeed, Schiller's complaints about modern society and individuals sound many of the same themes before, during, and after his
immersion into Kantian philosophy of freedom at the beginning of
the 1790s. Schiller's first play, *The Robbers*, is a portrait of rebellion. The first words of his first hero are a lament: "How this age of
puny scribblers disgusts me when I read of great men in my Plutarch."[3] The complaints about arbitrary rulers and unnatural conventions, the dissatisfaction with the soul-dividing spirit of modern
life when compared with the spirit of the Greeks, the disgust with

[2] G. W. F. Hegel, *Aesthetics*, in Hegel, *Werke*, 13:89; 1:61.

[3] F. Schiller, *The Robbers*, in *Werke*, Nationalausgabe, 3:20. Hereafter, except
where otherwise noted, references to works by Schiller will cite only the title of the
work and the volume and page number(s) of this German edition of his works. The
primary exception will be references to Schiller's *Letters on the Aesthetic Education
of Man*, which will cite Letter and/or page numbers of L. A. Willoughby's and
E. M. Wilkinson's bilingual edition. (As in previous chapters, a reference to the English translation of a particular work follows a semicolon after the reference to the
work in the original language.)

hypocrisy and servility, all expressed in *The Robbers* by Karl Moor, appear in Schiller's works at every stage of his career.

Moreover, the idea that art might lead the way beyond modern limitations, which receives its fullest development in his philosophic essays of the 1790s, appears in his poetry and prose of the preceding years as well. Schiller does not begin to study Kant's philosophy until 1791.[4] The *Letters on the Aesthetic Education of Man* (1793-1795) are among the fruits of his preoccupation with critical philosophy. Nevertheless, already in 1784, in his lecture on the moral value of the theatre, Schiller argues that we need the theatre to promote the aesthetic experience that provides a "middle state," a bridge between the two states of sense and thought, moral action and idea. A few years later (1789), he sets this idea to verse in the long poem "The Artists."

> What nature in her grand march
> From each other tears apart
> Is bound on stage and in song.[5]

Obviously, Schiller draws neither his dissatisfaction with modern society nor his exalted vision of the artist's vocation from Kant.

What he does draw from Kant is an explanation of the sources of his dissatisfaction with the modern world. Kant's philosophy of freedom allows Schiller to analyze his intuition about the connection between humanity and internal harmony without falling into the conceptual confusion about man's humanity that hinders his earlier attempts to develop this idea. By providing him with what he perceives as a clear definition and irrefutable defence of man's humanity, Kant's conceptual innovations allow Schiller to redefine the obstacle to a world without sources of dissatisfaction in a new and very significant way, which, in turn, transforms the character of his social discontent.

Schiller's early works seethe with disdain for the irrationality and arbitrariness of contemporary institutions which, in his view, turn modern men into servile hypocrites. These works are filled

---

[4] F. Schiller, Letter to Körner, March 3, 1791, in Schiller, *Briefe*, 3:134.
[5] *Werke*, 20:90, 1:207.

with Rousseauian rhetoric against the "men of our days," the "bourgeois" "who is good neither for himself nor for others."[6] The modern age, Schiller concurs with Karl Moor, is an age of "puny scribblers." One has to look in Plutarch for accounts of greatness.[7] "Man" is for Schiller, as for Rousseau, a term of distinction that modern individuals do not deserve to bear. Indeed, in an early ode (1782) Schiller celebrates Rousseau as a martyr who fell trying to make men out of modern individuals.

> Christians made him suffer, made him die
> Rousseau who would turn Christians into men.[8]

But the young Schiller does not share Rousseau's complex understanding of the problem of man's humanity. Like most of Rousseau's German admirers Schiller's exploitation of Rousseauian rhetoric is not based on careful analysis of his concepts. No German writer expresses as many Rousseauian themes—the worship of nature, the cult of sincerity, intoxication with republican virtue, contempt for the weakness of modern men—with as much fervour and eloquence as the young Schiller. Yet there is no evidence that Schiller read anything more of Rousseau before the end of the 1780s than his *Letter to d'Alembert on the Theatre* (though given the immense popularity of *La Nouvelle Héloïse* and *Emile*, it seems unlikely that Schiller was completely unfamiliar with these works). Most of his knowledge of Rousseau seems to have been taken from H. P. Sturz's pedestrian account of Rousseau's life and opinions.[9] It is not surprising, then, that one finds very little of Rousseau's analysis of man's social and political problems supporting Schiller's Rousseauian rhetoric.

[6] J.-J. Rousseau, *Emile*, 4:250; 40.

[7] In November 1790 Schiller writes to Körner that he would like to prepare a German translation of Plutarch. Such an undertaking, he suggests, would engage all of his interests, artistic, historical, philosophic, and moral (*Briefe*, 3:118).

[8] *Werke*, 1:163.

[9] Indeed, it was a Rousseauian remark reported in Sturz's book that inspired Schiller's second play, *The Conspiracy of Fiesco at Genoa*. See H. P. Sturz, *Denkwürdigkeiten von J. J. Roussèau*, 145-46. For a persuasive destruction of the "legend" of the young Schiller as a student of Rousseau, see W. Liepe, "Der Junge Schiller und Rousseau."

As already noted, Schiller, like Rousseau, uses man as a term of distinction. But what is the *qualité d'homme* according to Schiller? What is the quality that makes us human and that modern individuals seem to lack? Freedom, Schiller would most likely answer with Rousseau and most participants in the *Sturm und Drang*. But what freedom? The freedom of self-love or self-renunciation? Independence from convention or civic interdependence? Does the natural innocence of Don Carlos or the harsh republican virtue of Verrina in *The Conspiracy of Fiesco at Genoa* represent the freedom that defines man's humanity? Schiller points to both as if they were ultimately synonymous. He possesses nothing like Rousseau's conceptual distinction between natural independence and human freedom with which to clarify his views.

This conceptual confusion about the nature of freedom is far more disturbing to Schiller than to most of the other participants in the *Sturm und Drang*. Schiller does not share the disdain for political activity and political institutions expressed by most members of that generation of intellectual rebels.[10] However arbitrary and oppressive he thinks contemporary political institutions may be, he still sees politics as a realm in which man should be able to express his freedom. This concern for political reform makes the resolution of his conceptual confusion about human freedom a pressing problem for the young Schiller.

Moreover, Schiller has a greater respect for the need for conceptual clarity than do even the most profound participants in the *Sturm und Drang*, Goethe and Herder. He does not have to wait for Kant's philosophy to "spoil" his poetic inspiration with a compulsion for conceptual clarity.[11] Schiller's poetic sense had always been "spoiled" by this compulsion, although some may judge it one of his greatest achievements to have "made a seemingly intractable mass of intellectual matter available to poetry."[12] He turns to Kant's philosophy to satisfy his own needs, not because he is seduced by philosophy's siren call. Even the young Schiller does not

[10] R. Pascal, *The German Sturm und Drang*, 53.
[11] A claim often made by Schiller's readers and sometimes even by Schiller himself. See his letter to Körner of May 25, 1792, in *Briefe*, 3:201-2.
[12] I. Graham, *Schiller's Drama: Talent and Integrity*, 10-11.

hesitate to play out his conceptual struggles in prose and verse. Indeed, *Don Carlos*, the greatest drama of his youth, provides the best evidence of the young Schiller's struggles to resolve his confusion about the source of man's humanity.

The plot of *Don Carlos* centres on the conflict between King Philip of Spain and his son and heir, Carlos. Carlos and his childhood friend Roderigo, Marquis of Posa, share idealistic hopes for the end of tyranny in Spain and its Flemish empire, hopes that bring them into conflict with the despotic king. Carlos, however, does not yet possess sufficient emotional maturity to enter into competition with his father. He is an overly sincere young man who unfortunately has a very strong passion that he must hide from his father: his love for the queen, his stepmother, who was originally to be his bride. Posa, on the other hand, is in complete control of his emotions. Most of the action of the play follows from his attempts to manipulate Philip and Carlos into serving his idealistic ends. He tries to both gain Philip's confidence and use Carlos's passion for the virtuous queen, who shares Posa's ideals, to bring Carlos around to his duty. The failure of his intrigues lead to disaster for all concerned.[13]

The central theme of this long and complex play is the need for "real" men, individuals who are truly human. All of the main characters in the play are searching for such individuals. The king, surrounded by servile and hypocritical courtiers, longs for a real man and thinks he finds one in Posa. The crisis of the play develops out of Carlos's failure to behave like a real man. We watch as Posa tries to manipulate circumstances so as to educate him to manhood. The queen, who is at the centre of all the intrigue, frequently comments on the contrast between *Mann* and *Mensch*—between the mere man and the truly human man—throughout the play. By the end of the play, we see that there are two sides to a truly human character, two kinds of behaviour in tension with each other: the capacity to suppress one's inclinations in order to perform one's duty and the sincerity and honesty that come from always following one's inclinations.

[13] See Schiller's own account of the evolution of the play's plot and its inconsistencies in his *Letters on Don Carlos*, 12:137-77.

The union of both sides would provide the truly human character sought by the major characters of the play. The truly human individual would have to combine the qualities that Rousseau distinguishes as virtue and goodness. It is this combination that the queen first sees in Posa, and that she defines when she says she knows him to be both a "good human being and a great man" ("guten Mensch als einen grossen Mann").[14] But when she sees how Posa deceives and manipulates Carlos, albeit to serve the end the three of them share, she retracts her earlier judgment. Posa has the virtue of greatness but not of goodness. He is not a complete, fully human man.[15]

The lonely king also comes to an awareness of this distinction between *Mann* and *Mensch*. He seeks someone he can trust, a real man, since he is surrounded by flatterers and manipulators. He calls his adviser, Alba, a mere *Mann*, while his confessor is usually referred to as something less than a man. Posa's outspokenness and integrity attract him and eventually win his confidence. The king treats Posa in a way he does not treat his other subjects. "You may continue to be a man [*Mensch*]," he tells him. But he eventually realizes that he is also being used by Posa. In the end he recognizes Posa for what he is, not the sincere, openhearted man he sought as a friend, but the man of duty, a man "for all humanity."[16]

Finally, there is Carlos, who is human-all-too-human. Posa and the queen try to teach him to suppress his inclinations so that he will serve their idealistic goals. His failure to do so makes Posa's intrigues necessary and thus leads to catastrophe for all three. Posa and Carlos represent the two sides of a fully human character: one displays the greatness of virtue, the other the goodness of an innocent and uncorrupted character; one lacks sincerity, the other lacks strength.

Ironically, the only real *Mensch* in the play is the queen. Only she seems to combine the two sides of a human character that ap-

[14] *Don Carlos*, in *Werke*, 7: line 4011. Compare this description of Posa to Schiller's later distich, "Goodness and Greatness," (1:290): "There are only two virtues. May they ever be united: / Goodness ever great and greatness ever good!"
[15] *Don Carlos*, 7: line 4395. For an elaboration of this theme in the play, see V. Hell, *Schiller*, 110ff., 123.
[16] *Don Carlos*, 7: lines 2742, 2809, 5060.

pear separately in the male protagonists. Indeed, Schiller seems to believe that women naturally escape the divisions that men can overcome only with the greatest effort.

Overall woman yields before man; only in the highest
Does the most masculine yield before the most feminine.
. . . .
Man seems to be free. You are; forevermore
  You know of no choice, no necessity.
  Whatever you give, you give yourself fully, you are
    always whole.[17]

Schiller seems to believe that women's inclinations are naturally other-directed, so that for women virtue does not require the self-suppression it requires for men. Grace, the appearance of a lack of constraint on one's inclinations in voluntary movements, thus comes naturally to women.[18]

But no matter how high Schiller exalts his image of women, they represent mere *models* of the humanity that men should strive for, rather than living examples of that humanity. For a natural harmony of character, that cannot be otherwise than it is, is, for Schiller, not a human harmony.

Do you seek the highest, the greatest? The plants can teach
  it to you.
What they are without will, be through your will—that is it!

One could substitute "women" for "plants" in this distich and it would express the same idea for Schiller. For women's harmony is, like the plant's and the unity of all other natural things, something given, not something earned; they "know of no choice."[19] As such it provides an image of wholeness to inspire man's striving, but not an example of human harmony.[20]

[17] *Werke*, 1:287.
[18] See *Grace and Dignity*, 20:289.
[19] "The Highest," 1:259.
[20] In this, women are, for Schiller, like nature in general. Nevertheless, Schiller seems to be aware of the social conditions that produce such a character in women and thus relegate them to the role of providing a model for the striving of men. For this natural harmony disappears in the women in his plays as soon as they take up a

But in discussing Schiller's image of female harmony I have brought in conceptual distinctions that Schiller develops only some years after working on *Don Carlos*. While writing the play, he seems able only to present the tension between two aspects of man's humanity without being able to conceptualize the source of or solution to that tension. We can see Schiller's conceptual confusion clearly manifested in his *Letters on Don Carlos*, in which he tries to explain some of the problematic aspects of his play. Among the problems he deals with here are Posa's character and his changing role in the play as it evolved in Schiller's mind.

Posa used his friend, Schiller notes, because of his enthusiasm for an ideal of freedom. This, he suggests, should make us suspicious of moral and political enthusiasms; it is always safer to follow the voice of nature.[21] In a private letter, written during the same year, Schiller makes the same point. "The state is a work of man, man is a work of inaccessible nature"; nature is always a surer guide than the works of man.[22]

Yet Schiller also knows that simply following nature's voice will not lead to the virtue he expects of a truly human individual. The young Schiller seems deeply confused about virtue. On the one hand, he seems to share the *Sturm und Drang* faith that individual men of virtue will arise from the earth like Titans, as soon as the dead weight of law and convention is lifted from their shoulders. On the other hand, his dramas seem to question that faith. Posa, for example, pleads with the King that he need only grant freedom of thought to make real men out of his servile subjects.[23] Remove the conventional constraints on human behaviour and men will rise to the higher level you seek, Posa tells him. But Carlos's failure to do his duty, despite his obedience to nature's voice, brings that assertion into question. In *The Robbers* Karl Moor declares that "law has formed no great men." By freeing his men from conventional con-

---

public role—which the queen in *Don Carlos* does not. There is no greater contrast between rational calculation and natural openness in Schiller's plays than that between Queen Elizabeth and Queen Mary in *Maria Stuart*.

[21] See the eleventh letter of the *Letters on Don Carlos*.

[22] F. Schiller, Letter to Caroline von Beulwitz, November 27, 1788, in *Briefe*, 2:163.

[23] *Don Carlos*, 7: lines 3225ff.

CHAPTER FOUR

straints, he believes that they will regain the virtues of the ancients. With "an army of rogues like myself, a republic shall rise, next to which Rome and Sparta shall seem like nunneries." He is, in the end, sorely mistaken. Led by their unconstrained inclinations, Moor and his men become criminals on a grand scale rather than great men. In the last scene he admits that "two men like me would bring down the structure of the entire moral world."[24]

It seems that one cannot leave man's moral education to nature after all. Man too must become a work of man. But how can the individual become a work of man, how can he redirect his inclinations, without sacrificing his sincerity and integrity?

This is Schiller's dilemma in *Don Carlos*. If his idea of a truly human individual requires an integration of greatness and goodness, virtue and nature, then he needs a means of socializing individuals that will not do violence to their natural inclinations. In a way this is what Posa tries to do with Carlos. Guided and sometimes shocked by Schiller's explicit criticism of Posa, and assuming Schiller's unqualified commitment to sincerity, most commentators seem to forget that it is the defects in Carlos's character that force Posa to take the actions he does. Schiller's harsh words about Posa make us forget what a prize booby Carlos can be. His overflowing sentiments, his unlimited trust of questionable characters like the Princess Eboli, and his youthful sincerity all lead him toward the catastrophe that Posa tries, but fails, to prevent.

Posa tries to use Carlos's passion for the queen as the means of leading him back to his duty. He trusts in the queen's virtues, knowing that she will resist his advances and that she shares their commitment to political freedom. He hopes that she will redirect Carlos's passion for her toward the noble ideals they share—ideals that, in turn, will bring Carlos around to his duty without suppressing his inclinations. Thus, rather than attacking it directly, Posa encourages Carlos's passion for the queen.[25]

Such an eduction to virtue through sublimated sexual passion is worked out in great detail by none other than Rousseau, in *Emile*

[24] *The Robbers*, 3:21, 161.
[25] *Don Carlos*, 7: lines 4327ff.

and in *Julie, or the New Hélöise.*[26] This is Rousseau's way of leading men to virtue without "denaturing" their inclinations. The resemblance of *Don Carlos* to both *Emile* and *Julie* is striking in this regard. Posa corresponds to both Emile's tutor and Julie's husband, Wolmar, that is, to the omniscient, manipulative educator; Carlos to Emile and St. Preux, the lovesick men of natural feeling, who must learn self-restraint in order to live in society; and the queen to Sophie and Julie, the idealized objects of desire, who redirect men's inclinations toward virtuous ends.

Whether Schiller was directly influenced by Rousseau's works in pursuing such a form of education—as I noted above, there is little evidence that he was familiar with these works at the time he wrote *Don Carlos*—is unimportant here. (Schiller had already considered, in an essay he wrote, or more likely copied, when he was seventeen, the idea of using women to lead men to virtue.)[27] What is significant here is that both Schiller and Rousseau turn to the same remedy for the same problem, and that the remedy fails for both of them. Julie collapses under the pressure of her role, Emile can find happiness only by becoming a solitary,[28] and Carlos runs amok. Only after the shock of Posa's death does Carlos master his passion, but by that time the situation has degenerated beyond recovery. His frank outburst of grief and anger before the king seals his fate. When the queen realizes what Posa has tried to do with Carlos, she criticizes Posa severely, "for how much is risked when we ennoble passion with that noble name virtue."[29] Despite his acute understanding of character and situation, Posa loses control over the events he has initiated. He overestimates his freedom of action, a mistake he shares with a number of Schiller's tragic heroes. Once inspired, passions tend to defy direction and run their own course, as Carlos's erratic behaviour demonstrates. In Posa's attempted education of Carlos, we see Schiller suggesting and ultimately rejecting one means of harmonizing the two aspects of man's humanity.

[26] See J. Schwartz, *The Sexual Politics of Jean-Jacques Rousseau.*
[27] See F. Schiller, "On the Influence of Woman on the Virtue of Man," 17:69ff.
[28] See Rousseau's sequel to *Emile*, entitled *Emile and Sophie, or the Solitaries,* 4:881ff.
[29] *Don Carlos*, 7: line 4349.

This seems to be as far as the young Schiller can get in dealing with the problem of man's humanity. In the long poem "The Artists" (1789) he once again suggests that art can make man whole, and in "The Gods of Greece" he·suggests that art accomplished this task with the Greeks. But he still does not possess sufficient conceptual tools to analyze, let alone resolve, the problem of man's humanity. Kant's philosophy of freedom provides Schiller with these conceptual tools and thus makes possible his mature critique of dehumanization in modern society and his argument for aesthetic education as the means of overcoming it.

Kant's philosophy of freedom provides Schiller with a clear and, to him, irrefutable answer to the question about the *qualité d'homme*. "In the practical part of the Kantian system" is formulated the understanding of human dignity upon which "mankind has always been agreed."[30]

What makes him man is precisely this: that he does not stop short at what mere nature made of him but has the ability to retrace by means of reason the steps she anticipated for him, to transform the work of need into a work of free choice, and to elevate physical into moral necessity.[31]

Only moral freedom and reason make man a *human* being. Nevertheless, "if it is reason that makes man, it is sentiment that guides him." So runs the Rousseauian motto that Schiller places at the beginning of the first version of the *Letters on the Aesthetic Education of Man*.[32] Man's humanity rests on the ability to make unconditioned reason the determining ground of the will. No external influences can overwhelm or erase this capacity. But, Schiller argues, such an understanding of man's humanity need not devalue his inclinations, for no exertion of the free will can erase his externally conditioned impulses. The moral will can overcome sensual inclinations, but it cannot eliminate them. An externally conditioned inclination "will seek to realize its object no matter what rea-

[30] *Aesthetic Education*, Letter 1, 4-5.
[31] Ibid., Letter 3, 10-11.
[32] It is drawn from Rousseau's novel *Julie, or the New Héloïse*, 2:319.

son may say in addition."[33] Sentiment continues to influence our behaviour no matter how freely and rationally we are able to determine the will. Thus "anything that neutralizes the resistance offered to the law of duty favours morality" and the development of man's humanity.[34]

With these distinctions in mind, Schiller can conceptualize the problem of the division between the two aspects of man's humanity, and he does so in his discussion of aesthetic education. Moral freedom makes man human, and moral freedom requires the overcoming of all externally conditioned influences on the determination of the will. But "a complete anthropological evaluation," taking into account man as a whole "in which content counts as much as form," reveals man also to be a unique creature who combines reason and sense, freedom and natural inclination.

> Reason does indeed demand unity; but nature demands multiplicity; both these kinds of legislation make their claim upon man. The law of reason is impressed upon him by an incorruptible consciousness; the law of nature by an ineradicable feeling. Hence when ethical character can assert itself only by sacrificing the natural, it is always a sign of an inadequate education.[35]

To express man's humanity by devaluing his natural inclinations is to suppress another capacity that only human beings possess: the ability to harmonize their impulses with the demands of morality. Since reason itself can do nothing to redirect inclination—it can only resist externally conditioned impulses—we tend, Schiller argues, to think of these two expressions of man's humanity as mutually exclusive. Only if there is some third condition that mediates between sense and reason, that redirects sensual inclinations without imposing alternative externally conditioned ends upon them, can this obstacle to the full realization of man's humanity be removed. Building on Kant's suggestion that beauty is an image or symbol of moral freedom in which moral and sensuous experience

[33] F. Schiller, Letter to von Augustenberg, December 3, 1793, in *Briefe*, 3:402.
[34] *Werke*, 21:30.
[35] *Aesthetic Education*, Letter 4, 18-19.

appear to meet, Schiller believes he has found in aesthetic experience just such a "third condition."[36]

I do not intend here to analyze Schiller's new theory of beauty. My aim has been to show how Kant's philosophy of freedom leads Schiller to formulate a new understanding of the obstacle to a world without social sources of dissatisfaction. In his pre-Kantian works, Schiller expresses great dissatisfaction with the lack of humanity in modern individuals and institutions. But he can explain neither what humanity is, nor why we should lack it even though we know ourselves to be free and rational creatures. Thus in these works he cannot get beyond complaints about our lack of freedom and humanity or beyond a vague longing for unity.

By providing Schiller with a clear definition of man's humanity, Kant's philosophy of freedom allows Schiller to explain the source of his dissatisfaction. Moral freedom, he argues now, makes man human, just as Kant taught; but we will be dissatisfied as long as our humanity is not realized in our world. Kant's philosophy of freedom leads Schiller to formulate the problem of man's humanity in terms of the left Kantian question, How can our freedom be realized in the external world? Although he was dissatisfied with modern individuals and institutions long before he read Kant, it is only after he becomes familiar with Kant's conceptual innovations that he comes to equate the obstacle to human satisfaction with the obstacle to the realization of man's humanity in the external world.

Perhaps that is why Schiller's immersion in Kantian philosophy appears to be more an obsession than a conversion. It is not just the distraction from poetic activity that inspires Schiller's famous lament about Kant:

Two decades you cost me: ten years I lost
In grasping you, ten more in freeing myself from your grasp.

Other social critics, lacking Schiller's poetic vocation, have expressed the same obsession with Kant's dichotomies. For Kant's philosophy of freedom seems to open a path that could lead to the

[36] I. Kant, *Critique of Judgment*, 191, 196ff. Schiller builds his "objective" theory of beauty as "freedom in appearance" upon this suggestion in his so-called "Kallias" letters to his friend Körner. See especially *Briefe*, 3:232, 237-38, 245-46.

resolution of man's fundamental social problems and, at the same time, seems to stand guard against traveling along it. Such is the common reaction to Kantian philosophy of those who, in the previous chapter, I included in the Kantian left. Schiller is the first social critic to attempt to clear the obstacles from that path.

Schiller's Critique of the Spirit of Modern Society

The first ten letters of the *Letters on the Aesthetic Education of Man* present the sociopolitical analysis of his age that leads Schiller to suggest the "aesthetic way" to political freedom. All of the conditions described in the previous chapter as sources of the longing among post-Kantian intellectuals to overcome the dehumanizing spirit of modern society, and of the longing for total revolution, come together for the first time in Schiller's perspective on the limitations of modern society.

The work arises out of Schiller's discovery of a little suspected connection between the two subjects that most occupied his mind at the beginning of 1793: the course of political events in France and his new "objective" theory of beauty and humanity.[37] His correspondence with his friend Körner provides evidence that Schiller was simultaneously concerned with both subjects. At the same time as he writes Körner of his intention to speak out about events in France, he begins a series of letters, the so-called "Kallias" letters, in which he tries to work out his theory of beauty as "freedom in appearance."[38] The ethical-political implications of this theory of beauty, suggested already in the Kallias letters, become the main theme of the *Letters on Aesthetic Education*. Schiller argues:

> That I . . . put beauty before freedom, can, I believe, be justified on principle, not merely excused as my own inclination. I hope to convince you that this subject is far less alien to the needs of our age than to its taste and, moreover, that if man is

[37] Schiller wrote the first version of his work on aesthetic education in a set of letters which he sent at intervals to his patron, the Danish prince Count Friedrich Christian von Augustenberg, during the last half of 1793. He later expanded and published them in his new journal, *Die Horen*, in 1795.

[38] See especially his letter to Körner of December 21, 1792, in *Briefe*, 3:232-33.

ever to solve the political problem in practice he will have to take the aesthetic way, because it is only through beauty that man makes his way to freedom.[39]

"Were it true," he writes, "that law is raised to the throne and true freedom is made the principle of the political structure, then I would bid farewell forever to the Muses and devote all of my activity to the most splendid of all works of art, the monarchy of reason."[40] But it is not true. The revolutionaries have failed to put the moral law on the throne and rebuild the state on a foundation of moral freedom. Schiller believes that his understanding of the relationship between moral and aesthetic experience will explain why the French Revolution failed—and why any merely political revolution will always fail—to achieve this goal.

Since Schiller's perception that the Revolution had failed is one of the premises of his argument for aesthetic education, his advocacy of the aesthetic way to freedom is often viewed as an expression of disenchantment with the political ideals of his youth and with the hopes aroused by events in France. After all, many of the Revolution's staunchest partisans in Germany became bitter opponents of political reform after having their hopes dashed by the Terror and by French imperialism.

Schiller, however, is not one of them, if for no other reason than that he never was a great partisan of the revolutionary regime. Despite frequent reference to Schiller's "disillusionment" with the Revolution, there is no evidence that he ever shared the uncritical enthusiasm for the Revolution expressed by so many of his contemporaries. No public defence of the Revolution, like Fichte's, flows from his pen. No odes to the Revolution, like Klopstock's, are set in Schillerian verse.[41] Nor do we find even in his private correspondence any ringing expressions of enthusiasm for the Revolution. "The case of Schiller surprises us," writes one scholar. "That which one could call, in effect, the first period, that of support, joy,

[39] *Aesthetic Education*, Letter 2, 8-9.
[40] *Briefe*, 3:332.
[41] See J. Droz, *l'Allemagne et la Révolution française*, and G. P. Gooch, *Germany and the French Revolution*, for surveys and comparisons of the reactions of German intellectuals to the Revolution.

148

and enthusiasm, is scarcely visible.''[42] Yet so strong is the impression that Schiller's criticism of the Revolution must express disillusionment with earlier hopes for political change, that he concludes that this enthusiasm must have existed.

The only evidence that could support this conclusion lies in what Schiller wrote *before* the Revolution. Indeed, this conclusion rests on the assumption that the rebellious author of *The Robbers* and the "Republican Tragedy"—*The Conspiracy of Fiesco*—the celebrant of political freedom in *Don Carlos* and *The Revolt of the Netherlands*, must have greeted the overthrow of the old regime with enthusiasm before he began to criticize the new regime. This does not seem to be an unreasonable assumption. Indeed, the members of the French National Convention must have made this assumption when in 1792 they voted Schiller, along with Klopstock and other foreign partisans of the Revolution, an honourary citizen of the republic. Indeed, shortly before the Convention issued this decree, Parisians had cheered a new production of *The Robbers* in which Karl Moor had donned a Phrygian cap and waved the *tricouleur*.[43]

But it is, nevertheless, a false assumption. There is no reason to assume that Schiller greets the outbreak of the Revolution with any more enthusiasm than the cautious mixture of hope and fear he expresses in the months before the execution of the king.[44] His early plays, despite their violent challenges to the conventional authority, also voice fear of the consequences of a revolutionary attack against the established order. Each play points to the unexpected and unwelcome consequences that may follow from attempts to subvert the old order. Although in *The Robbers* Schiller celebrates rebellion against convention, he also points to the danger of complete independence from conventional authority. In the end Karl Moor admits that "two men like me would bring down the structure of the entire moral world," and he turns himself in to the authorities. The young Schiller has far more critical distance from his sentiments and protagonists than is usually recognized. Even

[42] M. Boucher, *La Révolution vue par les écrivains allemands*, 95.
[43] G. P. Gooch, *Germany and the French Revolution*, 216.
[44] See his letter to Körner, November 26, 1792, in *Briefe*, 3:231.

Moor's sacrifice at the end of the play, despite, or perhaps precisely because of, the Christlike pathos with which Schiller surrounds it, is brought into question. "Let him be," his companions comment, "it's the *Grossmannsucht*."[45] In *Fiesco* Schiller celebrates republicanism and republican virtue. But he also expresses his fear of Caesar figures, the false friends of the people who, like Fiesco, use rebellion against the old regime as the means to establish their own tyranny. The play ends with a great act of republican virtue, the killing of a tyrant. But, ironically, that act of republican virtue is performed to save the old despotic regime from the demagogic tyranny of the leader of the republican revolution. And in *Don Carlos* Schiller shows that reason cannot necessarily control the consequences of the revolutionary actions it initiates, and that most individuals, like Carlos, are not ready to be liberated.

Once we recognize the ambivalence of the young Schiller's attitude toward revolutionary change, there is no longer any reason to view his critique of the French Revolution as an expression of disillusionment with his earlier political hopes and ideals. We can thus take Schiller at his word when he states that his objective is the discovery of both the obstacles to the realization of political freedom and the means to overcome them.

Schiller begins his analysis of what went wrong in France with a reminder of "the principles by which reason is guided overall in political legislation."[46] These principles are the key to the analysis that follows in Schiller's essay. For they are "left Kantian" principles. The aim of the Revolution is to *realize* human freedom in the social interactions of man, not merely to develop a form of external political authority that a free and rational individual could accept. The failure to recognize Schiller's left Kantian understanding of political freedom has led, I shall argue, to a great deal of confusion and misunderstanding about his argument in the *Letters on Aesthetic Education*.

The first of "the principles by which reason is guided overall in political legislation" is a left Kantian definition of our humanity.

[45] *The Robbers*, 3:161-62.
[46] *Aesthetic Education*, Letter 2, 8-9.

What makes us human is the power "to transform the work of need into a work of free choice, and to elevate physical into moral necessity." Our humanity is expressed in our striving "to elevate physical into moral necessity," to bring our moral freedom into the world. Schiller's claim that "the construction of true political freedom" represents "the most perfect of all works achieved by the art of man"[47] is no mere rhetorical flourish. Rather it is a consequence of his first principles. True political freedom is a work of art, something that we must construct in the external world. But unlike all other works of art, the form and material of true political freedom are drawn from our humanity, our moral freedom. Since it represents the realization of what is highest in human beings, it is "the most perfect" of human artifacts.

In presenting this understanding of the fundamental principles of political freedom, Schiller seems to believe that he is simply drawing out the implications of Kant's understanding of moral freedom. He notes in the first letter his agreement with the moral part of Kant's system, and he confesses to his patron that "my thoughts on the main points of *Sittenlehre* are completely Kantian."[48] But as I have noted in the preceding chapter, these are not the political implications that Kant himself draws from his understanding of moral freedom.

Schiller uses this understanding of political freedom to analyze the origins and failure of the French Revolution. Nature, he argues, provides us with political institutions before we can construct them for ourselves. Individuals establish a political authority out of mutual fear and need long before they think of making the state an expression of their moral freedom. Thus when they finally awake from their "sensuous slumber," they find themselves already in a state—what Schiller calls the "natural state" (*Naturstaat*) or the "state of need" (*Notstaat*). He defines a natural state as "any political body whose organization derives originally from forces rather than from laws."[49] Schiller uses "laws" here as a term of distinction. He means the self-imposed laws of human freedom, not pos-

[47] Ibid., Letter 3, 10-11; Letter 2, 6-7.
[48] Ibid., Letter 1, 4-5; *Briefe*, 3:399.
[49] *Aesthetic Education*, Letter 3, 12-13.

itive laws. For he distinguishes the *natural state* from the *natural condition (Naturzustand)*, or state of nature—a condition in which no positive laws govern the interaction of individuals. The state of nature is a philosophical construct; no individuals live or have lived in this state. The natural state, on the other hand, has positive laws. It is a state in which the positive laws derive their authority from the externally conditioned impulses of fear and need, rather than from unconditioned moral reason—in short, the state as we know it in our own lives.

When man awakens from his "sensuous slumber" to consciousness of his moral freedom, "he neither could nor can rest content with this state of need." For "however firmly and skillfully, blind caprice [*Willkür*] may have grounded her work, . . . man may treat it all as if it never happened. For the work of blind forces possesses no authority before which freedom need bow." As a result, philosophers develop the idea of a pre-political state of nature in which individuals were completely independent of each other and thus free to choose the political principles under which they would associate with each other. They attribute to man "in this idealized natural condition a purpose of which he knew nothing in his actual natural condition and a power of choice of which he was then incapable." They proceed as if man, "starting from scratch, exchanged a state of independence for a state of contracts out of clear insight and free resolve." In this way they derive the principles of government that a free man would accept as replacements for those by which he finds himself bound in the natural state. And, in social practise, man comes to devalue and disregard the authority of the natural state. "This is the origin and justification of the attempt of a people grown to maturity to transform its natural state into a moral state."[50]

If the French Revolution was an attempt to transform the "natural state into a moral state," no wonder it was a failure. For the "moral state" as defined by Schiller demands more than a perfected set of political institutions; it rests on the actualization of man's autonomy in the interaction of individuals. If nothing has been done

[50] Ibid., Letter 3, 10-13.

to effect the externalization of human freedom, if, indeed, up to now one cannot even conceive of the possibility of such an externalization of human freedom, then the attempt to replace the natural state with a moral state will fail.

> True, the prestige of opinion has declined, arbitrary rule is unmasked and, though still armed with power, can no longer usurp the appearance of dignity. Man has roused himself from his long indolence and self-deception and is demanding, with an impressive majority of voices the restitution of his inalienable rights. But he does not just demand this; there and here he is rising up to take by force what, in his opinion, has been unjustly denied him. The fabric of the natural state is tottering, its rotting foundations are giving way, and there seems to be a physical possibility of setting law upon the throne, of finally honouring man as an end in himself, and making true freedom the principle of political association. Vain hope! The moral possibility is lacking, and so promising a moment finds a generation unprepared to receive it.[51]

The "physical possibility" for the transformation of the natural state exists at the end of the eighteenth century. Stripped of its prestige and dignity, the natural state can no longer maintain its authority, even by the use of naked force. Thus the natural state, and with it the *ancien régime*, falls when man arises to demand his rights. But "the moral possibility is lacking" for the realization of freedom, since to transform the natural state into a moral state we need more than the recognition of and demand for principles of freedom. We need freedom to serve already as the basis of our social interaction. Otherwise, "the gift of liberal principles [of government] will be a betrayal" of our aspirations.[52] As long as individuals still interact with each other on the basis of externally conditioned impulses of need and fear, the removal of the constraints of the natural state will only increase the role of external compulsion in our lives. Knowing no other way to interact with others, individuals

---

[51] Ibid., Letter 5, 24-25.
[52] Ibid., Letter 7, 44-45.

will feel free to pursue their particular needs with impunity, until finally the use of naked force, unadorned by conventional claims to legitimacy, is needed to establish order.

That is what happened in France, according to Schiller. The overthrow of the old regime pulls the "ladder of nature," the "natural" (externally conditioned) constraints of self-interest, out from under man's feet. Reason "takes from man something he actually possesses, and without which he possesses nothing, and refers him instead to something he could and should possess," thus depriving him of "the means of the physical existence [that is, self-preservation through the force exercised by the natural state] which is the very condition of his humanity." As a result, when the natural constraints of the *ancien régime* are removed, the lower classes, little influenced by cultural development of their natural inclinations, revert to a state of lawless self-interest. The better-educated classes, more deeply shaped by culture, languish in a state of paralyzed fear, worrying only about the loss of the comforts of social life, their natural inclination toward self-preservation extended through the whole range of their socially acquired needs. Schiller calls the former "savages," the latter "barbarians."[53]

Schiller saves his contempt for the more cultivated classes. "The savage despises civilization, and acknowledges nature as his sovereign mistress. The barbarian derides and dishonours nature, but, more contemptible than the savage, as often continues to be the slave of his slave."[54] Like Rousseau, Schiller argues that the modern arts and sciences, devised to liberate man from natural constraints, only broaden and deepen the empire of nature over us.

> Civilization, far from setting us free, in fact creates some new need with every power it develops in us. The fetters of the physical tighten ever more alarmingly so that fear of losing what we have stifles even the most burning impulse towards improvement, and the maxim of passive obedience passes for the supreme wisdom of life.[55]

[53] Ibid., Letter 3, 12-13; Letter 4, 20-21; Letter 5, 24-29.
[54] Ibid., Letter 4, 20-21.
[55] Ibid., Letter 5, 26-27.

The "tyranny" of nature in the civilized man is "a hundred times worse" than in the savage. For while the savage does follow his inclinations, unlike the barbarian he does not think that in doing so he is fulfilling his obligations as a civilized and rational being.[56] Only in questions of taste, where nature should rule, do modern individuals suppress nature. "We disown nature in her rightful sphere only to submit to her tyranny in the moral sphere."[57] We enslave nature to the passing fancies of fashion and conventional canons of taste and then let our slave rule us in moral matters.

Schiller concludes that only if we can bring into being a "third character" that "might prepare the way for a transition from the rule of mere force to the rule of law, and which, without in any way impeding the development of moral character, might on the contrary serve as a sensuous pledge of a morality as yet unseen," will we ever realize our political freedom.[58] In aesthetic experience, he hopes to prove, we have the basis of such a third character. Thus Schiller's argument for aesthetic education is presented as a means of overcoming the obstacle to the externalization of human freedom.

This "third character" is needed for two reasons: first, to "prepare the way" for the transition to the rule of law and second, to maintain the moral state by acting as a "sensuous pledge" between individuals of their moral freedom. The double function of aesthetic education, described at the end of the third letter, is emphasized again at the beginning of the fourth. "Only the predominance of such a character among a people makes it safe to undertake the transformation of a state in accordance with moral principles. And only such a character can guarantee that this transformation will endure."[59] The third character nurtured by aesthetic education is a necessary condition of both the transition from the natural to the moral state and the endurance of the moral state.

In order to understand the role that aesthetic education plays for Schiller in the realization of freedom, one needs to recognize that

[56] *Werke*, 21:23.
[57] *Aesthetic Education*, Letter 5, 26-27.
[58] Ibid., Letter 3, 14-15.
[59] Ibid., Letter 4, 16-17.

Schiller is pursuing a left Kantian rather than a Kantian goal: the realization of freedom in a moral state. A "moral state," for Schiller, is not merely a state in which all individuals act morally. It is a state in which all individuals recognize each other as acting morally, so that there is no need for external compulsion to settle disagreements. Moral freedom must somehow "show forth" in the behaviour of individuals[60] if we are to ever overcome the need for political coercion. For we have no way of recognizing each other's intentions except as they *appear* in the world of phenomena. "The setting up of a moral state involves being able to count on the moral law as an effective force, and free will is thereby drawn into the realm of cause and effect."[61] If we cannot count on the moral law as an effective force, if the freedom of each individual does not in some way show forth in the phenomenal realm, then we will still need the coercive apparatus of the natural state. No matter how well-intentioned the wills of our fellow citizens, we will still need the natural state, since we can never be sure of the meaning of our fellow citizens' behaviour. Without something like this third character, we may develop a state in which all individuals are moral, but we will not develop a moral state.

By focusing on this second of the two functions of aesthetic education, I present in the sharpest possible terms the problem that Schiller poses to himself. There must be a condition in which freedom, without losing its autonomous character, is in some way "drawn into the realm of cause and effect, where everything follows from everything else in a chain of strict necessity." Freedom must "show forth" in appearance, but show forth *as freedom*. The obstacle to true political freedom is thus for Schiller Kant's strict dichotomy between human freedom and natural necessity. And forms of society, like our own, that educate us in the spirit of this dichotomy are dehumanizing, for they prevent us from realizing our humanity in the world.

But why think that social interaction can be anything but dehumanizing, Schiller asks. "Such a portrait, you will tell me, does in-

---

[60] See *Briefe*, 3:285.
[61] *Aesthetic Education*, Letter 4, 16-17.

deed resemble mankind as it is today; but does it not also resemble any people caught up in the process of civilization?'' Must not the dichotomy between freedom and nature appear in every culture? We might think so, Schiller answers, were it not for the Greeks.

> The reputation for culture and refinement, on which we other-wise rightly pride ourselves vis-a-vis humanity in its merely natural state, can avail us nothing against the natural human-ity of the Greeks. For they were wedded to all the delights of art and all the dignity of wisdom, without, like us, falling a prey to their seduction. The Greeks put us to shame not only by a simplicity to which our age is a stranger; they are at the same time our rivals, indeed often our models, in those very excellences with which we are wont to console ourselves for the unnaturalness of our manners.[62]

''At that first fair awakening of the powers of the mind, sense and intellect did not as yet rule over strictly separate domains. . . . However high the mind might soar, it always drew matter lovingly along with it.''[63] When we consider the Greeks, the dichotomy be-tween freedom and nature, which at first seems to be an inescapable aspect of human existence, appears instead to be a historical and, therefore, a changeable condition. We come to recognize it as an as-pect of *our* limitations rather than of the limitations of human cul-ture. And we come to see in the spirit of modern culture the obsta-cle to the realization of humanity in the external world.

Schiller argues that while the division of human faculties has been a gain for the species, it has been a calamity for the individual. The new spirit of culture divides one's life into separate spheres. The Church fosters the spirit, the state protects the body. Labour is a private function performed in the service of self-preservation, rather than an activity associated with the common good and enjoy-ment of the community. In short, the inner being of an individual, one's reason and freedom, become separated from the external forms of one's life. And modern culture, culminating for Schiller in

[62] Ibid., Letter 6, 30-31.
[63] Ibid.

the *Critique of Pure Reason*, demonstrates that this is the way it must be.

Everlastingly chained to a single little fragment of the whole, man himself develops into nothing but a fragment; everlastingly in his ear the monotonous sound of the wheel he turns, he never develops the harmony of his being, and instead of putting the stamp of his humanity upon his own nature, he becomes nothing more than the imprint of his occupation or of his knowledge.[64]

Schiller's contrast of Greek wholeness with modern fragmentation in Letter 6 is probably the most famous section of the *Letters on Aesthetic Education*. Read in the light of the young Marx's critique of political economy, this argument has made Schiller appear to some twentieth-century intellectuals to be the prophet of their social discontent and the "father of the concept of alienation."[65]

Yet as Vicky Rippere has shown in a devastating critique of such reappropriations of Schiller's arguments, there is nothing particularly new or significant in Schiller's critique of modern fragmentation. The criticisms of modern self-contradiction and fragmentation were commonplaces of German writing and rhetoric at the time, as was the praise of Greek wholeness. The claim that Schiller is the "father" of the modern concept of alienation implies that his arguments in some way beget later concepts and feelings of alienation. But, in the end, all that can be maintained is the trivial assertion that Schiller, like many modern intellectuals before and after him, was disturbed by the fragmentation of the modern individual.[66]

The originality and significance of Schiller's critique of modern culture lies not in his eloquent description of the evils of fragmentation, but rather in his conception of the context within which this

---

[64] Ibid., Letter 6, 34-35, 40-41.

[65] D. Regin, *Freedom and Dignity: The Historical and Political Thought of Schiller*, 1. See also the treatment of Schiller in H. Popitz, *Der Entfremdte Mensch*, and in H. Marcuse, *Eros and Civilization*, for the most influential interpretations along these lines.

[66] V. Rippere, *Schiller and Alienation*, 48-49 and passim.

fragmentation occurs. Schiller is the first to analyze the phenomenon of fragmentation and alienation in the light cast by the left
Kantian perspective on human freedom and nature. From this perspective the contradictions and incompleteness of modern individuals take on an importance they never had in earlier formulations.
Now the fragmentary character of modern culture appears to be the
obstacle to the realization of human freedom in the external world,
rather than just a source of the limited accomplishments of modern
individuals. If Schiller's analysis of the fragmentation of the modern individual seems prophetic of Marxist theories of alienation,
then that is because Marx and his followers also look at fragmentation from the perspective of left Kantian questions, as I shall suggest in later chapters.

The idealized image of Greek culture bequeathed by Winckelmann to later generations of German intellectuals serves as a reproach to their own culture. But if Winckelmann tells German intellectuals *where* to look for an alternative model of cultural life,
Schiller provides them with the strongest reasons *why* they should
be looking for such an alternative. For from Schiller's point of view
the flaws of modern culture lead to the dehumanization of man, not
just to limitations in the cultural development of modern individuals. For this reason, "Schiller, much more than Winckelmann, became the father of that exaggerated enthusiasm for the Greek character" so characteristic of German intellectuals at the turn of the
nineteenth century.[67] He ties German nostalgia for Greek art and
life to the most powerful philosophic arguments of his time, the
Kantian critical philosophy.

Schiller's Kantian perspective on ancient versus modern culture
is clearest in his explanation of the decline and fall of Greek culture.
The condition that makes the harmonious spirit of Greek culture
possible is, in his opinion, a fortunate lack of clarity about the concepts of nature and spirit. As philosophic reflection matured among
the Greeks, it had to challenge the interpenetration of nature and
spirit that sustained Greek culture, for reason, Schiller insists, always gains clarity by separating and opposing our faculties. "The

---

[67] R. Fester, *Rousseau und die Deutsche Geschichtsphilosophie,* 112.

intellect was unavoidably compelled by the store of knowledge it already possessed to dissociate itself from feeling and intuition in an attempt to arrive at exact discursive understanding; . . . only a specific degree of clarity is compatible with a specific fullness and warmth."[68]

Schiller suggests that our greater clarity about the character and requirements of human freedom allows us to perceive the Greeks' limitations as well as our own. Greek harmony, he argues, depends on a systematic but unintentional confusion of freedom and nature. We thus cannot reproduce it without suppressing our own reason, something Schiller never advocates. If we are to seek a form of culture in which freedom shows forth in nature and nature is respected by freedom, it will have to embody somehow a higher level of self-consciousness than the harmonious spirit of Greek culture could bear. Thus Schiller's contrast between the spirit of Greek and modern culture leads him to suggest a third form of culture, a higher self-conscious harmony of freedom and nature, as the goal of aesthetic education. "It must be open to us to restore by means of a higher art the totality of our nature which the arts themselves have destroyed."[69]

But why presume that there is a path open to such a higher form of harmony? "Is this not," as Schiller, himself, asks, "to argue in a circle? Theoretical culture shall bring about moral [*praktische*] culture, and yet moral culture is to be the condition of theoretical culture? All improvement in the political sphere shall proceed from the ennobling of character—but how is character to be ennobled under a barbarous constitution?"[70] In other words, one cannot establish completely free political institutions until one has free and harmonious individuals. And one cannot educate such individuals as long as they are formed by the spirit of their unfree and unharmonious institutions. If the unharmonious spirit of modern society informs all social interactions, how can any intervention in our social behaviour produce the transformation of individual character that Schiller is looking for?

[68] *Aesthetic Education*, Letter 6, 38-41..
[69] Ibid., Letter 6, 42-43.
[70] Ibid., Letter 9, 54-55.

Schiller seems here to run into the obstacle to the founding of a free state that Rousseau describes and tries to overcome in the famous chapter of the *Social Contract* "On the Lawgiver."

> In order for an emerging people to appreciate the healthy maxims of politics, and follow the fundamental rules of statecraft, the effect would have to become the cause; the social spirit, which should be the result of the institution, would have to preside over the founding of the institution itself; and men would have to be prior to laws what they ought to become by means of laws.[71]

As long as men are what their governments make them, only individuals educated under free institutions would be ready to accept free institutions. As Schiller puts it, "[T]he state as presently constituted has caused the evil, while the state as reason conceives it, far from being able to found this better humanity would itself have to be founded upon it."[72]

Rousseau's solution to this problem is familiar. A free state needs a *deus ex machina*, the "lawgiver," to found its institutions. "The discovery of the best rules of society suited to nations would require a superior intelligence, who saw all of men's passions yet experienced none of them; who had no relationship at all to our nature yet knew it thoroughly." Such individuals are needed both to recognize the true demands of freedom in a corrupted society and to clothe free institutions in a form that would make them acceptable to individuals not yet educated to freedom. Their most successful strategy to the latter end, Rousseau notes, has always been "to have recourse to the intervention of heaven and to attribute their own wisdom to the Gods." In this way they are able "to convince by divine authority those who cannot be moved by human prudence."[73]

But Rousseau's solution to the problem of founding free political institutions is, for Schiller, no solution. First, it represents an explanation of how free states have come into existence, rather than a recommendation for action. The extraordinary individual in the

[71] J.-J. Rousseau, *Social Contract*, 3:383; 69.
[72] *Aesthetic Education*, Letter 7, 44-45.
[73] J.-J. Rousseau, *Social Contract*, 3:381, 383-84; 67-68, 69-70.

right place at the right time is a stroke of good fortune, not something we can produce at will. This is one reason why Rousseau shows so little interest in the implementation of his political proposals in the *Social Contract*. A more important objection, however, is that Schiller cannot accept the fraud implicit in Rousseau's solution to the problem of founding a free state. Schiller is working with a Kantian conception of human freedom. To impose free institutions on the basis of divine authority would violate the individual's autonomy, which the free state is supposed to realize. "To bestow freedom by means of freedom"[74] is the only solution to this problem acceptable to Schiller.

Schiller thus concludes that no political action can open a path to the transformation of the modern spirit of social interaction. But he denies that this means that "the conflict of blind forces shall endure forever in the political world." We need "to seek out some instrument not provided by the state, and to open up living springs which, whatever the political corruption, would remain pure and clear. . . . This instrument is fine art."[75] Here is the culmination of his analysis of the problem of political freedom. Aesthetic education, he suggests, can prepare unfree and unharmonious individuals for free institutions without the use of force or fraud.

Schiller had spoken of art as the mediator between man's opposing faculties long before he read Kant. After studying Kant he developed the conceptual means to present a theory of beauty that would express this early intuition. Once Schiller defines, in the manner discussed in the preceding pages, the obstacles to the realization of political freedom, his new theory of beauty and aesthetic experience appears to offer the instrument that will allow us to overcome our political problems. For he concludes from his analysis of the failures of the French revolutionaries that the obstacle to the realization of freedom lies not in the political power of the old regime, but in the spirit of social interaction that informs its political institutions and survives their demise. The limitation of the spirit of modern society that defeats attempts to replace the old state with

[74] *Aesthetic Education*, Letter 27, 214-15.
[75] Ibid., Letter 8, 48-49; Letter 9, 54-55.

a moral state is the opposition between reason and sense that continues to express itself in all of society's social and cultural institutions. This division prevents the moral freedom of individuals from being manifested in a way in that enables others to recognize it. A theory of beauty as ''freedom in appearance'' and aesthetic experience as something that engages man's rational and sensuous faculties simultaneously thus has political implications for Schiller that it does not for Kant, who does not view political freedom as the realization of autonomy. It appears to open up a path to the realization of political freedom, since it provides a means of developing the higher harmony of character whose absence Schiller sees as the fundamental obstacle to the realization of human freedom in the external world.

Aesthetic experience appears to offer a sub-political sphere of social interaction that escapes, or at least can potentially escape, the divisive spirit of modern society. In this way aesthetic education offers, for Schiller, the means of solving the problem of founding free political institutions without resorting to the pious fraud that Rousseau sees as that problem's only solution. If there is something about the very nature of aesthetic experience that challenges modern dichotomies between reason and sense, nature and freedom, then there is always a sphere of social communication that is not completely dominated by the modern spirit of social interaction.

In place of Rousseau's lawgiver, Schiller presents the artist as the legislator who makes political freedom possible. But though the artist needs the same combination of detachment from and knowledge of contemporary passions and customs that the lawgiver possesses, he need not be a special godlike genius to come by this disposition. The artist's love of beauty leads him to be dissatisfied with the contemporary spirit of social interaction and to search for alternatives, especially in classical antiquity, since the beauty of its art suggests that an alternative form of culture must be possible.

> The artist is indeed the child of his age; but woe to him if he is at the same time its ward or, worse still, its minion! Let some beneficent deity snatch the suckling from his mother's breast, nourish him with the milk of a better age, and suffer him to

come to maturity under a distant Grecian sky. Then, when he has become a man, let him return, a stranger, to his own century; not, however, to gladden it by his appearance, but rather, terrible like Agamemnon's son, to cleanse and purify it.[76]

The artist's love of beauty will draw him to the culture of ancient Greece and make him a "stranger to his own century." But in his mastery of aesthetic form he will still have a means of speaking to his own century. Thus he can return to modern society like Orestes, ready to murder the mother of modern culture and, in doing so, make possible the realization of human freedom.

To prove that aesthetic education can open up a path to such a transformation of the spirit of modern society, Schiller must show, first, that beauty and aesthetic experience do indeed have the character just described and, second, that aesthetic experience can, in some way, shape all other forms of social interaction, so that the transformation of this particular sphere of social interaction will effect a "total revolution in man's whole way of feeling."[77] These are the tasks which he sets for himself in the remaining letters.

Aesthetic Education and Political Community

I shall pass over Schiller's demonstration in Letters 11 to 26 of his concepts of beauty and aesthetic experience. His argument is long, complex, and suggestive, but not entirely successful.

Schiller's major problem is that he is trying to surpass Kantian dichotomies with concepts grounded in that dichotomy.[78] He wants to go beyond the letter of Kantian dichotomies in the true "spirit of the Kantian system."[79] Kant, himself, found nothing that contradicted his moral philosophy in the letter of Schiller's argument that moral freedom does not require the opposition of sensuous inclinations. A "joyous aesthetic character" may and should, in the best case, *accompany* acts of moral freedom. So Kant writes in response

---

[76] Ibid., Letter 9, 56-57.
[77] Ibid., Letter 27, 204-5.
[78] See D. Henrich, "Der Begriff der Schönheit in Schillers Aesthetik," 527-47, 540, 543.
[79] *Aesthetic Education*, Letter 13, 86-87n.

to Schiller's criticism—in *Grace and Dignity*—of his "Draconian" approach to moral duties. As long as the agreement of our inclinations does not become the necessary condition of our following the moral law, an inclination toward our duty does not diminish our freedom.[80] It is, ironically, more the spirit than the letter of Schiller's arguments that contradicts Kant's. An agreement of inclination with duty does not have the same moral and political significance for Kant as it does for Schiller. Kant is not seeking the means of "realizing" human autonomy in the world, and thus the harmonization of inclination and reason does not appear, as it does to Schiller, as the key to overcoming our political problems.

In the final letter Schiller describes the goal of aesthetic education, the form of social interaction he seeks to promote among human beings. I argued in the preceding section that aesthetic education represents Schiller's answer to the fundamental left Kantian questions: What are the obstacles to the realization of our humanity in the external world and how can they be overcome? Schiller has discovered that it is the unharmonious spirit of modern society that dooms to failure attempts to realize our freedom, and that we can only get beyond that spirit of social interaction by means of aesthetic education.

If this interpretation is accurate, the total revolution in human character brought about by aesthetic education should lead to the realization of the fully "human" community that follows, for the Kantian left, from the realization of human freedom. And, indeed, Schiller describes such a community in the last letter of the *Letters on Aesthetic Education*. Here is the key passage of that description.

If in the dynamic state of rights it is as force that one man encounters another, and imposes limits upon his activities; if in the ethical state of duties man sets himself over against man with all the majesty of the law, and puts a curb upon his desires: in those circles where conduct is governed by beauty, in the *aesthetic* state, none may appear to the other except as form, or confront him except as an object of free play. *To be-*

[80] I. Kant, *Religion within the Limits of Reason Alone*, 18n. See *Grace and Dignity*, 20:285.

stow freedom by means of freedom is the fundamental law of this kingdom. The dynamic state can merely make society possible, by letting one nature be curbed by another; the ethical state can merely make it (morally) necessary, by subjecting the individual will to the general; the aesthetic state alone can make society real, because it consummates the will of the whole through the nature of the individual. Though it may be his needs which drive man into society, and reason which implants within him the principles of social behaviour, beauty alone can confer upon him a *social character.*[81]

"Society" and "social character," as Schiller uses these concepts in this passage, are clearly terms of distinction. They have reference to a particular form, rather than to all forms, of social interaction among individuals. Our physical needs make "society," so understood, possible but not actual. In the "natural states" in which we currently live, states whose authority is based on needs and inclinations, there is thus no real "society." The moral law, Schiller suggests, makes the establishment of "society," so understood, obligatory "by subjecting the individual will to the general." This suggests that one of the defining characteristics of "society" is the agreement of the individual with the general will, which, for Schiller, is the universal unconditioned will of moral reason. The "aesthetic state," Schiller then argues, alone makes society *"real"* by somehow manifesting the universal will of moral reason in the will of the individual.

A "real" society, then, would be a community of individuals whose individual wills and behaviour manifest the universal will of moral reason. A "social character" is achieved only when the community that individuals share and that constitutes their character is fully "human," that is, only when it represents the manifestation of universal reason in the external world and the particular wills of individuals. The "society" that aesthetic education realizes thus represents the "human community," the realization of Kant's kingdom of ends, which the Kantian left seeks. The "aesthetic

[81] *Aesthetic Education*, Letter 27, 214-15.

state'' represents the form of interaction that allows the moral freedom of individuals to become manifest to each other in the phenomenal world, so that man's autonomy can be realized.

"All other forms of communication divide society," Schiller argues. "They relate exclusively either to the private receptivity or to the private proficiency of its individual members, hence to that which distinguishes man from man."

> The pleasures of the senses we enjoy merely as individuals, without the genus which is immanent within us having any share in them at all; hence we cannot make the pleasures of sense universal, because we are unable to universalize our own individuality. The pleasures of knowledge we enjoy merely as genus, and by carefully removing from our judgment all trace of individuality; hence we cannot make the pleasures of reason universal, because we cannot eliminate traces of individuality from the judgments of others as we can from our own. Beauty alone do we enjoy at once as individual and as genus, i.e., as representatives of the human genus.[82]

Society, as Schiller understands it, requires shared sentiments that would bind individuals together, and which, at the same time, would manifest man's universal humanity. Societies as we know them are founded on shared inclinations and disinclinations, the shared needs and fears of individuals. But in sharing the pleasures and pains of the senses, there is no genuine community, Schiller argues, for pleasure and pain affect us only as individuals. "The good of the senses . . . is founded on appropriation, and this always involves exclusion."[83] No matter how many individuals respond with pain or pleasure to the same external stimulus, their pain or pleasure is not something they share.

"The pleasures of knowledge," on the other hand, we gain only by abstracting from the external conditioning of our behaviour. We cannot truly share these pleasures "because we cannot eliminate

---

82 Ibid., Letter 27, 214-17.
83 Ibid., Letter 27, 216-17.

traces of individuality from the judgments of others as we can from our own." We know other individuals *only* as they appear to us. Thus we cannot know them in abstraction from their externally conditioned individuality and in that way share the truly "universal" sentiments associated with moral reason.

Aesthetic experience alone engages our sensuous individuality and rational universality simultaneously—at least if Schiller's understanding of it is correct, a very big "if"—and thus alone offers the means of realizing "society." Interpreted in this way, the total revolution in human character which Schiller seeks to effect through aesthetic education would do what Schiller claims it can do: make possible the replacement of the state of compulsion with a state of freedom.

Nevertheless, it is the opinion of the majority of Schiller's interpreters that his conclusions about the aesthetic state in the final letter diverge from the aim announced at the beginning of the *Letters on Aesthetic Education*: to demonstrate that "if man is ever to solve the political problem in practice he will have to take the aesthetic way, because it is only through beauty that man makes his way to freedom."[84] Given the celebration of the "aesthetic state" with which the *Letters on Aesthetic Education* closes, Schiller appears to many of his readers to have lost his way on the aesthetic road to political freedom. They suspect that by the end of the *Letters on Aesthetic Education* Schiller has become indifferent to political improvement, that it is not only "through" beauty, but *in* beauty that Schiller believes that man makes his way to freedom. Thus some of his readers see a "humanist reaction" against politics in Schiller's arguments, a reaction he shares with his famous friends in Weimar, Humboldt and Goethe.[85] Others speak of his flight from politics into an "aesthetic utopia."[86] The commonest criticism made of the *Letters on Aesthetic Education* is that they pursue two mutually exclusive goals: the realization of a "moral state" by means of aesthetic education—the political goal developed in the opening letters—and the realization of an "aesthetic state," of a higher free-

[84] Ibid., Letter 2, 8-9.
[85] See J. Droz, *l'Allemagne et la Révolution française*, 172ff.
[86] See especially G. Lukács, *Goethe und Seine Zeit*, 109ff.

dom transcending political and moral freedom, which Schiller seems to advocate in the later letters.[87]

Hans Lutz's analysis of the *Letters on Aesthetic Education* is the most sustained and influential attempt to demonstrate that Schiller's argument for aesthetic education contradicts itself. He argues that Schiller has two mutually exclusive theories of aesthetic education. The first treats aesthetic education as a means of promoting moral freedom. Aesthetic experience provides the ladder on which individuals can climb from natural inclination to moral freedom. We develop, as Schiller conceives it, in three stages, from the natural to the aesthetic to the moral condition. The aesthetic condition is thus, in this theory, a transitional condition which we pass through on the way to moral freedom. Schiller's second theory of aesthetic education, Lutz argues, treats the aesthetic condition as the final end toward which we develop, the higher synthesis of his nature and freedom, transcending moral and political relations. Lutz argues that Schiller moves back and forth between these two theories of aesthetic education throughout the *Letters on Aesthetic Education*, the first being more preponderant in the early letters, the second in the later letters. The clearest presentation and juxtaposition of the two theories appears, however, back-to-back in Letters 3 and 4. The moral development argument is put forward in the former and the aesthetic synthesis argument is expressed in the latter. Lutz explains the appearance of these two contradictory strands of argument in Schiller's work genetically, arguing that in the later drafts of the *Letters on Aesthetic Education* Schiller drifted more and more to the second theory and began superimposing it on the first.[88]

Willoughby and Wilkinson make many telling criticisms of Lutz's argument in their magnificent edition of the *Letters on Aesthetic Education*. They demonstrate that most of the conceptual contradictions on which Lutz bases his argument are not contradic-

---

[87] See especially H. Lutz, *Schillers Anschauungen von Natur und Kultur*. This argument has become the commonplace criticism of the *Letters*, as, for example, in R. Snell's brief introduction to his translation of the work for Frederick Ungar Press, 15ff.

[88] H. Lutz, *Schillers Anschauungen*, 221ff.

tions at all.[89] Nevertheless, there will always appear to be in Schiller's argument a contradiction that demands explanation, until we can explain how the realization of what Schiller calls the "aesthetic state" serves the original, political goal of his essay, the realization of the moral state. Unfortunately, Willoughby and Wilkinson do not address that issue, so that while they devastate the superstructure of Lutz's argument, they leave its foundations in place.

To uproot the foundations of that argument, one has to reconsider Schiller's original formulations of his goal in the early letters. It is easy to show that Schiller is aware, from the very beginning, that aesthetic education has two different functions. As noted above, he mentions the dual role of aesthetic education in *both* Letters 3 and 4. And he describes these two functions of aesthetic education in a way that leaves no doubt that they correspond to the two conflicting theories which Lutz, among others, finds in the work as a whole. We need the aesthetic condition, Schiller argues in Letter 3, *both* as "a transition from the rule of mere force to the rule of law" and to act as a "sensuous pledge" for a moral freedom that cannot otherwise be seen.[90] And then, at the beginning of Letter 4, he reiterates the point by stating that only the development of the character promoted by aesthetic education "makes it safe to undertake the transformation of the state in accordance with moral principles. And only such a character can guarantee that this transformation will endure."[91] We need aesthetic experience both as a transitory stage that leads us to a higher condition and as a continuing feature of the final stage of human development envisioned by Schiller. And note that he underlines this double role of aesthetic education in precisely those letters, 3 and 4, which Lutz claims represent the different strata and the conflicting theories of Schiller's argument.[92]

Do these two functions of aesthetic education contradict each other in some way? In interpreting these passages in the previous

[89] *Aesthetic Education*, lxiiiff. The glossary of Schillerian concepts in this edition is also very helpful in clarifying ambiguous terminology and multiple meanings that might, misunderstood, suggest self-contradiction in Schiller's arguments. Especially helpful is the entry on "*Natur*," 322-26.
[90] Ibid., Letter 3, 14-15.
[91] Ibid., Letter 4, 16-17.
[92] H. Lutz, *Schillers Anschauungen*, 170ff.

section I noted no contradiction. But do implicit contradictions between them perhaps become explicit when Schiller explains in the
later letters how aesthetic experience can transform human character?

I think not. As noted above, the reason why the two functions
appear to most readers to be mutually exclusive is because they do
not properly understand what Schiller means by a ''moral state.'' If
by a moral state Schiller means no more than a state made up of
individuals who respect the moral law as the only legitimate authority for determining the will, then aesthetic education could
serve nothing but a *transitional* role in the development of that
state. The role of aesthetic education would be to help individuals
come to recognize and follow the moral law by reducing the resistance to moral freedom offered by the inclinations. In this view, once
the moral state is reached, once all individuals recognize and follow
the moral law, aesthetic education no longer has any role to play. If
this is what Schiller means by the moral state, then, indeed, he contradicts himself when he speaks of a second function of aesthetic education without which the moral state would collapse.[93]

But, as we have seen in the previous section, this is not how
Schiller conceives of the moral state. A collection of moral individuals does not necessarily make a moral state. To transform the natural state into a moral state where law rules without compulsion, it
is not sufficient that individuals obey the moral law; they must also
recognize each other's moral freedom. Their freedom must show
forth somehow in the realm of phenomena, for we can only know
other individuals as they appear to us. Otherwise, we will always
be in doubt about their actions, for their actions will appear to us to
be conditioned by their fears and inclinations, and we will need a
common extra-moral authority (the sovereign) to resolve, by force
if necessary, our disagreements. Only when moral freedom manifests itself in the world of phenomena, when we have a ''sensuous
pledge'' of each other's moral freedom, can we ''exchange a state of
compulsion for a state of freedom.'' For only then can ''true freedom *become* the principle of political association.''[94]

[93] *Aesthetic Education*, Letter 4, 16-17.
[94] Ibid., Letter 4, 22-23.

171

The main focus of Schiller's explication of aesthetic education in Letters 10 to 27 is to show that aesthetic experience provides a path to moral freedom that does not suppress and devalue appearances and inclinations. He argues that to pass from a natural to a moral condition (*zustand*), we must pass through a third, aesthetic condition, which frees us from all determination, so that *unconditioned* reason may determine the will.

> In order to exchange passivity for autonomy, a passive determination for an active one, man must be momentarily *free of all determination*, and pass through a state of pure determinability. He must consequently, in a certain sense, return to that negative state of complete absence of determination in which he found himself before anything at all had made an impression upon his sense. . . . This middle disposition, in which the psyche is subject neither to physical nor to moral constraint, yet is active in both ways, pre-eminently deserves to be called a free disposition; and if we are to call the condition of sensuous determination the physical, and the condition of rational determination the logical or moral, then we must call this condition of real and active determinability the *aesthetic*.[95]

Without this intermediate condition of "determinability," moral freedom can be expressed only in reaction against inclination. Such an approach to moral freedom, which, for Schiller, corresponds to Kant's, has two disadvantages. On the one hand, it is too difficult for most individuals to sustain, since while reason can overcome sensuous inclinations, it can never stifle their promptings. On the other hand, it leads us to view appearance in a light that precludes it from manifesting our freedom. Thus such a view of moral freedom makes the achievement of a moral state, the realization of our freedom, impossible.

The aesthetic condition provides Schiller with an alternative path to moral freedom that has neither of these shortcomings. Aesthetic experience, Schiller suggests, suspends external conditioning, leav-

---

[95] Ibid., Letter 21, 140-41.

ing the individual in a state of pure "determinability" that restores to him "the freedom to be what he ought to be."[96] In doing so it "accomplishes no particular purpose, neither intellectual nor moral; it discovers no individual truth, helps us to perform no individual duty . . . By means of aesthetic culture, therefore, the personal worth of a man, or his dignity, inasmuch as this can depend solely upon himself, remains completely indeterminate."[97] But by suspending the determination of the will by physical influences, the aesthetic condition opens up a path to the moral condition that does not start with the suppression of externally conditioned inclinations.

> Through the aesthetic modulation of the psyche, then, the autonomy of reason is already opened up within the domain of sense itself, the domain of sensation already broken within its own frontiers, and physical man refined to the point where spiritual man only needs to start developing out of the physical according to the laws of freedom. The step from the aesthetic to the logical and moral state (i.e., from beauty to truth and duty) is hence infinitely easier than was the step from the physical state to the aesthetic (i.e., from merely blind living to form). The former step man can accomplish simply of his own free will, since it merely involves taking from himself, not giving to himself, fragmenting his nature, not enlarging it. . . . In order to lead aesthetic man to understanding and lofty sentiments, one need do no more than provide him with motives of sufficient weight. To obtain the same results from sensuous man we must first alter his very nature.[98]

It is in this context that Schiller speaks of three stages of human development that correspond to the natural, aesthetic, and moral condition. "Man in his *physical* condition merely suffers the dominion of nature; he emancipates himself from this dominion in the *aesthetic* condition, and acquires mastery over it in the

---

[96] Ibid., Letter 21, 146-47.
[97] See "On the Necessary Limitations of Beautiful Forms," 21:3-27.
[98] *Aesthetic Education*, Letter 23, 162-63.

moral."[99] But treating aesthetic experience as a middle condition that makes possible man's transition to moral freedom does not contradict the other function Schiller assigns to aesthetic education. For the "moral condition" (*Zustand*) and "moral state" (*Moralstaat*) have very different meanings in Schiller's usage.[100] When Schiller argues that the aesthetic condition makes possible man's transition from a natural condition to a moral condition, he is suggesting that aesthetic education is a means of leading individuals to recognize and act according to the moral law. Such a change in the character of individuals, such a transition to a "moral condition," is a necessary step toward the "moral state," but, as we have just seen, it does not bring us all the way there.

The "aesthetic state" that Schiller describes in the final letter of the *Letters on Aesthetic Education* neither supersedes nor yields to the moral state. It is concurrent with the moral state, a necessary support without which the moral state cannot exist. It alone makes the moral state "real" by providing the means through which our freedom "shows forth" to each other. The community that the aesthetic state makes possible is the "sensuous pledge" of our freedom, without which the elimination of the coercion of the natural state cannot take place.

The failure of most commentators to recognize the significance of this second function of aesthetic education makes Schiller's social discontent seem much closer than it really is to that of Weimar humanists like Humboldt and Goethe. They do not share his left Kantian understanding of human freedom. For them, individual cultivation is the end of social interaction. Social institutions are valuable as a means to that end, and they are sources of dissatisfaction when they pose obstacles to that end.

Schiller's friend Körner criticizes the first draft of the *Letters on Aesthetic Education* from this Weimarian "humanist" point of

[99] Ibid., Letter 24, 170-71.
[100] Unfortunately, Willoughby and Wilkinson, who recognize the importance of that distinction (ibid., xlvi), make it somewhat difficult to recognize in their translation, since they translate both *Zustand* and *Staat* as "state," distinguishing between the two merely by capitalizing the latter as "State." (See Letter 3, 10-13, Letter 23, 162-63, Letter 24, 170-71, and Letter 27, 214-215.)

view. "Aesthetic education," Körner insists, "is an end in itself. It needs no recommendation as a means. . . . The state is a mere means. Humanity alone is the end."[101] The ideal of humanity is a form of individual life for Körner, as it is for most of the Weimar humanists, not a form of social interaction. For Schiller, on the other hand, man's humanity is realized both in the individual and in the community among individuals.

> Every individual human being, one may say, bears within him, potentially and prescriptively, a pure ideal of humanity in itself, with whose unchanging unity it is his life's task to bring all his changing manifestations into agreement. This pure human ideal, which can be discerned, more or less clearly in every individual, is represented by the *state*, the objective, and so to speak, canonical form in which the diversity of individual subjects strives to unite.[102]

A comparison of Schiller's understanding of political freedom with that of his friend Humboldt, the most politically astute of all the major Weimar figures, including Schiller, gets to the heart of Schiller's differences with his Weimar friends. Schiller's *Letters on Aesthetic Education* and Humboldt's essay on *The Limits of State Action* are often linked together as complementary statements of the Weimar philosophy of individual cultivation. Indeed, Schiller read the manuscript of Humboldt's essay while preparing his own. But while they both pursue the means of developing man's humanity in their works, their views of political freedom and community differ greatly.

Humboldt argues that the fullest cultivation of the diverse potential of individuals is the aim of society. To that end, individuals should have the greatest freedom to think, act, and express themselves consistent with the same freedom of other individuals. Government is the means by which we secure the freedoms necessary for individual growth. Political interference in the lives of individ-

---

[101] F. Schiller, *Briefwechsel zwischen Schiller und Körner*, 3:148.
[102] *Aesthetic Education*, Letter 4, 16-17.

uals can only be justified by this need to secure the basic freedoms necessary to individual development.[103]

In essence, Humboldt argues that freedom from political and social constraint is one of the necessary conditions of individual cultivation. Schiller, on the other hand, argues, at least in the *Letters on Aesthetic Education*, that the proper cultivation of individuals is the necessary condition of the establishment of a free state. The former treats political freedom as means, the latter as end. Humboldt argues that political freedom produces culture; Schiller argues that culture produces political freedom.[104] While Humboldt believes that only freedom will mature the character of individuals, Schiller argues that individuals are not ready for freedom until their characters have been matured.

The young Schiller may have shared Humboldt's point of view. His idealistic hero, Posa, pleads with the king that if he would only grant freedom of thought to his subjects truly human individuals would blossom in his kingdom.[105] But, as we have seen, even in *Don Carlos* Schiller presents evidence that Posa may be mistaken. In his later works Schiller is certain that "every attempt at transformation of the state must be considered as untimely and every hope based upon it as chimerical, as long as the split within man is not first abolished."[106]

Political freedom becomes an end rather than a means for Schiller because, unlike Humboldt, he is looking for a form in which man's autonomy can be realized in the external world. "The state serves to represent that ideal and objective humanity which exists in the heart of each of its citizens."[107] All left Kantians seek some "objective," interpersonal realization of man's humanity in the external world, whether in the state or "beyond" the state, and thus they cannot accept the state/society, public/private distinctions that have made Humboldt's political thought attractive to English and Amer-

[103] W. von Humboldt, *The Limits of State Action*, chaps. 1 and 2.
[104] See R. Leroux, "Schiller: Theoricien de l'état," 25ff. Leroux's essay is, by far, the best study of Schiller's political thought.
[105] *Don Carlos*, 7: line 3215.
[106] *Aesthetic Education*, Letter 7, 44-45.
[107] Ibid., Letter 4, 20-21.

ican liberals. It follows from the left Kantian understanding of human freedom that man's freedom remains merely potential until it is realized in some objective form in the external world. Schiller's longing to merge state and society in a truly human community grows out of his left Kantian perspective on social and political problems.

To Become Whole Again

I find support for my account of Schiller's discontent with the spirit of modern society in the analysis of his dissatisfaction with the world that appears in the opening pages of his most famous essay, *On Naive and Sentimental Poetry* (1795). Schiller's lovely description of the sentimental interest in nature, which opens this essay, is well known.

> There are moments in our lives when we dedicate a kind of love and tender respect to nature in plants, minerals, animals, and landscapes, as well as to human nature in children, in the customs of country folk and of the primitive world, not because it gratifies our senses, nor yet because it satisfies our understanding or taste (the very opposite can occur in both instances), rather, simply *because it is nature*. Every person of a finer cast who is not totally lacking in feeling experiences this when he wanders in the open air, when he stays in the country, or lingers before the monuments of ancient times; in short, whenever he is surprised in the midst of artificial circumstances and situations by the sight of simple nature.[108]

Schiller's major aim at the beginning of the essay is to show that "this kind of satisfaction in nature," which he assumes his readers have experienced, "is a moral rather than an aesthetic satisfaction; for it is mediated by an idea, not produced immediately by observation."[109] The idea that provides the necessary condition of this interest in nature is a contrast between nature and human art that

[108] *On Naive and Sentimental Poetry* 20:413; 83.
[109] Ibid., 20:414; 84.

puts art to shame. Without such a contrast between nature and human art in mind, Schiller argues, nature as such would excite little interest in us. In pre-philosophic Greek culture, which, according to Schiller, did not make this contrast, one thus finds "little trace of the sentimental interest with which we moderns are attached to the scenes and character of nature."[110]

For us, "nature is nothing but . . . the subsistence of things on their own, their existence in accordance with their own immutable laws." We are drawn to nature when we compare its calm self-subsistence with our own internal conflicts, and we dream, like Rousseau imagining the state of nature, about what it would be like to live in complete harmony with our inclinations. "For what could a modest flower, a stream, a mossy stone, the chirping of birds, the humming of bees, etc., possess in themselves so pleasing to us? What could give them a claim even upon our love? It is not these objects, it is an idea represented by them which we love in them."[111] However pleasing nature often is to our senses, it is the idea of the harmonious self-identity that we feel we lack that produces our deep reverence for nature.

> Yet their [natural objects'] perfection is not to their credit, because it is not the product of their choice. They accord us then the rather unique delight of being our example without putting us to shame. . . . *In them*, then we see that which eternally escapes us, but for which we are challenged to strive, and which even if we never attain it, we may still hope to approach in endless progress. *In ourselves* we observe an advantage which they lack, and in which they can either never participate at all (as in the case of the irrational) or only insofar as they proceed by *our* path (as with childhood). They afford us, therefore the sweetest enjoyment of our humanity as idea, even though they must perforce humiliate us with reference to any particular condition of our humanity.[112]

The wholeness and self-subsistence of natural things, in themselves, merit no reverence, for with natural objects it could not be

110 Ibid., 20:429; 102.
111 Ibid., 20:413-14; 84-85.
112 Ibid., 20:414-15; 85-86.

otherwise. They have to be whole and self-contained. What we really long for when we revere nature is, Schiller argues, something that mere nature cannot achieve: a self-conscious harmony produced by our own efforts. When we envy nature's harmony we unconsciously "assign a will to the involuntary in our thoughts . . . making a virtue of its eternal uniformity, and envying its calm bearing as though there were really some temptation to be otherwise which it had resisted."[113] What we envy is the consciousness of having *achieved* harmony in the face of opposition, an achievement we impute to nature when we imagine *ourselves* in a purely natural state.

Once we recognize the source of our interest in natural things, then we understand that nature inspires in us a longing for a form of existence which, in fact, goes beyond natural things: a self-conscious and self-produced form of internal harmony. "They are what we were; they are what we should become again. We were nature just as they, and our culture, by means of reason and freedom, should lead us back to nature."[114]

It is this peculiar combination of delight, humiliation, and pride when we are "suprised in the midst of artificial circumstances . . . by the sight of simple nature" that defines for Schiller the sentimental attitude toward nature. Moreover, this attitude is, Schiller notes, "identical with that feeling which we have for the ancients." Indeed, one might argue that Greek culture is, for Schiller, the natural object of sentimental interest par excellence. For nature must surprise us to produce this interest. "The naive is childlikeness where it is no longer expected, and precisely for this reason cannot be ascribed to childhood in the most rigorous sense."[115] When we contrast nature or children or primitive peoples with ourselves we are surprised by their simplicity and harmony. But nowhere are we more surprised to find natural simplicity and wholeness than among those who "are at the same time our rivals, indeed often our models, in those very advantages which we are wont to console ourselves for the unnaturalness of our manners."[116] Our sentimental

[113] Ibid., 20:427; 100.
[114] Ibid., 20:414; 85.
[115] Ibid., 20:431, 419; 105, 90.
[116] *Aesthetic Education*, Letter 6, 30-31.

interest in Greek culture is therefore deeper and longer lasting than in any other object, since more than any other naive object of sentimental interest it appears as if it could be otherwise than it is. The longing to "become again" like nature, but "by means of our reason and freedom," is inspired, above all, by reflection on the spirit of Greek culture.

Schiller describes this interest in nature as a sentiment experienced by every "refined individual who is not completely lacking in a capacity for feeling."[117] But I think it would be better described as the reaction of every individual who views nature from the perspective of Kant's dichotomy between human freedom and natural necessity and finds it intolerable—that is, from the left Kantian perspective. The mediating "idea" which Schiller insists is the necessary condition of the sentimental interest in nature depends on two premises: that humanity and nature be viewed as opposed to each other and that those who see the world in this way consider this opposition intolerable. The first premiss corresponds to the fundamental dichotomy upon which Kant builds his philosophy of freedom. The second corresponds to the left Kantian reaction to this premiss. The combination of delight, pride, humiliation, and envy which Schiller describes as the "refined individual's" attitude toward nature follows from a left Kantian perspective on nature. For from this perspective nature is at once beneath and above us. It lacks self-determination, but it also lacks our self-contradiction. To realize our humanity in the external world is thus to become once again like nature—lacking self-contradiction—but "by means of our reason and freedom." In the fully human community that Schiller, like most left Kantians, longs for, our freedom would become the means by which we establish internal and external harmony.

That Schiller's account of this sentimental interest in nature should help explain the enthusiasm for nature of so many German intellectuals—so much so that Thomas Mann calls *On Naive and Sentimental Poetry* the "classic German essay which comprises all

[117] *Naive and Sentimental Poetry*, 20:413; 83.

the others and renders them superfluous''[118]—is due, I suspect, to the ubiquity of the left Kantian perspective among the idealists and romantics who established the foundations of post-Kantian German culture. Not that I am suggesting that the left Kantian perspective is the source of all the expressions of longing for natural simplicity and harmony that are found among German intellectuals. The contrast between Greek wholeness and modern fragmentation is already a commonplace of German rhetoric long before Kant develops his philosophy of freedom. Rather, I am suggesting that the Kantian philosophy of freedom is a source of one particular development of that theme which, since it includes the social criticism of Schiller, many romantics, the young Hegel, the left Hegelians, the young Marx, and Nietzsche, among others, is probably its most important and influential development. My point is that it is the Kantian philosophy of freedom that makes possible the reaction to nature which Schiller analyzes in his essay. For the Kantian dichotomy between humanity and nature provides the perspective on the world that allows nature both to appear in the light Schiller describes and to challenge us to re-create natural unity by means of our freedom and reason.

The Kantian perspective on nature and freedom also makes ancient-modern contrasts appear in a new light in Schiller's later works. Prior to Schiller's philosophic essays, this contrast was generally viewed as an either-or choice. One had to choose between the two models of culture, and, if one chose the ancient model, one then had to decide whether it could or could not be revived under modern conditions. But from Schiller's perspective, the contrast between the spirit of ancient and modern institutions comes to suggest, for the first time, the need for a higher, third stage of development that would transcend both.[119] For Greek culture appears, from Schiller's left Kantian perspective, as the unconscious overcoming of our dichotomies, and it thus suggests the final goal of human development: a conscious, that is, rational and free, establishment of inter-

[118] T. Mann, ''Goethe and Tolstoy,'' in Mann, *Essays of Three Decades*, 95.
[119] See M. Fuhrmann, ''Die 'Querelle des Anciens et des Modernes': Der Nationalismus und die Deutsche Klassiker,'' 117.

nal and external harmony, a fully human community between man and man and between man and nature.

Tripartite accounts of the history of human development become extremely popular among nineteenth-century German social critics, and, while it would be incorrect to trace their popularity to Schiller's influence, Schiller's is the first version of the most influential type of these accounts of human development: the account of man's recovery from self-alienation through the humanization of the external world—an account popularized by Romantic, left Hegelian, and socialist intellectuals. The three stages of Schiller's account, unconscious and unfree harmony, self-conscious and free disunity, and self-conscious and free harmony, provide an outline, as we shall see, for almost all of these accounts.[120] I shall try to show in the following chapters that the restoration of our internal and external unity "by means of our reason and freedom" becomes the goal of a most diverse group of social critics, from Novalis to Marx, from Moses Hess to Nietzsche.

These thinkers provide different historical reference points and use different language to describe free harmony, free disunity, and unfree harmony, so that it sometimes requires a little effort to recognize in their social criticism the tri-partite model just outlined. Novalis, for example, recasts the roles in Schiller's account of human development. The Catholic culture of the Middle Ages plays the role Schiller assigned to the Greeks. But he draws, nonetheless, essentially the same contrasts between modern and pre-modern culture and makes a demand for a post-modern culture that will return to the pre-modern at a higher level of self-consciousness. In the Middle Ages, before reason and science made "out of the infinite music of the universe a uniform rattling of a giant mill," nature, Novalis argues, was still alive with spirit. The universal rule of the Catholic Church promoted "the harmonious development of

[120] See H. Kuhn, *Die Vollendung der Klassischen Deutschen Aesthetik durch Hegel*, 84. I should emphasize here that naive/sentimental contrasts do not form the basis of a history of art for Schiller. He did not identify classical with naive art and modern with sentimental art, although Schlegel and Hegel later popularized such an outline of the history of art. See P. Szondi, *Poetik und Geschichtsphilosophie I*, 169-70.

all faculties,'' which Schiller describes as the glory of Greek culture. Indeed, Novalis's picture of mediaeval Catholicism is essentially pagan. Its definitive feature is the unconscious harmony between nature and freedom that is destroyed by the all-dividing spirit of Protestantism and scientific reflection. Novalis longs for that harmony, but at a higher level of self-consciousness that would protect it from the dissolution suffered by its earlier manifestation.[121]

Others, such as the young Hegel and the Polish young Hegelian, Cieszkowski, follow Schiller's outline more closely. Indeed, we shall see that Cieszkowski, one of the first philosophers to develop a ''left''-wing interpretation of Hegel's philosophy of freedom, uses Schiller's arguments to correct Hegel's philosophy of history and develop the tripartite account of human development toward full reconciliation between freedom and nature that he complains is missing from the mature Hegel's philosophy.[122]

The similarity in structure between this outline of human development and Christian interpretations of human history in terms of creation, fall, and redemption has suggested to a number of scholars that all of these accounts share a common source in Christian attitudes toward history. In particular, Joachim of Fiore's division of the history of human redemption into three periods, conforming to the three persons of the Trinity, is often cited as a source of the discontent expressed in these accounts of man's recovery from self-alienation. Indeed, the adjective ''Joachimite'' has come to serve, for some scholars, as a synonym for tripartite when referring to philosophies of history.[123] Lessing's suggestion that Joachim's '' 'Three Ages of the World' were, perhaps, not so empty a speculation after all'' provides some, if minimal, evidence of a process in which Joachim's Christian philosophy of history is ''secularized.'' For Lessing makes this suggestion in the midst of his own tripartite account of human development, an account that seeks to bridge the

---

[121] Novalis (F. von Hardenberg), ''Christendom or Europe,'' 128, 133, 137-38.

[122] A. von Cieszkowski, *Prolegomena zur Historiosophie*, 24-29, 81, 95. See my discussion of Cieszkowski's argument in the third section of Chapter 6.

[123] For example, see G. A. Kelly, *Idealism, Politics, and History*, 200. Karl Löwith makes the most extended and best-known argument for tracing modern discontent and philosophies of history back to ''Joachimite'' sources. See K. Löwith, *Meaning in History*, 145-59.

gap between Christian revelation and Enlightenment philoso-phy.[124]

In the following chapters I shall argue that we do not need to search for such evidence of a secularization process to explain the shared tripartite structure of the accounts of human alienation and self-recovery dealt with there. I shall try to show that they share the structure of Schiller's account because, like Schiller, their au-thors start with a left Kantian perspective on the world. Schiller's account, as the first to arise out of that perspective, gives the clear-est view of the way Kant's conceptual innovations make possible new forms of social discontent. As later thinkers comment upon and react to earlier reactions to Kant's dichotomy between human-ity and nature, the role of Kant's innovations in opening up new forms of discontent becomes obscured. But if we keep in mind Schiller's struggles with Kantian dichotomies, then, I believe, we will be better able to uncover the philosophic sources of the social discontent expressed by many later social critics.

---

[124] G. Lessing, "On the Education of the Human Race," 97.

F I V E

HEGEL: THE LONGING
TAMED

"A FREEDOM for which something is genuinely external and alien is no freedom; freedom's essence and its formal definition is that nothing is absolutely external."[1] Throughout his life, Hegel attempts to justify and explore the consequences of this understanding of human freedom. Like Schelling, his close friend at the Tübingen seminary, the young Hegel seeks to "subject every heteronomous power to our own autonomy."[2] He too starts with Kant's demonstration that we can eliminate heteronomy in the determination of the will, and he goes on to demand the elimination of heteronomy in the world. At the centre of this demand is a challenge to Kant: what good is an understanding of man's humanity that makes human dignity irrefutable, if its first premiss must be abstraction from all real conditions of interaction with the world? Like the other left Kantians, the young Hegel concludes that Kantian moral freedom is worth pursuing only if it can be realized in the external world.

The philosophy of freedom that he eventually devises to meet this challenge and that he teaches to a new generation of intellectuals in Berlin stills, for a time, the longings of many of his students for the realization of man's humanity in the external world. On the

[1] G. W. F. Hegel, *Natural Law*, in *GW*, 4:446; 89. Cf. the definition of freedom, written much later, in the *Philosophy of Mind*, paragraph 382. Hereafter, except where otherwise noted, citations of Hegel's works will include only the title of the work, appropriate volume and page number(s) of *GW* and, following a semicolon, page number(s) of translations cited in the Bibliography.
[2] F. Schelling, *New Deduction of Natural Law*, in *Werke*, 1:272.

one hand, his dialectical logic persuades his followers of the impossibility of maintaining Kantian dichotomies. On the other hand, his philosophy of spirit convinces them that it is the very essence of man's humanity to externalize itself. World history, he argues, can be understood as the process by which freedom is realized in the external world.

But there is a price to be paid for the way Hegel mediates the Kantian dichotomy between freedom and nature, a price not at first noticed by most of his followers. The hopes for social transformation expressed by the young Hegel are not fulfilled by his mature philosophy of freedom. The realization of man's humanity described by the Hegelian system does not transform society into the fully "human" community that left Kantians, including the young Hegel, had hoped for. Man is *fully* at home, Hegel eventually concludes, only in the realm of "Absolute Spirit," that is, in the community of shared knowledge, rather than in the social community. Only in the former can we completely eliminate externality, and thus only there are we completely free. In our social communities, however, otherness remains, no matter the extent to which our institutions realize our freedom. One result of this conclusion is that Hegel is willing to describe political institutions and forms of social interaction that leave untouched many of the deepest social sources of our dissatisfaction as the forms in which our humanity is realized in the world.

The combination of exhilaration about the inner might of the self-realizing spirit and resignation to the dissatisfactions of social life in Hegel's philosophy of freedom has long puzzled his readers. To those who still pursue the left Kantian goal of the realization of man's autonomy in a fully "human" community—and in the following chapters we shall see that there are many after Hegel who do—Hegel's legacy appears ambivalent. On the one hand, his philosophy of freedom demonstrates so conclusively for his followers the untenability of Kant's dichotomy between freedom and nature that they no longer feel the need to argue against it. On the other hand, Hegel appears as the great betrayer of their cause. For he recoils from what appears to them to be the implication of his philosophy of freedom: that we should not rest content with anything less than complete freedom, the elimination of externality, in our social interactions. His advice to seek satisfaction in the realm of speculative knowledge appears to them to be a flight from reality and a self-serving submission to conventional authority.

To set Hegel's philosophy of freedom free of his resignation and apparent flight from reality has been the aim of most of his more radical students. In the twentieth century this approach to Hegel has been encouraged by the rediscovery and publication of the mostly incomplete works he began before the *Phenomenology of Spirit* (1806). By focusing on these manuscripts, in which the hope for social transformation still burns intensely, and which anticipate many of the criticisms of the modern state and culture developed by Marx and Nietzsche, we can easily construct a more radical Hegel. We can then suggest that the resignation of his later years represents a failure to follow through on his own principles.[3] Hegel's willingness to make bold claims about the realization of freedom at the same time that he accepts the limitations of contemporary institutions makes Hegel's political thought an inviting target for radical critiques.

In this chapter I examine both Hegel's early dissatisfaction and his eventual reconciliation with the spirit of modern individuals and society. I suggest that the young Hegel follows Schiller in searching for means of realizing man's humanity in the world and in locating the source of dehumanization in the spirit of modern society. But, unlike Schiller, Hegel comes to question whether the satisfaction of his longing for the realization of humanity will remove the social sources of our dissatisfaction with the world. The first section of this chapter examines the young Hegel's social discontent, in particular, his search for institutional means of overcoming the dehumanizing spirit of modern society. In this section I use the left Kantian perspective discussed in Chapters 3 and 4 to help explain the peculiar character of the young Hegel's dissatisfaction and eventual reconciliation with the spirit of modern society. In the second section I try to clarify and elaborate on Hegel's reasons for resigning himself to the limitations of modern individuals and institutions. I suggest here that these reasons provide the basis for a

---

[3] The most influential reinterpretations along such lines have been G. Lukács, *The Young Hegel*, and A. Kojève, *Introduction à la lecture de Hegel.*

powerful argument that denies the possibility of ever achieving the fully human social community longed for by left Kantians before and after Hegel. Whether Hegel is justified in arguing that a full reconciliation between humanity and the world can be found in the speculative perspective of "Absolute Spirit," and whether modern political institutions represent the highest form in which freedom can be realized within the limitations of externality are not my concerns here. My purpose is not to defend Hegel's theory of the modern state or his philosophy of spirit. Instead, my aim is to show that (1) Hegel's portrayal of the obstacles to the satisfaction of our practical needs as inescapable is consistent with his philosophy of freedom, and that (2) only the acceptance of wildly unrealistic assumptions could deliver his philosophy of freedom from its resignation in the face of those obstacles.

This chapter thus serves a dual purpose. It is a further illustration of my argument about the philosophic sources of the longing for total revolution and it begins to lay the foundation of a Hegelian critique of those, like Marx and Nietzsche, who persist in demanding the full realization of man's humanity in the world. In this and the following chapters I suggest that we can mount a Hegelian critique of Marxist and Nietzschean social criticism that is at least as powerful as that which Marx, Nietzsche, and their followers have mounted against Hegel.

The Young Hegel's Social Discontent

In his first book, written in 1800, Hegel insists that "the need for philosophy" arises when "the might of union vanishes from the life of men." He sees his own era as such an age of dichotomy and his own philosophizing as a response to that era's need. There is a need, he writes, "for a philosophy which will recompense nature for the mishandling suffered in Kant's and Fichte's systems, and set reason in harmony with nature, not by having it renounce itself or become an insipid imitator of nature, but by reason recasting itself into nature out of its own inner strength."[4]

---

[4] *The Difference between the Systems,* 4:14, 8; 91, 83.

Why does Hegel think that there is a need to restore "the might of union" to our lives? Why does he think we need unity at all? And if we once had such unity in our lives and have now lost it, why does he think that philosophy can in some way restore it?

Hegel's answer to these questions appears to be that a need for such a philosophy of reconciliation arises out of the experience of division and contradiction in our daily lives. If we did not suffer from such contradictions in our daily lives we would never ask these questions. In other times and places, such as fifth-century Greece, where the "might of union" is present in social interaction, there is no need to search for such a philosophy of unity. The search only begins when that unity collapses, as it did at the end of the fifth-century and as it has, according to Hegel, in the modern world. "Dichotomy" in our lives "is the source of the need of philosophy."[5]

But the concepts with which Hegel describes dichotomy and restored unity point to a more philosophic source for his own need of philosophy. Intellectuals in many different times and cultures have complained about the lack of unity in experience and have longed for its creation or restoration. The idea of unity has had a certain "metaphysical pathos" for intellectuals in almost every culture.[6] But intellectuals have not always conceived of unity as a reconciliation between reason and nature, let alone as a compensation to nature for its "mishandling" by philosophers—a compensation that must be paid "by reason recasting itself into nature out of its own inner strength."[7]

Such a formulation gives expression to the experience of the isolation of the spirit from the world and the accompanying devaluation of nature which, I suggested in Chapter 3, follows, for many of Kant's disciples, from the acceptance of his philosophy of freedom. From the perspective of this experience, disunity is conceived of as the dichotomy between man's humanity, his autonomous reason, and nature. And unity is conceived of as the externalization of human reason and freedom that would both liberate our humanity

[5] Ibid., 4:12; 89.
[6] See A. Lovejoy, *The Great Chain of Being*, 10-14.
[7] *The Difference between the Systems*, 4:8; 83.

from its painful isolation and "recompense nature for the mishandling" by philosophers.[8]

An examination of the large collection of manuscripts Hegel wrote before 1800 discloses, I suggest, the left Kantian sources of his discontent. Without knowledge of these manuscripts, published only after Hegel's death, we might think that the starting point of Hegel's philosophy of freedom is a simple rejection of Kant's, since that is how he presents his position in the first of his published works. But we would be wrong. Hegel, unlike his friend Schelling, carries out his philosophic education in private. The growth of a philosophy of identity out of reflection on the implications of Kantian and Fichtean dichotomies, which is apparent in Schelling's published works from 1794 to 1800, appears in Hegel's work as well, but only in his unpublished manuscripts.[9]

For Hegel, as for Schiller, Kant's defence of the freedom and dignity of humanity represents the peak of intellectual enlightenment. Up to now, religion and politics have conspired together, according to Hegel, to teach "what despotism requires, contempt for the human race." But Kant has undermined that conspiracy. He has saved the concept of humanity from the insults of theologians, the scepticism of philosophers, and the dehumanizing "necessities" of statesmen. Hegel writes to Schelling in January 1795 that philosophers are finally able to teach respect for human dignity; the people must now "learn to feel it."

> From the Kantian system and its completion I expect a revolution in Germany. . . . I believe that there is no better sign of the times than that humanity is represented to itself as so worthy of respect; it is a sign that the halo about the heads of the oppressors and idols of the earth is disappearing. Philosophers prove this dignity, peoples will learn to feel it.[10]

But how can the people "learn to feel" their freedom if freedom, as it is understood by Kant, requires abstraction from feeling? This

[8] Ibid.

[9] For a discussion of Schelling's continuing dependence on Kant's philosophy of freedom, see W. Wieland, "Die Anfänge der Philosophie Schellings und die Frage nach der Natur," 406-440, especially 410-12.

[10] G. W. F. Hegel, *Briefe von und an Hegel*, 1:23-24.

is a problem which the young Hegel struggles with even before he discovers, in 1795, Schiller's formulation of the problem in the *Letters on the Aesthetic Education of Man*. The earliest of the so-called "Early Theological Manuscripts," those written in Tübingen and Bern in 1793 and 1794, represent Hegel's first attempts to deal with the problem of the realization of man's humanity in the external world. The religious vocabulary Hegel uses in these essays proves to be, on close examination, his way of reformulating the problem of feeling and freedom.

The problem that Hegel explicitly sets for himself in these essays is how "to make objective religion subjective."[11] By "objective religion" he means the universal truths, especially moral truths, that every religion worthy of the name should teach. "Subjective religion," on the other hand, "expresses itself only in feeling and actions." It represents the sentiments and inclinations that motivate moral action. "Everything depends on subjective religion," for only subjective religion gives us an interest in undertaking the moral actions objective religion prescribes. Hegel is "not inclined to dissociate religion and morality, but on the contrary consider[s] the latter to be the *primary purpose* of religious institutions—not something it merely promotes by means of the idea of God."[12]

The whole mass of religious evidences that go to make up objective religion may be the same for a great people, in principle they might be the same over the whole earth; it is interwoven in subjective religion, but makes up only a small and rather ineffective part of it—it takes a different form in every man— the most important point at issue in subjective religion is whether, and to what extent, the mind is disposed to let itself be controlled by religious motives—how far it is susceptible to religion; and further what kinds of images make a special impression on the heart.[13]

[11] G. W. F. Hegel, *Theologische Jugendschriften* (hereafter *Jugendschriften*), 49. The earliest of these essays are translated by P. Fuss and J. Dobbins in G. W. F. Hegel, *Three Essays*; see 79. For the most illuminating account of Hegel's understanding of these writings in general and of objective and subjective religion in particular, see H. S. Harris, *Hegel's Development toward the Sunlight 1770–1801*.

[12] *Jugendschriften*, 48; *Three Essays*, 78–79.

[13] Ibid., 7; 34.

The aim of subjective religion is to prepare "a genuine receptivity for moral ideas."[14] That Hegel identifies moral ideas, that is, objective religion, with the Kantian teaching on moral reason and autonomy is suggested by the parallels between his hope that the people shall "learn to feel" the dignity of their moral freedom as taught by Kant and his hope for the emergence of a subjective *Volksreligion*, which would make the people *feel* the moral obligations taught by objective religion.

Hegel states this identification of objective religion with Kantian morality more directly in another manuscript, written a few years later, entitled "The Positivity of the Christian Religion." He claims there that Jesus undertook "to raise religion and virtue to morality and to restore to morality the freedom which is its essence."[15] In this manuscript Christ's problem appears to be the same as the left Kantian's: how to make this pure moral freedom "subjective," how to make it a force in our lives, without debasing it. "Reason sets up morality, necessary and universally valid laws. Kant calls these laws 'objective.' . . . The problem is to make these laws subjective, to make them into maxims, to find motives for them." The Christian religion has failed, Hegel argues, to provide appropriate motives for the universal laws of objective religion that Jesus, like Kant, teaches. The way Christ's followers eventually institutionalize his religion debases the morality he proclaims. They replace respect for the moral law with a heteronomous motive for moral action—respect for the authority of priests and scripture. "The Christian religion proclaims the moral law is something outside us and something given." It thus rules out the "sole moral motive, respect for the moral law," which "can be aroused only in a subject in whom the law is itself the legislator, from whose inner consciousness this law proceeds."[16]

Hegel's attempts to discover "which institutions are required in order that the doctrine and force of religion should enter into the web of human feelings" can thus be seen as a variant of left Kantian attempts to seek the means of realizing man's freedom in his ac-

[14] Ibid., 8; 35.
[15] *Jugendschriften*, 154. The later essays in the *Jugendschriften* collection are partially translated by T. M. Knox in *Early Theological Writings*; see 69.
[16] *Jugendschriften*, 211-12; *Early Theological Writings*, 143-44.

tions.[17] Hegel's declaration that "we shall not be shocked when we are obliged to admit that sensibility is the principle factor in all the action and striving of men" corresponds to the Rousseauian motto that Schiller places at the beginning of his *Letters on Aesthetic Education*: "If it is reason which makes man, it is sentiment which guides him." Like Schiller, Hegel argues that "just as pure morality must, in the abstract, be sharply distinguished from sensibility in a system of morality, since sensibility is placed far below it—even so, in dealing with human nature and human life in general, we must take particular account of man's sensibility."[18] Rendering objective religion subjective requires some means of realizing man's moral freedom and reason in the naturally conditioned sphere of sensibility.

No wonder then that Hegel greets Schiller's *Letters on Aesthetic Education* as a "masterpiece."[19] Schiller's arguments directly address the problems Hegel was struggling to formulate in the first half of the 1790s. Much later, in his Berlin lectures on aesthetics, Hegel insists:

> It is Schiller who must be given credit for breaking through the Kantian subjectivity and abstraction of thinking and for venturing on an attempt to get beyond this by intellectually grasping unity and reconciliation as the truth and by actualizing them in artistic production. . . . In the conflict of these opposing sides, aesthetic education is precisely to actualize the demand for their mediation and reconciliation, since, according to Schiller, it proceeds by so developing inclination, sensuousness, impulse, and heart that they become rational in themselves; and in this way reason, freedom, and spirituality too emerge from their abstraction and, united with the natural element, now rationalized, acquire flesh and blood in it.[20]

Schiller's arguments must have reassured Hegel of the importance of the problems with which he was struggling, as well as given him hope that these problems were solvable. For these arguments

[17] *Jugendschriften*, 8; *Three Essays*, 38.
[18] Ibid., 4; 31.
[19] G. W. F. Hegel, *Briefe*, 1:25.
[20] G. W. F. Hegel, *Aesthetics*, in *Werke*, 13:89; 1:61-62.

suggest that the obstacle to the realization of man's humanity in the external world posed by Kantian dichotomies is not immovable.[21]

The influence on Hegel and his friends Schelling and Hölderlin of Schiller's argument for aesthetic education is most noticeable in the so-called "Systemprogram," the philosophic manifesto of 1796 which the three young former seminarians circulated among themselves.[22] The document begins by declaring an acceptance of Kant's limitation of future metaphysics to the realm of "moral theory." But it immediately adds that Kant "has only given an example of, and not exhausted," this realm. The "first idea" of a "complete system of all ideas or of all practical postulates" is suggested by Kant: "The presentation of my self as an absolutely free entity." The last idea, "which unites all the rest" is "the idea of beauty."

> I am now convinced that the highest act of reason, the one through which it encompasses all ideas, is the aesthetic act, and that *truth and goodness only become sisters in beauty*—the philosopher must possess just as much aesthetic power as the poet. Men without aesthetic sense; such are our philosophers-of-the-letter [*unsere Buchstabenphilosophen*]. The philosophy of the spirit is an aesthetic philosophy. . . . Poetry gains thereby a higher dignity, she becomes at the end once more, what she was in the beginning—the *teacher of mankind.* . . . Until we express the Ideas aesthetically, i.e. mythologically, they have no interest for the *people*, and conversely until mythology is rational the philosopher must be ashamed of it.[23]

The system of moral freedom initiated by Kant's philosophy of freedom, suggests the "Systemprogram," must be completed with

[21] Adrien Peperzak downplays the importance of Schiller's arguments for Hegel's development, since he finds little evidence of Hegel's directly adopting Schiller's formulations (*La jeune Hegel et la vision morale du monde*, 36n). I would suggest, however, that the real significance of the *Letters on Aesthetic Education* for Hegel's development is that they confirmed and reinforced his resolve to investigate problems he had only started to formulate.

[22] Which of the three actually wrote the document is not important here, since all three subscribed to its program. See the articles collected in R. Bubner (ed.), *Das Älteste Systemprogram.* For an argument in favour of Hegel's authorship, see H. S. Harris, *Hegel's Development*, 249ff.

[23] G. W. F. Hegel, *Dokumente zur Hegels Entwicklung*, 219-21. This manuscript is translated by H. S. Harris in *Hegel's Development*, 510-11.

an aesthetic philosophy that will allow us to express moral ideas in a way that enables philosophers to defend them and the people to gain a feeling for them. An aesthetic philosophy will solve the problems with which the young Hegel was grappling. Moreover, the higher standpoint established by this all-unifying aesthetic philosophy will allow one to "strip the whole wretched human work of the state, constitution, government, legal system—naked to the skin." Given the idea of man's humanity provided by Kant, in addition to the proof that man's humanity can be realized through aesthetic means, all coercive institutions lose their legitimacy. From this perspective, the state and all social institutions associated with it appear to form a "mechanical thing" which "must treat free men as cogs in a machine." "We must," therefore, "go even beyond the state!"[24]

With this last demand, the "Systemprogram" certainly goes beyond the letter of Schiller's arguments. But it does not go beyond its spirit. For the human community which the aesthetic state makes possible seems to render the political institutions of the state superfluous. It is difficult to conceive of what role political institutions could play in this fully human community that would not be coercive. In such a community, Schiller suggests, the state will be merely "the interpreter of his [the individual's] own finest instinct."[25] But if this finer "instinct" already guides individual behaviour, if moral freedom is realized in our social interactions already, what need is there of political institutions to interpret it? And if there is no such instinct already manifested in individual behaviour, then, according to Schiller's argument, attempts to establish noncoercive political institutions will always fail. If man's humanity is realized in a fully human community, as Schiller and most left Kantians hoped it would be, then the state appears to be either superfluous or "mechanical," either mere decoration or a coercive force that treats human beings as things rather than as ends in themselves. The demand that we "go beyond the state," made explicit here in the "Systemprogram" and later developed by

[24] Ibid., 220; 510.
[25] F. Schiller, *Aesthetic Education*, Letter 4, 20-21.

Marx, is thus rooted in the left Kantian longing to realize man's freedom in a fully human community.

One other point which the young Hegel shares with Schiller is the conviction that the spirit of modern society is the obstacle to the realization of freedom in the external world. "The spirit of the people," Hegel writes in 1793, "its history, its religion, the level of its political freedom cannot be treated separately either with respect to their mutual influence or in characterizing them—they are woven together in a single bond." The Greek spirit was "a son of fortune and of freedom, a pupil of beautiful fancy." "A different Genius," however, "has hatched in the [modern] West." While Greek religion established an all-harmonizing spirit of social interaction, "our religion aims to educate men to be citizens of heaven whose gaze is forever directed thither so that human feelings become alien to them." It is this unfortunate "genius," the spirit of modern society, which has erected a "dividing wall between life and doctrine."[26] Greek men and culture provide the young Hegel, as they provided Schiller, with evidence that the dichotomies analyzed and systematized by Kant's critical philosophy are *historical* rather than *human* limitations.

Hegel's image of classical Greek culture is, indeed, very similar to Schiller's, both because of the direct influence of Schiller's celebration of the Greeks and because they each turn to the Greeks with similar interests already in mind. Like Schiller, the young Hegel reinterprets the Winckelmannian image of Greek culture in the light cast by the Kantian dichotomy between human freedom and natural necessity. Greek culture suggests to him a challenge to that dichotomy. From this point of view the spirit of Greek individuals and institutions either represents a living refutation of Kantian dichotomies or a lucky and inimitable outgrowth of immaturity. The young Hegel chooses the former interpretation and thus treats these dichotomies as historical rather than human limitations.[27] The older Hegel, as we shall see, chooses instead the latter interpre-

[26] *Jugendschriften*, 26-29; *Three Essays*, 55-57.
[27] See *The Difference between the Systems*, 4:13-14; 90-92.

tation and argues that Greek culture grows out of a fortunate but unsustainable conceptual confusion.

In describing and accounting for the spirit of Greek society, the young Hegel places more emphasis on religious and political life than Schiller does. He provides an institutional focus for the aesthetic education that forms the Greek character: the Greek *Volksreligion*. It is in their religious experience that the Greeks learn to identify their humanity with the external world of nature, and thus learn to reject as unacceptable any public authority that they do not in some way share. Similarly, it is modern religion (Christianity) that teaches us to expect nothing but opposition and indifference from the external world of nature, and thus teaches us the need for submission to an external authority.

Rousseau's idea of a civil religion clearly suggests Hegel's concept of a *Volksreligion*. But Hegel adapts Rousseau's idea in such a way that it will simultaneously explain both Schiller's Athens and Rousseau's Sparta. Civil religion is, for Rousseau, one of the tools the legislator uses to "denature" the sentiments of the individuals who are to be transformed into citizens. For Hegel as well, religion is the means by which individuals are educated to identify their particular wills with the general will. But religion achieves this by *harmonizing* the individual will with the external world of nature and society, rather than by denaturing it.

No less than Rousseau's Spartan does Hegel's classical republican identify his own good with the common good of the polis.

As free men the Greeks and Romans obeyed laws which they gave themselves, obeyed men whom they had themselves appointed to office, waged wars which they had themselves decided, gave their property, exhausted their passions, and sacrificed their lives by the thousands for a cause that was their own. They practised, rather than learned and taught, the moral maxims which they could call their own. In public as in private and domestic life, each was a free man, each lived by his own laws. The idea of his country or of his state was the invisible, higher reality for which he laboured, which drove him; it was the final end of the world, or of his world, an end which he found represented in ordinary reality and which he himself helped maintain.[28]

But this freedom is not, and indeed cannot, be bought, according to Hegel, at the price of the denaturing of the individual's will and sentiments. Hegel sees in the denaturing of the will the abstraction, which Kant attempts, of the rational will from the external conditioning of natural and social influences. And as we have seen, Schiller and Hegel believe that the dichotomy between freedom and nature erected by Kant makes the "realization" of true political freedom impossible.

The freedom and patriotism described by Rousseau thus requires, for Hegel, an alternative explanation to the one Rousseau provides. What is needed is some way of explaining how one could "grant freedom by means of freedom,"[29] how individuals are led to identify their own good with the common good through, rather than against, their inclinations. This is the function of Hegel's concept of a *Volksreligion*.

Moreover, Hegel's understanding of the role of religion in shaping human character provides a focus for his reflections on the dehumanization of modern individuals. The longing to get beyond the spirit of modern society inspires in Hegel, as in other intellectuals, a search for the obstacle which prevents us from undertaking a transformation of that spirit of social interaction. If one can locate a particular sphere of social interaction which shapes all others, then actions altering that sphere would produce, as Schiller suggests, a "total revolution in [man's] whole way of feeling," which would completely transform the spirit of society. Religion is that sphere of social interaction for Hegel. The longing for a transformation of the religious conditions of modern life expressed in his early writings is a longing for the total revolution that would take us beyond the dehumanizing spirit of modern society.

As Schiller argues that without aesthetic education any attempt to make true freedom the principle of political association will fail, so Hegel argues that without a transformation of our religious life

---

[28] *Jugendschriften*, 221-22; *Early Theological Writings*, 154.
[29] F. Schiller, *Aesthetic Education*, Letter 27, 214-15.

our striving to realize our humanity in the world will be futile. Even in his later works Hegel argues that religious transformation is the necessary precondition of any successful political transformation. "It is nothing but a modern folly to try to alter a corrupt moral organization by altering its political constitution and code of laws without changing the religion,—to make a revolution without having made a reformation."[30] In these later works Hegel assumes that this "reformation" of religion which prepares the possibility of political freedom has already taken place. In the early works we are examining here, he expresses a longing for such a transformation. Luther's reformation of Christianity is not sufficient for the young Hegel because he has a much more demanding vision of political freedom than we find in his later works. To bring about the total revolution that would take us beyond the dehumanizing spirit of modern society, the character of modern religion must be completely transformed.

The major essays in the so-called *Early Theological Writings* represent Hegel's experiments with Christian sources to see whether they could be transformed in such a way as to effect this total revolution in our character. I have already discussed the kind of transformation needed. Christian religion would have to become the means of rendering "objective religion subjective." It would have to be adapted so as to provide the materials for the "mythology of reason" demanded in the "Systemprogram" as the means of leading the people to "feel" their freedom.

Hegel is far from alone in calling for a self-conscious, "rational" revival of mythology in Germany at the end of the eighteenth century. In 1800, for example, Schlegel declares the establishment of a rational mythology to be the aim of the romantic movement in literature. Schelling and Hölderlin also explore this theme, which is hardly surprising given that they too subscribed to the "Systemprogram's" demand for a mythology of reason.[31]

But in this atmosphere bursting with nostalgic dreams and fan-

[30] G. W. F. Hegel, *Philosophy of Mind*, paragraph 552.

[31] F. Schlegel, *Prosaische Jugendschriften*, 2:357-66. For Schelling, see *System of Transcendental Idealism*, 223. Overall see H. Freier, *Die Ruckkehr der Götter*.

tastic hopes, Hegel appears like a "sober man among the drunk."[32] What most distinguishes Hegel from the other German advocates of a conscious revival of mythology, from Schlegel to Nietzsche, is his determination to build such a mythology out of materials that are not foreign to the lives of modern individuals and to reject any self-contradictory or irrational materials as the foundation of the new mythology. Few German intellectuals are more deeply moved than Hegel by the charm of the Gods of Greece. Yet Hegel insists that we reconcile ourselves to the fact that however much pagan mythology may delight our imagination, it no longer moves our hearts. And if this is true of classical Greek mythology, it is all the more true of the mythology of pagan Germany. "The old German imagery has nothing in our day to connect or adapt itself to, it stands as cut off from the circle of our ideas, opinions and beliefs, and is as strange to us, as the imagery of Ossian or of India."[33]

The young Hegel's rejection of a revival of pagan mythology, and even of its imagery, manifests the realism which often emerges in his work where one least expects it. Christianity may have divided our lives, but it has also educated modern individuals in such a way that we cannot honour anything but spirit as divine. However much we may regret the *Entgöttlichung* of nature, we are simply incapable of honouring sensuous appearance as divine.

> If regret is felt about this new position of nature, it must also be granted that the beautiful union of nature and God is valid for fancy alone, not for reason. Even those who object so strongly to the de-divinization of nature and extol that identity, will all the same certainly find it very difficult to believe in a Ganga, a cow, a monkey, a sea, as God.[34]

We cannot take the old pagan mythology seriously whether we want to or not. Thus Hegel turns to Christian materials as the only available foundation for the mythology of reason he seeks.

The young Hegel's reinterpretations of Christian materials are very interesting and suggestive. But they are also extremely forced

---

[32] H. Kuhn, *Die Vollendung der Klassischen Deutschen Aesthetik durch Hegel*, 101.

[33] *Jugendschriften*, 217; *Early Theological Writings*, 149.

[34] G. W. F. Hegel, *Philosophy of Religion*, in *Werke*, 17:62; 2:185.

readings of the basic texts. Since they are experiments, which Hegel never published, he feels no need to avoid taking a position in one essay which might contradict a position taken in a previous essay. Thus in one manuscript Jesus appears as a propagandist for Kantian moral philosophy, while in another he is portrayed as the man who taught that "nature is holier than the temple" and whose "general drift is to elevate nature, which for the Jews is Godless and unholy."[35] It is hard to say which of these alternatives is more foreign to a genuine Christian perspective. What is important in the context of this study, however, is that Hegel eventually abandons these experiments and with them the attempt to effect a total revolution through the transformation of Christianity.

But the lack of religious means to effect this total revolution does not seem to shake Hegel's belief that the obstacle to the realization of human freedom posed by the spirit of modern society can be eliminated. Perhaps this is because from Hegel's fundamental philosophic perspective in these years—Schelling's philosophy of identity—it is dichotomy and disunity, that is, the spirit of modern society, that is abnormal and requires explanation, rather than harmony and unity.

This belief that it is cultural disunity that requires explanation is reflected in the young Hegel's comparisons between ancient and modern society. His account of the spirit of Greek culture differs from Schiller's in that he does not view its collapse as a result of its internal contradictions. For Schiller, the harmonious spirit of Greek culture is a happy accident which must collapse as soon as reflection reveals its internal contradictions.[36] Although Hegel tells much the same story in the *Phenomenology of Spirit* and the *Philosophy of History*, it is not the story he tells in these early works. And since the collapse of the Greek spirit is not made necessary by the very features that give it its harmonious character, Hegel need not conclude, as Schiller does, that the limitations of modern culture grow out of the inadequacies of ancient culture. Instead, he suggests, it was a contingent set of events and social developments that led to the collapse of the Greek spirit and the triumph of Christianity.

[35] Cf. *Jugendschriften*, 154 with 263; *Early Theological Writings*, 69 with 208.
[36] See F. Schiller, *Aesthetic Education*, Letter 6.

In early essays, such as "The Positivity of the Christian Religion," Hegel tries to bring to light the "still and secret revolution in the spirit of the age"[37] that made the triumph of Christianity over paganism possible. He points to political and social pressures external to the spirit of the polis as the source of its collapse. "Fortunate wars, increase of wealth, and acquaintance with luxury and more and more of life's comforts" corrupted the democratic spirit of public virtue in Athens and Rome. At first the people ceded power to an aristocratic elite as a temporary convenience. But "soon the preponderance freely granted to the rulers was upheld by force, and the fact that this could happen already presupposes the loss of that type of feeling and consciousness which, under the name of 'virtue,' Montesquieu makes the principle of a republican regime." Once virtue vanished "all political freedom vanished," for "the picture of the state as a product of his own energies disappeared from the citizen's soul."[38] Greeks and Romans were ready to be swallowed up by the universal despotism of the Roman empire.

Such are the conditions, Hegel argues, that made possible the triumph of Christianity.

> Reason could never give up finding the absolute, self-sufficient, and practical principles somewhere or other; but these were no longer to be met with in man's will. They now showed themselves in the deity proffered by the Christian religion, beyond the sphere of our powers and our will but not of our supplications and prayers. Thus the realization of a moral ideal could now no longer be willed, but only wished for (since what we wish for we cannot achieve ourselves, but expect to acquire without our action). . . . Thus the despotism of the Roman princes had chased the human spirit from the earth and spread a misery which compelled men to seek and expect happiness in heaven; the theft of freedom forced the human spirit, its eternal and absolute element, to take flight into the deity. God's

---

[37] *Jugendschriften*, 220; *Early Theological Writings*, 152.
[38] Ibid., 222-23; 155-57.

objectivity goes along with the corruption and slavery of man.[39]

For the young Hegel, the Greek community *is*, at least in principle, the fully human community he longs for and would like to reconstruct under the altered conditions of modern social life. Greek customary morality is, for him, a *"pure* morality," in which "the moral commandments of reason, which are subjective, were not treated or set up as if they were objective rules with which the understanding deals."[40] We do not have to go beyond the spirit of the polis to discover human freedom and "pure morality," as Schiller believes we must.

Hegel scoffs here at the idea that it was the intellectual and moral inadequacies of Greek religion that led to the collapse of the Greek spirit. Those who speak of the need for "intellectual enlightenment" as the source of Christianity's triumph over paganism are completely mistaken. They are misled by the fact that

> it is so very easy for us to make any child understand how silly is the belief in a troop of Gods up in heaven, like those the heathens believed in, who walk about, eat, drink, indulge in horseplay, and do other things that any decent person would be ashamed to do on earth. But anyone who has made the simple observation that the heathen too had intellects, and that in everything great, beautiful, noble, and free they are so far our superiors that we can hardly make them our examples but must rather look up to them as a different species at whose achievements we can only marvel . . . will find unsatisfactory the usual answers to the question about the supersession of paganism.[41]

The "Greeks and Romans were satisfied with Gods so poorly equipped because they had the eternal and self-subsistent within their own hearts."[42] If Greek *Volksreligion* could reproduce the "eternal and self-subsistent" in the hearts of Greek citizens, then

[39] Ibid., 224, 227-28; 158, 162-63.
[40] Ibid., 211; 143.
[41] Ibid., 221; 153-54.
[42] Ibid., 224; 157.

who are we to laugh at its incongruities? The Greek religion must
be seen as a source of, rather than an obstacle to, the establishment
of "pure morality" and political freedom.

At this stage of his development, Hegel values the "immediacy"
of the identity between individual and community—the lack of recognition of the individual's subjective particularity, which he later
comes to consider the essential limitation of the polis—as the greatest virtue of Greek political life. In the works produced from 1800
to 1804 in Jena, Hegel describes ethical life as a "sheer identity of
universal and particular." "[The] absolutely ethical has its own organic body in individuals, and its movement and vitality in the
common being and doing of everyone is absolutely identical as both
universal and particular." "Singulars are no more; it is absolute
substance, it is the spirit of the people."[43]

Yet a few years after writing these descriptions of the polis, Hegel
argues that making "the individual will identical to the universal"
is the limitation and undoing of the Greek political community,
even if it is also the essential condition of "the beautiful and happy
freedom of the Greeks which is and has been so envied."[44] In Greek
political life, as most fully realized in the Spartan republic and most
fully conceptualized in the Platonic republic, "the outer actual freedom of the individuals, in their immediate existence, is lost." "The
higher principle of the modern era," which makes free government
"independent of the self-knowledge and individual character of rulers," is "unknown to Plato and the ancients."[45] In the Greek polis
public freedom and rationality was dependent on the character of
individuals, on their public virtue, their "sheer identity" of individual and general will.

These statements, written sometime during 1805 to 1806, mark
a decisive break in Hegel's attitude towards the Greek polis. Hegel
here suggests the outline of the argument he later develops at
length in the *Philosophy of Right*. The spiritual and institutional
foundations of modern society allow the realization of public free-

[43] *Natural Law*, 4:479, 470; 126, 115. *Jenaer Realphilosophie I*, 6:315.
[44] *Jenaer Realphilosophie II*, 8:262, 262n. This manuscript has been translated by
L. Rauch as *Hegel and the Human Spirit*; see 159, 159n.
[45] Ibid., 8:263; 160.

dom without rooting out the individual's self-preference. These foundations make the modern state both stronger and freer than the polis.[46] After 1806 he never again sets up the polis as the form of political community which follows from the realization of freedom in the external world. This break in the development of Hegel's understanding of the polis and political freedom is rooted, as Manfred Riedel has persuasively argued, in the fundamental shift in Hegel's philosophic perspective away from Schelling's philosophy of identity. At the beginning of the 1800s, Hegel is still an advocate and defender of Schelling's standpoint. From this perspective, the individual appears related to the community in a free and rational society as accident is related to substance.[47] The apparent submersion of the Greek citizen in his community is the greatest virtue of the polis, since it corresponds to this understanding of the identity between nature and freedom.

But by 1806, Hegel has begun to assert his own understanding of the reconciliation between nature and freedom, the understanding which provides the foundation for all of his major works. This understanding of the reconciliation between nature and freedom in absolute spirit rejects Schelling's philosophy of absolute identity as a colourless uniformity which fails to grasp either the multiplicity of the world or the special dignity of human freedom. Schelling's absolute is, in Hegel's famous phrase, "a night in which all cows are black."[48] From Hegel's new perspective, the purported immediacy and total identity of the Greek citizen with his community represents a limitation rather than a virtue. Social institutions that submerge the individual subject in the state's "substantive" identity no longer correspond to Hegel's understanding of the realization of man's freedom and humanity in the world. Hegel rejects the Greek polis, like Schelling's absolute, as a substance that ignores subjective freedom.[49] From this point on in Hegel's writings, the Greek

[46] See especially *Philosophy of Right*, paragraph 273, in which Hegel argues that the ancient republics' need of the "political virtue," rightly pointed out by Montesquieu, is a sign of their institutional weakness rather than of their strength. Cf. *Jenaer Realphilosophie II*, 8:263n with *Philosophy of Right*, paragraph 185.

[47] M. Riedel, "Hegels Kritik des Naturrechts," 180, 188, 191.

[48] *Phenomenology of Spirit*, 9:17; 9.

[49] Cf. the treatment of the polis as a "substantive" ethical order in the first part of

polis no longer puts the spirit of modern social institutions to shame.

After he adopts this new philosophic standpoint, Hegel begins to discuss the internal inconsistencies and tensions in Greek culture. The first and most famous of these discussions, his commentary on the conflict in Sophocles' *Antigone*, forms the first chapter of the "Spirit" section of *Phenomenology*. Antigone's resistance to the orders of the state, he suggests, reveals the fundamental contradictions of the "substantive" morality of the polis.

In Hegel's interpretation of the play, Kreon, confident of the ethical law enforced by the state, opposes Antigone and the divine law governing burial which she defends, only to discover that the ethical law's authority over the mind of the individual depends on the obscure customs of the divine laws of the dead. Customary beliefs, developed unconsciously over the ages, are the foundation of the citizens' identification with the state, despite their belief in its and their autonomy. When the ethical will of the state attacks the divine law of the underworld, it unknowingly cuts its own roots. It destroys the immediate "substantial" identity between the individual and the community by forcing him or her to choose between religious custom and the city's law. In the polis citizens believe that they rule themselves, but this conflict makes them realize that their laws and customs are dependent upon developments external to their will. For in the "substantial" community of the polis the individual is recognized merely as something insubstantial. "He counts only as a shadowy unreality," that is, as the departed spirit honoured by the divine law. Their identification with the community's law shattered by this conflict, the citizens now begin to see political and religious authority as external forces of fate to which they must either submit or escape. Thus, in this account, the destruction of the Greek spirit by Roman despotism is prepared by the internal contradictions of Greek culture, rather than merely by external political and social developments, as Hegel had argued earlier.[50]

---

chapter 6 of *The Phenomenology of Spirit* with the insistence in the preface of that work (9:18; 17) that "everything turns on grasping and expressing the true, not only as substance but equally as subject."

[50] *Phenomenology of Spirit*, 9:251, 260-61; 279, 289-90.

In his Berlin lectures on world history and on philosophy, Hegel uses the execution of Socrates to illustrate the internal contradictions of the customary morality of the polis. The Athenian community cannot accommodate Socrates' demand that its laws and institutions be judged by the standards of subjective reason without uprooting the customary morality which is its foundation. But by opposing Socrates, the city nevertheless brings its customary morality into question. For with the execution of Socrates, Hegel suggests, the subordination of subjective freedom to the political community, which has remained up to that point implicit, now becomes explicit to all.

> With Socrates the tragedy of the Greek spirit is performed. He is the noblest of men, morally unblameworthy; but he brought the principle of a supersensible world to consciousness, a principle of the freedom of pure thought that is absolutely justified in and for itself. This principle of inwardness with its freedom of choice means destruction for the Athenian state. Thus his fate is the highest tragedy. His death can appear as the highest injustice, since he completely fulfilled his duties to his country and opened up to his people the inner world. On the other hand, however, the Athenian people were completely right when a deeper consciousness told them that this inwardness would weaken the authority of the law and undermine the Athenian state. As deeply justified as Socrates was, so were the Athenian people against him.[51]

Greek customary morality rests, according to Hegel, on the identification of the spiritual and the natural. In his early works, Hegel takes that identification as a model to be imitated. In his later works he argues, like Schiller, that that identification grows out of a fortunate confusion that cannot survive the maturation of human reason. "The fundamental characteristic of the Greek spirit is that its freedom of spirit is conditioned by and essentially related to a natural stimulus. Greek freedom is excited by something other than

[51] G. W. F. Hegel, *Vorlesungen über die Philosophie der Weltgeschichte* (herefter *Vorlesungen*), 645-46. The English translation by J. Sibree, *Philosophy of History*, was made from an older, less inclusive edition of Hegel's lectures.

itself, and it is only free to the extent that it alters and reproduces that stimulus on its own." When Socrates demonstrates through his life and ideas that "the world of thought is man's true home," he reveals the secret of Greek customary morality: the duties taken by the Greeks to be natural growths are actually products of the human spirit.[52]

The Greeks, Hegel argues in his later work, were able to locate the spiritual in the natural without devaluing either only because of their unconscious confusion about spirit and nature. The Greeks discovered meaning and value in nature only after setting aside what is "contingent, decayed, inauthentic, and inessential" in nature. "Man, therefore, expresses what nature means," even for the Greeks; "that meaning belongs merely to man."[53] The unique achievements of Greek culture depended, however, on continuing to treat this humanly developed meaning as the work of nature itself. By demonstrating it to be the work of men, subject to the standards established by human reason, Socrates upset the delicate but confused balance which supported the Greek spirit. We, Socrates' heirs, who recognize the human source of meaning, can never re-create the beautiful freedom of the Greeks.[54]

In the *Phenomenology of Spirit* Hegel abandons the spirit of the polis as the standard by which to measure modern social life, never to raise it again. The beauty of Greek culture may seem a reproach to our lives, but our freedom is a greater reproach to theirs.

> The statues are now mere corpses from which the living soul has flown, just as the hymns are words from which belief has

[52] *Vorlesungen*, 570, 645; *Philosophy of History*, 238, 270. In contrast, some of Hegel's early essays portray Socrates as the philosophic protector of customary morality. See H. S. Harris, *Hegel's Development: Night Thoughts*, 131-34, 193-94.

[53] *Vorlesungen*, 560, 564.

[54] One consequence of that recognition, Hegel argues, is our inability to reproduce the level of artistic achievement we find in ancient Greece. For the highest forms of art, he argues, depend upon our recognizing the sensuous manifestation of human meaning. The Greeks reached the peak of artistic achievement because the fundamental principle of their culture was the reading of man's humanity into sensuous natural forms. I discuss Hegel's argument about the death of art in the third section of Chapter 8, where I raise it as a response to Nietzsche's demands for the rebirth of tragic culture.

gone. The tables of the gods provide no spiritual food and drink, and in his games and festivals man no longer recovers the joyful consciousness of his unity with the divine. The works of the Muse now lack the power of the spirit, for the spirit has gained certainty of itself from the crushing of gods and men. They have become what they are for us now—beautiful fruit already picked from the tree, which a friendly fate has offered us, as a girl might set the fruit before us. . . . But, just as the girl who offers us the plucked fruits is more than the nature which directly provides them—the nature diversified into their conditions and elements, the tree, air, light, and so on—because she sums all this up in a higher mode, in the gleam of her self-conscious eye and in the gesture with which she offers them, so, too the spirit of fate that presents us with those works of art is more than the ethical life and the actual world of that nation, for it is the *inwardizing* in us of the spirit which in them was still *outwardly* manifested.[55]

With this sad farewell to the polis, one might expect Hegel to return to something like Schiller's position on the limitations of modern society: we should try to reproduce the harmony with nature that the Greeks had, but at a higher level, by means of the freedom and self-conscious reason that raises us above Greek society. This is not, however, Hegel's conclusion. His farewell to the polis is also his farewell to the left Kantian goal of transforming modern society into a community in which man's humanity is fully realized in the external world. When he bids farewell to the "beautiful and happy freedom of the Greeks," he bids farewell to the pursuit of any kind of freedom that can be "beautiful and happy."[56] Why this should be so is the subject of the next section of this chapter.

Hegel's Resignation to the Limitations of Human Freedom

From Hegel's new and final philosophic standpoint, the spirit of modern society no longer appears to be an obstacle to the realization

---

[55] *Phenomenology of Spirit*, 9:402; 455-56.
[56] *Jenaer Realphilosophie II*, 8:262; *Hegel and the Human Spirit*, 159.

of freedom. Indeed, in his philosophy of spirit, Hegel goes so far as to reverse his earlier position and argue that the spirit of modern society *is* the form in which man's freedom and humanity are realized in the world. In effect, Hegel declares that the left Kantian demands for the externalization of man's humanity have been satisfied. Thus those demands should no longer inspire dissatisfaction with modern men and institutions.

Yet Hegel's account of freedom realized abandons almost all the hopes that he and the rebellious generation of the 1790s attached to the left Kantian project. The realization of freedom produces no great transformation of human character. It brings no outburst of beauty and human greatness. The modern world, as Hegel conceives it, offers no revival of the grandeur and nobility of Greek political life, no refreshment of the aesthetic sense, no soothing, world-enlivening *Volksreligion*. Modern citizens are free, but they still look and act like the same much maligned bourgeois they are. Art is reduced to irony and imitation. And the religion of free individuals is a lukewarm and uninspiring version of Protestantism.

Little wonder then that Hegel has been charged with the betrayal of his generation's emancipatory dreams. If the mature Hegel still believes what the young Hegel believed, that the realization of freedom in the external world would remove the social sources of dissatisfaction from our lives, then his philosophy of spirit would provide a great deal of evidence to support the charge. For if Hegel finds no source of dissatisfaction in the institutions and social practises which, he argues, realize freedom in the modern world, then his standards have indeed fallen drastically. His critics' charges that cowardice, ambition for worldly success, and the complacency of middle age led him to abandon his critical sense would be very easy to defend.

If the realization of freedom still has the same meaning for Hegel in his maturity that it did in his youth, then his portrayal of the modern world does represent the epitome of bourgeois, philistine self-satisfaction that his critics complain about. In this section, however, I shall try to show that the realization of freedom does not have the same meaning for the older Hegel as it did for him in his youth. The realization of freedom does *not* remove the obstacle to a world without social sources of dissatisfaction for the author of the *Science of Logic,* the *Encyclopedia of the Philosophic Sciences,* and the *Philosophy of Right.* This discovery about the realization of freedom leads Hegel to reconcile himself to the limitations of modern institutions. Given his mature philosophy of freedom, those limitations are not dehumanizing.

Freedom "realized" is, for the older Hegel, freedom externalized. It is the sphere of "Objective Spirit," the sphere in which our humanity is made manifest to us through the alterations that social actions impose on the appearance of the world. For freedom to be able to manifest itself for us, there must be something "other" than freedom in which it can become manifest. This sphere of "otherness," or externality, is nature. Natural necessity provides the essential contrast to the self-directed purposiveness of human freedom. When our freedom becomes manifest in the external world, the world shaped by the necessity of natural forces and their indifference to human purpose, then our freedom is realized.

But "realized" freedom, "Objective Spirit," is also limited freedom. It cannot be the complete "self-identity," the "absence of dependence on another," which defines absolute freedom for Hegel.[57] The very definition of "Objective Spirit" is *externalized* freedom, freedom as it appears in the "otherness" of natural necessity. In "Objective Spirit" the contingency of nature, its indifference to human ends, becomes the means by which freedom manifests itself for us. But this does not mean that contingency is conquered and disappears. Rather, it means that the forms in which freedom has manifested itself are shaped by the contingencies that enable them to develop in the first place.

> In law and its actualization, for example, my rationality, my will and its freedom, are certainly recognized; I count as a person and am respected as such; I have property and it is meant to remain mine; if it is endangered, the court sees justice done to me. But this recognition and freedom are always solely confined to single relative matters and their single objects: this house, this sum of money, this specific right, this specific law,

[57] G. W. F. Hegel, *Philosophy of Mind,* paragraph 382.

etc., this single action and reality. What confronts consciousness here are single circumstances which indeed bear on one
another and make up a totality of relations, but only under
purely relative categories and innumerable conditions, and
dominated by these, satisfaction may as easily be momentary
as permanent. . . . The content of this freedom and satisfaction remains *restricted*, and thus this freedom and self-satisfaction retain too an aspect of *finitude*. But where there is finitude, opposition and contradiction always break out again
afresh, and satisfaction does not get beyond being relative.[58]

"Opposition and contradiction always break out again afresh" in
modern social interaction, as they always have in the past, even if
modern institutions represent to Hegel the realization of human
freedom. Neither the modern state nor any state or social community can become the fully "human" community in which the
"otherness" of nature has been entirely tamed. For "in this world
freedom presents itself under the shape of necessity."[59]

The national spirit contains nature-necessity, and stands in external existence: the ethical substance, potentially infinite, is
actually a particular and limited substance; on its subjective
side it labours under contingency, in the shape of its unreflective natural usages, and its content is presented to it as something *existing* in time and tied to an external nature and external world.[60]

Hegel does try to refute with his philosophy of freedom the strict
Kantian dichotomy between humanity/freedom and nature. He
tries to demonstrate that we only know our humanity to the extent
that it has manifested itself in the external world, in our laws and
in our moral practises. This is his major complaint about Kant's
moral philosophy. The moral law and duties that Kant derives from
his conception of autonomy, from man's ability to make *unconditioned* reason the determining ground of the will, he in fact derives,

[58] G. W. F. Hegel, *Aesthetics*, in *Werke*, 13:136; 1:99.
[59] G. W. F. Hegel, *Philosophy of Mind*, paragraph 385.
[60] Ibid., paragraph 552.

claims Hegel, from the moral and social practises of the modern European world. The fundamental institution that shapes the *Sitten* of that world is Christianity, with its emphasis on the infinite worth of the individual and his subjective freedom. It is this fundamental aspect of modern moral practises that is registered in the way Kant defines man's humanity in terms of his ability to abstract from external conditioning.

But Hegel's refutation of Kantian dichotomies does not support the assertion that freedom *is* the world of nature, or that man's activity *humanizes* nature, neutralizing its contingency and indifference to human ends. In Hegel's own system, nature's otherness is mediated but never overcome. We know nature, Hegel argues, only in its opposition to human freedom, in its otherness. That is the condition of experiencing something as natural. In itself, in its unmediated being, nature remains opaque. Nothing can be said about the sheer being of a thing except that it is, which is to say nothing about it that distinguishes it from anything else. To insist on the being of nature apart from human purpose is to say nothing at all about it.[61]

This opposition of nature to freedom, however, is also the necessary condition of our self-knowledge. Far from denying nature's contingency and indifference to human ends, Hegel makes them a necessary part of his philosophic system. Indeed, Dieter Henrich goes so far as to suggest that Hegel's "is the only philosophic theory which recognizes absolute contingency."[62] The contingency of nature is the necessary condition of the realization of freedom. Nature's indifference to purpose allows it to be shaped by man and allows us to recognize the meaning and purpose in the world as our own. Its contingency, however, also limits the extent of the realization of human meaning and purpose in the external world. The forms freedom takes in the world are shaped by the opportunities

[61] Thus the first argument of the *Science of Logic*, which attempts to prove the equivalence of being and nothing as conceptual categories. See also the Introduction to Hegel's *Philosophy of Nature*.

[62] D. Henrich, "Hegels Theorie über die Zufall," in Henrich, *Hegel im Kontext*, 59. See also M. Theunissen, *Hegels Lehre vom Absolute Geist als Theologisch-Politischer Traktat*, 27ff.

for development offered by the contingencies and coincidences of natural events and naturally conditioned sentiments. The actualization of freedom in the world makes use of the contingency of nature but is thereby limited in its turn.

Since the realization of freedom in the external world does not eliminate natural contingencies as influences on our social actions, it does not eliminate the obstacle to a world without social sources of dissatisfaction in the way that the young Hegel hoped it would. What it does do for Hegel, however, is eliminate the obstacle to a world without *theoretical* sources of dissatisfaction posed by the opposition between human purposiveness and natural contingency. Once freedom has been realized in our institutions and practises, then theoretical activity is liberated from its dependence on otherness. For now mind knows mind, spirit knows spirit when it views the world.

Such knowledge, the self-consciousness of spirit that Hegel calls "Absolute Spirit," "is the resolution of the highest opposition and contradiction."

> In it validity and power are swept away from the opposition between freedom and necessity, between spirit and nature, between knowledge and its object, between law and impulse, from opposition and contradiction as such, whatever forms they may take. Their validity and power *as* opposition and contradiction are gone.[63]

Hegel does not mean to suggest that contingency and external necessity disappear from one's life as soon as one becomes a philosopher. The philosopher, as much as anyone else, is buffeted about by external necessities beyond his control. What Hegel suggests is that nature's externality loses its absolute opposition to human freedom and reason when viewed from a theoretical perspective. When freedom is realized, natural contingency becomes the means of self-knowledge, the indispensable condition by which our own freedom and reason can become manifest to us, rather than the perpetual obstacle to our satisfaction. Its indifference to our practical

[63] G. W. F. Hegel, *Aesthetics*, in *Werke*, 13:137-38; 1:100.

ends, which it constantly frustrates, is no longer a source of dissatisfaction when we view the world from this theoretical perspective.

According to Hegel, the social and political development of man does make possible a fully "human" community in which man is completely at home. But that community is the community of self-knowledge, not the community of social interaction. The first and essential premiss that makes us members of this community is our ability to abstract from the externally conditioned ends we pursue in social interaction and to turn toward the pursuit of an end which we all share as *human* beings: self-knowledge. During the week we pursue the former set of ends, with varying degrees of success. Only on our days of rest, our philosophic Sabbaths, do we become members of this fully human community and lose our dissatisfaction with the external world.[64]

Hegel does reproduce something that corresponds to Schiller's tripartite scheme of human development culminating in man's free and self-conscious harmony with external nature. But he does so in an account of the history of metaphysical attitudes, not in his account of the historical development of "Objective Spirit."

In the first stage of the development of philosophy, which comprises ancient metaphysics, there is an immediate reconciliation between nature and mind. "Thinking," for the ancients, "is not anything alien to the object, but rather its essential nature, things and the thinking of them . . . are explicitly in full agreement, thinking in its immanent determinations and the true nature of things forming one and the same content." The ancients have confidence that their concepts reflect the true nature of things. Such a position maintains the unity of mind and nature, and manifests "a higher conception of thinking than is current today." But it gains that unity by subordinating the freedom of the mind to something external, the "true nature" of things.[65] It corresponds to the harmonious, but unfree, relationship between nature and humanity that Schiller discovers in Greek social life.

In the second period man conceives of thought as "reflective un-

---

[64] G. W. F. Hegel, "Inaugural Address," in Hegel, *Berliner Schriften*, 16ff.
[65] *Science of Logic*, 21:29; 45.

derstanding." That period "stands for the understanding as abstracting, and hence as separating and remaining fixed in its separations." It maintains "that thoughts are *only* thoughts" which we impose on our experience of the external world. Although "in this self-renunciation on the part of reason, the notion of truth is lost," it is, nonetheless, "based on something more profound on which rests the elevation of reason into the loftier spirit of modern philosophy." For in the characterization of thought as reflective understanding, man discovers the essential feature of thought and, indeed, of humanity: autonomy.[66] This period, which comprises modern philosophy from Descartes to Kant, corresponds to the period of free and self-conscious disunity, which Schiller argues begins with the fall of the polis and continues up to his own time.

The final period, inaugurated by Hegel's philosophy, corresponds to Schiller's final period of human social development, the return to natural wholeness by means of our freedom and reason. In it we have the "liberation from the opposition of consciousness" for which Schiller and the left Kantians longed.[67]

In contrast with his account of the history of metaphysics, Hegel's account of the historical development of "Objective Spirit" in the *Philosophy of History* does not follow this tripartite pattern of unfree harmony, free disunity, and free and self-conscious harmony. It has, surprisingly, four parts: the Oriental, Greek, Roman, and German (modern) worlds. More important than the number of stages, though, is their character. The stage of self-conscious dichotomy, which is the second in his account of the development of metaphysics and in Schiller's account of human development, is here the final stage. And though Hegel leaves the future open, he makes no suggestion that it might hold the possibility of the free and self-conscious harmony with the external world that Schiller had forecast.

The final epoch Hegel describes is one in which the realization of the true concept of freedom, first introduced by Christianity, takes place. The process of freedom's realization has three steps: revela-

[66] Ibid., 21:29-30; 45-46.
[67] Ibid., 21:33; 49.

tion (the birth of Christianity), reformation, and revolution. The completion of this process, the end of the social convulsions begun by the French Revolution, does not, however, raise social life to a new and higher level of self-conscious harmony with the external world. Rather, it makes possible the third stage of metaphysical development by manifesting freedom in the world so that it can be recognized as such by the self-knowing mind. The history of the world thus represents a "theodicy," according to Hegel, for it makes possible the ideal overcoming of otherness in absolute spirit.[68] It does not, however, represent for him a *redemption* of the world, an elimination of the obstacles placed in the way of our ends by natural contingencies, as becomes clear when one examines the rational state in which he argues freedom and reason have been realized.

The rationality of the state Hegel describes and justifies in the *Philosophy of Right* is limited and conditional. Political rationality does not entail for him the elimination of the effects of contingency as it does for Plato in the *Republic*, to cite the author whose political philosophy Hegel uses most often as a contrast to his own. In the *Republic* everyone and everything is in the right place: the individual in the job to which his nature suits him, things in the hands of the individuals who can best use them. The entire regime is arranged so as to eliminate the contingencies of birth, class, gender, ambition, and individual self-preference, contingencies that keep individuals out of the positions they deserve and things out of the hands of the individuals who can make the best use of them. The conventional privileges and the individual liberties which leave room for such inappropriate distributions have been eliminated in the *Republic*. The conventions that are established by the regime, summarized in what Plato calls the noble lie, are those required to allow the continual restoration of individuals and things to their appropriate places. And at the top of the social hierarchy, reason rules directly in the figure of an omniscient philosopher-king.

Hegel's rational state, on the other hand, is shot through with contingency from top to bottom. At the top, the ruler owes his po-

---

[68] *Vorlesungen*, 938; *Philosophy of History*, 457.

sition to his birth. His qualification for sovereignty is precisely his lack of qualifications other than the sheer contingency of his birth.[69] In general, individuals choose and perform their vocations according to their own choice, whether or not they are especially suited to them. Plato excludes such subjective freedoms because they would upset the rationality of the political order. "For Plato subjective freedom does not count, because people have their occupations assigned to them by the guardians." Hegel argues against Plato that the "higher principle" of modern states allows subjective freedom full play without upsetting the rationality of political order.[70]

Political rationality, for Hegel, means primarily impersonality, not correctness. Rational institutions are those that establish and administer laws which eliminate the power of the personal opinions and wills of individuals over each other, rather than those which lead to the right decisions being made by the right people at the right time. "Despotism," Hegel writes, "means any state of affairs . . . where the particular will as such, whether of a monarch or a people (ochlocracy) counts as law or rather takes the place of law."[71] Hegel's claim is that the peculiar configuration of the modern state—by which he means the post-Napoleonic constitutional monarchies of Western Europe—succeeds in avoiding despotism so defined, while still recognizing and protecting the subjective freedom of individuals.

Were the claim true, it would be a tremendous achievement. Hegel celebrates that achievement in the *Philosophy of Right* and the *Philosophy of History*. But it would *not* remove the social sources of dissatisfaction from our lives. For, on the one hand, such institutional arrangements only allow us to deal with the sources of our dissatisfaction in a nondespotic way. A free and rational political order does not "subject heteronomous powers" to our own auton-

[69] G. W. F. Hegel, *Philosophy of Right*, paragraphs 280-81. For the argument supporting this interpretation, see my article "The Rationality of Hegel's Concept of Monarchy."

[70] G. W. F. Hegel, *Philosophy of Right*, addition to paragraph 262, paragraph 185. (The "additions" to the *Philosophy of Right*, taken from Hegel's lectures, are included in G. Lasson's edition and T. M. Knox's translation of the *Philosophy of Right*).

[71] Ibid., paragraph 278.

omy. And, on the other hand, even this achievement is contingent upon developments which we have no control over and cannot reproduce on our own—for example, the development of a general acceptance of the claim of one noble family to sovereignty combined with a general disapproval of its use of that power to initiate policies according to its own judgments. The development of such ambivalent sentiments is essential to the proper functioning of Hegel's rational state, but it rests on the contingent development of social forces and attitudes peculiar to Western Europe. One cannot will this arrangement into existence. Nor is there any reason to assume, even if, as Hegel claims, it does now exist, that it will last for a very long time even in Western Europe.[72]

The realization of freedom in the world thus does not conform to some eternal model of rationality. The course of human development is shaped by all of the contingencies of nature that regularly intrude on human ends—geography, climate, natural disaster, heredity, and bad luck. "The laws of freedom, when they actually appear, always have a positive side marked by reality, externality, and contingency." As a result, "the laws of freedom" are both limited and precarious. "Satisfaction does not get beyond being relative" in this world. For "where there is finitude, opposition and contradiction always break out again afresh."[73] History may be the story of the realization of our freedom; but it is also a story "in which the periods of happiness are written on blank pages."[74]

We modern individuals, Hegel argues, have a self-awareness that will always leave us dissatisfied with the ways of the world. For we know ourselves as free beings. We recognize in ourselves that capacity to abstract from external conditioning and choose the ends that will guide us. Only compliance with our ends would remove the sources of dissatisfaction from the external world of nature and society. Indeed, that is what the Kantian left demands when it calls on us to subject heteronomous powers to our own autonomy. But since the best that world can do is manifest our freedom, rather

[72] See B. Yack, "The Rationality of Hegel's Concept of Monarchy," 712-15, for this interpretation of the *Philosophy of Right.*

[73] G. W. F. Hegel, *Philosophy of Religion,* in *Werke,* 17:195; 2:337. Idem, *Aesthetics,* in *Werke,* 13:136; 1:99.

[74] G. W. F. Hegel, *Lectures on the Philosophy of World History,* 79.

than bow to our control, we are always going to be dissatisfied with it.

> Vexation is the sentiment of the modern world; the feeling of vexation presupposes an end, a demand of the will, which authorizes and justifies this feeling when the end is not fulfilled. Thus modern man easily develops a mood in which he loses heart for everything else, and does not even seek to reach ends which he could reach. . . . This is the feeling of vexation; it could not have formed the character of the Greeks; their grief over the necessary is only a simple kind of grief. The Greeks set themselves no end as absolute, essential, which must be reached; their grief is therefore the grief of resignation.[75]

Hegel does offer an escape from that feeling of vexation. But that escape also requires an escape from the desire of seeing our practical goals realized. The world is not vexing if one looks at it from a theoretical perspective. That is Hegel's claim. The relief from longing he offers is at the same time a resignation to the limitations of our ability to achieve our practical ends in society.

Hegel appears to be a vulgar philistine who celebrated the life and morals of the German bureaucrat as the peak of human perfection only when one ignores the theoretical character of the complete reconciliation he offers. Most of his critics have done just that. They usually portray his philosophy of reconciliation as an attempt to satisfy practical needs. Yet "Hegel does not only not say this, but rather insisted bluntly and repeatedly" that the complete reconciliation he offers takes place "only in the world of thought."[76]

This misperception of Hegel's argument has become common, in part, because the reformulation of his ideas by radical social critics has generated much of the recent interest in his work. Social critics from Ruge and Marx to contemporary philosophic Marxists and critical theorists enthusiastically adopt Hegel's refutation of Kantian dichotomies while rejecting the idealist foundations on which that refutation rests. From their perspective,

[75] G. W. F. Hegel, *Philosophy of Religion*, in *Werke*, 17:131-32; 2:263.
[76] H. Stuke, *Die Philosophie der Tat*, 43.

Hegel is guilty of being doubly half-hearted: first in that, while declaring that philosophy is the mode of existence of the Absolute Spirit, he refuses to recognize the actual philosophical individual as the Absolute Spirit; second, in that he lets the Absolute Spirit as Absolute Spirit make history only *in appearance*. For since the Absolute Spirit becomes *conscious* of itself as the creative world spirit only *post festum* in the philosopher, its making of history exists only in the consciousness, in the opinion and conception of the philosopher, i.e., only in the speculative imagination.[77]

Marx and other radical critics complain not only about the idealism of Hegel's philosophy of freedom, but also about its halfheartedness. In effect, they ask: If Hegel *really* believes that "Absolute Spirit" makes history and it is the philosopher's consciousness that manifests "Absolute Spirit," why does he not take charge of things himself and stop hiding behind the excuse that the "Absolute Spirit makes history only *in appearance*"?

But, as we have seen, it is only *in appearance*, that is, as conceived from a theoretical perspective, that the realization of spirit directs the course of world history. One can so characterize the world only by abstracting from the residual and surrounding natural contingencies which, according to Hegel, are opaque to human reason. Left Hegelians like the young Marx demand not only the "realization" of Hegel's idealist philosophic premises, but also the "realization" of the reconciliation between nature and freedom offered in his philosophy of "Absolute Spirit." They demand that the process of historical development be so conceived as to be capable of eliminating the obstacles posed by nature's contingencies to our practical as well as to our theoretical ends.

I do not want to defend here either the philosophic premises of Hegelian idealism or his characterization of post-Napoleonic constitutional monarchy as the realization of freedom. But I do believe that the preceding discussion shows, at least, that Hegel is not inconsistent in applying those premises. And I also want to suggest that it is, at least in part, the greater "realism" of Hegelian idealism

[77] K. Marx and F. Engels, *The Holy Family*, in *MEW*, 2:90; *CW*, 4:86.

that keeps him from pursuing the goals which his left Hegelian critics demand of a lover of freedom.

By his greater "realism," I mean his denial that any form of society could eliminate the obstacles to a world without *social* sources of dissatisfaction posed by the indifference of nature to man's practical ends. To argue otherwise, social critics would have to make, from Hegel's point of view, one of two wildly unrealistic assumptions. They would have to argue either that nature, in itself, serves human purposes or that the power of the human will is so great that it can destroy the forces of nature rather than merely redirecting them and mitigating their effects.

To make the first assumption would be, in effect, to assume that from the start the *actual is rational*, something Hegel never does. He argues that "the rational is actual" and therefore "the actual is rational."[78] Our understanding of human reason is something we derive from reflection upon the human meanings manifested in the external world, in actuality. Reason develops through a process by which human meanings are introduced into the world—the rational becomes actual—where they are apprehended and interpreted by the mind as the world's meaning—the actual thus is rational.

To reverse this statement, to argue that the actual is rational and therefore the rational is actual, as, interestingly, Engels does, is to suggest that reason and human purpose are somehow implicit in the forces of nature.[79] (Indeed, Engels makes such a suggestion when he argues, in the *Dialectics of Nature*, that natural forces are guided by the same kind of dialectic laws that govern human development.) The only way to avoid this assumption, and still argue that the obstacles to satisfaction of our practical needs posed by natural contingencies can be eliminated, is to assume that man can *impose* his ends on an indifferent world and its forces not "only in the speculative imagination," but in reality.[80]

[78] See Hegel's explanation of this famous statement in the *Logic: Part One of the Encyclopedia of the Philosophical Sciences*, paragraph 6.

[79] In F. Engels, *Ludwig Feuerbach and the End of Classical German Philosophy*, 10. See F. Rosenzweig, *Hegel und der Staat*, 2:79-82, and E. Fackenheim, "On the Actuality of the Rational and the Rationality of the Actual," 690-98, for discussion of Engel's reversal and its significance.

[80] K. Marx and F. Engels, *The Holy Family*, 2:90; *CW*, 4:86.

Hegel's left Hegelian critics, least of all Marx, can accept neither of these two assumptions, both because of their wildly unrealistic character and because the demand for a return to common sense from the abstract and counter-intuitive premises of Hegelian philosophy is one of their most effective rhetorical weapons. Consequently, they cannot build an argument that would demonstrate that the obstacles to our social satisfaction posed by nature's contingency can be removed. They focus instead on locating and analyzing those obstacles. In particular, they try to unmask the obstacles to the subjugation of all heteronomous powers to our own ends (which the philosophers up to and including Hegel teach us are natural and therefore immovable), as in reality created and imposed by human actions. Instead of demonstrating man's ability to realize his autonomy, they "demystify" the obstacles to that realization.

Hegel seems to remove the obstacle to the "control and conscious mastery" of the forces that govern our world[81] by refuting the strict Kantian dichotomy between human freedom and natural necessity. Thus his philosophy of freedom encourages the belief that the fully human community that left Kantians had longed for is within our grasp. If one could only "realize," bring into the real world of social interaction, the reconciliation between nature and freedom which Hegel proves to be possible for philosophic speculation, then that longing would be satisfied. For this reason, the "realization of philosophy" becomes the main project of left Hegelian social criticism.

In this section I have previewed some of the conceptual problems that plague this project. One of the premises that allows Hegel to refute Kantian dichotomies and develop in his philosophy of "Absolute Spirit" a full reconciliation between human freedom and natural necessity rules out, I suggest, the possibility of such a "realization" of that reconciliation. Attempts to realize Hegel's philosophy of reconciliation develop internal inconsistencies when they continue to rely on his refutation of Kantian dichotomies, as we shall see in the following chapters.

[81] K. Marx, *The German Ideology*, in *MEW*, 3:37; *CW*, 5:51.

PART THREE

SIX

THE SOCIAL DISCONTENT
OF THE HEGELIAN LEFT

As THE realization of freedom is the left Kantian call to arms, so the realization of philosophy is the cry that rallies the Hegelian left. The philosophers most often described as left Hegelians—Ciesz-kowski, Feuerbach, Ruge, the Bauers, Hess, and the young Marx—all demand that philosophy be "realized" in what they call "praxis."[1] Their intellectual efforts focus on uncovering and over-coming the obstacles to the realization of philosophy. Their social discontent expresses itself, characteristically, as dissatisfaction with all institutions that fall short of this goal.

This demand for the realization of philosophy registers two kinds of dissatisfaction. On the one hand, it expresses dissatisfaction with the abstraction from the contingencies of social life that seems to be the price of Hegel's philosophic reconciliation. The realization of philosophy is needed to return philosophy to the "real" limits of human experience and action. On the other hand, this demand ex-presses dissatisfaction with all forms of human activity and social interaction that fall short of the full reconciliation between human freedom and nature that Hegel locates exclusively in the sphere of "Absolute Spirit." The realization of philosophy would also make the overcoming of nature's resistance to our practical ends "real."

Thus, in calling for the realization of philosophy, the left Hege-lians simultaneously demand a return from Hegelian idealism to "common sense" reality and an unprecedented transfiguration of that reality. They demand, like Marx, that the philosopher be re-

[1] See H. Stuke, *Die Philosophie der Tat.*

turned to his feet from the awkward position on his head that Hegel advises him to take. But they also demand that the world be, so to speak, turned upside down, so that natural contingency will no longer create any serious social obstacles to the satisfaction of human ends.

In this chapter I suggest that this longing for the realization of philosophy grows out of the same fundamental conceptual perspective as the left Kantian longing for the realization of freedom. I try to show how a particular reaction to Hegel's philosophy of freedom reopens for many of Hegel's followers the dichotomy between man's humanity and his nature that Hegel sought to close. I also point out the parallels between their speculations about the obstacles to the realization of humanity and those of left Kantians like Schiller and the young Hegel. They too come to focus on the spirit of modern society as the source of the dichotomies they want to overcome, and they seek to locate the key spheres of social interaction whose transformation would lead to a total revolution in the character of modern individuals and society.

My discussion of left Hegelian social criticism will be much briefer than the comparable discussion of the Kantian left in Chapter 3. One reason for the brevity of this chapter is that, since I suggest left Hegelian social criticism revives something very close to the left Kantian perspective on man and society, much of my discussion of how the left Kantian perspective makes possible new forms of social discontent is relevant here as well. Moreover, in Chapter 3 I coined a new term, *left Kantian*, the usefulness and appropriateness of which I was obliged to defend. *Left Hegelian*, on the other hand, is an old and familiar term. Ever since D. F. Strauss suggested that we should divide Hegel's disciples into left, right, and centre groups,[2] scholars have used the term to categorize post-Hegelian philosophers and their arguments. In accepting left Hegelian as a useful and appropriate interpretive category,[3] I rely on

---

[2] D. F. Strauss, *Streitschriften zur Verteidigung meiner Schriften über der Leben Jesu*, 3:95.

[3] I have relied most heavily on John Toews's recent work, *Hegelianism*, the best and most comprehensive account, in any language, of the Hegelian school in the 1830s and early 1840s.

the work of other scholars. Of course, there have been disagreements about the use of the term and the relationship between "young" and "left" Hegelians. Some scholars use the term *young Hegelian* to characterize the individuals described here as left Hegelians.[4] Some have denied the appropriateness of the term for any of Hegel's followers.[5] Such debates can never be decided finally one way or the other. I accept John Toewes's account as establishing a plausible case for the use of the term. He rightly makes a point, however, of distinguishing between Hegelians critical of contemporary political institutions and the Hegelian left. There had been such Hegelian social critics from Hegel's first years in Berlin. But these "old" Hegelian social critics should be distinguished from the members of the "new" Hegelian left of the late 1830s, with their demand for the realization of Hegel's philosophy. I follow Toews in treating this demand as the characteristic feature of left Hegelian criticism.[6]

My aim in this chapter is to bring to light particular characteristics and problems of left Hegelian social criticism rather than to offer an attempt to redefine the term in question. In particular I shall try (1) to make a plausible case that some of the most characteristic left Hegelian demands grow out of a reformulation of the conceptual perspective described as left Kantian in previous chapters and (2) to point to conceptual difficulties that manifest themselves in the left Hegelians' attempts to realize Hegel's philosophy. In pursuing these aims I prepare the ground for my interpretation and critique of Marx's social criticism in Chapter 7, since I shall argue there that Marx's innovations represent, at least in part, attempts to answer left Hegelian questions.

These questions continue to be asked today, and not only by Marxists. But, beginning with Marx, new ideas about the obstacles to the realization of humanity tend to obscure the conceptual prem-

---

[4] For example, W. Brazill, *The Young Hegelians*; H. Stuke, *Die Philosophie der Tat*; and J. Gebhardt, *Politik und Eschatologie: Studien zur Geschichte der Hegelschen Schule 1830-1840*.

[5] See, for example, Z. Rosen, *Bruno Bauer and Karl Marx*, 34-35.

[6] J. Toews, *Hegelianism*, 206. Apart from Toews's book, Karl Löwith's *From Hegel to Nietzsche* and Horst Stuke's *Die Philosophie der Tat* seem to me to offer the most insightful philosophic treatments of left Hegelian thought.

isses that would lead one to demand the realization of humanity in social interaction in the first place. By recovering these conceptual premises, we gain not only a better understanding of the social discontent of the intellectuals who ask these questions but also a better position from which to evaluate their social criticism, for we are then able to measure the premises that underlie their proposed remedies to the limitations of modern individuals and institutions against the premises that allow them to identify those limitations in the first place. These two sets of premises contradict each other, as I suggest in this chapter and shall try to demonstrate in my analysis of Marx's social criticism in Chapter 7.

Hegel and the Hegelian Left

Like Kant, Hegel was celebrated by his disciples as a vindicator of human dignity and a conqueror of self-doubt and cynicism. But Hegel's conceptual innovations, unlike Kant's, did not immediately pose new and more painful dilemmas for his followers as they resolved old ones. While Kant's greatest students began to look for ways beyond his dichotomies almost as soon as they adopted his philosophy of freedom, Hegel's students tended to form a school of disciples who applied the master's teaching to different areas of research. The former saw themselves as explorers and system-builders, while the latter thought of themselves as epigones, wondering how to divide up the empire Hegel conquered.[7]

An explanation of the different reactions to the two philosophies is not difficult to find. Kant defends human freedom and dignity by distinguishing man's humanity from the world in which man lives, Hegel by reintroducing man's humanity into that world. By mediating disunity rather than introducing new dichotomies, Hegel's philosophy of freedom tends to still old longings without stirring up new ones. If one identifies, as do many of his contemporaries, the dichotomy between man and world as the obstacle to a satisfac-

---

[7] One eulogist at Hegel's funeral compared the position of Hegel's students to that of Alexander the Great's generals as they debated how to carve up the conqueror's empire. See K. Rosenkranz, *Hegels Leben*, 552.

tory world, then Hegel's philosophy of freedom seems to promise a world without sources of dissatisfaction.[8]

Nevertheless, Hegel's philosophy of freedom plants the seeds of a new dichotomy, a dichotomy between philosophy and world, between theory and practise. I argued in the preceding chapter that Hegel recognizes that the price of his mediation between spirit and nature is resignation to the inevitability of our practical dissatisfaction with the world. That distinction between theoretical and practical satisfaction with the world, though at first unnoticed, eventually begins to stir up once again among some of Hegel's followers the longing for the realization of man's humanity in the world.

In their eagerness to appropriate Hegel's philosophy of freedom, with its refutation of all previously held dichotomies, many of his disciples fail to notice his denial of the possibility of complete practical satisfaction with the world. For example, in the famous letter he sent to Hegel in 1828 along with his doctoral dissertation, Ludwig Feuerbach expresses the expectations of a transformation of our ordinary lives that Hegel's philosophy so often inspires among his followers. Hegel has, he writes, plucked "the Idea out of the heaven of its colourless purity" and filled the world with spirit. He has reconciled the age-old opposition between heaven and earth, between spirit and nature.[9] Hegel's philosophy has prepared the way, Feuerbach writes, for a "third world period" in which we will see the "actualization and, so to speak, the secularization [*Verweltlichung*] of the idea, which is what the *ensarkosis* or incarnation of the pure *logos* would be called." This third epoch would be a "*Reich der Idee*" that would take us beyond the contradictory and dehumanizing spirit of modern society.[10]

Hegel's philosophy of history, as we have seen, does not end in such a *Reich der Idee*, so Feuerbach must project the hopes that Hegel inspires into the future, into an imminent "third world period." Hegel's philosophy of freedom apparently does not reconcile Feuerbach to the limitations of human ends and aspirations in the world.

[8] See J. Gebhardt, *Politik und Eschatologie*, 53ff., for examples of the enthusiasm expressed by so many Hegelians on the discovery of their master's philosophy.
[9] L. Feuerbach, *Kleine Schriften*, 8.
[10] Ibid.

Instead, by outlining in his account of "Absolute Spirit" a realm of experience in which contradiction and otherness cease, Hegel offers Feuerbach a new definition of the obstacle to a world without sources of dissatisfaction: the opposition between "Absolute" and "Objective Spirit," between philosophy and world. Thus instead of stilling Feuerbach's longing for world transformation, Hegel's conceptual innovations give it a new object: a world without the opposition between philosophy and reality, a world in which philosophy is realized.

To demand that Hegel's philosophy be completed with the realization or "incarnation" of the idea of freedom seems, at first glance, strange, since Hegel's philosophy of freedom is nothing if not an attempt to show that it is the very essence of the idea of freedom to embody itself in the world. But the embodiment of the idea of freedom that Feuerbach demands is far from the one Hegel provides. "Realized" freedom is no *Reich der Idee* for Hegel. Freedom, though it manifests itself in the external world, has no empire over it. Realized or incarnate freedom means something very different for Feuerbach than it does for Hegel. It means the overcoming of nature's opposition to human ends, the establishment of an earthly empire in which the world is completely humanized. The realization of freedom described by Hegel in his philosophy of "Objective Spirit" is merely a prelude to the realization of freedom Feuerbach expects. Hegel's realization of freedom overcomes the opposition between natural contingency and human purpose only for theory. In effect, Feuerbach demands the realization of Hegel's realization of freedom. Without this further realization of the idea, there remains a gap between nature and humanity.

The gap Feuerbach sees here between philosophy and reality is, I suggest, at least in part the dichotomy between natural necessity and human freedom that left Kantians also located as the obstacle to a world without social sources of dissatisfaction. It is the still unconquered opposition between natural contingency and the purposiveness of human freedom that creates the gap between the harmony of "Absolute Spirit" and the disharmony of "Objective Spirit" in Hegel's philosophy. In longing to close that gap, Feuerbach thus expresses a new form of the longing for the realization of man's humanity in the world.

When he asks for the realization of philosophy, Feuerbach is demanding something that he believes Hegel's philosophy promises to deliver. The realization of philosophy means for Feuerbach here the last stage in Hegelian world history, not a critique of Hegel's philosophy. But in the years following Hegel's death this last stage of history begins to look increasingly remote, given the resurgence of Protestant orthodoxy and the growing hostility to Hegelianism in the Prussian government. As a result, some of Hegel's disciples begin to wonder whether Hegelian philosophy itself shares the limitations of the unreconciled world in which it first develops. Otherwise, why would Hegel have celebrated contemporary institutions as the realization of human freedom?

If we believe that Hegel's philosophy of freedom promises the elimination of the social sources of our dissatisfaction with the world, then how do we account for the continuing, even growing irrationality and arbitrariness of our institutions? One response would be to ignore these limitations and idealize our institutions, as some Hegelians did in the 1830s.[11] Another response would be to suggest that these limitations of the present are anachronisms in the present regime, remnants of an old regime doomed to eventual extinction. This response becomes more and more difficult to support as the strength of the rationalizers in the Prussian administration wanes throughout the 1830s.[12] Finally, we could respond by denying that Hegel had properly understood what the realization of freedom requires, for if he had properly understood it, he never could have suggested that reason and freedom are realized in the current regime. That is the response that, I suggest, defines the left

[11] The worst cases by far of this "right Hegelianism" occurred among Russian intellectuals like Bakunin and Bielinsky who, before appropriating left Hegelian arguments in the 1840s, celebrated Nicholas I's obscurantist and extremely repressive regime as the complete realization of reason in the world. Many of the German thinkers designated as right-wing Hegelians, on the other hand, had reformist, even liberal views. See H. Lübbe, *Die Hegelsche Rechte*. Most of the strongest intellectual supporters of Prussian reaction in the 1830s were deeply opposed to Hegelian philosophy.

[12] See J. Toews, *Hegelianism*, 221-23.

Hegelian reaction to Hegel's philosophy of freedom in the late 1830s.[13] Like Feuerbach, a group of Hegel's followers begins to demand the completion of what it believes Hegel's philosophy promises: the full realization of human freedom in a new epoch of world history. But, unlike Feuerbach in 1828, they also come to the conclusion that the philosophy that makes that promise first must be "realized" itself, that is, purged of its abstraction from ordinary reality. Before humanity can be fully realized, our concepts of humanity and nature must be made more realistic.

In a sense, the left Hegelians demand the completion of the left Kantian project. Hegel's conceptual innovations have overcome in theory the Kantian dichotomies blocking the realization of man's humanity; it is time now, they say, to finish what he started by bringing his reconciliation of nature and freedom into social practise. The realization in social practise of the reconciliation of nature and freedom is precisely what the young Hegel, like other left Kantians, sought to achieve. In his later years, however, Hegel no more believes it possible to "realize" his theoretical overcoming of nature's contingency than Kant believes it possible to realize autonomy. Nevertheless, his theoretical overcoming of the Kantian dichotomy between natural necessity and human freedom appears to many to remove the major obstacle to the full realization of man's humanity in the world and to the elimination of the social sources of dissatisfaction that were thought to follow from the removal of that obstacle. Thus Hegel's philosophy of freedom revives, for many of his followers, the intense longing for a fully humanized world that he himself felt so strongly in his youth.

Cieszkowski and the Third Epoch of "Praxis"

August von Cieszkowski's *Prolegomena zur Historiosophie* (1838) is the first major work to formulate the left Hegelian demand for the realization of philosophy. Many scholars have speculated about the importance of this work to the development of Marx's social

[13] See ibid., 206. Toews also notes here the resemblances between the demands for the actualization of Kantian and Hegelian philosophy.

thought.[14] And its influence on the social criticism of other left Hegelians, including Moses Hess and Alexander Herzen, is beyond doubt.[15] But I am interested in it here less for its influence on later thinkers than for the striking parallels it reveals between left Kantian and left Hegelian social criticism. An examination of Cieszkowski's arguments uncovers the left Kantian foundations of the longing for the realization of philosophy.

Moreover, Cieszkowski also comes to argue that the modern spirit of social interaction is the obstacle to the realization of philosophy. The contradictions and dichotomies that persist in Hegel's philosophy of spirit, he insists, reflect the limitations of the spirit of modern society. As Schiller and the young Hegel suggest about Kant, Cieszkowski suggests about Hegel: his philosophy of freedom represents the limitations of modern society come to self-consciousness, the highest form of intellectual endeavour possible under those limiting conditions. In making these arguments, Cieszkowski insists that the external conditions of social life, not the conceptual problems that Hegel uncovers, represent the real obstacle to the realization of philosophy. Thus, like Schiller and the young Hegel, he comes to long for the overcoming of the dehumanizing spirit of modern society.

Cieszkowski has nothing but praise for the Hegelian system up to the end of the philosophy of "Objective Spirit." But he suggests that Hegel's philosophy of history is incomplete, for it ends not in complete reconciliation, but rather in the set of objective conditions that make philosophic reconciliation possible. Hegel's philosophy of history lacks a "third period" beyond the modern "German" world described by Hegel, a final world epoch "that would realize the idea of beauty and truth." Social life and activity must achieve, he insists, the full reconciliation of spirit and nature achieved in philosophic contemplation. The contradiction "between being and thought must therefore dissolve in praxis, the contradiction be-

---

[14] For example, S. Avineri, *The Social and Political Thought of Karl Marx*, 124-28.

[15] See A. Liebich, *Between Ideology and Utopia: The Political Philosophy of August von Cieszkowski*, for a general account of Cieszkowski's influence.

tween art and philosophy in social life."[16] We must reject as inadequate and dehumanizing anything less than such a harmonious form of social activity and interaction.

"The same reproach which Hegelian philosophy makes against Kantian philosophy (namely, that it falls back again upon subjective one-sidedness)," Cieszkowski insists, "one must make against Hegelian philosophy itself, but on a higher unprecedented plane." Hegelian philosophy "collapses back into absolute idealism" because the Kantian dichotomy between spirit and nature is reopened with the dichotomy between the harmony of "Absolute Spirit" and the disharmony of "Objective Spirit."[17] In demanding the realization of philosophy, Cieszkowski seeks the final overcoming of the Kantian dichotomy between humanity and nature. And like the left Kantians before him, he seeks this overcoming in a full realization of man's humanity in the spirit that informs his social activity. It is this unlimited realization of man's humanity in social interaction that Cieszkowski designates as "praxis."

If Hegel had been consistent in the application of his dialectic logic, Cieszkowski argues, his philosophy of history should have been completed with this third period of human development, even if that epoch had to be projected into the future. Instead, Hegel abandons his dialectic method when dealing with the development of "Objective Spirit." He divides history into four epochs rather than the three epochs that would correspond to immediacy, negation, and negation of negation. To correct his philosophy of history we should collapse Hegel's first three epochs, the Oriental, Greek, and Roman worlds, into one, and make the modern Christian epoch the second rather than the culminating epoch of history. We should then project a third age of "praxis" that would negate and transcend our present limitations.[18]

Hegel fails to establish such a vision of history, Cieszkowski suggests, because his notion of reconciliation corresponds to the limi-

---

[16] A. von Cieszkowski, *Prolegomena zur Historiosophie*, 29, 112. Excerpts from this work are translated by A. Liebich in L. Stepelevich (ed.), *The Young Hegelians*, and in A. Liebich (ed.), *Selected Writings of August Cieszkowski*.
[17] A. von Cieszkowski, *Prolegomena zur Historiosophie*, 112-13; see also 3-4.
[18] Ibid., 24ff.

tations that inform social interaction in the modern age. Hegel can conceive of absolute freedom only in terms of theoretical activity because of the limited forms of social interaction with which he is familiar. His philosophy of reconciliation represents the modern age's self-consciousness about its limitations. Just as the ancient world could conceive of such reconciliation only in terms of art, so the modern age can envision it only in terms of a form of activity that abstracts from the contingencies of the external world. In the post–modern age that Cieszkowski longs for, the transformation of society will make possible the realization of that reconciliation in social interaction itself.[19]

Cieszkowksi's three epochs correspond to Schiller's three stages of human development discussed at the end of Chapter 4. Those stages are characterized by unfree harmony, free disunity, and free harmony, respectively. The reconciliation through art, character- istic of antiquity, is for Cieszkowski, as for Schiller, a "natural iden- tity" that must be dissolved with the "moral consciousness" that goes along with subjective freedom. Indeed, Cieszkowski quotes with approval Schiller's demand for a "new, higher unity" that would reproduce Greek harmony with nature at a higher level of moral self-consciousness. He defends Schiller against the charge of sacrificing moral freedom for the sake of a return to Greek whole- ness. Schiller's major limitation, according to Cieszkowski, is that he believes that such a higher unity can be achieved through art and aesthetic experience. On this point Cieszkowski follows Hegel. Art, as the sensuous manifestation of the idea, is limited to an "imme- diate," natural, and thus non-self-conscious form of identity.[20]

Cieszkowski speaks of the higher unity he seeks as the integra- tion of art's sensuous reconciliation of spirit and nature with phi- losophy's free, reflective reconciliation. Nevertheless, his goal re- mains essentially the same as Schiller's. "Mankind will shape, to a certain extent, a return to the ancient world, but without alienating itself from the modern. It will be the exhilaration of life without the loss of its deep-set interiority." The age of praxis "will not be a re-

[19] Ibid., 26-27, 101ff., 130.
[20] Ibid., 26-27, 81-87.

turn and descent to life, but rather a withdrawal and elevation of the life of nature to our level."[21] In other words, we will return to an identity with the natural world, but at a higher level, accomplished, as Schiller demands, "by means of reason and freedom."

In the preceding chapter we have seen that Hegel deems such a unity of aesthetic and philosophic reconciliation in social life impossible. Cieszkowski never addresses Hegel's objections to this goal directly. He never tries to redefine humanity in such a way that a fully human spirit of social activity would not seem contradictory. Instead, he maintains that since Hegel's arguments are tied to the forms of social interaction characteristic of modern society, they do not represent valid objections to a future form of society that transcends present limitations. For Cieszkowski, the spirit of modern society appears to be the obstacle to a world without sources of dissatisfaction. His longing for social transformation thus takes the form of a longing to get beyond the dehumanizing spirit of modern society—a longing very similar to that expressed by Schiller and the young Hegel.

Left Kantian Echoes in Left Hegelian Social Criticism

Despite their often violent disagreements, most left Hegelian social critics share Cieszkowski's opinion that the spirit of modern society is the obstacle to the realization of philosophy. The need to define and overcome that dehumanizing spirit of social interaction touches off among them an explosion of speculation that resembles in many ways the philosophic ferment of the 1790s. Once again manifestoes and system-programs tumble forth one after another, each predicting the dawn of a new epoch in human history.[22] And each new manifesto usually begins with an assertion that preceding manifestoes share in the limitations they claim to expose. Most left Hegelian polemics, as a result, are directed at other left Hegelians.[23]

[21] Ibid., 144.
[22] The major difference between the two explosions of speculation is that left Hegelian speculation does not culminate in the kind of system building characteristic of the left Kantians (though Marx may be an exception). On the fragmentary character of most left Hegelian efforts, see K. Löwith, *From Hegel to Nietzsche*, 67.
[23] Very few of these polemics attain the monumental length of Marx and Engels's

The angry and tiresome accusations that the left Hegelians throw out at each other tend to obscure their shared belief that the spirit of modern society dehumanizes man by preventing the realization of philosophy's reconciliation of spirit and nature. Their disputes, I suggest, grow, in part, out of disagreements about how to characterize the humanity we have lost and where to locate the source of dehumanization in modern society. Feuerbach and Bauer tend to define the obstacle to the realization of humanity in terms of religious institutions and attitudes, and they look to atheism as the means of realizing man's humanity. Ruge and, until 1843, Marx look instead toward political institutions and attitudes and see the realization of a fully human community in democracy. Hess and, beginning in 1844, Marx locate the obstacle in the social relations that grow out of productive relations and the full realization of humanity in socialism. Bakunin comes to see in institutional authority itself the obstacle and looks to anarchism as the form in which man's humanity is fully realized.

Though these thinkers all come to disdain each other's views, they all begin with similar questions—questions that betoken a conceptual perspective and a form of longing that they share not only with each other, but also with Rousseau and the left Kantian thinkers examined in the preceding chapters. Following are a few examples of left Hegelian social criticism that I believe illustrate this contention. I can here only illustrate my claim about the left Kantian foundations of left Hegelian social discontent, since an adequate defence of it would require much more detailed studies of the various left Hegelians than are appropriate within this book. My aims are only to suggest the plausibility of this characterization of left Hegelian social discontent and to explore some of the conceptual problems created by the attempts to realize Hegel's philosophy of freedom.

In a public letter to Ruge in 1843, Marx makes the following plea.

The self-confidence of human being, freedom has first of all to be aroused again in the hearts of these people. Only *this feel-*

---

in *The Holy Family* and *The German Ideology*, however. The latter work devotes almost three hundred pages to the ridicule of Max Stirner.

ing, which vanished from the world with the Greeks, and under Christianity disappeared into the blue mist of the heavens, can again transform society into a *community of human beings*, united for the highest aims, into a democratic state. . . . Despotism's sole idea is *contempt for man*, the *dehumanized* man.[24] (Emphasis added.)

The hopes expressed in this letter recall those expressed by Hegel in his famous letter to Schelling of January 1795.

From the Kantian revolution and its completion I expect a revolution in Germany. . . . I believe that there is no better sign of the times than that humanity is represented to itself as so worthy of respect; it is a sign that the halo about the heads of the oppressors and idols of the earth is disappearing. Philosophers prove this dignity, peoples will learn to *feel it*. . . . Formerly, religion and politics taught what *despotism* required, *contempt for the human race*.[25] (Emphasis added.)

Marx's stated end here is the realization of freedom in a "community of *human* beings," the same end as the young Hegel's. More important, he shares with Hegel an understanding of the obstacle to that end: the specifically modern political sentiments that prevent modern individuals from *feeling* their freedom in the way the ancient Greeks did. Now that philosophers have stripped despotism of its theoretical foundation by refuting the arguments supporting its contempt for man, Marx, like the young Hegel, demands that the freedom whose existence philosophers have proved come to shape the life of individuals—that it be realized in their activity. "This feeling" of freedom, "which vanished from the world with the Greeks," is what the young Hegel seeks to inculcate through "subjective religion." Marx, of course, scorns religious means of bringing freedom down from "the blue mist of the heavens"; but he shares the young Hegel's end, whatever the means he chooses to pursue it.

Arnold Ruge's social criticism, on the other hand, more often re-

[24] K. Marx, *MEW*, 1:238-39; *CW*, 3:137-38.
[25] G. W. F. Hegel, *Briefe*, 1:23-24.

calls Schiller's. Like Schiller, he insists that the spirit of social interaction, not traditional political constraints, represents the obstacle to a humanized world. He states that "to expect the salvation of the world from the reformation of politics is the old mistake of liberalism; everything lies in the reformation of consciousness."[26] The goal of such a reformation of consciousness is for Ruge much the same as it is for Schiller: the realization of human autonomy in our actions and social interaction. "The principle around which everything turns is the autonomy of *Geist*." If man is to be free, the state cannot remain an "alien condition."

> Man must be theoretically and ethically autonomous. The state is an end in itself. Its concept is misunderstood. For state is a bad, dead word. Public life is better, or history, *Reich des Geistes*, freedom. From these names one can see immediately that here the human subject is its substance and end. Our time demands now this empire of freedom in its self-conscious and self-determined movement, as the public and thoroughly realized reason of the people. This is ethical autonomy.[27]

What is needed, according to Ruge, is "a new consciousness that in all spheres raises free man to his principle and the people to an end, in a word, the dissolution of liberalism in democracy."[28] Although, unlike Schiller, Ruge identifies the "new consciousness" with democracy, he shares with Schiller the longing to see man's autonomy realized in his social interaction and political institutions.

Alexander Herzen's *From the Other Shore* provides even closer parallels to Schiller's social criticism. In this work, Herzen draws from the failure of the 1848 revolutions many of the same conclusions that Schiller draws from the failure of the great Revolution of 1789. In Herzen's opinion, the fatal error of the Parisian republicans of 1848 was to "throw themselves into the task of liberating others before they had liberated themselves."[29] Like Schiller, Her-

---

26 A. Ruge, "Selbstkritik des Liberalismus," in Ruge, *Gesammelte Werke*, 3:110.
27 A. Ruge, "Theorie und Praxis," in *Gesammelte Werke*, 3:30-31.
28 A. Ruge, "Selbstkritik des Liberalismus," 3:116.
29 A. Herzen, *From the Other Shore*, 57-58.

zen argues that one cannot free men from external constaints without already having free men. The failure of the 1848 revolutions teaches him that we must turn to the transformation of human character if we seek to liberate human beings from external constraints. In particular, we must seek the means to "unite freely and harmoniously these two ineradicable elements of human life," egoism and moral freedom, rather than try to impose the common good by sheer force of will.[30] Like Schiller, Herzen looks for some way of realizing our moral ends in our naturally conditioned individual interests.

These parallels between Herzen's and Schiller's social criticisms are not that surprising, given the intellectual environment in which Herzen received his education. That environment was saturated with the concepts of German idealism, and with Schiller's language in particular.[31] Nowhere, outside of Germany, did post-Kantian speculative philosophy have a deeper and more immediate impact than in nineteenth-century Russia. Moreover, like many members of the newly vocal class of intellectuals in the 1840s, Herzen excitedly followed post-Hegelian philosophic debates in Germany.[32] His first extended works are attempts to reconcile Hegel's philosophy of freedom and the spirit of empirical science. He too tries to "realize" Hegel's philosophy of freedom.[33] And as with Hess and Marx, these attempts to realize Hegelian philosophy lead him toward the advocacy of a new conception of socialism.

Herzen's compatriot, Bakunin, makes the kinship between left Kantian and left Hegelian social discontent obvious in an article he contributed to one of Ruge's journals. "The realization of freedom: who can deny that this expression stands today at the head of the agenda of history?" Hegel represents to Bakunin what Kant represented to the left Kantians: "unconditionally, the greatest philosopher of present times, the highest summit of our modern one-sided,

[30] Ibid., 138-40.
[31] See M. Malia, *Alexander Herzen and the Birth of Russian Socialism*, 38-98, 218-56.
[32] On Herzen's debt to Cieszkowski in particular, see A. Liebich, *Between Ideology and Utopia*, 60.
[33] See A. Herzen, *Selected Philosophical Works*, 59ff., 72, 98.

theoretical cultural formation." Hegel formulated the principle of a "new practical world," a world created by "an original act of the practical, autonomous spirit." But the limitations of our "one-sided, theoretical cultural formation" led him to abstract that principle from practise and apply it only to theory. Once we actualize the principle underlying Hegelian theory then, according to Bakunin, we can expect "a qualitative transformation, a new life-giving revelation, a new heaven and a new earth, a young and magnificent world in which all present discords will resolve themselves into harmonious unity."[34]

The demands for socialism made by Hess and Marx, as the demand for anarchism later made by Bakunin, certainly go beyond the aims of left Kantian social criticism. But without minimizing the importance of changing social conditions in inspiring this demand, I want to emphasize that for both Hess and Marx socialism represents an answer to questions that they share with the Kantian and Hegelian left. One reason they are drawn to socialism is that it appears to provide the form of social interaction, the praxis, in which man's humanity, as defined by Kant and Hegel, could be realized. We cannot know whether they would have become advocates of socialism if they had not asked such questions about the realization of humanity. But we can be quite certain that the socialism they might have pursued would have taken a very different form if they were not seeking answers to these questions.

That socialism represents for Hess an answer to left Kantian questions about how to realize man's autonomy is fairly easy to recognize. The essential social problem, as Hess perceives it, is to resolve the dichotomy between man's universality—his capacity for autonomous behaviour—and his naturally conditioned particularity. "All attempts to resolve theoretically the difference between the particular man and the human species must miscarry." For even if one knows humanity and nature to be reconciled, as does

[34] M. Bakunin, "The German Reaction," in Bakunin, *Selected Writings*, 37, 47, 40. For an attempt to show that romantic and left Hegelian longings for self-realization provide the key to Bakunin's intellectual and political development, see A. Kelly, *Michael Bakunin: A Study in the Psychology and Politics of Utopianism*, 21, 115, 193, 197-98, 291.

the Hegelian philosopher, man remains in actuality sundered as long as the division of man is not *practically* overcome. "But this separation will only be resolved through socialism—that is, if men unite themselves in their communal life and activity."[35]

Socialism represents for Hess the form of social interaction in which Hegel's theoretical reconciliation between spirit and nature becomes actual. "Our whole history—up to this point—is nothing but the history of a social animal world." We are less than human in our society, even if we are conscious of our character as free beings. If a reconciliation of our universality and our particularity is not realized in our social interaction, then we live in an "animal" world, a world that dehumanizes us. And the "history of the social animal world is nothing but the history of egotist unions."[36] A non-animal society would be one in which we overcome egotism as a principle of association, one in which our humanity, that is, our autonomy, is the fundamental principle of association. That is the form of community that Hess finds in socialism. Like Schiller, he seeks a form of community in which "true freedom is the principle of association." Hess thus asks a left Kantian question: How does one realize human autonomy as a principle of social interaction? Discontent with all forms of community that fail to achieve this end is something he shares with the Kantian left.

Marx, of course, quickly comes to ridicule "true" German socialists for claiming as a mark of superiority that they "'arrived at socialism by way of metaphysics that then changed into anthropology, [and] are both finally resolved in humanism.'"[37] Marx's own path to socialism is not, however, much different. He distinguishes himself from the true socialists by claiming that, unlike Hess, he does not use socialism to resolve the problems suggested by German metaphysics and anthropology. In the following chapter I shall argue that his claim is unjustified. I shall show that the way he formulates his basic socioeconomic concepts, especially socialism, the capitalist mode of production, and the proletariat, registers his con-

[35] M. Hess, "The Recent Philosophers," 360.
[36] Ibid., 367, 373.
[37] K. Marx, *The German Ideology*, in *MEW*, 3:445; *CW*, 5:458.

tinuing need to answer left Hegelian questions about the realization of autonomy in the external world.

These examples, however brief, provide some evidence of the longings shared by left Kantians and left Hegelians. Of course, there are many attitudes that the two groups do not share. The most important of these, in the context of this study, is the left Hegelians' formulation of their goal as the realization of philosophy rather than as the realization of freedom. They believe their task is to return from philosophic speculation to reality, to stand Hegel on his feet, rather than to complete the speculative revolution introduced by their teacher, as the Kantian left perceives its task.

But the concept of "praxis," which left Hegelians use to escape Hegelian abstraction from reality, is highly problematic. Their return to praxis is more than a return to common sense reality, more than a return to the externally conditioned needs that seem to shape social behaviour. Praxis also represents for the left Hegelians the realization of Hegel's reconciliation of humanity and nature. Though they portray it as the "concrete" reality from which Hegelian speculation abstracts, their concept of praxis rests on an even greater abstraction from externally conditioned needs than does Hegel's concept of externalized freedom.

As Rüdiger Bubner has pointed out, praxis, as conceived by the left Hegelians, represents an abstraction from an abstraction, rather than a simple return to physically and socially conditioned needs. Hegel achieves his theoretical reconciliation of spirit and nature only by abstracting from the portion of natural contingency—by far the largest portion—untouched by spirit. The left Hegelians demand not only renewed interest in the natural contingencies that Hegel ignores; they demand in addition Hegel's theoretical reconciliation minus its abstraction from reality. But that reconciliation depends upon a certain abstraction from nature. The left Hegelians criticize Hegel for abstracting from concrete social practise in his understanding of man and society. But praxis, as they understand it, represents nothing concrete. It is rather the way one would conceive of social reality if one abstracted from the abstraction from natural contingency contained in Hegel's philosophy of reconciliation. Their "concept of praxis . . . is defined as what theory is not."[38]

What theory is not is, on the one hand, realistic and, on the other hand, capable of satisfying our practical needs. "Defined as what theory is not," praxis represents a conception of social interaction as simultaneously dependent upon natural contingency and fully satisfying our practical ends. Left Hegelian praxis is thus defined in terms of two mutually incompatible conceptions of the relationship between human freedom and natural necessity. One negation of theory defines praxis in terms of the persistence of natural contingency, the other in terms of its subordination to human purpose. One demands a recognition of nature's unalterable otherness, the other demands nature's transfiguration into a human form.

By defining social reality in terms of an abstraction from Hegel's abstractions, the left Hegelians are compelled to affirm and deny the major premiss of German idealism: the dichotomy between human freedom and natural necessity. They must both deny man the capacity to abstract from contingent and externally conditioned ends and affirm his capacity to overcome the externality and otherness of natural forces. For they must, in the first place, argue against any notion of our humanity that distinguishes its expression from naturally conditioned ends and actions. If they do not make such an argument, then the path always lies open to Hegel's argument that fully *human* satisfaction does not lie in the satisfaction of our practical ends. But they must also reaffirm such a notion of our humanity in order to portray social practise as a process by which our humanity is realized and the otherness of nature is overcome.

By appealing at the same time to both common sense reality and transfigured reality as standards by which to criticize social institutions, left Hegelians from Ruge and Bauer to twentieth-century critical theorists can reject as unacceptable any trace of heteronomy in our institutions, without invoking an overtly idealistic standard of autonomy by which to judge them.[39] The power and suggestive-

[38] R. Bubner, *Theorie und Praxis: Eine Nachhegelsche Abstraktion*, 7.
[39] See ibid., passim, and M. Theunissen, *Gesellschaft und Geschichte*.

ness of left Hegelian social criticism depends, to a great extent, on its ability to mask this contradictory understanding of social reality. But the left Hegelians' failure to resolve this contradiction is one reason why "their writings are manifestoes, programs, and theses, but never anything whole, important in itself."[40] In the following chapter on Marx's social discontent, I shall try to show that the attempt to satisfy the left Hegelian longing for the realization of philosophy did, indeed, compel the most important and influential of the left Hegelian social critics to contradict himself.

Feuerbach and the Return to Nature

The left Hegelians' need for an understanding of humanity that would in some way both affirm and deny the idealist dichotomy between humanity and nature helps explain their tremendous enthusiasm for Feuerbach's anthropology and philosophy of nature. Feuerbach's return to nature in the early 1840s seems to provide just the kind of realization of Hegel's concept of humanity for which left Hegelians were searching.

Writing at the end of the nineteenth century, Engels vividly recalls the enthusiasm inspired by Feuerbach's philosophic anthropology in the 1840s.

> Then came Feuerbach's *Essence of Christianity*. With one blow it pulverized the contradiction, in that without circumlocutions it placed materialism on the throne again. Nature exists independently of all philosophy. It is the foundation upon which we human beings, ourselves products of nature, have grown up. Nothing exists outside of nature and man, and the higher beings our religious fantasies have created are only the fantastic reflections of our own essence. The spell was broken; the .system was exploded and cast outside, and the contradiction shown to exist only in our imagination, was dissolved. One must have experienced the liberating effect of this book to

---

[40] K. Löwith, *From Hegel to Nietzsche*, 67.

get an idea of it. Enthusiasm was general; we all became Feuer-bachians.[41]

Feuerbach's critique of religion provided the crowning touch to left Hegelian religious criticism. Religion represents, in his presentation, man's self-objectification in an alienated form, and nothing more. But, as can be seen from Engels's recollections, Feuerbach's philosophy of nature did something more for his followers than give Christianity a *coup de grâce*. It "pulverized the contradiction" between nature and humanity. It proved that "nature exists independently of all philosophy," that "it is the foundation upon which we human beings, ourselves products of nature, have grown up." Spirit, or any other understanding of man's humanity that opposes itself to man's nature, is thus revealed as "only the fantastic [reflection] of our own essence."

Feuerbach's philosophy of nature "realizes" Hegel's philosophy of freedom in both senses demanded by left Hegelian criticism. It returns us to common sense reality by restoring the priority of nature to humanity. Humanity again proceeds from nature, rather than nature from humanity as humanity's posited otherness. But it also makes the capacity for self-realization that characterizes *Geist*, according to Hegel, a natural quality. Feuerbach thus naturalizes Hegel's understanding of humanity without losing the special dignity bestowed on man by idealism's opposition of human freedom to natural necessity. The idealist dichotomy between humanity and nature disappears, but humanity retains a value found nowhere else in nature.

Feuerbach argues that the opposition between humanity and nature is an idealistic illusion, the invention of a philosophy that inherits Christianity's disdain for material reality. "Hegel pluralizes and splits up the simple self-identical essence of nature and man in order later to bring together forcibly what he has split up."[42] Human nature is a "simple self-identity," according to Feuerbach, not the dialectical difference within unity that Hegel describes. Man is a sensuous being like all other natural beings. Feuerbach argues

[41] F. Engels, *Ludwig Feuerbach and the End of Classical German Philosophy*, 17.
[42] L. Feuerbach, "Preliminary Theses on the Reform of Philosophy," in Feuerbach, *The Fiery Brook: Selected Writings of Ludwig Feuerbach*, 156.

that we need not go beyond sensuousness to account for the characteristics that distinguish man from all other animals. What distinguishes man is his "universal" sensuousness. Man is indifferent to any particular material; he can and does turn his senses to every kind of object. It is this universal sensuousness that makes man a "universal being." Man's freedom and rationality should be seen as manifestations of his universal sensuousness, and thus one need not oppose free mind to sensuous nature in order to account for freedom, reason, and thought.[43]

In Feuerbach's conception, man is both completely natural and yet sets himself apart from nature as a whole. "Nature is *being not distinguished* from existence; man is *being* that *distinguishes* itself from existence."[44] (Feuerbach's emphasis.) Man differs from nature in that, unlike all other beings, man distinguishes himself from being. Only man opposes himself to his existence and makes an object for himself—his religious ideas—in which he recognizes himself. Man is thus a double creature. He is the passive, sensuous creature of nature and nature's active negator.[45]

Feuerbach tries to present this understanding of man's relationship to nature as a "simple self-identity." Yet it is anything but simple. It would better be described with the Hegelian concept he rejects: difference within unity. The dichotomy between being and thought persists in Feuerbach's philosophy of nature; Feuerbach merely uses a conception of nature rather than a conception of spirit to mediate that dichotomy.[46] In man, according to Feuerbach, nature opposes itself to itself in the same way that Hegelian spirit opposes itself in the world. It develops this self-opposition, according to Feuerbach, because of man's universal sensuousness. But what makes man's sensuousness universal? What gives human senses the capacity to abstract from any given object or direction in a way no other sensuous being can, if not something like the capacity to distinguish itself from all external objects, which, for Hegel, defines free mind? Feuerbach does not answer this question, so it is difficult

[43] L. Feuerbach, "Principles of the Philosophy of the Future," in *The Fiery Brook*, 242. Idem, "Preliminary Theses," 168.
[44] L. Feuerbach, "Preliminary Theses," 169.
[45] L. Feuerbach, "Philosophy of the Future," 182, 224.
[46] See F. Gordon, "The Contradictory Nature of Feuerbachian Humanism," 37.

to avoid the conclusion that Hegel's opposition between nature and spirit reappears in Feuerbachian anthropology, thinly disguised by naturalistic rhetoric.[47]

Feuerbach proclaims that "the only source of salvation lies in a return to nature."[48] But like many later critics of the idealist philosophy of freedom, he reproduces idealist dichotomies in his account of human nature. "Everything which Feuerbach attacked in Hegel, he brought back as an essential feature of his own thought."[49] Feuerbach's response to Hegel's philosophy of freedom, in the end, resembles Schiller's response to Kant's. Like Schiller, Feuerbach proposes a "complete anthropological view, where content counts no less than form, and living feeling too has a voice" to compensate for the imbalance of an overly idealist philosophy.[50] Schiller, however, recognizes the idealist foundation on which he is attempting to build his anthropological view that takes into account both the "reason that makes man" human and the "sentiments that guide him."[51] Feuerbach does not.

The nature to which Feuerbach bids us return is a strange and new concept. It is dynamic, even dialectical. It is divided between active and passive elements, the human and the nonhuman. This nature acts in man in a qualitatively different way than it acts anywhere else. Through man it overcomes itself. Feuerbach's concept of human nature allows us to keep man in the exalted position in the scheme of things to which idealism has raised him but without incurring the costs of idealism's justification of that lofty position. But lurking behind that elevation of man's humanity lies an idealist understanding of man's humanity as something that opposes itself to the natural necessity that governs the rest of existence. In the following chapters I suggest that Hegel's *Geist* haunts Marx and, even more surprisingly, Nietzsche in much the same way.

---

[47] For a similar critique of Feuerbach, see G. Dicke, *Der Identitätsgedanke bei Feuerbach und Marx*, 63ff.

[48] L. Feuerbach, "Towards a Critique of Hegelian Philosophy," in *The Fiery Brook*, 94.

[49] F. Gordon, "Feuerbachian Humanism," 31.

[50] F. Schiller, *Aesthetic Education*, Letter 4, 18-19.

[51] Ibid., Epigraph, 1.

MARX AND SOCIAL
REVOLUTION

MOST SCHOLARS have focused on Marx's vision of communism in order to identify and account for the peculiar character and intensity of his social discontent. After all, Marx insists that we reject and overthrow all social institutions that fall short of the "control and conscious mastery" of our social forces that communism will bring.[1] Statements like this one suggest that it is a vision of social perfection under communism that sours Marx's appreciation of the more limited achievements of non-communist institutions.

In this chapter, however, I suggest that we can best identify and account for the peculiar character of Marx's social discontent in terms of a new understanding of the obstacle to social perfection, rather than in terms of a new vision of social perfection itself. Even those who look to Marx's vision of communism to explain his discontent usually admit that that vision remains extremely vague and undeveloped. It seems unlikely that so weak a vision as that communicated by Marx's writings could have inspired such powerful longings. Not surprisingly, many scholars feel the need to advance supplementary hypotheses to explain how such an undeveloped image could have taken hold over Marx's mind. They suggest, for example, that Marxian communism represents a secularized version,

---

[1] K. Marx, *The German Ideology*, in *MEW*, 3:37; translated in *CW*, 5:51. Hereafter, except where otherwise noted, citations of the German texts of Marx's writings will include the title of the work and the appropriate volume and page number(s) of the Dietz Verlag edition cited here as *MEW*. As in the preceding chapters, reference to the translation of each work will follow a semicolon after the reference in the original language.

a "pseudomorphosis," to use Karl Löwith's expression, of the otherworldly perfection that has fired the discontent of Messianists, Gnostics, and religious fanatics for more than two thousand years.[2] Or they point to the conflict in Marx's thought between utopianism and scientific determinism, a conflict that leads Marx to suppress and underplay his utopian visions of social perfection.

We can, however, avoid such supplementary hypotheses, and the acrimonious debates that swirl around them, once we recognize the way Marx's new understanding of the obstacles to desired goals inspires new longings for social transformation. It is Marx's discovery of what he deems the true obstacle to a world without social sources of dissatisfaction, the capitalist mode of production, that gives his social discontent its new and peculiar form. In the capitalist mode of production Marx discovers an obstacle to our satisfaction that is historically specific and therefore, in principle, changeable. Moreover, unlike the other understandings of the obstacle to a world without sources of dissatisfaction discussed so far, it is a target we can surely hit. Our actions can undoubtedly destroy the capitalist mode of production. Given this understanding of the obstacle to our satisfaction, a world without social sources of dissatisfaction seems to be within our grasp.

The question that I address in this chapter is how Marx comes to view capitalism as the obstacle to a world without social sources of dissatisfaction. Why should the overcoming of the capitalist mode of production in communism lead, for Marx, to the "control and conscious mastery" of the powers that "have till now overawed and ruled men as powers completely alien to them?"[3] Why not conceive of capitalism rather as the obstacle to a fairer, less constricting, more productive way of organizing our societies in the face of a world that we cannot completely control?

I suggest that Marx conceives of the capitalist mode of production in this way because it represents for him the obstacle to the overcoming of the dehumanizing spirit of modern social interaction which he, like most left Kantians and left Hegelians before him, was

[2] K. Löwith, *Meaning in History*, 44-45.
[3] *German Ideology*, 3:37; CW, 5:51-52.

looking to discover. It represents the fundamental sub-political sphere of social interaction that shapes all social phenomena in the modern epoch and thus explains its dehumanizing character. Capitalism comes to represent the obstacle to social perfection only because Marx, along with the Kantian and Hegelian left, already had defined the obstacle to social perfection in a particular way: the dehumanizing spirit of modern society. In short, I argue that Marx's longing for a communist revolution represents a new species of the longing for total revolution, as I have defined it in this book.

It is not difficult to show, as I try to do in the first section of this chapter, that, up until 1844 and his turn to political economy, Marx locates the obstacle to a world without social sources of dissatisfaction in the dehumanizing spirit of modern society. Nor is it difficult to show that, up to that point, Marx shares with the Kantian and Hegelian left the conceptual premises that, I have argued, make that state of mind possible. My challenge lies in showing that he continues to think of the obstacle to social perfection in this way *after* his turn to political economy and the advocacy of a workers' revolution.

Marx's violent rejection of the modes of social criticism that he had shared with the Hegelian left makes this challenge seem very difficult. In *The German Ideology*, Marx proclaims his rejection of even the questions posed by the left Hegelians. For "not only in their answers, already in their very questions there was a mystification."[4] After his self-described "leap" from philosophy to "reality,"[5] Marx's questions have a completely different focus. He turns from the search for the obstacle to the realization of philosophy and humanity to the structure of capitalist production, the obstacles to collective ownership of the means of production, and the means of organizing the working class.

I suggest in the middle sections of this chapter, however, that the *way* Marx conceptualizes his new subjects of interest—communism, capitalism, and proletarian revolution—registers his continuing need to answer left Hegelian questions about the explanation

[4] Ibid., 3:19; 5:28.
[5] Ibid., 3:218; 5:236.

and overcoming of the dehumanizing spirit of modern society. Questions about communism, capitalism, and proletarian revolution, the subjects which now command Marx's attention, are derived from his new answers to old questions. Indeed, Marxism as a whole, I suggest, is best characterized as an attempt to use the categories of political economy to provide answers to left Hegelian questions.

Another challenge to my account of Marx's social discontent, growing out of my designation of his longing for proletarian revolution as a new species of the longing for total revolution, lies in his explicit rejection of the dichotomy between human freedom and natural necessity. For this dichotomy is one of the conceptual premisses, I have argued, that make the longing for total revolution possible. Either I am wrong in my account of the conceptual sources of the longing for total revolution or Marx's social criticism must still, in some way, rest on this opinion about freedom and nature despite his claims to the contrary. In the final section of this chapter I suggest that Marx does indeed implicitly affirm something like the Kantian dichotomy between man's humanity and his nature and, furthermore, that he must both affirm and deny this premiss in order to represent communism as man's "control and conscious mastery" of the forces created by social interaction.

By pointing to the importance of the conceptual context of Marx's social discontent, I do not mean to dismiss social and institutional sources of his longing to change the world. After all, the social conflicts that Marx tries to analyze are not philosophic inventions. To a certain extent, we all take sides in them, no matter the conceptual perspective from which we view them. Nevertheless, I agree with Dieter Henrich that although Marxism "may be more than a mere conceptual problem for us, it is also that, and in the beginning, only that."[6] Marx might very well have become a partisan of communism and the working class even if he had not asked the questions about the realization of humanity emphasized here. But Marxism, as a particular understanding of communism and the

[6] D. Henrich, "Karl Marx als Hegels Schuler," in Henrich, *Hegel im Kontext*, 207.

needs of the working class, owes its origin to the conceptual perspective from which Marx interpreted economic organization and working-class needs. Marx's conceptualization of communism as the "control and conscious mastery" of our social world, I suggest, grows out of a characterization of the obstacle to social perfection made possible by the conceptual innovations I have been examining in this book.

Marx's Categorical Imperative

In his "Introduction" to the critique of Hegel's *Philosophy of Right*, Marx insists that the critique of religion and philosophy should lead us to "the *categorical imperative to overthrow all conditions* in which man is a debased, enslaved, abandoned and contemptible being—conditions that cannot be better described than by the Frenchman's exclamation about a proposed tax on dogs: 'Poor dogs, they want to treat you like men.' "[7] (Emphasis added.) That Marx should express indignation at such conditions and demand that we work to overthrow them hardly seems remarkable in itself. No one but sadists, tyrants, and misanthropes are pleased by conditions that degrade and debase human beings. There are surely intellectuals in every epoch who would accept this categorical imperative.

But when we view this demand in the left Hegelian conceptual context out of which it arises we recognize that it expresses a much more specific and exclusive state of mind. Marx calls on us to attack the relations that render men "contemptible," relations that treat human beings as if they were animals. His complaint is more specific than a general complaint about cruelty, that is, about the inhumane treatment of human beings. It is rather a complaint about social conditions that turn human beings into animals, that is, conditions that dehumanize individuals.

Moreover, Marx intentionally contrasts his categorical imperative to Kant's. Kant's categorical imperative obliges us to treat all

[7] "A Contribution to the Critique of Hegel's 'Philosophy of Right': Introduction" (hereafter "Introduction"), 1:385: *CW*, 3:182.

individuals with the respect due human beings, to treat all individuals not only as means but as ends in themselves. Marx's obliges us to attack the *conditions* that fail to respect man's humanity. If Kant demands that we overcome heteronomy in the will, Marx demands that we overcome heteronomy in the world. Such a demand suggests that Marx sees the obstacle to the overcoming of dehumanization in the spirit of social interaction that informs modern conditions. Thus his "categorical imperative" expresses a longing to get beyond the dehumanizing spirit of modern society.

An examination of Marx's social criticism up to the time he makes these demands confirms my interpretation. Marx still clings to a very Hegelian understanding of humanity up until the end of 1843. Like Hegel, and Kant for that matter, Marx defines man's humanity in terms of a capacity for self-rule that distinguishes truly human from naturally conditioned ends. "Freedom," he writes in 1842, "is so much the essence of man that even its opponents actualize it even while combatting its reality."[8] The discovery of man's true humanity is the modern world's great achievement. "Antiquity was rooted in nature, in the substantive. Its degradation and profanation means a fundamental break with the solid substantive life. The modern world is rooted in spirit and can be free."[9]

Still following Hegel, Marx insists that "laws are the positive clear general norms in which freedom has gained an impersonal theoretical existence, independent of the arbitrary will of individuals. The law book is the people's Bible of freedom."[10] To doubt that freedom is the real essence of man, as do the sceptics of the Enlightenment, or to believe that laws represent nothing but contingent and irrational conventions, as do the members of the "historical school of law," is to degrade man by leaving "only what is animal in man" intact. "Hugo misinterprets his teacher Kant by concluding that because we cannot know what is *true*, we must allow the *untrue*, if it exists at all, to pass as *fully valid*. He is a *sceptic* with regards to the necessary essence of things, so as to be a *courtier* with

---

[8] "Debates on Freedom of the Press," 1:51; *CW*, 1:155.
[9] K. Marx, "Notebooks on Epicurean Philosophy," in Marx & Engels, *Werke, Erganzungsbände* (hereafter *MEW, Ebde.*), 1:59-60; *CW*, 1:423.
[10] "Debates on Freedom of the Press," 1:58; *CW*, 1:162.

regards to their *accidental appearance.*"[11] Just like Schelling and the rest of the Kantian left, Marx reacts indignantly to the suggestion that Kantian philosophy be used to justify the proposition that man's freedom cannot be realized in human laws. He reacts this way because he has inherited their conceptual perspective from Hegel. In other words, he both separates man's humanity from his nature by defining it in terms of contra-causal freedom and rejects all institutions that fail to realize autonomy.

In his earliest social criticism, his essays of 1842 to 1843 in the *Rheinische Zeitung,* Marx explains the various deficiencies of contemporary laws and institutions in terms of their failure to realize human freedom. "Censorship cannot, anymore than slavery, ever become lawful, even if it exists a thousand times as a law." For "where law is real law, . . . it is the real existence of human freedom."[12] Censorship laws usurp the name of law because they constrict rather than realize human freedom.

Marx's first foray into the realm of socioeconomic criticism, his essay on the "Debates on the Law on Wood Thefts" in the Rhineland Assembly, touches on similar themes in explaining what is wrong with laws that legitimize the economic deprivation ·of the poor and the customary privileges of the rich.

> By the so-called customs of the privileged are understood to mean *customs contrary to the law.* The date of their origin falls in the period in which human history still formed a part of natural history, and in which, according to Egyptian legend, all gods concealed themselves in animal forms. Mankind appeared to fall into definite species of animals which were connected not by equality, but by inequality, an inequality fixed by laws. The world condition of unfreedom required laws expressing this unfreedom, for while human law is the mode of existence of freedom, animal law is the mode of existence of unfreedom. Feudalism in the broadest sense is the *spiritual animal kingdom,* the world of divided mankind. . . . The cus-

[11] "The Philosophical Manifesto of the Historical School of Law," 1:81, 79; *CW,* 1:206, 204.
[12] "Debates on Freedom of the Press," 1:58; *CW,* 1:162.

tomary rights of the aristocracy conflict by their *content* with the form of universal law. They cannot form law because they are formations of lawlessness.[13]

"Private interest seeks to degrade" the state and its laws. Marx insists that the state, as the realization of human freedom, must recognize "only *spiritual forces*. The state interlaces all of nature with spiritual nerves, and at every point it must appear that it is the form, not the material, which dominates, the nature of the state, not nature without the state, the free human being, not the unfree object." It must cry out at attempts to disguise private interest in the form of law: "Your ways are not my ways, your thoughts are not my thoughts!"[14]

By pointing to the abstract and philosophic character of Marx's first attempts at economic criticism, I do not mean to suggest that they bring into question the seriousness of his concern about economic inequalities at this, let alone any other, stage of his career. Rather, my purpose is to recover the basic questions that shape the form of Marx's social criticism. Marx certainly recognized that censorship laws impose unnecessary constraints on society and that laws legitimizing economic privilege unfairly divide wealth. But to explain why such sources of dissatisfaction exist in our institutions, he turns to his understanding of man's essence as an autonomous, self-realizing being. The obstacle to a world without such constricting and unjust laws appears to him to be whatever blocks the full realization of human freedom. Thus the fundamental questions that guide the young Marx's social criticism concern the obstacle to the realization of human freedom and how we overcome it, rather than the obstacles to a more equitable distribution of goods. Marx is certainly not uninterested in economic distribution. Far from it. My point is simply that the questions raised by economic inequality are, for Marx, secondary, since the underlying obstacle to economic equality remains the dehumanization of man.

Like other intellectuals who derive from the Hegelian philosophy

[13] "Debates on the Law on Wood Thefts," 1:115-16; *CW*, 1:230-31.
[14] K. Marx, "On the Commissions of the Estates in Prussia," in *MEW*, *Ebde.*, 1:419; *CW*, 1:306. "Debates on the Law on Wood Thefts," 1:126; *CW*, 1:241.

of freedom a longing for the full realization of human autonomy in the world, the young Marx has to confront the gap between "Absolute" and "Objective Spirit." Marx's reaction to this gap clearly marks him as a left Hegelian. He decries the dichotomy between theoretical reconciliation and practical disharmony as both an idealistic delusion and a moral disgrace. Like other left Hegelians, he comes to view the obstacle to the realization of humanity in terms of this dichotomy and thus calls for the realization of philosophy.

Marx treats Hegel's political philosophy as if it were meant to be an account of the institutions that fully reconcile nature and freedom, the particular and the universal, in the everyday lives of individuals.[15] Given this understanding of Hegel's aims, it is no wonder that Marx is so dismissive of Hegel's *Philosophy of Right*. If one thinks of Hegel's political philosophy as an attempt to describe and justify a state in which "only spiritual interests" count, it must appear to be a ridiculous failure. For, as I noted in my discussion of Hegel, everywhere one looks in the *Philosophy of Right*, the general, "spiritual interests" are mediated by particular, natural interests.

Marx wants "the general interest *actually*—and not, as with Hegel, merely in thought, as an *abstraction*—becoming the particular interest, which is itself only possible as a result of the *particular* interest becoming the *general* interest."[16] What he finds instead in the *Philosophy of Right* is a depiction of the state as the actualized general interest of the community—a depiction that seems to ignore the fact that the state is tied to real individuals only through the mediation of non-generalized particular interests. Thus "Hegel falls everywhere from his political spiritualism into the crassest materialism." To portray the state as the realization of freedom, he abstracts from the real interests that motivate individuals, but to organize his state, he repeatedly falls back on the most material and least rational standards, such as hereditary monarchy.[17]

Marx's critique of the *Philosophy of Right* leads him to give up his earlier identification of the realization of freedom with law.

[15] H. Stuke, *Die Philosophie der Tat*, 48.
[16] *Contribution to the Critique of Hegel's "Philosophy of Right,"* 1:250; CW, 3:48.
[17] Ibid., 1:310; 3:105.

What in his first attempts at social criticism he viewed as the opposition between genuine and non-genuine laws, he now begins to see as a contradiction between the formal universality of legal and political institutions and the particularity of actual behaviour, a contradiction characteristic of modern society. To seek the realization of freedom in the reform of political legislation and institutions will only solidify the dichotomy between theory and practise that Marx discovers in Hegel's political philosophy.

"Political emancipation," Marx now insists, must be distinguished from "human emancipation." "Political emancipation is a reduction of man, on the one hand to a member of civil society, an independent, egoistic individual, and on the other hand, to a *citizen* of the state, to a moral person."[18] Liberal political and legal reforms remove the painful constraints on individual interests characteristic of previous regimes, and then ask individuals to abstract from those interests and act, as citizens, according to the general interest. Not surprisingly, the general interest remains an abstract desideratum while the liberated particular interests guide behaviour.

Political emancipation falls short of "human" emancipation because it fails to realize man's humanity, that capacity of individuals to direct their own actions toward the general good. With the transformation of political institutions, such as took place in the United States, "man was not liberated from religion; he received religious liberty. He was not liberated from property; he received the liberty to own property. He was not liberated from the egoism of business; he received the liberty to engage in business." Like Schiller, Marx complains that political liberty does not, in itself, make men free.

> Human emancipation is complete only when the real individual has taken back into himself the abstract citizen, when as an individual, in his empirical life, in his work, and in his relationships, he has become a *species-being*, and only when he has recognized and organized his own powers as social powers so that he no longer separates social power from himself in the form of *political* power.[19]

[18] "On the Jewish Question," 1:370; *CW*, 3:168.
[19] Ibid., 1:370; 1:168.

This statement reveals the full significance of Marx's categorical imperative. Marx's categorical imperative reformulates the left Kantian call to arms voiced by Schelling: "Subject every heteronomous power to your own autonomy."[20] "Human emancipation" means, for Marx, the realization of man's humanity, what he calls here, following Feuerbach's attempt to naturalize the idealist concept of humanity, "species-being," "in his empirical life, in his work, and in his relationships." All conditions that fall short of this fully human condition enslave man and render him contemptible. The need to locate and analyze the actual conditions that produce this gap between man's humanity and his world drives Marx's theoretical activity for the rest of his life.

New Answers to Old Questions

"One must 'leave philosophy aside,' one must leap out of it and devote oneself like an ordinary man to the study of reality."[21] After this leap from the concepts and categories of left Hegelian philosophy to those of English political economy, Marx scoffs at the "innocent and child-like fancies [that] are the kernel of young-Hegelian philosophy." The left Hegelians, Marx complains, would have us believe that

[h]itherto men have always formed wrong ideas about themselves, about what they are or ought to be. They have arranged their relations according to their ideas of God, of the normal man, etc. The fantastic products of their brains have taken them to task. They, the creators, have bowed down before their creations. Let us liberate them from these fantastic creatures, the ideas, dogmas, imaginary beings under whose yoke they are wasting away. Let us revolt against this rule of thoughts. . . . [A]nd existing reality will collapse.

Marx's monumental polemic in *The German Ideology* aims at "uncloaking these sheep, who take themselves and are taken for

[20] F. Schelling, *Werke*, 1:272.
[21] *German Ideology*, 3:218; *CW*, 5:236.

wolves. . . . Its aim is to ridicule and discredit the philosophic struggle with the shadows of reality, which appeals to the dreamy and drowsy German nation."[22]

Marx still speaks of the need for a "total revolution." But the total revolution he demands now is the rebellion of one disadvantaged class, the proletariat, against its oppressors rather than the "total revolution in man's whole way of feeling" demanded by Schiller and his heirs.[23] Total revolution represents for Marx the transformation of the organization of production that that victory will bring rather than the mere transformation of "consciousness" that he claims the German tradition of social criticism has sought.

Marx's "leap . . . into the study of actuality" marks a significant break with the tradition of social criticism I have been examining. None of the social critics thus far examined in this study ever advocate the social revolution of an oppressed class as Marx does. Indeed, the concept of total revolution developed by Schiller and some of the others studied here develops in response to what are seen as the limitations of social revolution. Schiller argues, as we have seen, that the removal of social and political constraints on human behaviour will not be feasible until individuals have been prepared to act autonomously. The real revolution required by human emancipation is the "transformation of consciousness," not the transformation of institutions. Left Hegelian social critics, like Ruge, echo this argument when they complain that "to expect the salvation of the world from the reformation of politics is the old mistake of liberalism; everything lies in the reformation of consciousness."[24]

Marx, on the other hand, consciously returns to the revolutionary tradition from which the social criticism of the best-known German philosophers had departed. Marx's revolution is to be a "social convulsion." It is to be the "total revolution" awaited by the par-

[22] Ibid., 3:13-14; CW, 5:23-24.
[23] Ibid., 3:38-39; 5:54. *Totale Umwalzung* is rendered in this translation of *The German Ideology* as "complete revolution." Cf. F. Schiller, *Aesthetic Education*, Letter 27, 204-5.
[24] A. Ruge, "Selbstkritik des Liberalismus," in *Gesammelte Werke*, 3:110.

tisans of the French Revolution, the completion of the uprising of the oppressed begun in 1789.[25]

But Marx's turn to economic analysis and class interest is also the means by which he answers the questions left Hegelians had been asking. For in the study of reality he believes he has discovered the "material elements" that will realize the "idea" of total revolution "expressed a hundred times already" by German social critics. In ridiculing the left Hegelians, Marx insists that

> if these material elements of a total revolution are not present—namely, on the one hand the existing productive forces, on the other the formation of a revolutionary mass, which revolts not only against particular conditions of the prevailing society, but against the prevailing "production of life" itself, the "whole activity" on which it was based—then it makes no difference at all for practical development whether the *idea* of this revolution has been expressed a hundred times already, as the history of communism proves.[26]

Marx too had made a distinction in his earlier work between the political emancipation that removes direct governmental constraints on certain aspects of our lives and the "human emancipation" that puts us in control of the world we created.[27] What distinguishes his later position from Ruge's and Schiller's is that he believes that a social revolution led by a particular oppressed class can overcome the obstacles to human emancipation.

In what follows, I suggest that Marx's longing for a proletarian revolution represents a species of the longing for total revolution. I suggest that the obstacle to a successful proletarian revolution, the capitalist mode of production, is also, for Marx, the obstacle to the elimination of dehumanization in the modern world. The place to begin a defence of these assertions is with Marx's understanding of communism, that is, with the negation of the capitalist mode of production. For communism, I suggest, represents for Marx the ne-

---

[25] For "total revolution" as conceived by the revolutionary tradition, see J. Billington, *Fire in the Minds of Men*, 78, 88.

[26] *German Ideology*, 3:38-39; *CW*, 5:54.

[27] In "On the Jewish Question," 1:370; *CW*, 3:168.

gation of man's subjection to external, nonhuman forces and thus the fully human community, for which left Kantians and left Hegelians long.

Communism

So far association . . . has been nothing but an agreement about those conditions within which individuals were free to enjoy the fruits of blind chance [*Zufälligkeit*]. . . . This right to the undisturbed enjoyment, within certain conditions, of blind chance has up till now been called personal freedom. Communism differs from all previous movements in that it overturns the foundations of all previous production and exchange relations, and for the first time consciously treats all naturally developed conditions as the creations of hitherto existing men, strips them of their natural character and subjects them to the power of the united individuals. . . . The existence which communism creates is precisely the real basis for making it impossible that anything should exist independently of individuals, insofar as the present is nothing but a product of the preceding intercourse of individuals.[28]

Statements such as these, taken from *The German Ideology*, the high-water mark of Marx's anti-philosophic rhetoric, rather than from the "humanist" speculations of the *Economic-Philosophic Manuscripts*, remind us that Marx's interpretation of socialism is, despite its enormous influence, only one interpretation of socialism—and a rather peculiar one at that. For Marx, communism certainly represents a fairer and more productive way of organizing society than does capitalism. But justice and efficiency are not the primary criteria supporting his preference for communism.[29] His primary reason for advocating communism is that he sees in it the means by which individuals can eliminate the effects of "blind chance" on their social relations. Communism creates an "existence" that renders "it impossible that anything should exist inde-

[28] *German Ideology*, 3:75, 70; *CW*, 5:80-81.
[29] See J. Elster, *Making Sense of Marx*, 82ff.

pendently of individuals." Stripping these contingencies "of their natural character," that is, showing them to be "the creations of hitherto existing men," somehow "subjects them to the power of the united individuals." Communism, for Marx, thus represents the "control and conscious mastery" of the forces created by our interaction with nature and each other.[30]

It is clear from these and other statements that any lack of control over these forces, is, for Marx, intolerable. One can hardly miss in these statements the left Kantian and left Hegelian longing for the realization of humanity which would "subject every heteronomous power" to man's autonomy. For in Marx's description that is precisely what communism appears to do. It "subjects" all external forces of social interaction "to the power of the united individuals." It strips them of their externality and treats them as human powers, that is, as powers created and controlled by man.

Communism subjects external forces to the power of the "*united* individuals," which means, for Marx, the general will of all individuals, rather than the collection and distillation of the opinions of particular individuals. According to Marx, any institutional or personal means of collecting and distilling opinions would reintroduce some fortuity and chance into the forces that control our lives. One "naturally evolved" premiss that communism strips is the "cleavage between the particular and common interest."[31] Communism subjects the external forces that influence our social interaction to the control of the general will, of the autonomous human subject. In doing so it actualizes our general will.

With this conceptualization of communism, Marx "realizes" Hegel's philosophy of freedom in both senses aimed at by the Hegelian left. He returns to the materially conditioned needs from which Hegel abstracts in his philosophy of "Absolute Spirit," and he also relocates the full overcoming of the world's externality, which for Hegel is bought only at the price of such abstraction, in the world created by our interaction with nature and each other.

[30] *German Ideology*, 3:37; *CW*, 5:51.
[31] Ibid., 3:33; 5:47.

Thus it is not surprising to hear in one of Marx's early descriptions of communism an echo of Hegel's descriptions of "Absolute Spirit." In a famous passage from one of the *Economic-Philosophic Manuscripts*, Marx describes communism in the following terms.

> It is the *genuine* resolution of the opposition between man and nature and between man and man, the true resolution of the rupture between existence and essence, between objectification and self-confirmation, between freedom and necessity, between the individual and the species. It is the riddle of history solved, and knows itself as this solution.[32]

Compare this description of communism to Hegel's description of "Absolute Spirit."

> In it validity and power are swept away from the opposition between freedom and necessity, between spirit and nature, between knowledge and its object, between law and impulse, from opposition and contradiction as such, whatever forms they may take. Their validity and power *as* opposition and contradiction is gone.[33]

The parallels are obvious. Hegel had argued that "where there is finitude, opposition and contradiction always break out again afresh, and satisfaction does not get beyond being relative."[34] Thus, for Hegel, the full reconciliation of freedom and necessity, spirit and nature, comes only with the transcendence of finitude in "Absolute Spirit." The "riddle of history" that communism solves for Marx is how man can strip the forces that control his life of their dehumanizing externality without abstracting from the finitude of his interaction with nature and other individuals.

Communism represents Marx's answer to the left Kantian and Hegelian questions about the form which a fully human community would take. Marx begins his search for such a community long before he turns to political economy for answers. In some of his

[32] K. Marx, *Economic-Philosophic Manuscripts*, in *MEW, Ebde.*, 1:536; *CW*, 3:296.
[33] G. W. F. Hegel, *Aesthetics*, in *Werke*, 13:137-38; 1:100.
[34] Ibid., 13:136; 1:99.

early writings, he treats democracy as the fully human community for which he is searching. But the conception of democracy that Marx develops in his 1843 critique of Hegel's *Philosophy of Right* differs as greatly from our usual conceptions of democracy as Marx's conception of socialism differs from our usual conceptions of socialism. Democracy, he insists, "is a *human manifestation*; whereas in other state forms man is a *legal manifestation*. That is the fundamental distinction of democracy." "True democracy" represents for Marx something more than a form of government in which power is widely or universally shared. "The *political* republic" is merely the "abstract state form of democracy." "In true democracy the *political state is annihilated*. This is correct insofar as the political state *qua* political state, as constitution, no longer passes for the whole."[35]

What, then, for Marx is the "concrete" state form of democracy? The general will actualized. "The political sphere has been the . . . only sphere in which the content as well as the form has been species-content, the truly general; but in such a way that at the same time, because this sphere has confronted the others, its content has become formal and particular." The democratic republic as a mere constitutional form stands as a means of opposing and controlling the private interests of society. "It is obvious that the political constitution as such is brought into being only where the private spheres have won an independent existence."[36]

In true democracy, however, the private spheres win no independent existence. In true democracy, the general will is actualized in the particular wills of individuals. "The abolition of the bureaucracy is only possible by the general interest *actually*—and not, as with Hegel, merely in thought, as an *abstraction*—becoming the particular interest, which is itself only possible as a result of the *particular* interest becoming the *general* interest."[37] That is why, for Marx, the "political state" disappears in "true democracy," just as it does in "true" communism. When the general will has been actualized in particular interests, then a collective authority to

---

[35] *Critique of Hegel's "Philosophy of Right,"* 1:232; *CW*, 3:30-31.
[36] Ibid.
[37] Ibid., 1:250; 3:48.

coerce compliance with the general will, organized democratically or in any other manner, becomes superfluous.

From his advocacy of democracy in 1843 to his advocacy of communism in 1846 Marx asks the same question: What are the means of actualizing man's humanity so that he can subject the forces that shape social interaction to his general interest? The answers change, and with them the entire focus of Marx's theoretical and practical activity. But the question persists, a question which the young Hegel, Schelling, and Hölderlin already asked when they too declared that we must go "beyond the state."[38]

Some scholars see in Marx's later works indications that Marx finally abandons his hopes that communism might eliminate natural contingencies from man's social life.[39] In a letter written in 1868, Marx notes that "natural laws cannot be abolished, only the *form* in which these laws assert themselves."[40] And in the famous passage from the third volume of *Capital*, Marx insists that communist production "still remains a realm of necessity." "In fact, the realm of freedom actually begins only where labour which is determined by necessity and mundane considerations ceases; thus in the very nature of things it lies beyond the sphere of actual material production."[41]

Clearly these passages indicate that Marx eventually abandons his hopes that nature itself, the whole realm of necessity, could be humanized.[42] But that does not necessarily mean that he abandons his hopes that communism would eliminate natural contingency in our social relations, so that we could gain "conscious mastery and control" of the forces created by our social interaction. In the very passage of *Capital* just quoted Marx describes the freedom created

[38] In the so-called "Systemprogram" of 1796, discussed in the first section of Chapter 5 above.

[39] For recent commentaries on Marx that make this point, see R. N. Berki, *Insight and Vision: The Problem of Communism in Marx's Thought*, 132-33, 155, and P. Kain, *Schiller, Hegel, and Marx: State, Society, and the Aesthetic Ideal of Ancient Greece*, 122-24, 133-36.

[40] Letter to J. Kugelmann, July 1, 1868, in Marx & Engels, *Selected Correspondence*, 246.

[41] *Capital, Vol. 3*, 25:828; 820.

[42] Hopes expressed in his *Economic-Philosophic Manuscripts*, especially in the short essay entitled "Private Property and Communism."

by the communist mode of production in terms that suggest he clings to these hopes. "Freedom in this field [material production] can only consist in socialized man, the associated producers, rationally regulating their interchange with nature, bringing it under their common control, instead of being ruled by it as by the blind forces of nature."[43] This description of communist production coincides with the descriptions in *The German Ideology*, which I quoted at the beginning of this section. The elimination of the "blind forces of nature" in the social organization of production still defines Marx's concept of communism here. Natural necessity, he admits, is an immovable obstacle to the humanization of nature; but he does not admit that it is an immovable obstacle to the complete control of the forces created by our social interaction. Communism still represents for him the form in which our freedom and humanity is manifested in our world, a form of social organization that eliminates the *social* sources of dissatisfaction with the world.[44]

The Capitalist Mode of Production

"The whole of human servitude is involved in the relation of the worker to production, and all relations of servitude are but modifications and consequences of this relation."[45] This is the great discovery that inspires Marx's experimentation in the *Economic-Philosophic Manuscripts*. It gives him, I suggest, the target at which he aims his theoretical and practical efforts for the rest of his life. For

[43] *Capital, Vol. 3*, 25:828; 820.

[44] In the final section of this chapter I shall argue, however, that Marx can portray communism as the "control and conscious mastery" of our social forces only if he assumes something like the complete humanization of nature which he explicitly rejects in his later work. Thus I agree, in the end, with R. N. Berki's suggestion that Marx both affirms and denies in his work the transcendence of natural necessity. I add, however, that the famous passage in *Capital, Vol. 3*, about the realms of freedom and necessity is itself indirect evidence of Marx's affirmation, as well as direct evidence of his denial, of the possibility of transcending natural necessity. See R. N. Berki, *Insight and Vision*, 155, 132-33.

[45] K. Marx, *Economic-Philosophic Manuscripts*, in *MEW, Ebde.*, 1:521; *CW*, 3:280.

in the concepts and categories of political economy he finds the explanation of the dehumanizing character of modern social life.

Even while writing his thesis, as thoroughly Hegelian a document as he ever produced, Marx suggested that the achievement of left Hegelian goals would require the abandonment of philosophy.

> The world confronting a philosophy total in itself is a world torn apart. This philosophy's activity therefore also appears torn apart and contradictory; its objective universality is turned into the subjective forms of individual consciousness in which it has life. . . . At such times half-hearted minds have opposite views to those of whole-hearted generals. They believe that they can compensate losses by cutting the armed forces, by splitting them up, by a peace treaty with the real needs; whereas Themistocles, when Athens was threatened with destruction, moved the Athenians to abandon the city entirely and found a new Athens at sea, in another element.[46]

In the mid-1840s Marx discovers in political economy the other "element" in which he can found his "new Athens at sea."

As we have seen in the previous chapter, Marx demands nothing new in asking for the "realization" of Hegel's philosophy of freedom and its transfer into "another element" rooted in the concrete "praxis" of human activity. He breaks with his former comrades more through the manner in which he carries out this project. Marx complains that the left Hegelians are half-hearted and inconsistent in pursuing their demands for the realization of philosophy. While they are willing to deny that philosophy itself has the power to heal the world, they still seem to think that ideas have the power to shape and distort it. Though they deny that theory can eliminate the illusions and self-estrangement rooted in the actual conditions of life, they still trace the origin of these illusions to theoretical ideas.

"German theory too was confronted with the question . . . how did it come about that people 'got' these illusions 'into their heads'?" But it offered no answers.[47] In *The German Ideology*

---

[46] K. Marx, "Notebooks on Epicurean Philosophy," in *MEW, Ebde.*, 1:215-16; *CW*, 1:491-92.

[47] *German Ideology*, 3:217; *CW*, 5:236.

Marx claims that he was confronting this question already in his essay "On the Jewish Question" and in his "Introduction" to the critique of Hegel's *Philosophy of Right*. But the "philosophical phraseology" in which he expressed his ideas there, "the traditionally occurring philosophical expressions such as 'human essence,' 'species,' etc., gave the German theorists the desired occasion for misunderstanding the real development and believing that here again it was merely a question of giving their worn-out theoretical robe a new turn." To answer the questions they raise, in particular, to locate the source of dehumanization in the modern world, one must " 'leave philosophy aside,' one has to leap out of it and devote oneself to the study of reality."[48] It is a left Hegelian question that suggests the need to abandon left Hegelian philosophizing.

Marx's "leap" into "the study of reality" and his discovery there of the source of modern man's dehumanization occur simultaneously in the *Economic-Philosophic Manuscripts*. In these notes and incomplete essays Marx experiments with using the categories and concepts of political economy to answer left Hegelian questions about modern man's dehumanization. It is difficult to know what Marx's ultimate opinion of these experiments was. But one thing, at least, is clear. Marx became convinced through them that he had located the field—political economy—which would, after further study, answer his questions.

We need not underestimate the significance of Marx's break with left Hegelian questions. The hardheaded conceptual vocabulary of English political economy that he uses in *Capital* represents something more than a Trojan horse concealing the "philosophical phraseology" of his early essays. Certainly, the questions that he raises there *are* drawn from the questions raised by classical political economy. But behind these questions lies Marx's continuing need to locate the obstacle to the realization of man's humanity. This continuing need is registered in the *way* he conceptualizes the categories of classical political economy and capitalism in general.

As Leszek Kolakowski suggests:

The fundamental novelty of *Capital* consists in two points which entail a wholly different view of capitalist society from

---

[48] Ibid.

that of the classical economists with their labour theory of value. The first of these is the argument that what the worker sells is not his labour but labour power, and that labour has two aspects, the abstract and the concrete. . . . In the second place, having discovered the dual nature of labour as expressed in the opposition between exchange-value and use-value, Marx is able to define capitalism as a system in which the sole object of production is to increase exchange-value without limit; the whole of human activity is subordinated to a non-human purpose, the creation of something that man as such cannot assimilate, for only use-value can be assimilated. The whole community is thus enslaved to its own products, abstractions which present themselves to it as an external alien power.[49]

The core of the first volume of *Capital* is a theory of value creation and profit that explains the structure and development of production peculiar to capitalism. In particular, Marx seeks to demonstrate that the same set of productive relations among individuals has unleashed the unprecedented, uncontrolled growth of productive forces in the modern world and legitimized the oppression and exploitation of workers. The definitive feature of capitalist production, according to Marx, is, as in every other system of production, the way in which surplus value is created by labour. The relations between individuals that lead them to produce more than they need for their subsistence gives a "mode of production" its specific character.

The key social relationship that shapes capitalist production is the sale of labour power by individuals to other individuals who have the wherewithal to invest in their product. The essential precondition of this relationship is that both labour and capital no longer be tied to any specific means of production. So that they can meet as seller and buyer in the market, the owners of labour power and capital must be free to alienate what each owns.

Marx's major complaint against classical political economists is that they take this relationship between the seller and buyer of labour power to be a natural relationship without historical precon-

[49] L. Kolakowski, *Main Currents of Marxism*, 1:264.

ditions, and thus they point to it as the foundation of production per se. They fail to see that this relationship is the basis of capitalist production in particular. "The historical conditions of its existence," Marx insists, "are by no means given with the mere circulation of money and commodities."

> Nature does not produce on one side owners of money or commodities, and on the other owners of nothing but their own labour-power. This relation no more has a natural basis than it has a social basis common to all historical periods. It is clearly the result of a previous historical development, the product of many economical revolutions, of the extinction of a whole series of older forms of social production. . . . It arises, only when the owner of the means of production and subsistence chances upon the free labourer selling his labour-power in the market. This one historical condition comprises a world history.[50]

Without an awareness of the historically specific character of the wage labour-capital relationship, Marx argues that one cannot properly understand the structure of capitalist production, let alone its development. "The capitalist epoch is therefore characterized by this, that labour-power takes in the eyes of the labourer himself the form of a commodity which is his property; his labour consequently becomes wage labour."[51]

This commodification of labour power provides the key to the structure and development of capitalist production. For it allows us to explain, Marx argues, how capital gains profits through purchasing labour power. "In order to extract value from the consumption of a commodity our owner of money must be so lucky as to discover, within the sphere of circulation, in the market, a commodity whose use-value itself possesses the peculiar property of being a source of value, whose actual consumption, therefore, is itself an embodiment of labour, and consequently, a creation of value." The

[50] *Capital, Vol. 1,* 23:183-84; 189.
[51] Ibid., 23:184 n. 41; 189 n. 1.

capitalist finds just "such a special commodity in capacity for labour or labour-power."[52]

Labour is a very special kind of commodity. "The value of labour power is, like that of every other commodity, determined by the labour-time necessary for the production, and consequently also the reproduction, of this special article."[53] But labour power is unlike any other commodity in that its consumption creates new value. "The consumption of labour-power is at one and the same time the production of commodities and of surplus value." Here we discover "the secret of profit making."[54] The purchase of a commodity which itself produces values for exchange far beyond its own exchange value allows the purchaser to make a profit through his purchase.

What is wrong with such a system of production? For one thing, there is the grinding poverty to which the sellers of labour power are reduced. For another, there are the crises that periodically hamper and, Marx predicts, will eventually end productive growth. But even in *Capital*, loss of control and dehumanization, rather than injustice and inefficiency, remain the primary reasons for Marx's condemnation of capitalism. Under the capitalist mode of production man loses control of the productive forces his labour has created.

> The means of production are at once changed into means for the absorption of the labour of others. It is now no longer the labourer who employs the means of production, but the means of production that employ the labourer. Instead of being consumed by him as material elements of his productive activity, they consume him as the ferment necessary to their own life-process, and the life-process of capital consists only in its

[52] Ibid., 23:181; 186.

[53] Ibid., 23:184-85; 189. "In contradistinction to the case of other commodities, there enters into the determination of the value of labour-power a historical and moral element," since "the extent of his so-called necessary wants, as also the ways of satisfying them, are themselves historical products" and thus depend, to a certain extent, upon the customs and habits peculiar to a given epoch. "Nevertheless, in a given country, at a given period, the average quantity of the means of subsistence necessary for the labourer is understood" (ibid., 23:185; 190).

[54] Ibid., 23:189; 195.

movement as value constantly expanding, constantly multiplying itself.[55]

According to Marx, such a system of production *appears* to represent the maximum of human freedom in economic relations, the "very Eden of the innate rights of man." For "both buyer and seller of a commodity, say of labour power, are constrained only by their own free will. They contract as free and legally equal persons. The contract is but the form in which they give their will a common legal expression."[56] But though "in their imaginations, individuals seem freer under the dominance of the bourgeoisie than before, because their conditions of life seem to them accidental; in reality, of course, they are less free, because they are to a greater extent subsumed by material forces," that is, by the nonhuman powers of "blind chance [*Zufälligkeit*]."[57]

> Since, before entering the process, his own labour has already been alienated by the sale of his labour power, appropriated by the capitalist and embodied in capital, it must, during the process, be objectified in an alien product. Since the process of production is at the same time the process by which the capitalist consumes labour-power, the product of the labourer is constantly transformed, not only into commodities, but into capital, into value that sucks up the value-creating power, into means of subsistence that buy persons, into means of production that employ the producers. The labourer therefore is constantly producing material wealth as capital, as an alien power that dominates and exploits him.[58]

Capital attempts to prove that the very relationship that gives capitalist production its distinctive character, the free sale and consumption of labour power, turns the forces created by our social interaction into "alien" powers that "employ its producers." One might say that *Capital* explains our subjection to "heteronomous powers," our dehumanization. This is not to say that Marx has two

[55] Ibid., 23:329; 339.
[56] Ibid., 23:189–90; 195.
[57] *German Ideology*, 3:78–79; CW, 5:78–79.
[58] *Capital, Vol. 1*, 23:596; 625.

sets of concerns in *Capital*: "humanist" concerns about dehumanization and more "concrete" concerns about the injustice and inefficiency of the capitalist mode of production. Rather, I am suggesting that, just as in his very first discussions of socioeconomic relations, Marx continues to explain the problems of injustice and inefficiency that we encounter in our socioeconomic relations in terms of our failure to realize our humanity in our social world. The underlying obstacle to overcoming injustice and inefficiency is the obstacle to the realization of our humanity posed by the capitalist mode of production.

Indeed, when we look more closely at the dependence of the capitalist mode of production on the commodification of labour, we recognize in Marx's account of capitalism a new species of the dehumanization argument we have been examining throughout this study. According to Marx, to *commodify* labour is to treat something that gives commodities their value as itself a mere commodity. It is to treat something distinctively human as no different from the objects that human labour creates. When he sells his labour power, the worker, "like Esau, surrenders his creative power, he surrenders his birthright for a mess of potage."[59] The "birthright" that he surrenders—and that he has no choice but to surrender at this stage of development—is not only the direction of his own creative powers, but also the "control and conscious mastery" of the forces created by social interaction. Marx's analysis of capitalist production attempts to demonstrate that the commodification of labour power introduces a relentless expansion of production that necessarily must escape our control.

Marx's demonstration that the structure of production peculiar to capitalism is also the obstacle to overcoming dehumanization is made possible by two conceptual innovations that he introduces in the 1840s. Both represent examples of his use of categories drawn from political economy to "realize" the Hegelian philosophy of freedom. The first is his redefinition of man's humanity in terms of his labour, a definition that makes the commodification of labour "dehumanizing." The second is his contention that the "mode of

[59] K. Marx, *Grundrisse*, 307.

production," the fundamental relationships between individuals that characterize productive activity in a given epoch, shapes the character, or "spirit," of *all* activity and social interaction in that epoch. This latter innovation allows Marx to argue that the dehumanization of man imposed by the commodification of labour will shape social interaction as a whole, rather than just the immediate relationship between worker and capitalist.

Marx introduces the first of these innovations in his *Economic-Philosophic Manuscripts*. He does so as part of an effort to purge of its abstraction from material reality what he views as a valid Hegelian insight. The "negative" power toward the external world, which defined for Hegel man's freedom and humanity, is, Marx insists, actually physical labour. And the objective "manifestation" of man's humanity in the world, which Hegel described as the realization of freedom, is the world of objects that labour produces. The "great thing" in Hegelian philosophy is that Hegel "grasps the essence of labour and conceives of objective man—true, that is, real, man—as the outcome of his own labour." But Hegel recognizes, Marx argues, only "mental labour" as human, and thus, though he sees man's humanity as something realized in the world, he recognizes only those aspects of human behaviour that transcend worldly limitations, the *geistliche* sphere, as being human. The need to "realize" Hegel's concept of humanity leads Marx to assert that it is in the world of production, the world of objects created by human labour, that man manifests his humanity in the world.[60]

According to Marx, to treat labour as another commodity to be bought and sold is to degrade labour to the nonhuman level of a thing, a means rather than an "end in itself." Thus Marx does not hesitate to argue here that "a forced increase in wages would be nothing but *better payment for the slave* and would win neither for the worker nor for labour their human status and dignity."[61] (Marx's emphasis.) In the "Critique of the Gotha Program," written more than thirty years after the *Economic-Philosophic Manuscripts*, Marx asserts again that labour must become "not only a

[60] K. Marx, *Economic-Philosophic Manuscripts*, in *MEW, Ebde.*, 1:574; *CW*, 3:332-33.
[61] Ibid., 1:520-21; 3:280, 276-77.

means of life but life's prime want."[62] And as we have seen, Marx's analysis of capitalist production, written in the years between these two statements, rests on an interpretation of labour as a distinctively human, value-creating capacity.

Moreover, the labour theory of value allows Marx, in *Capital*, to portray production as the way this distinctively human capacity realizes itself in the world. The value of commodities, he suggests, is "a mere *congelation* of homogenous human labour, . . . crystals of *social substance*."[63] (Emphasis added.) Marx sets out to eliminate the "metaphysical subtleties and theological whims" that surround our understanding of commodities.

> The mystery of the commodity's form consists simply in this: in the commodity the social character of men's labour is portrayed to men as an objective character of things, as its natural quality; hence the social relation of producers to their collective labour is portrayed to them as a social relation between objects existing apart from them.[64]

But Marx himself introduces a concept, "social substance," the embodiment, congelation, or crystallization of labour in the world, that suggests quite a bit of "metaphysical subtlety."[65] For the author of *Capital*, labour still introduces man's humanity into the world. To treat value as a relation among things rather than a quality introduced by man into the world is to worship things as if they possess the creative power that distinguishes man—the famous "fetishism of commodities." (In the last section of this chapter I discuss whether Marx can conceptualize labour in this way without falling into self-contradiction.)

---

[62] "Critique of the Gotha Program," 19:21. This essay is translated in R. Tucker (ed.), *The Marx-Engels Reader*, 531.

[63] *Capital, Vol. 1*, 23:52; 45.

[64] Ibid., 23:85-86; 81, 83.

[65] In the first volume of *Capital* Marx notes and tries to explain Aristotle's failure to recognize the common substance that removes value from the realm of convention and opinion (ibid., 23:73-74; 69). One can imagine an Aristotelian response to Marx, beginning with a challenge to the strange metaphysical ideas implied by the notion of congealed labour as the "social substance" embodied in all of our products. See C. Castoriades, "From Marx to Aristotle and from Aristotle to Ourselves," 260-319.

Marx unveils the second innovation, his interpretation of the "mode of production," as part of his anti-Hegelian polemic in *The German Ideology*.

> The social structure and the state are continually emerging from the life-process of definite individuals, not, however, as they appear in their own or others' imagination, but as they *really* are, i.e., as they act, produce materially, and hence as they work under definite material limits, presuppositions and conditions independent of their will. . . . The opposite assumption is only possible if in addition to the spirit of the real, materially evolved individuals another distinct spirit is presupposed.[66]

These "definite material limits, presuppositions and conditions independent of their will" are what Marx terms the mode of production.

The mode of production represents Marx's answer to the question he claims the left Hegelians never got around to asking: How is it that "people 'got' " dehumanizing theoretical "illusions 'into their heads' " if philosophy is powerless to shape reality in its image? It is the way individuals produce that explains the illusions in their heads, rather than the other way round. For

> this mode of production must not be considered merely as the reproduction of the physical existence of the individuals. Rather it is a definite form of activity of these individuals, a definite form of expressing their life, a definite *mode of life*. As individuals express their life so they are. What they are, therefore, coincides with their production, both with *what* they produce and with *how* they produce. Hence what individuals are depends on the material conditions of their production.[67]

Marx's use of the mode of production to explain the character of social thought and activity in a given epoch, the key doctrine of historical materialism, also represents an attempt to realize a Hegelian

[66] *The German Ideology*, 3:25, 26n; *CW*, 5:35-36, 36n.
[67] Ibid., 3:21; 5:31-32.

concept: the *Volksgeist*. Marx assumes here the existence of the phenomenon he uses the mode of production to explain: the singular character of social thought and activity in a given epoch. (In the last section of this chapter I ask whether he can do so without relying on idealist premises that he explicitly rejects.) For Marx, the mode of production answers a *how* rather than a *why* question. In particular, it explains how the "mode of life" that characterizes any epoch acquires its character. It does not explain why a particular society or epoch should be informed by a single "mode of life."

Marx's ability to locate the obstacle to overcoming the dehumanizing spirit of modern society in the capitalist mode of production rests on his ability to realize Hegel's concepts of humanity and *Volksgeist* in this way. If man expresses his humanity in productive labour, then the commodification of labour, characteristic of capitalism, will appear dehumanizing. And if the fundamental relations of production, as a mode of production, informs every aspect of a society's life, then in order to change that mode of life we must transform its mode of production. Thus to overcome the dehumanization characteristic of modern society we must, in Marx's view, eliminate the capitalist mode of production.

Proletarian Revolution

A general revolt by the working class represents the means by which Marx expects the obstacle to the realization of man's humanity, posed by the capitalist mode of production, to be eliminated. Marx's proletarian revolution is at the very core an *"emancipation of the human being,"* rather than the mere negation of the constraints that currently torment workers. According to Marx, the working class "cannot emancipate itself without . . . emancipating all other spheres of society, . . . and hence can win itself only through the *complete rewinning of man.*"[68]

One could easily explain Marx's identification of proletarian revolution with human emancipation, without invoking left Hegelian questions about the realization of humanity, by arguing that Marx

[68] "Introduction," 1:390; CW, 3:186.

himself is no exception to the theory of ideology creation that he formulates in the *The German Ideology*.

[E]ach new class which puts itself in the place of one ruling before it is compelled, merely in order to carry through its aim, to present its interest as the common interest of all the members of society, that is, expressed in ideal form: it has to give its ideas the form of universality, and present them as the only rational, universally valid ones. The class making a revolution comes forward from the very start, if only because it is opposed to a *class*, not as a class but as the representative of the whole of society, as the whole mass of society confronting the one ruling class.[69]

Marx would, of course, reject this explanation, since he denies that the proletariat is merely one more class seeking to dominate. But Marx himself warns us to reject such denials; every ideologist makes such claims. His theory of ideology suggests that his own portrayal of proletarian revolution as the liberation of humanity is just another example of the self-delusion typical of ideologists.

This portrayal of Marx's understanding of proletarian revolution as ideological exaggeration can help us account for much of the universalistic rhetoric that surrounds Marxist theory and social movements. But it is limited as an explanation of Marx's own commitment to proletarian revolution, since it assumes that Marx's advocacy of a revolutionary redemption of "humanity" grows out of his advocacy of a workers' revolt. The evidence of his intellectual development shows, however, that, if anything, the exact opposite is true. Marx's search for the means of realizing man's humanity in the world precedes and, I suggest, leads to his advocacy of proletarian revolution.

It is at this point that some of Marx's most perceptive readers and critics feel compelled to introduce religious analogies, along with the explanations they suggest, to account for Marx's portrayal of proletarian revolution. They suggest that Marx's vision of proletarian revolution represents a "religion of revolution," a "pseudo-

---

[69] *German Ideology*, 3:47-48; *CW*, 5:60.

morphosis" of Judeo-Christian visions of Messianic redemption, and that it rests upon a "hidden soteriological myth." In short, they insist that Marx's vision of revolution is "quite unintelligible" apart from its Jewish and Christian sources.[70]

In my account of Marx's social criticism, as well as in the chapters that have preceded it, I have tried to show that Marx's ideas about capitalism and communism, even the most visionary among them, are quite intelligible without reference to religious visions of redemption. This is no less the case with regard to Marx's concept of proletarian revolution. It too, in part, represents a new answer to left Hegelian questions about how man's humanity can be realized. This answer differs from the ones I have discussed so far in that Marx's commitment to proletarian revolution precedes his "leap" from philosophy to political economy.[71]

The way Marx conceptualizes proletarian revolution registers his continuing need to find "material weapons" with which to realize the goals forged by the "spiritual weapons" of "philosophy,"[72] a problem faced by both left Kantians and left Hegelians. Marx's identification of the capitalist mode of production as the obstacle to the overcoming of the dehumanizing spirit of modern society allows him to satisfy that need. It allows him to argue that the total revolution he longs for represents the real interest of an oppressed and ever-growing class, rather than a theoretically discovered desideratum.

The search for the "material weapons" with which to realize the philosophy of human emancipation is a concern of left Kantian and Hegelian social critics as far back as Schiller.

> Reason has accomplished all that she can accomplish by discovering and establishing the law; its execution requires firm will and living feeling. If truth is to win out in her conflict with forces, she must herself first become a force and appoint as her

[70] See R. Tucker, *Philosophy and Myth in Karl Marx*, 25, 12-22; K. Löwith, *Meaning in History*, 44-45; L. Kolakowski, "The Myth of Human Self-Identity," 18; and R. N. Berki, *Insight and Vision*, 44.

[71] On this point, see S. Avineri, *The Social and Political Thought of Karl Marx*, 27ff.

[72] "Introduction," 1:391; CW, 3:187.

champion a drive in the realm of phenomena; for drives are the only forces in the sensible world.[73]

Schiller's *general* aim is also Marx's: to make man's humanity, his "true freedom," the basis of his association, so that the forces that shape our lives will be "human" powers within our control. To realize man's humanity in such a way "involves being able to count on the moral law as an effective force, and free will is thereby drawn into the realm of cause and effect where everything follows from everything else in a chain of strict necessity."[74] Since man's humanity is defined by his capacity to abstract from the externally conditioned interests that shape social interaction, the realization of humanity requires that freedom find "as her champion a drive" in the realm of those interests.

The search for such a champion persists throughout left Kantian and left Hegelian speculation. Marx's originality comes from his willingness to entertain the possibility that the interests that drive a social revolution could become the interests that champion man's humanity in the realm of social interaction. Schiller believes that the course of the French Revolution demonstrates the untenability of such a hypothesis. His notion of interests that favour human emancipation opposes itself to the notion of interests that ignite social convulsions. In this he is followed by most left Hegelians, no matter how radical their rejection of contemporary institutions. Even Moses Hess, who becomes a propagandist for socialism and the working class, fears social conflict as an obstacle rather than a means to human emancipation.[75]

But Marx is firmly convinced that, in the proletariat, human emancipation has found its champion in the realm of conditioned interests. "Philosophy," he insists, "cannot be realized without the abolition [*Aufhebung*] of the proletariat, the proletariat cannot be abolished without the realization of philosophy."[76] Given this conviction, he feels free to scoff at his predecessors' fears, claiming that

[73] F. Schiller, *Aesthetic Education*, Letter 7, 48-49.
[74] Ibid., Letter 3, 16-17.
[75] See M. Hess, "The Recent Philosophers," 360-61.
[76] "Introduction," 1:391; CW, 3:187.

these fears betray a lack of resolution or, worse, self-serving mystification. It is his discovery of this "material weapon" that allows Marx to chastise his predecessors for their lack of seriousness and good faith about their shared goal, the realization of philosophy.

Marx devises, at various times in his career, different strategies for demonstrating that the proletariat's class interest directs it against the dehumanizing spirit of modern society, rather than against a less inclusive target. The most elaborate appears in his first celebration of the proletariat in his critique of Hegel (1843-1844). What is needed "for general emancipation" in Germany, he argues there, is a class that "is forced by its *immediate* condition, by *material* necessity, by its *very chains*" to revolt against dehumanization.

> [A] class with *radical chains*, a class . . . which has a universal character by its universal suffering and claims no *particular right* because no *particular wrong* but *wrong generally* is perpetrated against it; which can no longer invoke a *historical* but only a *human* title; . . . which cannot emancipate itself without emancipating itself from all other spheres of society and without thereby emancipating all other spheres of society, which, in a word, is the *complete loss* of man and hence can win itself only through the *complete rewinning of man*. This dissolution of society as a particular estate is the *proletariat*.[77] (Marx's emphasis.)

Its "universal suffering," in this characterization, seems to make the proletariat a "universal class." The suffering of the proletariat, Marx argues, cannot be blamed upon natural forces beyond man's control. The proletariat represents an "artificially impoverished" mass and is coming to recognize itself as such. To relieve its suffering, it must effect a total revolution in the spirit of social interaction, for only such a revolution will remove the obstacle to regaining the control of the forces created by the interactions of individuals, the forces that impose upon the proletariat its suffering.[78]

[77] Ibid., 1:390; 3:186.
[78] Ibid., 1:391; 3:187.

His later location of the obstacle to overcoming dehumanization in the capitalist mode of production allows Marx both to characterize the proletariat as the class that will bring about the total liberation of man and to do so without having to rely on his earlier philosophic assumptions. As a political economist, Marx now claims that a continual downward pressure on wages is built into the relationship between capital and wage labour, and that this pressure will both obstruct economic development and compel the working class to destroy the capitalist mode of production.

Because subsequent economic developments have discredited a narrowly economic interpretation of Marx's pauperization thesis, many Marxists have tended toward a broader interpretation of Marx's argument, emphasizing the general decline in quality of life as capitalism develops. There is certainly evidence in *Capital* for such an interpretation. Marx insists that "to the extent capital accumulates, the position of the labourer, be his payment high or low, must grow worse. . . . Accumulation of wealth at one pole is, therefore, at the same time accumulation of misery, agony of toil, slavery, ignorance, brutality, moral degradation, at the opposite pole." In short, capitalism creates conditions that increasingly render man "a debased, enslaved, neglected and contemptible being."[79] Marx still follows his old categorical imperative to overthrow such dehumanizing conditions. The pauperization thesis makes it the proletariat's imperative as well.

Although it is clear that Marx means more by pauperization than a mere decline in wages, the downward pressure on wages is important enough to him that he is willing, in a rare deviation from his usual behaviour, to suppress data that suggest its inaccuracy.[80] It is so important to him because, without it, he would have to admit that it is the acceptance of a particular *interpretation* of the quality of life, rather than sheer economic need, which leads to the overthrow of capitalism. Such an interpretation would have to rely on an idea of humanity that would enable us to distinguish a truly human from a dehumanized life. But then everything would turn

[79] *Capital, Vol. 1*, 23:675; 708-9. "Introduction," 1:385; *CW*, 3:182.
[80] See B. Wolfe, *Marxism: 100 Years in the Life of a Doctrine*, 322-23.

again on the correctness of one's conception of humanity, the left Hegelian position that Marx scorns and tries to escape. Marx could no longer represent his social criticism as the expression of working class needs and experience. The need for a total revolution, he would have to admit, does not arise necessarily out of the social experience of workers; workers must view their experience from a particular philosophic perspective, they must have a particular understanding of man's humanity and the obstacles to its realization, before they will even long for a total revolution in the mode of production, let alone actually revolt.

Such an admission would suggest that there is a disjunction between the worker's and the critical philosopher's perspective that must be closed before Marx's proletarian revolution can take place. Marx is loath to admit this disjunction or address the problems it creates. But the reluctance of workers' organizations, in the years following Marx's death, to seek the total revolution that Marx insists is their greatest need has compelled his twentieth-century followers to face this disjunction. The reaction of Marxist intellectuals to the disjunction between the proletarian's and critical intellectual's perspective has defined, I suggest, the different paths that Marxism has taken in this century. Most Marxists have chosen one of the following three alternatives: (1) to try to impose the philosophic perspective on the workers and, in this way, to seek the total revolution Marx longed for; (2) to follow the workers' self-expressed interests and, as a result, to turn away from total revolution as Marx conceived it; (3) to continue to seek total revolution, but without expecting the working class to have any special place in the revolt against the dehumanizing spirit of capitalist production. The first alternative is that chosen by Lenin and all Marxist-Leninist parties; the second is chosen by the social democratic parties of Western Europe; the third is chosen by the many twentieth-century Marxist intellectuals, like the members of the Frankfurt school, who continue to demand a total revolution against modern society, but who have lost Marx's faith in the existence of the material weapons with which to bring it about. From the perspective of Marx's works all three alternatives are one-sided. The Leninist position denies the workers' freedom and tries to will rather than follow the transformation of social conditions; the social democratic position accepts the continuation of dehumanizing forms of social life; the critical theorist's position returns us to the ineffectual hopes of the left Hegelians. All of these alternatives lose something that Marx deemed essential, so none can claim to be the "genuinely" Marxist position. But Marx avoids a one-sided interpretation of his own ideas only by ignoring the need to choose among them.

Marx's reluctance to address the possibility of a disjunction between proletarian and philosophic perspectives manifests itself most clearly in his response to Bakunin's criticisms. In *Statism and Anarchy* Bakunin argues that Marx's dictatorship of the proletariat would, when actualized, become a dictatorship of the intellectuals over the proletariat.

> Thus no matter from which side you look at the question, you will always arrive at the same, sad conclusion—the rule of the majority by a privileged minority. . . . However these representatives will be passionately convinced, as well as educated, socialists. The terms educated socialists and scientific socialism, which are encountered continuously in the writings of the Lasalleans and the Marxists, themselves demonstrate that the alleged popular state will be nothing more than the despotic rule of the popular masses by a new and numerically small aristocracy of real or imagined scholars. The people have not been educated and will, therefore, be freed entirely from the cares of government, and placed entirely into the governed herd. A fine liberation! The Marxists sense this contradiction and, recognizing that this scholarly government would be the most burdensome, offensive, and despicable in the world, that in spite of all the democratic reforms it would be a real dictatorship, console us with the idea that this dictatorship will be temporary and short.[81]

Marx copied this passage in the notes he made on Bakunin's book. Knowing that on this point, at least, Bakunin's prophecies

---

[81] M. Bakunin, *Statism and Anarchy*, 270.

were fulfilled, we are eager to hear Marx's response to the suggestion that the dictatorship of the proletariat will become the dictatorship of the Marxist party of intellectuals. Yet Marx barely responds to Bakunin's critique. Beside the words "scholarly government" he exclaims, "*quelle rêverie!*" In addition, he merely notes that Bakunin has misunderstood the dictatorship of the proletariat; it will *not* necessarily be short.[82] Bakunin, Marx insists, does not understand the difference between social management and political ruling, and therefore he misunderstands the role that its intellectual leaders will play in the proletariat's life. But Marx assumes here the identity of interest between workers and critical intellectuals that Bakunin asks him to demonstrate. He simply does not take Bakunin's charges seriously.[83] Once he discovered in the working class a material force with which to realize total revolution, Marx never faces the possibility that workers and intellectuals may have different perspectives and different needs.

The most serious and influential attempt to bridge the disjunction between the proletarian and philosophic perspectives in Marxist thought, Georg Lukács's arguments in *History and Class Consciousness*, merely reformulates this disjunction. Lukács sets out to distinguish "the authentic class consciousness of the proletariat" from the ordinary "psychological" consciousness of workers. What defines "authentic" proletarian consciousness, if not the workers' conscious aims and experience? The way Lukács answers this question, I suggest, makes it clear that, for him, it is the Marxist perspective on human history and well-being that defines authentic proletarian consciousness.

To say that class consciousness has no psychological reality does not imply that it is a mere fiction. Its reality is vouched

---

[82] "Conspectus on Bakunin's *Statism and Anarchy*," 18:636.
[83] Shortly before his arrest and expulsion from East Germany, Rudolf Bahro urged his fellow Marxist intellectuals to recognize the prescience of Bakunin's criticisms and to try to develop a Marxist explanation for the "contradiction between science and the working class" that led to the dictatorship of the Communist Party. "It was probably necessary," he suggests, "to be both an anarchist and a Russian to perceive behind the authority of Marx and his doctrine in the year 1872, the shadow of Stalin. Marx did not see this shadow, he could not and would not see it" (R. Bahro, *The Alternative in Eastern Europe*, 41-42).

for by its *ability to explain* the infinitely painful path of the proletarian revolution, with its many reverses, its constant return to its starting point, and the incessant self-criticism of which Marx speaks in the celebrated passage of *The Eighteenth Brumaire*. Only the consciousness of the proletariat can point to the way that leads out of the impasse of capitalism. . . . And if the proletariat finds the economic inhumanity to which it is subjected easier to understand than the political, and the political easier to understand than the cultural, then all these separations point to the extent of the still unconquered power of capitalist forms of life in the proletariat itself.[84] (Emphasis added.)

The working class may not understand the political and cultural inhumanity that capitalism imposes on it, but "the unique element in its situation is that its surpassing of immediacy represents an *aspiration towards society in its totality*, regardless of whether this aspiration remains conscious or unconscious for the moment."[85] Lukács defines "authentic" proletarian consciousness in terms of the ability to explain the contemporary world and guide a revolution. That ability is possessed by those who look at the world from the perspective of Marx's understanding of history and humanity (for Lukács, the Communist party). From this perspective one sees the completeness of the inhumanity that capitalism imposes on man—political and cultural as well as economic dehumanization—and thus comes to long for a total revolution against the capitalist mode of production. That most workers do not share this longing Lukács explains by pointing to "the still unconquered power of capitalist forms of life in the proletariat itself." But this explanation implies that it is philosophic knowledge, the attainment of a particular understanding of man, that conquers the "power of capitalist forms" in the workers' lives. The disjunction between proletarian and philosophic experience becomes clear. Only to the extent to which workers raise themselves to the Marxist philosophic perspective on human history will they free themselves from capitalist ide-

[84] G. Lukács, *History and Class Consciousness*, 75-76.
[85] Ibid., 174.

ology and commit themselves to a Marxist total revolution. As Alvin Gouldner suggests, the charges of "false consciousness" which Marxists so often throw at workers and their organizations can plausibly be reversed and thrown back at Marxists. "Marxism," he suggests, can be interpreted as "the false consciousness" of radicalized bourgeois intellectuals, who convince themselves that the working class pursues and is freed by the goals conceived by and for those intellectuals.[86]

Marx, I have suggested, never adequately addresses the disjunction between proletarian and philosophic perspectives on the world. If he did address this problem, he would have to turn our attention back to the concepts that underlie his philosophic perspective and that allow him to identify the capitalist mode of production as the obstacle to overcoming the dehumanizing spirit of modern society. In the following section I suggest that Marx has more to fear from such a return to his philosophic premises than the waste of time that could be better used in the organization of the proletariat and in the analysis of the obstacles to proletarian revolution. For I shall argue that Marx is able to identify the capitalist mode of production as the obstacle to the "control and conscious mastery" of our world only by relying on self-contradictory philosophic premisses.

Contradictions Underlying Marx's Concept of Communism

One problem with trying to argue that Marx's longing for proletarian revolution represents a species of the longing for total revolution, as I have defined that longing here, is that Marx explicitly denies the freedom/nature dichotomy and, indeed, any dichotomy between man's humanity and his nature. In what follows, I suggest that Marx implicitly relies on such a dichotomy despite his explicit denials.

Beginning in 1844, Marx defines man's humanity in terms of his special capacity for socially productive labour. As we have seen in the previous section, he derives this definition simultaneously from political economy's labour theory of value and from a realization of

---

[86] A. Gouldner, *The Future of the Intellectuals and the Rise of the New Class*, 75-76.

Hegel's philosophy of freedom. According to Marx, "Hegel's standpoint is that of modern political economy. He grasps *labour* as the *essence* of man." But Hegel's standpoint is limited, in Marx's eyes, by its reliance on defining human labour in terms of man's mental or spiritual capacities, that is, in terms of those capacities through which man seems to resist external conditioning by material forces and natural needs. "The only labour which Hegel knows and recognizes is *abstract mental* labour." The capacity to abstract from external conditioning that defines philosophy becomes for Hegel the creator of man's world.[87]

Marx takes over Hegel's conception of man's humanity as a capacity for self-actualization and seeks to "concretize" it by showing that it is physical labour, precisely the labour conditioned by material forces and natural needs, that is the bearer of man's humanity. That Kantian and Hegelian idealism oppose man's humanity to his naturally conditioned needs is merely a sign of the self-estrangement or dehumanization imposed on modern individuals by their conditions of production. The conditions under which modern individuals labour compel them to view labour as "merely a *means* to satisfy needs external to it," rather than as "the satisfaction of a need." As a result, individuals feel human only in their escape from labour, in their satisfaction of needs at leisure.[88]

Both the political economists' and the idealists' concepts manifest this self-estrangement, according to Marx. Both groups characterize man's humanity in terms of his escape from physical labour. The former, however, view leisure as the escape from a specific externally imposed pain—labour—while the latter glorify leisure as the resistance to external conditioning in general. Marx persists, throughout his career, in deriding such views as reflections of man's loss of the true meaning of his humanity. Labour should represent "life's prime want," he insists, rather than a pain one suffers only as a means to other goals.[89]

But the persistence of a freedom/nature dichotomy in Marx's

[87] K. Marx, *Economic-Philosophic Manuscripts*, in *MEW Ebde.*, 1:574; CW, 3:333.
[88] Ibid., 1:514-15; 3:274-75.
[89] See K. Marx, "Critique of the Gotha Program," 19:21; translated in *The Marx-Engels Reader*, 531. See also K. Marx, *Grundrisse*, 611-12.

new definition of humanity becomes evident once one tries to answer the following question: What is it that distinguishes "human" production from that of animals such that labour should be treated as an "end in itself" rather than as a means to other ends?[90] Marx tries to answer this question in a number of different ways throughout his career. But though he never admits it, the underlying premiss of each answer is that it is mental freedom from external conditioning that distinguishes human activity from all other natural activity.

In the *Economic-Philosophic Manuscripts* of 1844 Marx offers an adaptation of Feuerbach's answer to this question. Feuerbach, as we have seen, argues that man and nature represent a "simple self-identity." The distinctively human capacities arise from our "universal sensuousness," rather than from our resistance to the external conditioning to which our sensuousness makes us vulnerable. Marx argues that man is the "universal" producer. Animals are limited to the material to which their natural needs lead them. Human beings are indifferent to every particular material. They shape them all and thus reproduce all of nature.

But what explains man's ability to turn to any particular material and use it for production? Why is it that man, and man alone, escapes the dependence on particular objects of satisfaction that rules in the rest of nature's realm? The unstated premiss of Marx's argument, as of Feuerbach's, is that man possesses the negative capacity to resist identification with any particular external condition, the capacity Kant and Hegel use to define man's humanity and special dignity.[91]

Marx's indignation at labour's being reduced to a means of securing the wherewithal to satisfy physical needs registers his residual Kantianism. "Certainly eating, drinking, procreating etc., are also genuinely human functions. But taken abstractly, separated from the sphere of *all other human activity* and turned into sole and exclusive ends, they are animal functions." (Emphasis added.) Consequently, when productive labour "appears to man primarily

[90] K. Marx, *Economic-Philosophic Manuscripts*, in *MEW, Ebde.*, 1:521; *CW*, 3:280.
[91] Ibid., 1:516-17; 3:276.

as a *means* of satisfying a need—the need to maintain physical existence"—then "what is animal becomes human and what is human becomes animal."[92]

Are "eating, drinking, procreating etc. . . . genuinely human functions" in themselves, or only to the extent that they are shaped by "other human activity"? If the former, then however much we narrow our humanity by subordinating other activities to the satisfaction of our physical needs, we certainly do not thereby lose our humanity. If the latter, then it is only a particular capacity manifested in those other activities that renders those "animal" needs human. And, given the way Marx speaks of the "animal" and the "human" here, it is difficult to see what capacity that would be except the ability to abstract from naturally conditioned ends.

In the *Grundrisse* Marx tries to account for the distinctive character of *human* production by referring to the distinctive character of human sociality. Social production among humans differs from social production among gregarious animals—bees, for example— in the kind of sociality that makes their production possible. Borrowing a concept from Aristotle, Marx suggests that "the human being is in the most literal sense a *zoon politikon*."[93]

Unfortunately, Marx never explains the "literal sense" in which man is a political rather than a merely social animal. For Aristotle, it is *logos*—reason, argument, speech—that makes man a political animal. Human communities differ from animal communities, most of which are far better unified than human communities, in that they are founded upon the need to justify actions in speech with reference to some commonly shared standard of judgment.[94] Marx, of course, cannot accept this explanation of man's political nature without himself resorting to the use of mental labour, *logos*, as the defining characteristic of man's humanity. Without such an explanation, however, Marx's description of man as a political animal merely indicates that Marx thinks humanity represents something more than he tells us it represents. It is not surprising, then, that in *Capital* Marx withdraws this characterization of man, af-

[92] Ibid., 1:515-16; 3:275-76.
[93] K. Marx, *Grundrisse*, 84.
[94] See Aristotle, *Politics*, 1253a.

firming only that "man is by nature, if not as Aristotle contends, a political, in any case, a social animal."[95]

In *Capital* Marx implicitly admits the point I am making, but without facing its implications for his understanding of man's humanity. Here he notes that "what distinguishes from the start the worst architect from the best bee" is the mental image of his product that guides his activity.[96] It is man's mind, the negative freedom of his imagination, that distinguishes human from animal production. What makes human labour *human* is the mental freedom that underlies it, not the act of production itself. From this point of view, one must conclude that material production represents only one facet of the "human" activity free mind makes possible.

Marx insists that labour is one of nature's "own forces." In labour, man

> faces nature as one of her own forces. He sets in motion the natural forces of his body, arms and legs, head and hands, in order to appropriate nature's productions in a form useful to his own life. While these movements affect and later alter external nature, they change his own nature at the same time.[97]

This characterization of labour captures the essential ambiguity of Marx's conception of humanity. Human labour is a natural force with which man opposes himself to nature and puts the stamp of his humanity on the materials that come into his hands. It is both entirely natural and opposed to nature as such.

As Alfred Schmidt argues, Marx tries to conceive of nature and humanity as "a differentiated unity."[98] The question is whether he succeeds in doing so. The metaphors with which he describes that unity, I suggest, betray the dualism that still characterizes his perspective on man and society. Marx calls labour the "living ferment" within nature, as if everything else in nature were dead. It is the "form-giving fire," the "organic" force, which the capitalist

---

[95] *Capital, Vol. 1*, 23:346; 358. Nancy Schwartz argues otherwise in "The Distinction between the Private and the Public Life: Marx on the Zoon Politikon," 245-66.

[96] *Capital, Vol. 1*, 23:193; 198.

[97] Ibid., 23:192; 197-98.

[98] A. Schmidt, *The Concept of Nature in Marx*, 45.

mode of production degrades by treating as an "inorganic" force.[99] Man "opposes himself to nature as one of her own forces," Marx says. He characterizes such opposition as "living," "organic" force, in contrast to the other forces of nature. Such a characterization can only be taken metaphorically, since man is hardly the only organic creature in the universe. But the metaphor implies that labour is to nature as life is to inorganic existence, and that human and natural forces belong to separate categories, rather than that labour is one of nature's own forces. Such metaphors betray Marx's lingering Kantianism. The fundamental distinction within the world of experience is, from Marx's perspective, still the dichotomy between the "living" human forces and the dead forces of nature.

If this dichotomy shapes Marx's perspective on the world, why then does he labour so hard to deny it? Why the ridicule of left Hegelians such as Bruno Bauer, who "goes so far as to speak of 'the antitheses in nature and history,' as though these were two separate 'things,' " when Marx, too, analyzes them as two separate things, no matter how much they mutually mediate each other?[100] What compels him to both affirm and deny the humanity/nature dichotomy that underlies his own longing for total revolution?

The most common response to this question is that Marx's assertions of materialist monism arise from his desire to give his arguments a "scientific" claim to our attention that would distinguish them from the overblown humanistic rhetoric of left Hegelian social criticism. As Leszek Kolakowski puts it, "[O]nce he had come to the conclusion that socialism would be achieved not by humanitarian sentiment but by the paroxysm of the class struggle," Marx "avoided any expressions which might . . . imply that the world could be transformed by ideals and emotions which transcended class enmity."[101] Such motives might lead Marx to deny categorically the philosophical foundation of such ideals: the idealist's dichotomy between humanity and nature.

This response goes a long way toward answering my questions. But it is not only Marx's commitment to a scientific approach that forces him to suppress his idealist understanding of man's human-

[99] *Capital, Vol. 1,* 23:200; 206. Idem, *Grundrisse,* 361, 489, 542.
[100] *German Ideology,* 3:43; *CW,* 5:39.
[101] L. Kolakowski, *Main Currents of Marxism,* 1:265.

ity. Marx's *emancipatory project itself* bears the seeds of self-contradiction, apart from any pretensions to scientific objectivity. The
left Hegelian project, the realization of Hegel's philosophic reconciliation of freedom and nature, requires, as we have seen in the
previous chapter, the simultaneous affirmation and denial of the
humanity/nature dichotomy. In the preceding section I suggested
that Marx's theory of proletarian revolution represents an answer
to left Hegelian questions about how to realize philosophy. If that
characterization of Marx's longing for proletarian revolution is correct, then it should not be surprising that Marx too is compelled to
both affirm and deny this dichotomy in order to portray the negation of the capitalist mode of production as the means of gaining
"control and conscious mastery" of our world.

Like most left Hegelians, Marx recognizes that it is Hegel's continuing adherence to an understanding of man's humanity as distinct from nature that leads him to argue that in the finite world of
social action "satisfaction does not get beyond being relative."[102]
Such prospects of merely relative satisfaction compel Marx to deny
Hegel's dichotomy between spirit and nature. By defining man's
humanity in opposition to his nature, Marx complains, Hegel
makes alienation an inescapable consequence of the objectification
of man in the external world.[103] Objectified man represents, for Hegel, humanity as it develops in the realm of the opposing forces of
nature, even if such objectification is the product of physical labour.
We cannot gain the "control and conscious mastery" of the forces
created by our interaction with nature and each other if that interaction takes place in an "alien" environment, an environment indifferent to human purpose. For then, no matter how mediated by
social interaction the forces that control our lives may be, they
would maintain an element of contingency that would resist efforts
to strip "them of their natural character and [subject] them to the
power of the united individuals."[104]

But while Marx must deny the humanity/nature dichotomy to

[102] G. W. F. Hegel, *Aesthetics,* in *Werke,* 13:136; 1:99.
[103] K. Marx, *Economic-Philosophic Manuscripts,* in *MEW, Ebde.,* 574ff.; *CW,*
3:333ff.
[104] *German Ideology,* 3:70; *CW,* 5:81.

maintain the possibility of overcoming dehumanization, he must also make use of that dichotomy to portray the negation of capitalism as the return of the forces that govern society to "control and conscious mastery." If Marx does not affirm such a dichotomy, then what does he mean by the "control and conscious mastery" of the forces created by our mutual interaction? What is "mastering" what? What is the difference between "human powers" that "master" those forces and "objective forces" which master us? Marx complains in *The German Ideology* that "in imagination, individuals seem freer under the dominance of the bourgeoisie than before, because their conditions of life seem accidental." "In reality, of course, they are less free," he argues, "because they are to a greater extent *subsumed by material forces [sachlicher Gewalt]*."[105] (Emphasis added.) Does this statement imply that freedom is measured by the extent to which we eliminate the influence of material forces on our lives? I think so. When we are governed by forces created by our own actions, but which have escaped our control, then we are governed "by material forces." But when we recognize those forces as our own creations, and the material conditions exist for the overthrow of the system of relations those forces have created, those material forces become "human powers" subject to our control.

Marx needs to make a distinction between human powers and material forces. And the basis of that distinction is conscious control—subjection of material constraints to human purposes. If Marx does not make such a distinction, then what could possibly be gained from the recognition that the material forces that govern our lives are our own creation, other than the none-too-comforting discovery that the particular external constraints that burden us will pass—into another set of constraints? The mere knowledge that the forces governing social life are mediated by our actions does not necessarily grant us control over them.[106] For that matter, purely

[105] Ibid., 3:76; 5:78-79.
[106] J. Elster, *Making Sense of Marx*, 100-101. Elster also discusses passages in which Marx seems to recognize this point, but he concludes that Marx most often jumps from evidence that social forces are not purely natural to the conclusion that human beings can control them.

natural forces are sometimes far easier to control than those created by the social interaction of human beings, since cause and effect are often easier to identify in natural phenomena. To describe communism in the way he does, Marx must assume the existence of two kinds of forces in the world: the forces of nature, forces characterized by their indifference to human purpose and the forces created by the interaction of human beings with nature and each other, forces characterized by purposiveness and the susceptibility to conscious direction.

Marx's need to both deny and affirm the idealist's dichotomy between "human" powers—that is, freedom—and material forces is made manifest by his attempts, in *The German Ideology*, to argue that the "common interest does not exist merely in the imagination, as a 'universal,' but first of all in reality, as the mutual dependence of the individuals among whom labour is divided."[107] To portray our dependence as our common interest actualized, Marx must first deny the freedom/nature dichotomy. In particular, he must deny that individuals can arrive at an understanding of their common interest by abstracting from their naturally conditioned individual interests. According to Marx, by abstracting from individual interests, we establish a merely "illusory community." "Particular interests, which *actually* constantly run counter to the common and illusory common interests, necessitate *practical* intervention and restraint by the illusory 'general' interest in the form of the state." But, as we have seen already, such formulations of common against particular interests by the state represent the universalization of class interests, the celebration of the liberation of a class from its particular constraints as the liberation of humanity from external constraints.[108] If our humanity were defined in contrast to our naturally conditioned interests, then mutual dependence would be what Rousseau portrayed it to be: the means of our ever-deepening enslavement.

In addition, Marx must deny the idealist's dichotomy in order to portray the forces created by our mutual interaction as the only

[107] *German Ideology*, 3:33; CW, 5:46.
[108] Ibid., 3:34; 5:47.

forces that govern social life. "The social structure and the state are continually emerging from the life-process of definite individuals, . . . i.e., as they act, produce materially, and hence as they work under definite material limits, presuppositions and conditions independent of their will." Individuals interact with each other in such a way as to expand their ability to produce the means of satisfying their natural needs. The way they interact socially to produce these means has unintended consequences: it creates new forces that shape their lives. The "opposite assumption," Marx suggests in a passage that originally followed this depiction of the essence of historical materialism, "is only possible if in addition to the spirit of the real, materially evolved individuals another distinct spirit is presupposed." If such a "spirit is presupposed," then Marx could no longer argue that "what they [individuals] are coincides with their production, both with *what* they produce and *how* they produce."[109] Not only their real interests but also the real forces that shape their lives might then conflict with the forces created by our mutual dependence in social production.

On the other hand, Marx must affirm something like the Kantian-Hegelian dichotomy between human universality and naturally conditioned particularity in order to portray our mutual dependence as our *common* interest actualized. For Marx means to discover a genuinely common interest in our mutual dependence, not just the recognition that we share an interest in maintaining the means by which we satisfy our individual interests. He portrays these forces of interdependence not just as contingent forces created by our interaction with the forces of nature and each other, but as "man's own deed," the realization of all individuals' "own united power."

There would be nothing contradictory in Marx's description of these forces as "man's own deed," if all he meant by that characterization is that these forces arise out of the interaction of individuals with the forces of nature. One could argue that we constantly mistake constraints created by such interaction as purely natural forces. Indeed, one might go so far as to argue that we experience

109 Ibid., 3:25-26, 26n, 21; 5:35-36, 36n, 31-32.

the constraints of natural forces *only* as mediated by the forms created by such interaction.

But Marx wants to say more than this.

> The *social power,* i.e., the *multiplied productive force,* which arises through the co-operation of different individuals conditioned by the division of labour, appears to these individuals, since their co-operation is not *voluntary* but has developed *naturally,* not as their own united power, but as an alien force existing outside them, a force of whose origin and goal they are ignorant, which they are no longer able to govern, which on the contrary passes through a peculiar series of phases and stages independent of the wishes and actions of man, nay even directing these wishes and actions.[110]

Marx portrays the "multiplied productive force," the forces of production created by the interaction of individuals with nature and each other, as a singular, integrated "social power." His theoretical efforts here, and throughout the rest of his career, concentrate on explaining why these forces appear otherwise to us. But to the more fundamental question, *why* these forces represent a "social power," a single, controllable force that can, at least in principle, be used by individuals to serve their common interests, Marx has no answer. Why should the forces created by our social interaction with nature represent anything more than aimless forces that sometimes support and other times collide with the purposes of individuals, and with each other? His only explicit answer to this question, at least after 1844, is his repeated arguments that these forces are "creations of hitherto existing men" rather than natural forces.

But Marx's insistence on the historical character of social and economic constraints does not answer this question. Marx only demonstrates that no *particular* configuration of aimless forces need constitute our "multiplied productive force." He does not demonstrate that our productive powers represent anything more than the changing configurations of forces that follow from the unintended consequences of individual actions.

[110] Ibid., 3:48; 5:48.

In offering these arguments as answers to the question I have posed, Marx assumes that historically changing forces of production represent potentially controllable "social powers." Such an assumption rests on an unstated premiss implicit in his arguments: forces created by the social interaction of individuals and natural forces are not contingent and aimless, like natural forces. Demystifying them strips them of their pseudonatural character and "subjects them to the power of the united individuals."[111] In other words, for Marx, there are two kinds of forces in this world: the aimless forces of nature and the purposeful forces that man introduces into the world through his interaction with nature. The history of human development is the process by which the former are subordinated to the latter. It is the process by which something nature lacks comes to dominate nature's forces. In short, it is the process by which man's humanity comes to realize itself in the world. Marx's claim that communism brings us the "control and conscious mastery" of the forces that govern social interaction thus rests on the idealist assumption of a dichotomy between aimless, contingent natural forces and free, purposive human forces, an assumption he explicitly subjects to ridicule.

Marx could avoid contradicting himself in this way by falling back on one of the two positions discussed at the end of Chapter 5. He could, on the one hand, portray nature's forces as, in themselves, directed toward the satisfaction of human ends. According to this position, communism's overcoming of opposition to human purpose would represent nature's own self-realization, rather than man's imposition on its aimless forces. By taking this position, Marx could relieve himself of the need to affirm the idealist's dichotomy between freedom and nature. On the other hand, he could assume that man is possessed of sufficient power to wrest control of his life from the "material forces" of nature. According to this second position, communism would represent the "humanization" of the natural world and the elimination of natural necessities. This position could relieve Marx of his need to deny the dichotomy between humanity and nature.

[111] Ibid., 3:70; 5:81.

Although Marx toys with both positions during his career,[112] he ultimately rejects them both because of the absurdly unrealistic assumptions on which they rest. Marx himself realizes that the former position requires a teleology far more anthropocentric than any mediaeval, let alone Greek, philosopher would have dared to suggest, while the latter position demands an idealism that would make even Fichte and Hegel blush. But without the support of one of these positions, Marx is compelled to say yes and no to idealism.

Even the most fundamental doctrine of historical materialism, that every sphere of social life and action is shaped by the mode of production, requires this self-contradictory reaction to the dichotomies of idealism. To justify explaining all social phenomena in terms of the mode of production, one must treat society as a "totality," as a coherent, integrated whole informed by a particular character. Lukács rightly insists that Marx treats social production in this way.[113] In the *Grundrisse*, Marx not only describes each mode of production as a "totality," "an organic system" whose development "consists precisely in subordinating all elements of society to itself";[114] he also makes use of almost all of the conceptual categories Hegel devised to analyze totalities. He analyzes production, distribution, and consumption as "distinctions within a unity." He uses Hegel's logic of essence to analyze the contradiction between exchange-value and use-value. And in trying to conceptualize the totality of capitalist social production, he even makes use of Hegel's concepts of "good" and "bad" infinity.[115]

However, like Lukács and his many followers, Marx never addresses the question of how one can justify treating production as a coherent, let alone purposive, totality. He justifies his approach

---

[112] For the former, see A. Schmidt, *The Concept of Nature in Marx*, 76-78; for the latter, see especially K. Marx, "Private Property and Communism," in the *Economic-Philosophic Manuscripts*. As I have already noted, the famous passage in the third volume of *Capital* about the persistence of the realm of necessity under communism indicates Marx's final rejection of the latter position (*Capital, Vol. 3*, 25:828; 819-20).

[113] G. Lukács, "What is Orthodox Marxism?" in Lukács, *History and Class Consciousness*, 1-26.

[114] K. Marx, *Grundrisse*, 278.

[115] Ibid., 99, 100-102, 137-40, 197.

merely by contrasting the greater realism of situating the source of society's coherence and integration in the mode of production with situating it in some supranatural *Volksgeist*, as Hegel does. That society represents such a totality he takes for granted or, to be more precise, he learns from Hegel. His concern is to "realize" Hegel's concept of social totality.

But Hegel's treatment of society as a totality rests on idealistic premises that Marx must reject. Hegel argues that we can treat historical epochs as coherent wholes because the mind can comprehend only what is rational, coherent, and purposive in history. When we look at the world rationally, that is, with a mind shaped by the historically developed categories that we use to look at the world, the world looks rationally back at us. The phenomena we see fit into those categories that we use to guide our vision. When we look at the world without such categories, all we get is a blank stare. The mind can know only what corresponds to itself in the world. It cannot integrate unmediated contingencies into its understanding. The sheer "being" of things apart from their mediation by the mind's concepts remains opaque to the human mind. The mind's knowledge of social totality is a form of self-knowledge. Society is thus *conceived* by Hegel as a totality. Whether it *is* a totality apart from the categories in which we conceive it is not a meaningful question for Hegel.[116]

Gerald Cohen rightly emphasizes, in his defence of historical materialism, that Hegel's view can only produce a "reading" of history, not a "theory" of historical development.[117] But a "reading" of history is all Hegel thinks we can have. Hegel believes he can show that, *for the mind*, history is a process of the realization of freedom through a series of social totalities, and that such is historical reality as we can know it.

Marx, of course, is not content with mere *readings* of history. "Marxism requires not only the perception of society as totality, it also assumes that society is totality."[118] It is not enough for him to

---

[116] See K. Hartmann, *Die Marxsche Theorie*, 21ff.

[117] G. Cohen, *Marx's Theory of History: A Defence*, 27.

[118] M. Theunissen, *Hegels Lehre vom Absolute Geist als Theologisch-Politischer Traktat*, 5.

show that we must and do *conceive* of society as a totality; society must *be* a totality. If Marx cannot demonstrate this, his whole argument about the advantages to be gained by the negation of the capitalist mode of production collapses. For his arguments locate in the fundamental relations of production under capitalism the source of *all* social conditions that make man a "debased, enslaved, neglected and contemptible being."

What grounds does Marx have for arguing that societies are totalities? Is nature so ordered that human beings organize themselves into historical epochs, each with its own set of all-encompassing laws? Or are human beings so powerful that their interactions not only mediate but actually overcome the direction of natural forces such that the only real forces that govern our lives are those created by the configuration of social forces in different historical epochs? Marx rejects both of these possible grounds. But he offers no other in their place. Instead, he takes for granted that Hegel successfully demonstrates that societies represent totalities.

But Hegel's characterization of societies as totalities rests on unashamedly idealistic premises. As Michael Theunissen points out, "Hegel, though he wanted to conceive of society as a totality, never argued that totality is social," as Marx does; "society can only be conceived of as a totality if he does not conceive of totality as social."[119] Only if there is something human beyond social reality, that is, only if the totality of things includes something like the idealist dichotomy between mind and reality, is it legitimate to conceive of society as a totality. Marx's conception of society as a totality rests, then, on an idealist premiss that he must immediately deny in order to argue that his conception corresponds to the way things are, that social reality so conceived *is* the totality of human life. Once again, we see Marx simultaneously affirming and denying idealist dichotomies.

If such a simultaneous affirmation and denial of the humanity/nature dichotomy is a necessary foundation of Marx's characterization of socialism, then it is not surprising to discover that it was Feuerbach's anthropology that originally provided Marx with a

[119] Ibid., 5. See also K. Hartmann, *Die Marxsche Theorie*, 21ff.

MARX AND SOCIAL REVOLUTION

"philosophic basis for socialism." For, as we have seen in the preceding chapter, Feuerbach's philosophy of man concealed such a self-contradictory position in the guise of his demand that philosophy "return to nature."

In the early fall of 1843 Marx is still hesitant to advocate socialism as the form that a fully human community would take. In September of that year he describes communism as a "dogmatic abstraction," merely "a special expression of the principle of humanism, which is still infected by its opposite, the private system." Communism expresses only half the truth. "The whole socialist principle in its turn is only one aspect that concerns the *reality* of the true human being. But we have to pay just as much attention to the other aspect, to the theoretical existence of man."[120] The material reality introduced by socialism does not represent man's full humanity. There must be something more.

But only one month later, Marx writes to Feuerbach that in his "Principles of the Philosophy of the Future,"

> you have provided—I don't know whether intentionally—a philosophic basis for socialism. The unity of man and man, which is based on the real difference between men, the concept of the human species brought down from the heaven of abstraction to the real earth, what is that but the concept of socialism?[121]

It is Feuerbach's philosophy of man, not some socioeconomic or historical analysis of the social relations of production, that eliminates Marx's objections to socialism. For Feuerbach's characterization of man's humanity as his "species-being" brings the concept of humanity "down from the heaven of abstraction to the real earth." One need no longer consider the satisfaction of man's material interests in socialism as a one-sided "special expression of the principle of humanism," since Feuerbach's conception of humanity shows that the sensuous manifestation of man's humanity *is* his humanity. Humanity is man's species-being, his development within sensuous constraints rather than against them.

[120] "Letters from the *Deutsch-Französisches Jahrbuch*," 1:344; CW, 3:142-43.
[121] K. Marx, Letter to Feuerbach, October 3, 1843, in CW, 3:354.

From this discovery of "a philosophic basis for socialism" there follow the excited declarations of an identity between communism, humanism, and naturalism that Marx makes in the *Economic-Philosophic Manuscripts* and other writings of the period. "Communism, as fully-developed naturalism, equals humanism, and as fully-developed humanism equals naturalism." "Society is the complete unity of man with nature—the true resurrection of nature—the accomplished naturalism of man and the accomplished humanism of nature." "*Human nature* is the *true community* of men."[122]

Marx's excitement about these identities stems from his discovery that, with Feuerbach's conception of species-being, the realization of man's humanity in the world need not be portrayed as man's escape from and subjugation of nature's forces. Rather it can be portrayed as an accomplishment of nature itself. The fully human community can now be portrayed as the development of man's nature, "the accomplished naturalism of man and the accomplished humanism of nature." This discovery allows Marx to view social production, the pursuit of the means of satisfying naturally conditioned needs, as the realization of "human" powers rather than the development of further constraints on man's humanity. Moreover, it allows him to identify the obstacles to the full development of man's productive powers as the obstacle to the realization of his humanity.

Feuerbach is able to make this conceptual breakthrough only because he writes into his concept of nature the idealist's dichotomy between humanity/freedom and natural necessity. "Nature is *being not distinguished* from existence; man is *being* that *distinguishes* itself from existence."[123] Through man nature overcomes itself.

Marx soon abandons the concept of species-being as too unhistorical a conception of man's humanity. "In reality" the "human essence . . . is the ensemble of its social relations." He complains

---

[122] K. Marx, *Economic-Philosophic Manuscripts*, in *MEW, Ebde.*, 1:529, 531; *CW*, 3:296, 298. "Critical Notes on the Article: 'The King of Prussia and Social Reform,' " 1:408; *CW*, 3:204.

[123] L. Feuerbach, "Preliminary Theses," in *The Fiery Brook*, 169.

that Feuerbach locates "the human essence" in a natural quality in each individual. Feuerbach's conception of humanity thus "assumes an abstraction: the *isolated* human individual." That abstraction, Marx argues, is a reflection of the social basis of the "old materialism" that Feuerbach advocates: the socially imposed atomism of capitalist " 'civil' society." "The standpoint of the new materialism" that Marx advocates "is human society, or social humanity."[124]

Marx is wise to abandon the concept of species-being. But I do not see how he can support his new standpoint, "socialized humanity," without something like it, that is, without a concept of man's humanity that simultaneously affirms and denies the Kantian-Hegelian dichotomy between human and natural forces. For without such a concept, he cannot portray the productive forces created by social intercourse as "man's own deed," as the "social power" of a "socialized [that is, realized] humanity." The bridge that allows Marx to cross over to socialism is shaky. But though he burns it behind him, Marx never builds a stronger one to take its place.

Instead, Marx devotes almost all of his theoretical energy in the years following his rejection of Feuerbachian anthropology to demonstrating that the capitalist mode of production represents the obstacle to overcoming the dehumanizing spirit of modern society. "When things are seen in this way, as they really are and happened, every profound philosophical problem is resolved . . . into an empirical fact. For instance, the important question of the relation of man to nature."[125] In particular, the discovery of the true obstacle to satisfaction with our social world resolves the "unresolved antinomies" between spirit and matter, thought and reality, freedom and nature, bequeathed by idealist philosophy to later generations.[126]

In this section I have tried to show that historical materialism does not resolve "every profound philosophical problem," least of all the "question of the relation of man to nature." What Marx provides is a new and immensely fruitful approach to identifying and explaining some of the forces that impede the satisfaction of our

[124] "Theses on Feuerbach," 3:6-7; *CW*, 5:4-5.
[125] *German Ideology*, 3:43; *CW*, 5:39.
[126] G. Lukács, *History and Class Consciousness*, 148.

needs. His claim, however, that the negation of the obstacles to human satisfaction so identified would yield man "control and conscious mastery" of the forces that shape human life rests on self-contradictory assumptions. If Hegel asks us, in the name of philosophic consistency, to deny common sense and look for satisfaction in the realm of "Absolute Spirit," then Marx asks us, in the name of the satisfaction of human needs, to stifle our demands for consistency.

In one of the major theses of his doctoral dissertation, Marx defends Epicurus as a more praiseworthy thinker than Democritus precisely because he subordinated logical consistency to the satisfaction of human needs. Democritus, Marx admits, was the greater philosopher. He had a "lust for knowledge" that led him to travel throughout the world seeking wisdom from all peoples and places. Epicurus, on the other hand, was a dogmatist who stayed in his Athenian garden, learned only from himself, and wanted to know only as much as was needed to maintain his peace of mind. He taught absolute trust in sense data, even when that trust led to absurd conclusions, such as that the sun is really no more than a few feet in diameter.[127] Epicurus reaps Marx's praise for putting human needs above the search for truth. Despite their contradictions, Marx insists that his ideas deserve to be respected as plausible or possible accounts of the world, since they are designed to satisfy our need for independence and peace of mind.

Marx's subordination of theory to practical needs displays a striking affinity to the behaviour he praised in Epicurus. Many have admired Marx for his willingness to subordinate the needs of theory to the needs of practise. But such willingness to avoid considering the implications of conceptual contradictions no more makes the external world amenable to our "control and conscious mastery" than Epicurus's willingness to believe that the sun is only a few feet wide reduces its size.

That Marx's vision of communism, like other left Hegelian visions of a truly human praxis, turns out to be an abstraction from

[127] K. Marx, *The Difference between the Democritean and Epicurean Philosophy of Nature*, in *MEW, Ebde.*, 1:273ff., 277, 282-83, 304-5; *CW*, 1:41ff., 45, 50-51, 72-73.

an abstraction proves nothing in itself about the effectiveness of communist institutions as means of organizing ourselves to deal with the impact on our lives of forces beyond our control. But it does rule out communism as *Marx* understands it as a viable end of human striving.

E I G H T

NIETZSCHE AND CULTURAL
REVOLUTION

PHILOSOPHIC criticism teaches us "the categorical imperative to overthrow all conditions in which man is a debased, enslaved, abandoned and contemptible being."[1] These words are Marx's, but they may as well have been Nietzsche's. They express the guiding aim, or, one might say, the only aim of his intellectual career. Every conceptual innovation, every bold critique that Nietzsche undertakes grows out of his longing to overthrow the conditions that degrade man. All of the different streams of his thought flow toward this goal.[2] Nietzsche's imperative, like Kant's, admits of no limiting conditions or prudential calculations. *All* conditions that make man a contemptible being must be overthrown. All comforting illusions that hinder the development of human greatness must be swept away, no matter how necessary to the peace of society or to the individual's peace of mind. Whatever conditions are necessary to produce greatness—slavery, world war, cruelty to oneself and to others, willed self-contradiction to the point of risking one's sanity—we must not merely tolerate but welcome. We must *dare* to accept what others found contradictory or distasteful, dare to do all that is necessary to bring man to his greatest depth and true dignity. That is the challenge with which Nietzsche attempts to rouse us to battle.

Such a characterization of Nietzsche's discontent contradicts many of Nietzsche's own descriptions of his aims. Nietzsche, after

[1] K. Marx, "Introduction," 1:385; *CW*, 3:182.
[2] For a similar opinion about the coherence of Nietzsche's work, see R. Schacht, *Nietzsche*, 267.

all, ridicules the "improvers of mankind" who seek to heighten man. "The last thing I should promise would be to 'improve' mankind. No new idols are erected by me; may the old ones learn what feet of clay mean."[3] Nietzsche associates the improvement of man, indeed, the very concept of "humanity," with the moral idealism of Kant and Hegel, a philosophic tradition for which he expresses even less respect than Marx does.[4] Thus it is not surprising to find him celebrated today as the great emancipator of modern philosophy from the Kantian and post-Kantian concern with human dignity and worldly dehumanization. For example, in his very influential study of Nietzsche's philosophy, Gilles Deleuze insists that Nietzsche's project "runs counter not only to Kantianism, but to the whole Kantian inheritance." Nietzsche is not, as Deleuze recognizes, the first German philosopher to attempt to break the spell of the Kantian philosophy of freedom. But he is the one who finally gets the job done.[5]

That Nietzsche tries to break with the premises of the Kantian philosophy of freedom is undeniable; whether he succeeds is another question. I shall argue here that in his social criticism he fails to overcome these premises, and that his explicit rejection of them only leads him into self-contradiction. In particular, I shall suggest that Nietzsche shares the longing for the realization of man's humanity that the Kantian philosophy of freedom made possible, and, as a result, that the conceptual innovations examined in this book provide us with a context that best makes sense of the most striking elements of his social discontent.

I shall thus treat Nietzsche's revolt against the spirit of modern

[3] F. Nietzsche, *Twilight of the Idols*, in *Sämtlichte Werke* (hereafter *SW*), 6:98-102; this is translated in *The Viking Portable Nietzsche*, 501-505. Idem, *Ecce Homo*, in *SW*, 6:258; 218. Hereafter, except where otherwise noted, citations of works by Nietzsche will include only the title of the work and the appropriate volume and page number(s) of *SW*. (In this chapter, as in previous chapters, a reference to the English translation follows a semicolon after the reference to the work in the original language.)

[4] He also associates the concept of humanity with humanitarianism and with what he calls the Rousseauian "religion of pity." See *The Gay Science*, 3:630; 339, in which he exclaims, "Humanity! Has there ever been a more hideous old woman among old women—unless it were truth?"

[5] G. Deleuze, *Nietzsche and Philosophy*, 88-89.

culture as a continuation of Rousseau's, Schiller's, and the young Hegel's earlier revolts. This is, of course, not the only interesting story to be told about Nietzsche's dissatisfaction with modern individuals and institutions. As long as we have an interest in breaking with religious, moral, and philosophical legacies, Nietzsche's claims to novelty will interest us. His insight and renown will lend support to attempts to break with older forms of discourse. Nietzsche's innovations represent something more than new answers to older questions; but they represent that as well. By treating Nietzsche as another defender of man against the dehumanizing spirit of modern society, I do not mean to provide a comprehensive description or evaluation of his work. I merely choose to focus on one element of his social criticism, an element that is frequently ignored because of Nietzsche's often exaggerated claims to novelty. When we bring that element into focus, some of the ambiguities and tensions in Nietzsche's social thought become easier to understand. In particular, I shall suggest that his continuing need to overcome the dehumanizing spirit of modern society leads Nietzsche, like Marx before him, to deny the Kantian conceptual roots of his social discontent even while his arguments implicitly confirm Kantian dichotomies.

If asked why he took all of the intellectual self-doubt and anguish of modern man onto his own shoulders, Nietzsche probably would have answered, like his alter ego Zarathustra, I have "gone under" because "I love man." Perhaps he loves man infinitely more than man deserves. Nietzsche often entertains that doubt. But that doubt cannot shake his love of man or his vigilance for man's future.

> For this is how things stand: the dimunition and equalization of European man hides *our* greatest danger, for the sight of him makes us weary. . . . Precisely here lies Europe's doom— along with our fear of man we have also lost our love of him, our reverence for him, our hopes for him, even the will to him. The sight of man now makes us weary—what is nihilism today, if not that?—We are weary of *man*.[6]

[6] *On the Genealogy of Morals*, 5:278; 44.

Despite endless talk of humanism and idealism, despite the cen-
turies-old attack on religion's dimunition of human capacities,
Nietzsche fears we do not really value man. We have lost the
ground for our special valuation of man, along with the supersen-
sible world of religion and philosophy that our critical sense compels us to abandon. This is the problem of modern nihilism. "The
highest values devalue themselves."[7] The love of truth engendered
by the ideal of an eternal and consistent world has compelled us to
abandon that very ideal as untrue. But with that ideal goes our justification for believing that man is something especially worthy of
our love.

Our problem, then, goes far beyond mere cultural decadence, according to Nietzsche. The "last man," whom Nietzsche fears, has
lost not only Europe's old aristocratic culture but also his very *humanity*. It is the dehumanization of man that Nietzsche fears.
Moreover, because he too treats historical epochs as coherent
wholes integrated by a single spirit of social interaction, it is the dehumanizing spirit of modern culture with which he sets out to do
battle.

To render such an interpretation of Nietzsche's social discontent
plausible I must show (1) that Nietzsche does indeed rely on the
conceptual innovations I have described as the philosophic sources
of the longing for total revolution and (2) that these conceptual innovations shape his social discontent by leading him to define the
obstacles to satisfaction with society in the way I have just described.

I shall rely heavily on Nietzsche's early essays to substantiate
these claims[8]—too heavily, I suspect, for many of Nietzsche's interpreters, who tend to accept his claim that the innovations introduced in *Thus Spoke Zarathustra* and later works represent an entirely new starting point in his own philosophy. But as Allen Megill
has noted, "[I]mportant aspects of his 'mature' position are already
in place in the early writings. And the historical roots of that position are much more clearly visible in the early than in the later

[7] F. Nietzsche, *The Will to Power*, 9.
[8] I refer here to the works Nietzsche published from 1870 to 1876, especially *The Birth of Tragedy* and the four *Untimely Meditations*.

writings."[9] I focus so heavily on his early works because there is a greater continuity between Nietzsche's concerns at the beginning and end of his career than is usually recognized and because Nietzsche is more willing to acknowledge his intellectual debts in his first essays. In the second half of this chapter I argue that the conceptual innovations of his later works represent, in part, new solutions to the problems raised by his earlier critique of modern culture, rather than the discovery of an entirely new set of questions. And, as I did with Marx, I shall try to show that the new answers Nietzsche develops require him to deny the conceptual premises that led him to ask the questions in the first place—premises most evident in his earlier works, but which persist in the later ones.

Human Dignity and the "Bildungsphilister"

Nietzsche's revolt against the spirit of modern individuals and institutions begins with his unmasking of the German intellectual's pretence of culture. As the young Marx rages at the Hegelian *Burgerphilister*, the young Nietzsche rages at the Hegelian *"Bildungsphilister."* Both see in Hegelian ideas a source and justification of philistine self-satisfaction. "Hegel's disciples," Nietzsche later complains, "are the real educators of Germany."[10] But despite their great erudition, they remain cultural philistines in his eyes.

It is not unfair to suggest that Hegel's resignation to the lack of artistic and human greatness in the modern world becomes, for some of his followers, a self-satisfied feeling of superiority. This is especially true of D. F. Strauss, Nietzsche's model for the portrait of the *Bildungsphilister* in the first of his *Untimely Meditations*. Strauss's demythologizing *Life of Jesus*, published in 1835, was the opening salvo of the left Hegelian critique of Christianity. At that time, his freethinking inspired controversy in the universities and enthusiasm among the more rebellious of Hegel's disciples. By

[9] A. Megill, *Prophets of Extremism: Nietzsche, Heidegger, Foucault, Derrida*, 35. Tracy Strong also notes the relevance of these early essays to explanations of some of Nietzsche's most striking later innovations (T. Strong, *Nietzsche and the Politics of Transfiguration*, 236-37).
[10] *Human-all-too-Human*, 2:623-24.

1871, however, when Strauss published his life's testament, *The Old Faith and the New*, his freethinking was somewhat stale and conventional. It still inspired enthusiasm—the book was reprinted again and again—but now among the broad middle class of intellectuals rather than the rebellious fringe. It outraged only orthodox and dogmatic clerics.

The new faith with which Strauss proposes to sustain life is an amalgam of deference to the authority of natural science, reverence for the cosmos, Darwinian theory, and the Hegelian philosophy of freedom. The heaven of the new faith is in this world. It lies in our enjoyment of the great peaks of culture. For example, Strauss calls the Goethe-Schiller correspondence one of the "sacred relics" of the new faith. He can think of no greater bliss than a dream concert in which Haydn is served as "soup," Mozart as the main course, and Beethoven as "dessert." We are extremely lucky, he argues, in that we can appreciate all of the peaks of culture, no matter how much their styles clash with each other. Geniuses like Schiller do not share our good fortune. They cannot, for example, enjoy both the earnestness of Gluck and the rustic humour of Haydn.[11]

After reading Strauss's testament, one finds it difficult to avoid sharing Nietzsche's disgust. The man was certainly a cultural philistine in some very important sense. Strauss's love of culture is well informed, but it appears ridiculous, even disrespectful. It seems, in his presentation, as if the greatest achievements of art and culture have been brought forth merely to titillate a self-professed voyeur. As Nietzsche puts it, "[T]he Straussian philistine lodges himself in the work of our great poets and musicians like a worm that lives on what it destroys, marvels at what it devours, and offers itself to what it digests."[12]

But why does this *Bildungsphilister* haunt Nietzsche so? Why does Nietzsche not just laugh and forget him? Certainly, the popularity of Strauss's work must have been annoying. But Nietzsche

[11] D. F. Strauss, *The Old Faith and the New: A Confession*, 375-76, 408. Nietzsche retorts that "his Haydn soup and Beethoven dessert are not our Haydn and Beethoven" (*David Strauss: The Confessor and the Writer*, 1:185; this is translated by R. J. Hollingdale in *Untimely Meditations*, 22).
[12] *David Strauss*, 1:188; *Untimely Meditations*, 25.

always professes disdain for the opinion of the many, especially the cultured many. His audience, he insists over and over again, is the few. Why not ignore the popular philistines of the day?

The answer, I suggest, is that Nietzsche loves man—not the few great individuals alone but, despite his overheated aristocratic rhetoric, man in general. The most "characteristic threat to culture in our times" is, he argues, the "hardening" of the soul produced by the vulgarity and mediocrity that surrounds us. "Talent without that longing" to be surrounded by truly cultured men stifles the growth of real culture.[13] We must not lose faith in the potential of our contemporaries.

In his polemic against Strauss Nietzsche suggests that F. T. Vischer, Strauss's friend and another prominent Hegelian, reveals the *Bildungsphilister's* deepest secret when he says of Hölderlin: " 'His spirit had too little hardness. He lacked the crucial weapon of humour; he could not admit that one is not necessarily a barbarian if one is a philistine.' " Nietzsche explodes at Vischer's suggestion that one can be a philistine and still be a man of culture.[14] A man of culture is, for him, a completed whole, someone worthy of the respect due to a truly human being. The philistine is contemptible. How can one be both? This problem weighs on Nietzsche's mind as it did on Hölderlin's. We ordinarily contrast the cultural philistine with the connoisseur. But in Strauss and his kind we recognize connoisseurs who remain, nevertheless, philistines. For all their knowledge of culture, they never possess any culture. A connoisseur without taste, without a single unified style, Nietzsche insists, is not a man of culture. For "culture is above all the unity of artistic style in all the manifestations of the life of a people."[15]

It is not difficult to recognize a philistine, even when he possesses *Bildung*. We sense one immediately in Strauss. The question is how to react to such a figure. Vischer cautions us that the philistine is not necessarily a barbarian; lack of humanity is not his crime. Nietzsche insists that he is a barbarian, and in doing so he insists

---

[13] *Schopenhauer as Educator*, 1:357; this is translated by R. J. Hollingdale in *Untimely Meditations*, 142.

[14] *David Strauss*, 1:172; *Untimely Meditations*, 13.

[15] Ibid., 1:163; 5.

that we redefine our notion of barbarism. Barbarism is not the opposite of civilization, of knowledge of the arts and sciences, as is commonly supposed. Barbarism is the opposite of culture. The philistine is a barbarian, no matter how refined his knowledge of civilization may be. Nietzsche revives the critique of the arts and sciences we have seen in Rousseau and Schiller, but he replaces their moral critique of the value of the arts and sciences with an aesthetic critique. Knowledge of the arts and sciences must be limited because it destroys cultural, rather than moral, greatness.

Nevertheless, I suggest that Nietzsche's critique of unlimited cultural knowledge issues from the same general source as Rousseau's and Schiller's: fear of the diminution of man. "[T]he goal of culture is to promote the emergence of truly *human beings,* and nothing else."[16] Rousseau, as we have seen, insists that "all institutions which put man into contradiction with himself are worthless." Since modern institutions produce the "bourgeois, a nothing," they are worthless and deserve to be overthrown. Nietzsche's reasoning follows similar lines. Modern culture produces the *Bildungsphilister* as its crowning achievement. Such a figure is less than human, and thus the institutions that produce him deserve to be destroyed. Nietzsche's redefinition of barbarism puts man's humanity at stake in the striving for culture. The fighter for culture is a fighter for truly human beings. He fights against the dehumanization imposed by the spirit of modern culture. Nietzsche's indignation at the existence of the *Bildungsphilister* expresses something more than an aesthete's longing for great art and cultural genius. It expresses a longing to overcome what appears to be the pervasive dehumanization of man.

This interpretation of Nietzsche's early cultural critique suggests not only that Nietzsche has a concept of human dignity, a concept that allows him to distinguish a truly human from a dehumanized existence, but also that his concept of humanity is defined, like Rousseau's and Kant's, in contrast to a concept of nature. Nietzsche explicitly denies both suggestions in his early writings. His rejection of the concept of human dignity and of humanity/nature di-

---

[16] *Schopenhauer as Educator,* 1:387; *Untimely Meditations,* 164.

chotomies can best be seen in his early essays on "The Greek State" and "Homer's Contest." "The Greeks," he writes there, "did not need such conceptual hallucinations" as "human dignity" to develop their culture. Illusions like human dignity arise out of our unwillingness to face nature as it is.

> When we speak of *humanity*, the idea is based on what separates and distinguishes man from nature. But there is in reality no such separation: the so-called "natural" qualities and truly "human" qualities grow together inseparably. Man, in his highest and noblest powers, is fully natural and bears his uncanny double character in himself.[17]

But Nietzsche's language in his early cultural criticism raises doubts about his rejection of humanity/nature dichotomies. As we have seen already, he understands the "goal of culture" to be "the emergence of truly *human* beings," the renewal and continuation "of the human as such."[18] Moreover, he repeatedly contrasts such a "truly human" existence with the existence of animals and non-human nature. In *Schopenhauer as Educator*, for example, Nietzsche suggests that with truly human beings "nature, which never leaps, takes her only leap." The knowledge gained by such beings "transfigures nature." Their activity brings about "the redemption of nature from the curse of the life of the animal."[19] "All nature presses toward man, . . . who is nature's sole concern."

> Yet let us reflect: where does the animal cease, where does man begin? . . . As long as anyone desires life as he desires happiness he has not yet raised his eyes above the animal's horizon, for he only wants more consciously what the animal seeks through blind impulse. But that's how it is for us throughout the greater part of our lives: we rarely emerge out of animal-

[17] SW, 1:764-65, 783. For direct denials of the humanity/nature dichotomy in the works of Nietzsche's middle period, see especially *The Dawn*, 3:41, and *The Gay Science*, 1:474; 174.
[18] *Schopenhauer as Educator*, 1:387; *Untimely Meditations*, 164. *Richard Wagner in Bayreuth*, 1:453; this is translated by R. J. Hollingdale in *Untimely Meditations*, 213.
[19] *Schopenhauer as Educator*, 1:380, 378; *Untimely Meditations*, 159, 157.

ity, we ourselves are animals who seem to suffer senselessly. But there are moments *when we realize this*: then the clouds are rent asunder, and we see that, together with all nature, we are pressing towards man as towards something that stands high above us. . . . Yet we do not achieve even this momentary emergence and awakening through our own power; we must be raised to it—and who are they who raise us? They are those true *men, those who are no longer animal, the philosophers, artists, and saints*; nature, which never leaps, takes her only leap with their appearance.[20] (Nietzsche's emphasis.)

In creating the men who raise us above the power of blind impulse that keeps us in an animal condition, nature leaps above herself. Our humanity is defined in them in opposition to the ordinary forces and impulses of nature. Nietzsche insists that the leap nature takes in creating truly human individuals is toward its own perfection; in redeeming man "from the curse of the life of the animal," nature is redeeming itself. But the dichotomies Nietzsche draws between human and animal being, conscious self-overcoming and blind impulse, the willing of meaning and senseless suffering all suggest the persistence of a dichotomy between human freedom and natural necessity as the basis of his distinction between man and animal.

Schopenhauer provided Nietzsche with a philosophic perspective that sought to erase the dichotomy between human and natural being—a perspective that Nietzsche invokes in these accounts of man's humanity. Will is for Schopenhauer "the key to the knowledge of the innermost being of the whole of nature"; he "intends every force in nature to be conceived as will."[21] But, unlike Schopenhauer, Nietzsche repeatedly tries to distinguish human will and elevate it over the mere "blind impulses" of nature. Even while celebrating Schopenhauer, Nietzsche feels compelled to distinguish the " 'obscure impulse' " in nature from the "conscious willing" necessary to "the production of true *human beings*."[22] Celebrating

---

[20] Ibid., 1:378-80; 157-59.
[21] A. Schopenhauer, *The World as Will and Representation*, 1:109-11.
[22] *Schopenhauer as Educator*, 1:387; *Untimely Meditations*, 164.

as nature's leap over itself the elevation of the truly human over the natural impulses that rule animals merely adds to the humanity/ nature dichotomy the assertion that humanity is somehow natural as well. I have no doubt Nietzsche believes this to be true; but whenever Nietzsche tries to distinguish human and animal existence, he falls back on Kantian and post-Kantian dichotomies between human freedom and natural necessity.

Thus, for Nietzsche, humanity is, I suggest, something that man must assert against nature and realize in the world. If the goal of culture is the production of truly human individuals, then its goal is the realization of humanity in the world. A form of culture that precludes the development of such individuals keeps us at an animal level of existence. It degrades and dehumanizes us. It represents the real conditions that make man "a debased, enslaved, neglected and contemptible creature," the conditions Nietzsche must attack.

And strange as it may seem, I insist that Nietzsche's categorical imperative compelled him to take up this battle for human dignity in the name of man in general, not just for the sake of the few great individuals. He wanted his example to redeem "whole peoples."[23] Nietzsche may have accepted the title of "aristocratic radical," a title that Georg Brandes suggested characterized their shared perspective. But "missionary of culture," a title that Brandes, a more genuine cultural aristocrat, could not accept, better captures the peculiar vocation Nietzsche imposed upon himself.[24]

I asked before why Nietzsche could not simply satirize a cultural philistine like Strauss and then forget about him. If great individuals are the rarest flowers of nature, why care about philistines and failures? If Nietzsche's aristocratic convictions are so firm, why not shrug off philistines' existence? Why not simply dismiss the *Bildungsphilister* as the aristocratic minister answered the calumniator's pleading that he too had to eat: "I don't see the necessity"?

Despite Nietzsche's shrill and often offensive aristocratic rhetoric, he cannot leave the cultured philistines and the uncultured mob aside. He cannot leave them condemned to a less than human life.

[23] Ibid., 1:350; 136.
[24] G. Brandes, *Friedrich Nietzsche*, 64, 66.

In his own way, he wants, like Marx, to overthrow the conditions that make men, all men, contemptible. In the first pages of *The Gay Science*, Nietzsche makes an ironic but very revealing admission— an admission that forces us to qualify his violently aristocratic rhetoric.

> To stand amid this *rerum concordia discor* and the wholly wonderful uncertainty and ambiguity of existence *without questioning* . . . that is what I feel to be *contemptible* and this is the feeling for which I look first in everybody. Some folly keeps persuading me that every human being, as a human being, has this feeling. This is my kind of injustice.[25]

Nietzsche calls this feeling about man his "injustice" because he believes that, in fact, most people are incapable of living with such questioning. By expecting each individual to live up to his expectations, he does not give each individual his due; he treats unequals equally. His love of man forces him to be unjust. Nietzsche goes on to mention that the pride of the ancient philosophers, which allowed them to dismiss the majority of men as incapable of human behaviour and to treat them as mere slaves no matter what their position in life, is impossible today, for himself as much as for anyone else.[26] He confesses, surprisingly, that he cannot completely share the aristocratic sentiments he so often celebrates. The dignity of the individual forces such "justice" out of his mind. For all his blasts at the slavishness and herd-morality of the many, it pains Nietzsche to see individuals who do not realize their full humanity. Like the egalitarian Rousseau, he longs for a transformation of modern institutions that will turn contemptible individuals into fully *human* beings.

I must add immediately that Nietzsche's idea of a society in which human dignity in each individual is truly realized is one in which the vast majority devote themselves to the cultivation of a few great individuals. But Nietzsche is in earnest about this understanding of human dignity. All individuals receive their due as *hu-*

[25] *The Gay Science*, 3:373-74; 76-77.
[26] Ibid., 3:388-89; 91.

man beings in a grossly inegalitarian society. A healthy culture requires both genius and spectators worthy of being an audience and environment for genius. "The human being only has dignity in so far as he is, consciously or unconsciously, a tool of genius."[27] I draw this quotation from the essay on "The Greek State," the very essay Nietzsche begins by rejecting human dignity as a "hallucinatory concept." In the end, Nietzsche seems to redefine rather than reject the concept of human dignity.

In *Schopenhauer as Educator* Nietzsche complains that "as quickly as an individual will resolve to sacrifice his life to the state, so slowly and thoughtfully will he behave when an individual, rather than the state, requires this sacrifice."[28] Nietzsche follows Rousseau and Kant in conceiving of man's humanity in terms of a capacity for self-overcoming that raises man above nature. What he rejects is their understanding of the kind of self-overcoming that makes us human. Rousseau and many others have treated patriotic self-sacrifice as the activity that brings forth man's true dignity. Nietzsche would say the same of self-sacrifice for the sake of another's greatness. What greater honour is there, he asks, for an individual without genius than to be a means to it? The overriding goal of Nietzsche's critique of modern culture is the realization of man's humanity in the lives of all individuals, genius and spectator, ruler and ruled.

The Historical Sense and the Spirit of Modern Culture

From where does Nietzsche derive such an understanding of man's humanity and dehumanization? Certainly not through the direct influence of Rousseauian or Kantian works. Whatever similarities one may discover between Nietzschean and Rousseauian arguments, Nietzsche treats Rousseau and his ideas as a sickness that we must overcome.[29] As for Kantian arguments, it is quite clear that in

[27] "The Greek State," 1:775-76. See also *Richard Wagner in Bayreuth*, 1:431; *Untimely Meditations*, 197.
[28] *Schopenhauer as Educator*, 1:384; *Untimely Meditations*, 162.
[29] For interesting discussions of Nietzsche's unstated affinities as well as his explicit rejection of Rousseau, see W. D. Williams, *Nietzsche and the French*, xxi, 103-

his early cultural criticism Nietzsche shares some Kantian or, more accurately, neo-Kantian epistemological ideas. Each of his two guides to philosophy, Schopenhauer and Lange, tried to save what they considered the most valuable insight of Kantian philosophy—the recognition that we have no access to reality unmediated by intellect—from Kant's other, less defensible claims.[30] Indeed, one reason Nietzsche gives for dismissing the Hegelians is that in their attempts to go beyond Kant they lapse into an uncritical realism.[31] But however much indebted Nietzsche is to Kantian and neo-Kantian epistemology, there is little evidence of any debt to Kantian moral philosophy and the understanding of man's humanity that it develops.

In the next two sections, I suggest that Nietzsche's concern with the realization of humanity stems from his interest in the renewal of modern culture—an interest based on insights derived from a study of Greek culture. As I have already shown in Chapters 3 and 4, the Kantian philosophy of freedom provided Schiller, among others, with a new way of formulating and interpreting the contrast between ancient and modern culture. In this new version, ancient culture stands for the unconscious and unfree harmony of reason and nature, humanity and world, while modern culture, epitomized by Kantianism, stands for a dehumanizing, yet free and self-conscious disharmony between man and nature. The project suggested by such a contrast is the free and self-conscious restoration of harmony between man and nature. We must become again what we were, naturally whole, "by means of our reason and freedom."[32] I suggest here that Nietzsche's understanding of the ancient-modern contrast is shaped, sometimes directly, sometimes indirectly, by this post-Kantian formulation and interpretation, and thus that he

5, 128, 169-70, and P. Heller, "Nietzsche in his Relation to Voltaire and Rousseau," 116-25.

[30] See A. Schopenhauer, *The World as Will and Representation*, 1:417-18. For Nietzsche and Lange, see G. Stack, *Lange and Nietzsche*, 16-17, 195ff.

[31] *David Strauss*, 1:191-92; *Untimely Meditation*, 27-28. *The Birth of Tragedy*, 1:188ff.; 112ff. The neo-Kantian influence on Nietzsche's early work is most evident in the unfinished essay (1873), "On Truth and Lie in an Extra-Moral Sense," 1:875-90.

[32] F. Schiller, *On Naive and Sentimental Poetry*, 20:414.

derives his interest in the realization of humanity from his understanding of the cultural crisis of modern man.

Given his training as a philologist, it is hardly surprising that Nietzsche is drawn into the traditional German debates about ancients and moderns. But Nietzsche also shares a particular way of looking at the world with post-Kantian cultural critics like Schiller and the young Hegel, a perspective that opens his mind to their construction of the crisis of modern culture. He shares with them the view that epochs form coherent wholes, each integrated by a single spirit of social interaction. He shares with them a particular form of what Nietzsche calls the "historical sense." Neither Kant nor Schopenhauer share this historical sense, and, as a result, neither of them speak of a crisis of modern individuals or institutions.[33] More than anything else, I suggest, it is his historical sense of man's problems that separates Nietzsche from Schopenhauer and leads him to a completely anti-Schopenhauerian concern with the problems peculiar to modern man.

Why should culture be the means and the obstacle to the realization of man's humanity? One would think that the intrepid individuals whom Nietzsche describes as the crowning achievement of nature could exist in isolation or call out to each other over the centuries-wide chasms that separate them. But, as Nietzsche understands them, fully human individuals cannot develop by themselves. Like every living thing they need the nurturing environment of a cultural horizon.

This is a universal law: a living thing can be healthy, strong and fruitful only within a horizon; if it is incapable of drawing a horizon around itself, and at the same time too self-centered to enclose its own view within that of another, it will pine away slowly or hasten to its timely end.[34]

If conditions are such that they can break down these life-giving horizons, then man's humanity will wither away even in these great

[33] For Schopenhauer's rejection of the importance of historical perspectives, see A. Schopenhauer, *The World as Will and Representation*, 1:273.
[34] *On the Uses and Disadvantages of History for Life*, 1:251; this is translated by R. J. Hollingdale in *Untimely Meditations*, 63.

individuals, let alone among the masses who are shaped by them. And the breakdown of these horizons and the resulting dehumanization of life are precisely, Nietzsche insists, what modern individuals are experiencing.

The obstacle to the realization of humanity, as Nietzsche understands it, is the peculiar spirit of modern culture. Modern culture provides a very peculiar kind of horizon—a horizon that destroys horizons. Like any other horizon it expresses a limited point of view, a prejudice. Its prejudice is that we are capable of appreciating the achievements of every other culture. Such a prejudice destroys the "unity of artistic style in all the manifestations of the life of a people," which is the prerequisite of true culture.[35] Though we gorge ourselves on the achievements of the past, they merely sit in our stomach like "indigestable knowledge stones." Their "rattling betrays the most distinctive property of modern man: the remarkable opposition of an inside to which no outside and an outside to which no inside corresponds, an opposition which ancient peoples never knew."[36] Our knowledge of culture has little or no effect on our external appearance or behaviour. How could it, given the variety of conflicting styles we try to appreciate?

The defining and dehumanizing feature of modern cultures is the unrestrained "historical sense." Some historical sense is not something we are free to choose or dismiss, Nietzsche suggests at the beginning of his essay *On the Uses and Disadvantages of History for Life*. Animals cannot remember; humans cannot help but remember.

> Consider the herds that are grazing yonder; they know not what yesterday or tomorrow is; they move about, eat, rest, digest and move again, from morning through night, from day to day bound to their pleasure and displeasure, to the mercy of the moment, feeling neither melancholy nor satiety. It hurts man to look at this because he boasts of his humanity over the beast and still gazes jealously at its happiness—for the single

---

[35] *David Strauss*, 1:163; *Untimely Meditations*, 5.
[36] *On the Uses of History*, 1:272; *Untimely Meditations*, 78.

thing he wants, to live without satiety or pain like the beast, is in vain because he does not want to become like the beast.[37]

We envy the contentment of a cow chewing its cud. We would like to be able to forget the knowledge that sets us apart from the present moment, the knowledge that multiplies our woes by compelling us to relive the pains of the past and anticipate the pains of the future. But we cannot. The historical sense, as Nietzsche understands it, raises us above the animals. But an unrestrained historical sense, the feeling that everything is worth remembering, dehumanizes man. It makes superficial and tasteless erudition the hallmark of culture. In short, it produces the *Bildungsphilister* as its crowning achievement.

Nietzsche's attacks on the unrestrained historical sense lead him to minimize the extent to which he shares the historical perspective of thinkers like Hegel and Marx on the organization of human life. Nevertheless, Nietzsche shares Marx's disdain for unhistorical English social critics like Bentham, who, "with the driest of naiveté, . . . take the modern shopkeeper, especially the English shopkeeper, as the normal man."[38] The lack of historical sense is for him a fundamental defect of all previous philosophy, and thus, in the end, he counts the historical sense among "our virtues."[39] Nietzsche ridicules our attempts to appreciate the cultural achievements of every age and every historical style, but he knows he attempts to do so as well. Aeschylus and his contemporaries may indeed have found Shakespeare laughable, as Nietzsche insists in *Beyond Good and Evil*.[40] But Nietzsche can laugh at neither Aeschylus nor Shakespeare. He feels compelled to understand and appreciate both.

Fortunately, the historical sense has its uses as well as its abuses.

When I contemplate the present age with the eyes of some remote age, I can find nothing more remarkable in present-day

---

[37] Ibid., 1:248; 60.
[38] K. Marx, *Capital, Vol. 1*, 23:636-37 n. 63; 668 n. 2.
[39] In Chapter 7 of *Beyond Good and Evil*, entitled "Our Virtues." See also *Human-all-too-Human*, 2:225.
[40] *Beyond Good and Evil*, 5:159; 152.

humanity than its distinctive virtue and disease which goes by the name of "the historical sense." This is the beginning of something altogether new and strange in history: If this seed should be given a few centuries and more, it might ultimately become a marvelous growth with an equally marvelous scent that might make our old earth more agreeable to live on.[41]

One reason Nietzsche values the historical sense is that the interest it inspires in the spirit of other epochs often promotes longing to get beyond the limitations of one's time. The three "useful" kinds of history discussed in his essay *On the Uses and Disadvantages of History for Life*—monumental, antiquarian, and critical history—all gain their utility from this capacity to inspire dissatisfaction with the present.[42] A similar appreciation of the usefulness of modern man's historical sickness is also expressed in Nietzsche's later writings.

> German philosophy as a whole—Leibniz, Kant, Hegel, Schopenhauer, to name only the greatest—is the most fundamental form of romanticism and homesickness there has ever been: the longing for the best that has ever existed. One is no longer at home anywhere; at last one longs back for that place in which alone one can be at home because it is the only place in which one would want to be at home: the Greek world! . . . [W]e are growing more Greek by the day, at first, as is only fair, in concepts and evaluations, as Hellenizing ghosts, as it were; but one day, let us hope, also in our bodies. Herein lies (and always has lain) my greatest hope for the German character.[43]

In the homelessness produced by the historical sense lies Nietzsche's "greatest hope for the German character." A modern individual cannot envisage a truly cultured existence without it. Nietzsche does everything he can to sharpen the historical sense into a deadly weapon for use in his battle with the spirit of modern

[41] *The Gay Science*, 3:564; 267-68.
[42] *On the Uses of History*, 1:258-70; *Untimely Meditations*, 67-76.
[43] F. Nietzsche, *The Will to Power*, 225.

culture. Genealogies of modern attitudes and practises thus become his favorite form of social and cultural criticism.

Nothing better demonstrates the affinities between Nietzsche's perspective on history and that of earlier cultural critics like Schiller and the young Hegel than his reliance on this genealogical approach to social criticism. Nietzsche's interest in the past, especially the classical past, is inspired, like Schiller's and Hegel's, by an awareness of the limitations of the present. His genealogies represent attempts to define the character and sources of modern limitations through contrast with earlier cultures, rather than through accounts of the historical development of ideas and institutions.[44] Only through the reconstruction of alternative spirits of social interaction can we articulate the limitations of our own. "[I]t is only to the extent that I am a pupil of older times, especially the Greek, that I was able to acquire such untimely experiences about myself as a child of the present time."[45] Without the interest in such "untimely experiences" we have no way of recognizing our limitations. Thus Nietzsche would surely agree with Schiller when he warns:

> The artist is certainly the child of his time; but woe to him if he is at the same time its ward or, worse still, its minion! May some beneficent deity snatch the suckling in time from his mother's breast, nourish him with the milk of a better age, and let him come to maturity under a distant Greek sky. Then, when he has become a man, may he return, a stranger, to his own century; not, however, to gladden it by his appearance, but rather, terrible like Agamemnon's son, to purify it.[46]

Schiller's image of the artist as an Orestes who returns home to purify his age by killing the mother of modern culture is, perhaps, too violent to describe Schiller himself; but it fits Nietzsche perfectly. Schiller, after all, "gladdened" his time with his poetry and plays. It was Nietzsche who returned from his study of the Greeks demanding blood. With his account of the origins and dissolution

---

[44] For a good account of Nietzsche's genealogical approach see T. Strong, *Nietzsche and the Politics of Transfiguration*, 37ff., 189ff.

[45] *On the Uses of History*, 1:247; *Untimely Meditations*, 60.

[46] F. Schiller, *Aesthetic Education*, Letter 9, 54-57.

of the underlying spirit that gave birth to Greek tragedy, in the contrast between the "plastic power" of Greek culture and the open horizons of modern historical culture, Nietzsche adds to a tradition of social and cultural criticism begun by Schiller and the young Hegel. Nietzsche shares with them the belief that "we no longer understand altogether what was most familiar and frequent [for the Greeks], for example, the day and waking. . . . All experiences shone differently because a god shone through them."[47] And he shares with them his interest in reconstructing those experiences for use as a critical weapon against the spirit of modern culture. But such a weapon is only effective to the extent one assumes that every epoch has a particular spirit of social interaction that underlies and informs all human experience and action within it. Nietzsche, I suggest, also shares this assumption with Schiller and Hegel.

Nietzsche's Longing for Tragic Culture and Hegel's Acceptance of the "Death of Art"

Nietzsche's first book, *The Birth of Tragedy*, is also his first attempt to make use of the genealogical method outlined above as a means of social criticism. Although subsequent interest in the book generally has focused on the value of its contribution to the study of the origins of Greek culture or to aesthetic theory, Nietzsche's interest in his reconstruction of Greek tragic consciousness clearly goes beyond historical explanation and aesthetic analysis. For him, that reconstruction provides the means of judging and condemning modern experience, as well as the means of defining a project for cultural transformation. He does not simply seek to reproduce the cultural spirit that gave rise to Greek tragic consciousness. Nietzsche's goal is to build a new tragic culture on a new kind of consciousness, that of a "Socrates who practises music."[48] By bringing to light what we lack and, at the same time, the sources of the dissolution of tragic consciousness, his genealogy of the Greek spirit establishes his goal for modern man: a rebirth of tragic con-

---

[47] *The Gay Science*, 3:495; 196.
[48] *The Birth of Tragedy* 1:102; 98.

sciousness and a new form of tragic culture that will be immune to the Socratic criticism that destroyed Greek tragic culture.

Moreover, Nietzsche's interest in the rebirth of tragic culture goes beyond an interest in the renewal of a powerful and creative aesthetic tradition. Why should we care so much whether our culture is capable of producing tragic drama? Because, Nietzsche answers in his fourth *Untimely Meditation*, "all the ennoblement of mankind is enclosed in this supreme task." Nietzsche's interest in tragic culture represents an interest in "the unity and continuance of the human as such."

> The individual must be consecrated to something supra-personal—that is the meaning of tragedy; . . . this is what it means to have a *tragic sense*; all the ennoblement of mankind is enclosed in this supreme task; the final rejection of this task would be the bleakest picture a friend of man could bring to mind. That is how I see it! There is only one hope and one guarantee for the future of humanity: that the *tragic sense* does not die out. An unheard-of cry of distress would resound across the earth if mankind should ever lose it completely; and, conversely, there is no more rapturous joy than to know what we know—that the tragic idea [with Wagner's music] has again been born into the world. For this joy is completely universal and supra-personal, the rejoicing of mankind at the guarantee of the continuity and persistence of the human as such.[49]

For Nietzsche, the tragic sense represents the "one hope and one guarantee for the future of humanity," the one influence that may raise man to a "supra-personal" standpoint and thus save him from the loss of his humanity. Dehumanization is clearly the danger that Nietzsche, the "friend of man," fears in modern, nontragic culture. The spirit of modern culture poses for him an obstacle to the "persistence of the human as such." Thus his interest in the rebirth of the tragic sense represents an interest in overcoming the dehumanizing spirit of modern culture. Although Nietzsche later ridicules the offensively Hegelian "smell" of *The Birth of Tragedy*, he still

[49] *Richard Wagner in Bayreuth*, 1:453; *Untimely Meditations*, 213.

recognizes it as his first attempt at a "transvaluation of all values."[50] This first attempt at a "transvaluation of all values," as all of his subsequent attempts, grows out of his longing to get beyond what he saw as the dehumanizing spirit of modern culture.

Nietzsche uses Schopenhauerian concepts to reconstruct the nature and meaning of the tragic sense. But he does so in the name of a most un-Schopenhauerian project: to save modern man from dehumanization. As a result, Schopenhauer's philosophy, though it deeply influences Nietzsche's understanding of the tragic sense, is a poor guide to the interpretation of the general project undertaken in *The Birth of Tragedy*. Schiller's cultural criticism, I suggest, provides a far better guide to the analysis of that project.

Much has been written about the influence of Schiller's aesthetic philosophy on Nietzsche's arguments in *The Birth of Tragedy*.[51] If one is familiar only with Nietzsche's later dismissal of Schiller as "the moral trumpeter of Sackingen,"[52] as is the case with many readers, then it comes as a shock to discover how important Schiller's ideas were for Nietzsche's early criticisms of modern culture. One of Nietzsche's biographers, Charles Andler, has suggested that "no doctrine had more influence on Nietzsche's youth; none had as durable an effect upon him."[53] By the end of the 1870s, Nietzsche begins to make fun of Schiller's appeal to "callow youth." He may well be thinking of himself. For though he eventually lines Schiller up with the enemies of his untimely attitude,[54] Nietzsche originally considered him the very model of the untimely fighter against his time. Among those who fight for the future, he proclaims from the lectern in 1871, "there are the hopeful, whose noblest and sublimest expression stands before our eyes in our great Schiller."[55]

But I am less interested here in Schiller's direct influence on

[50] *Ecce Homo*, 6:310; 270.
[51] See especially B. Bennet, "Nietzsche's Idea of Myth: The Birth of Tragedy from the Spirit of 18th Century Aesthetics," 420-33, and U. Gaede, *Schiller und Nietzsche als Verkünder der Tragischen Kultur*. For Nietzsche and early Romantic aesthetics in general, see E. Behler, "Nietzsche und die Frühromantische Schule," 59-87.
[52] *Twilight of the Idols*, 6:111; *Portable Nietzsche*, 513.
[53] C. Andler, *Nietzsche, sa vie et sa pensée*, 1:46.
[54] *Human-all-too-Human*, 2:605-8. *Twilight of the Idols*, 6:111; *Portable Nietzsche*, 513.
[55] *On the Future of our Educational Institutions*, 1:646.

Nietzsche's arguments than I am in the parallels between their critical projects and the light these parallels shed on Nietzsche's social discontent. Schiller, like Nietzsche, believes that it is man's very humanity that is at stake in the fate of culture. The spirit of modern culture threatens man with dehumanization, so Schiller looks to ancient Greek culture to determine what we moderns lack. We lack an appreciation of the intrinsic value of the external world of nature and social interaction. Our understanding of humanity, an essentially Kantian understanding, devalues what is external and natural, and as a result we become divided and disharmonious beings. To the extent we are human, we feel compelled to reject the external world as valueless; to the extent we enjoy that world, we feel less than human. The source of our internal disharmony is the "all-dividing" spirit of modern culture.[56] The task Schiller sets for himself is the "realization" of our humanity, now imprisoned by modern culture in a noumenal world, in the phenomenal world of cultural and social interaction. But Schiller's contrast between ancient and modern culture also brings to light what ancient culture lacks: freedom and self-consciousness, essential attributes of man's humanity which it is the great merit of the moderns to have discovered. Thus he conceives of his project as an attempt to return man to the wholeness and harmony of the Greeks, and of nature in general, by means of the reason and freedom that raise man above nature.

The general project announced by Nietzsche in *The Birth of Tragedy*—the conscious reimposition of myth, the need for a "Socrates who practises music"[57]—runs parallel, I suggest, to Schiller's project as I have formulated it. The three stages of development Nietzsche outlines there, tragic culture, Socratic or Alexandrian culture, and a reborn, self-conscious tragic culture, parallel Schiller's three stages of unconscious harmony, conscious disharmony, and self-conscious, self-imposed harmony. Of course, Nietzsche rejects Schiller's interpretation of all the key concepts—nature, freedom, humanity, harmony—that Schiller uses to formulate his cultural criticism. Above all, he fears taking a naive view of Greek

[56] F. Schiller, *Aesthetic Education*, Letter 6.
[57] *The Birth of Tragedy*, 1:102, 147-49; 98, 135-37.

naiveté. His greatest innovation in *The Birth of Tragedy*, the assertion that Greek tragic culture grows out of a balance between the conflicting Apollonian and Dionysian drives, represents, in part, a challenge to Schiller's claims about the naive attitude that underlies the best of Greek culture. Nevertheless, for all of his ridicule of the typical German image of the Greeks as naive, cheerful children, Nietzsche still distinguishes the Greeks from the moderns by their ability to appreciate what seems to us the superficial surface of things. They find themselves in that surface, while we value only inner depth. As Nietzsche notes some years later in *The Gay Science*: "Oh, those Greeks! They understood how to live. For that one has to stop courageously at the surface, the fold, the skin, to adore appearance, to believe in forms, tones, words, in the whole Olympus of appearance. Those Greeks were superficial—*out of profundity.*"[58]

However profound Greek superficiality may be, whatever dark and fascinating secrets it may hide, the fundamental difference between them and us remains, for Nietzsche, that while the Greeks started with an unconsciously developed identity between nature's appearance and man's humanity, we moderns start with an opposition between nature and humanity and will have to impose any identity between the two upon ourselves. Although Nietzsche describes the unity of the Apollonian and Dionysian drives in Greek tragedy as "a metaphysical triumph of the Hellenic 'will',"[59] he does not think of Greek culture as being consciously self-imposed. The "will" to which he refers here, and rightly places between quotation marks, is the Schopenhauerian *will*, the noumenal force that underlies all existence, rather than a conscious volition. Both the Apollonian and Dionysian drives develop *spontaneously* out of religious sources. Their simultaneous development and ultimate synthesis is the miracle that made Greek culture what it was.

The Apollonian world of myth, the world of dreamy forgetfulness, will not return spontaneously. We must impose myth upon ourselves because our reason teaches us it is necessary to a truly hu-

[58] *The Gay Science*, 3:352; 38.
[59] *The Birth of Tragedy*, 1:25; 33.

man culture.[60] Socrates' criticism destroys the Greek tragic sense, since its contradictory attitude toward the world—the combination of Dionysian immersion in its meaningless suffering with Apollonian illusion to shield us from revulsion at that suffering—cannot withstand demands for consistency. Socrates' demand, know thyself, forces his and later generations to search their minds for contradictory attitudes, attitudes they must sacrifice on science's altar of consistency. But the quest for self-knowledge that Socrates initiates eventually leads us to recognize, first of all, that the scientific ideal of consistency is itself a form of illusion and second, that we must limit our search for self-knowledge, since it damages the mythic horizons that every creative culture needs.[61] The Socratic quest for self-knowledge thus eventually forces us to deny the possibility and desirability of universally valid truths.

"The extraordinary courage and wisdom of Kant and Schopenhauer," Nietzsche notes, have succeeded in gaining victory over Socratic and scientific optimism. "With this insight a culture is inaugurated which I venture to call tragic culture."[62] Like Schiller, Nietzsche sees Kant's critique of reason as the culmination of the drive for knowledge that destroyed the spirit of Greek culture and as the inaugurator of a new culture that will take us beyond modern limitations. We *know* that we must limit our knowledge. That is our special self-knowledge. We are thus, according to Nietzsche, heirs of Socrates who recognize our need to reestablish the kingdom of myth that he overthrew. To restore the identification with the world as it is provided by the tragic sense, we must consciously use the knowledge we have gained about our need to limit our knowledge. In short, we must impose myth upon ourselves, by means of our reason and freedom.

Nietzsche draws similar conclusions in his essay *On the Uses and Disadvantages of History for Life*. It is our openness to alternative cultures that teaches us what a healthy culture requires: a limiting horizon of forgetfulness. Our remembrance of other cultures is what teaches us to forget them. The need to limit historical knowl-

[60] Ibid., 1:147-49; 135-37.
[61] Ibid., 1:147; 135.
[62] Ibid., 1:118; 112.

edge is itself derived from historical knowledge. If we lose interest in alternative cultures, then we will no longer remember what it is we have to forget in order to transcend our limitations.

This need for self-conscious forgetfulness is already implied in Schiller's demand that we return to a harmony with nature by means of our reason and freedom. It is our reason and freedom that separate us from nature. Schiller, in effect, asks us to return to unity with nature by means of the very faculties that oppose our ends to nature's. If we ever achieved such harmony, we would have to forget somehow the character of the means of its achievement in order to maintain it. But if we forget that we have imposed this harmony on ourselves by means of our reason and freedom, that harmony loses its special, human value. Thus in the end we must simultaneously forget and remember the freedom that distinguishes us from nature in order to achieve Schiller's goal.

Nietzsche not only accepts this need for self-conscious forgetting, he glorifies it. It is not only our dreadful burden, it is our greatest opportunity, the path to superiority over even the Greeks. "Even in the past this higher type has often appeared—but as a fortunate accident, as an exception, never as something *willed.*" "He who really is convinced that the goal of culture is the production of true human beings and nothing else, . . . will think it necessary finally to replace that 'obscure impulse' with a conscious willing."[63] Nietzsche distills Schiller's teaching to its most paradoxical form and argues that we have no choice but to accept this paradox if we love man. We must remember to forget the meaninglessness of nature. Self-conscious forgetting is the remedy that Nietzsche, the self-appointed doctor of sick cultures, prescribes. *Hic Rhodus hic saltus.*

Nietzsche was not the first to suggest that we might have to leap over Rhodes in this way in order to realize man's humanity in a post-modern culture. Hegel, for one, came to recognize that Schiller's critique of modern culture ultimately issues in a demand for self-conscious forgetting. But Hegel shunned such a need as absurd

---

[63] *The Antichrist,* 6:170; this is translated in *The Viking Portable Nietzsche,* 570. *Schopenhauer as Educator,* 1:387; *Untimely Meditations,* 164.

and self-destructive. If the *full* realization of man's humanity in the world requires such conscious self-contradiction, then, he concludes, that project must be rejected.[64] The novelty of Nietzsche's position lies less in its analysis of modern man's predicament than in the reckless daring with which he invites us to will self-contradiction, to impose limits on ourselves that we do not truly respect. A comparison of Nietzsche's critique of modern culture with Hegel's teaching about the "death of art" in the modern age makes it easier to recognize the extent to which Nietzsche shares a philosophic perspective on modern men and culture with Schiller and Hegel.

The young Nietzsche's critique of modern culture is extremely perceptive, strikingly presented, and, to a large degree, persuasive. It is not, however, quite as novel as he insists it is. The portrait of historical, "Alexandrian" culture which he paints in his early essays corresponds to Hegel's description in his lectures on aesthetics of "ironic," post-romantic art and culture.[65] Nietzsche does not seem to have been familiar with these lectures. Indeed, most of his knowledge of Hegel seems secondhand. Most often he relies for his understanding of Hegel's ideas either on the works of contemporary Hegelians he despised, like Strauss and Vischer, or on the interpretations provided by thinkers whom he admired, but who despised Hegelianism, for his understanding of Hegel's ideas. With teachers like Schopenhauer and Burckhardt, it is not surprising that Nietzsche shows little familiarity or appreciation of the range of Hegel's achievements.[66]

It is surprising, then, to discover that Nietzsche reproduces so much of Hegel's comparison between ancient and modern cultures. The most striking example is Nietzsche's understanding of the collapse of Greek culture. Like Hegel, Nietzsche portrays this collapse as a failure to withstand Socrates' demand for a rational examination of the understanding of man and world that supports Greek culture. Nietzsche claims that in *The Birth of Tragedy* "Socrates is

[64] See the final section on Hegel in Chapter 5, above.

[65] See especially G. W. F. Hegel, *Aesthetics*, in *Werke*, 13:223-42; 1:593-611.

[66] In 1870, Nietzsche writes a friend that he is learning Hegel's philosophy from Burckhardt's lectures on philosophy of history (F. Nietzsche, *Briefwechsel*, 2:155).

recognized for the first time as the instrument of Greek disintegration." No modern before him, he asserts, has recognized the justice of Aristophanes' attack on Socrates.[67] But, as we have seen in Chapter 5, not only does Socrates play a central role in Hegel's account of the collapse of Greek culture and political life, but Hegel also acknowledges the justice of the Athenians' accusations against him. For Hegel, Socrates' execution is a tragedy in which right clashes against right.[68]

Nietzsche's diagnosis of the disease that affects modern culture provides another example of his reproduction of Hegelian sociocultural analysis. Hegel suggests that in the modern age—which for him commences in the nineteenth century, following the French Revolution—art begins to lose the significance it had in previous ages. Art and aesthetic experience, Hegel claims, "no longer serve our highest needs"; our longing for the re-creation of the artistic greatness we envy in the Greeks thus cannot be satisfied.[69] The modern, that is, "ironic" or post-romantic, artist finds no material inherently more valuable than any other. This spells the end of art as we have known it, for, as Nietzsche puts it, the artist must "love his act infinitely more than it deserves."[70] In Hegel's language, aesthetic experience rests on the "sensuous manifestation of the Absolute," that is, on the experience of something sensuous as containing within itself what we recognize as the meaning and value of the world. The self-knowledge of modern individuals, their recognition that it is the freedom of the mind, and the freedom of the mind alone, that brings value into the world, precludes their experiencing anything sensuous as the complete manifestation of human meaning. That is why Hegel argues that artistic production "no longer serves our highest need." Try as we might, we cannot revere the sensuous form of the work of art. We cannot "bend the knee" like the Greek before a statue of a god or the mediaeval Catholic before an image of a saint. We are still moved by art; but what we revere is the artist's mind and skill, or their effect on our mind,

---

[67] *Ecce Homo,* 6:311; 271. *The Birth of Tragedy,* 1:88ff.; 86ff.
[68] G. W. F. Hegel, *Vorlesungen,* 644-45; *Philosophy of History,* 270.
[69] G. W. F. Hegel, *Aesthetics,* in *Werke,* 13:24; 1:10.
[70] *On the Uses of History,* 1:254; *Untimely Meditations,* 64.

not the object itself. When we admire a statue of a god we are inspired to wonder at the state of mind that allowed the Greeks to produce such works, and we wonder about our state of mind that seems to keep us from producing such works. We are "not in earnest," Hegel concludes, about the sensuous forms themselves.[71]

As a result of this lack of earnestness, post-romantic culture is open to all forms and materials. Like Nietzsche, Hegel points to the lack of a unified style in contemporary culture.

> The artist thus stands above specific consecrated forms and configurations and moves freely on his own account, independent of the subject-matter and mode of conception in which the holy and eternal was previously made visible to human apprehension. No content, no form, is any longer immediately identical with the inwardness, the nature, the unconscious substantial essence of the artist; every material may be indifferent to him if only it does not contradict the formal law of simply being beautiful and capable of artistic treatment. Today there is no material which stands in and for itself above this relativity, and even if one matter may be raised above it, still there is no absolute need for its representation by art.[72]

Without a shared conception of meaningful forms, culture becomes the knowledge of culture which, Nietzsche complains, replaces real culture in the modern world. To get at the meaning of art, it is not enough merely to gaze at its surface. We moderns, Hegel suggests, have to probe beneath the surface. We have to speculate about the artist's state of mind and his methods in order to appreciate his work. Or we have to bring in critics with aesthetic theories to explain the work and its effect on our state of mind to us. In other words, art becomes dependent on concepts, the philosopher's tool; for it is only in concepts, not in sensuous appearance, that we recognize meaning.

From Hegel's point of view, twentieth-century artists' proud boast of creative independence is actually an admission of their increasing irrelevance to our spiritual life. We no longer have any

---

[71] G. W. F. Hegel, *Aesthetics*, in *Werke*, 13:24, 242, 14:233; 1:10, 103, 603.
[72] Ibid., 14:235; 1:605.

need to have particular subjects represented to us sensuously, so artists' voices are only added to the other voices expressing their subjective standpoints in journalistic and scholarly prose. Artists can rebel against this subjective independence, as many artists in this century do, and they can try to impose limitations upon themselves—distorted perspectives, arbitrarily chosen forms, chance composition, and so on. But even in this rebellion against formlessness and independence it is the artists' state of mind that continues to command our attention. When confronted with works of this sort we cannot help but wonder what artists aim at by *choosing* to impose these limitations upon themselves—for we know that they are chosen.

Hegel concludes that art cannot mean for us what it meant in the past. Aesthetc experience no longer serves our deepest needs, so it can no longer reach the heights we envy in past cultures. Of course, artistic production continues. But something essential is lost, something that gnaws at us every time we gaze in wonder at the great works of the past. We must resign ourselves to this loss, Hegel argues, for it is an inescapable consequence of our discovery of the *human* source of meaning and purpose.[73]

Nietzsche rebels against Hegelian resignation to the death of art. With regard to this issue, Deleuze is correct in suggesting that there can be "no possible compromise" between Hegel and Nietzsche.[74] Nevertheless, Nietzsche only rebels against Hegel's evaluation of our predicament, not against his diagnosis. Nietzsche reproduces much of Hegel's diagnosis of art's mortal illness in the modern age. How should we account for these parallels?

Karl Hillebrand, one of his few critics whom Nietzsche admired,[75] suggests the most obvious answer to this question. In a generally favourable review of Nietzsche's first *Untimely Meditation*, Hillebrand complains about Nietzsche's compulsion to "out-

[73] For interesting discussions of Hegel's arguments about the "death of art," see E. Heller, "The Artist's Journey into the Interior," in Heller, *The Artist's Journey into the Interior and Other Essays*, 99-170; D. Henrich, "Kunst und Kunstphilosophie der Gegenwart," 11-36; and K. Harries, "Hegel and the Future of Art," 677-97.

[74] G. Deleuze, *Nietzsche and Philosophy*, 195.

[75] See R. F. Krummel, *Nietzsche und der Deutsche Geist*, 23-24, and *Ecce Homo*, 6:318; 279.

Schopenhauer Schopenhauer" in his ridicule of Hegel. Nietzsche's violent rejection of Hegelianism is embarrassing, Hillebrand suggests, because so many of his arguments have Hegelian foundations. Like it or not, Nietzsche, like the whole of German cultural life in the nineteenth century, has drunk "the Hegelian philosophy with his mother's milk."[76] Even if Nietzsche does not have much knowledge of Hegel's arguments, and rejects those with which he is familiar, he cannot help but make use of some of Hegel's insights, given the way Hegelianism has influenced nineteenth-century German cultural life.

Hillebrand, it seems to me, is surely correct in tracing Hegelian affinities in Nietzsche's thought to the Hegel-saturated cultural environment in which he comes to maturity. My analysis in this chapter of Nietzsche's revolt against the spirit of modern culture helps specify what he shares with the Hegelian tradition he rejects. The parallels between Nietzschean and Hegelian analyses of the predicament of modern culture grow out of the understanding of humanity and the coherence of historical epochs, which, I have suggested, Nietzsche shares with Hegel and Schiller. Schiller's cultural criticism, to which the young Nietzsche is deeply indebted, may have played a role in transmitting these new perspectives to Nietzsche. But by Nietzsche's time, they are already old and familiar elements of German culture. Nietzsche does not have to go back to Schiller and Hegel to become familiar with them.

By reproducing Hegel's portrait of modern culture and rejecting as dehumanizing his resignation to the death of art, Nietzsche, in effect, returns to Schiller's perspective on the problem of modern culture, but with a clearer understanding of the need for self-conscious forgetting as the means of getting beyond the dehumanizing spirit of modern culture. Hegel argues that we cannot resurrect the kind of culture Nietzsche longs for because we *know* that our objects are not infinitely valuable. Nietzsche agrees that we know this, but he argues that, given this knowledge and the knowledge of what makes a culture healthy, we must impose such limitations upon

---

[76] K. Hillebrand, "Einiges über den Verfall der deutschen Sprache und der deutschen Gesinnung," 2:291-310, 303-4. Hillebrand discusses the second and third *Untimely Meditations* in 2:314-38 and 2:353-66, respectively, of the same collection.

ourselves, knowing all the while that they are *without* any inherent justification.

How can one will forgetfulness, while remembering what and why one must forget?[77] Again and again, Nietzsche returns to this problem, for it poses the obstacle to the rebirth of a truly human culture. In the more sceptical essays of his so-called middle period, Nietzsche seems more inclined to resign himself, like Hegel, to the immovability of this barrier. In *Human-all-too-Human*, he even plays with the idea that artistic culture must die. "Perhaps never before was art so deeply and soulfully grasped as now when the magic of death seems to play around it. . . . The artist will soon come to be regarded as a splendid relic."[78]

But such moments of Hegelian resignation are short-lived. With the revelations first introduced in *Thus Spoke Zarathustra*, with the startling conceptual innovations that have brought him fame—superman, eternal return, and will to power—Nietzsche revives his demands for self-forgetfulness as the means of overcoming modern culture and its dehumanizing effects. In the following section I shall try to show how these conceptual innovations represent, at least in part, answers to the questions about the need for self-conscious forgetfulness suggested by Nietzsche's earlier critique of modern culture. In particular I shall try to show how they grow out of Nietzsche's longing to overcome the dehumanizing spirit of modern society and the understanding of man and history which, I have argued, make this longing possible for Nietzsche as much as for Schiller and the young Hegel.

"The Most Interesting Animal": Nietzsche's Later Understanding of Man's Humanity

In the writings of his so-called middle period, *Human-all-too-Human*, *The Dawn*, and *The Gay Science*, Nietzsche backs off a little from the project of cultural revolution that he advocates in his early

---

[77] See J. Elster, *Ulysses and the Sirens: Studies in Rationality and Irrationality*, 50-51, and *Sour Grapes: Studies in the Subversion of Rationality*, 44-52, for interesting discussions of the problem of self-conscious forgetting.

[78] *Human-all-too-Human*, 2:185-86. See Allen Megill's commentary on this passage in *Prophets of Extremism*, 68-69.

essays. His critique of modern culture remains just as sharp, and his interests broaden. But these writings lack the clear sense of mission found in the early essays. Perhaps Nietzsche's recognition that the fighters for a cultural revolution in Germany—Wagner, Schopenhauer, and Schiller—whom he celebrated in his early works, share the vices of modern culture dampens that sense of mission. Whatever the reasons, Nietzsche seems content with the role of gadfly in these middle works.

But with the writing of *Thus Spoke Zarathustra*, Nietzsche again becomes a man with a mission. He becomes the prophet of a cultural revolution that promises to raise humanity to new, "superhuman" heights. Nietzsche presents this mission as a new beginning rather than as a return to the problems raised by his earlier cultural criticism. His project is, indeed, built upon the new foundation provided by Nietzsche's three most famous conceptual innovations: superman, eternal return, and will to power. This new foundation is certainly meant to mark a complete break with the premises of the German philosophy of freedom, in particular, and with the entire Western tradition of philosophy beginning with Socrates, in general.

Does Nietzsche succeed in breaking with the conceptual foundation underlying German idealism, let alone the entire Western philosophic tradition? In the end, I think not. I do not mean to challenge the novelty of Nietzsche's conceptual perspective by pointing to earlier suggestions of his three new concepts. One can, of course, find in the works of Nietzsche's predecessors interesting precedents for each of these ideas. But by trying to bring these three concepts together as the foundation of a single philosophic approach, Nietzsche surely attempts something new. My suspicion that Nietzsche's new approach rests on old German foundations grows instead out of reflection upon his interest in bringing these three concepts together. I suggest that underlying and integrating Nietzsche's conceptual innovations is a continuing concern about man's fate in the modern world, in particular, a concern with what he perceives as the dehumanization imposed on modern individuals by the spirit of modern culture. This concern links Nietzsche's later works not only to his earlier cultural criticism, but also to the post-

Kantian tradition of sociocultural criticism examined in this book. Nietzsche's later innovations, like Marx's, represent, I have suggested, new answers to old questions. I shall try to show that the new answers he develops require him to deny the premises that suggested the old questions in the first place, especially the Kantian dichotomy between humanity and nature. But I shall also try to show that these new answers are important to Nietzsche only to the extent that he still finds the old questions relevant. Thus I conclude that Nietzsche, again like Marx, is compelled to affirm and deny the humanity/nature dichotomy he inherits from post-Kantian philosophy.

How does one go about justifying such assertions, given Nietzsche's tendency to question and even undermine every premiss he uses? How does one demonstrate self-contradiction in an author who rejects the Aristotelian principle of noncontradiction?[79] Obviously, only with extreme caution, and with the ever-present suspicion that one has missed something important. However, I believe that we fail to take Nietzsche seriously if we allow the fear of being accused of naiveté to prevent us from searching for underlying contradictions in his thinking.[80]

One way of uncovering the foundations underlying Nietzsche's conceptual innovations is by exploring his understanding of man's distinctive character. What kind of creature is man? What makes his needs so special? Does anything justify his boast of bearing an unmatched value and dignity in the world?

It is not inappropriate to pose such questions to Nietzsche. Despite his historicism, he presents the specifically human characteristics of man as something distinct, as something we can fall below or rise above. And despite his teaching of eternal recurrence, he is no morphologist of historical development, like his disciple Spengler. When he warns of modern decadence, he is speaking of the decadence of *man*, not of the degeneration that occurs at the end of

---

[79] F. Nietzsche, *The Will to Power*, 279.

[80] Wolfgang Müller-Lauter's book *Nietzsche: Seine Philosophie der Gegensätze und die Gegensätze seiner Philosophie* provides not only a splendid model of criticism of Nietzsche's contradictions based on careful and sympathetic interpretation, but the best account of Nietzsche's philosophy of contradiction as well.

a culture's life cycle.[81] The nihilism that knocks on our door threatens man as man. It is the culmination of all previous historical development, rather than a stage in the life of all cultures. It is Europe's "destiny" to become "weary of man." "Along with our fear of man we have also lost our love of him, our reverence for him, our hopes for him, our will to him."[82]

What then is so special about man that he is worth saving from the threat of nihilism? Why risk our peace of mind and physical comfort just to raise man to some conception of his true value and dignity? Nietzsche, like Marx, usually tries to avoid answering such questions, since they suggest, in their very asking, idealistic answers. To speak of man's special character is to suggest that his peculiar capacities, capacities usually associated with his mind, raise him somehow above the rest of nature. Nietzsche never misses an opportunity to ridicule such suggestions. "The development of consciousness, the 'spirit,' " he insists, "counts for us only as a symptom of a relative imperfection of the organism. . . . We deny that anything can be done perfectly as long as it is still done consciously."[83]

Yet despite his mockery of idealism's celebration of human dignity, Nietzsche devoted his life to the analysis and overcoming of the conditions that degrade and enslave man. Even while rejecting man's claims to a special dignity among nature's creatures, he rarely fails to qualify his descriptions of the human animal with a telltale superlative. Man, he says, is the "sickest" animal, and thus "the most interesting animal." He is "the cruelest animal against himself."[84] Man is wholly animal for Nietzsche; yet he is something more as well, something that makes him especially "interesting."

---

[81] See O. Spengler, *The Decline of the West*, 1:38-40. Spengler's un-Nietzschean advice is to adapt ourselves to what is possible at this stage of our culture's life cycle, rather than to try to get beyond the spirit of our culture. Great art is impossible for us—better to be a good engineer than a bad artist, Spengler insists.

[82] *On the Genealogy of Morals*, 5:278; 44.

[83] *The Antichrist*, 6:181; *Portable Nietzsche*, 581.

[84] *On the Genealogy of Morals*, 5:253, 365; 65-66, 120-21. *The Antichrist*, 6:180; *Portable Nietzsche*, 580-81. *Thus Spoke Zarathustra*, 4:273; this is translated in *The Viking Portable Nietzsche*, 330.

Nietzsche's fear of reproducing the naiveté he finds in his predecessors' celebration of human dignity makes it extremely difficult to identify with any precision his understanding of the *qualité d'homme*. Nevertheless, some understanding of man's special character stands at the centre of his later philosophic thought and social criticism. *Thus Spoke Zarathustra*, the first of his later works, begins with Zarathustra's proclamation that "Man is a rope, tied between beast and superman—a rope over an abyss."[85] His later works are filled with many such evocations of man's uniqueness. But we find little sustained discussion of the meaning of and justification for such a view of man. We thus have to reconstruct for ourselves, from the hints he gives us, Nietzsche's understanding of man's humanity.

In the second essay of *On the Genealogy of Morals* there is a passage that is particularly useful for such a reconstruction of Nietzsche's understanding of man's humanity. In this passage Nietzsche diagnoses the sickness that makes man such an interesting animal. "All instincts that do not discharge themselves outwardly turn inward—this is what I call the *internalization* of man: thus it was that man developed what was later called his 'soul.' " Social barriers to the external discharge of our instinctual energies have forced human instincts to turn on themselves. The consequence of such self-laceration is the birth of the "bad conscience" and the "ascetic ideal." This "internalization" of instincts, Nietzsche suggests, is unique to man. And with the creation of this "animal soul turned against itself," nature once again overleaps itself. "Let us add at once that, on the other hand, the existence of an animal soul turned against itself, taking sides against itself, was something so new, profound, unheard of, puzzling, contradictory, *and pregnant with a future* that the aspect of the earth was essentially altered."[86]

This passage is best known as the most striking suggestion in Nietzsche's works of a theory of sublimation. But although the ideas expressed here suggest new approaches to the study of man,

[85] *Thus Spoke Zarathustra*, 4:16; *Portable Nietzsche*, 126.
[86] *On the Genealogy of Morals*, 5:323; 85.

like Freud's, they also point back to older approaches. With this internalization of instincts, man once more stands apart from and opposed to the rest of existence, and, as a result, "the aspect of the earth was essentially altered." Nature, which never leaps, leaps beyond itself by producing something that breaks the laws that guide all its other creations: "an animal soul turned against itself"—man.

The quality that distinguishes man from the rest of natural existence is whatever quality it is that gives man, and man alone, this capacity for self-overcoming first witnessed in the internalization of his instincts. For all that Nietzsche may envy the "good conscience" and unreflective enjoyment of the noble beasts described in the first essay of the *Genealogy of Morals*, they no more resemble *human* beings than cows grazing in the field. There is no essential distinction between their spontaneous enjoyment of life and the cow's unshakable but silent contentment. They too never bring their self-satisfaction into question; it thus has no value in Nietzsche's eyes, for, as I have noted already, a life "without questioning" is, to Nietzsche, contemptible.[87] Much as he envies Greek self-satisfaction and despises Jewish self-contempt, he still associates profundity with the latter. "The whole of European psychology is rich with Greek superficiality, without that little bit of Judaism. . . ."[88] Man gains value and profundity only when he asserts himself by denying the external direction of his drives. By denying himself, man becomes sick, but he also becomes human.

Many of the notes made in preparation for *The Will to Power* indicate that Nietzsche tries to use the concept of will to power as a means of accounting for man's uniqueness without reintroducing any of the traces of dualism suggested by the passage I have been discussing. All life, he insists in these notes, down to the level of single cells and protoplasm, represents the interplay and overcoming of conflicting wills. All life is will to power. The "sole objective measure of value" is "the quantum of enhanced and organized power." "There is nothing to life that has value, except the degree

[87] *The Gay Science*, 3:373-74; 76-77.
[88] F. Nietzsche, Letter to Franz Overbeck, February 23, 1887, in Nietzsche, *Selected Letters of Friedrich Nietzsche*, 261.

of power."[89] From this perspective, man is something special only to the extent that he is capable of a greater degree of power than any other creature.

What gives man the capacity for producing higher degrees of power? "In contrast to the animals," Nietzsche answers, "man has cultivated an abundance of *contrary* drives and impulses within himself."[90] To make man capable of the greatest "quantum" of power, Nietzsche must characterize him as a battlefield of conflicting forces, a battlefield found nowhere else in nature. All life may be a battle among conflicting wills to power, but the conflict *within man* is essentially different from the conflict anywhere else in the world. Man must have some unique capacity for self-opposition and self-overcoming in order to explain the "abundance of contrary drives and impulses" that Nietzsche finds in him. Though he develops the will to power as a means of explaining all life, Nietzsche cannot resist using it as a means to distinguish man from the rest of nature. "That which partly necessity, partly chance has achieved here and there, the conditions for the production of a stronger type, we are now able to comprehend and consciously *will*."[91] The explanation of man's being in terms of the will to power thus returns to an understanding of man as an "animal soul" capable of turning "against itself." The capacity for self-denial and self-overcoming still distinguishes man from the rest of nature's creatures.

Of course, the creation of a capacity for self-overcoming is for Nietzsche also the source of the sickness and world devaluation that afflicts modern man. Nietzsche's ambivalent evaluation of man's internalization has much of the flavor of Rousseau's evaluation of man's transition from the state of nature to civil society. For Rousseau too, civil society destroys man's innocent self-love and unreflective enjoyment of life. It ends his independence, imposes burdensome obligations, and gives him insatiable desires. Yet Rousseau affirms civil society and for much the same reason as Nietzsche affirms man's internalization. By destroying his innocent dependence on natural instinct, civil society gives man a chance

[89] F. Nietzsche, *The Will to Power*, 356, 57.
[90] Ibid., 507.
[91] Ibid., 477.

to order his own life as befits a *human* being. It "changed him from a stupid, limited animal into an intelligent being and a man."[92] Nietzsche shuns Rousseau's language of moral uplift when he talks about the heightening and deepening of man. Nevertheless, the overcoming of externally given ends remains for him, as for Rousseau and Kant, the measure of man's humanity.[93]

Indeed, Nietzsche often gives the same name to this capacity for resisting externality that Rousseau and Kant gave it: freedom.

> How is freedom measured in individuals and peoples? According to the resistance that must be overcome, according to the exertion required to remain on top. The highest type of free men should be sought where the highest resistance is constantly overcome: five steps from tyranny, close to the threshold of the danger of servitude.[94]

This description of freedom is, of course, intended to invert the egalitarian description advanced by Rousseau and Kant. He agrees with them that freedom requires "that one has the will to assume responsibility for oneself." But he has a rather different interpretation of the "responsibility" that one assumes with one's freedom. The free individual must "maintain the distance that separates us," and "sacrifice human beings for one's cause, not excluding oneself," rather than treat every individual as an end in himself.[95] Nevertheless, he shares Rousseau's and Kant's admiration for self-overcoming. What he objects to is their insistence that the overcoming of resistance is admirable only in pursuit of moral, universalistic ends. If it is the overcoming of resistance that inspires their admiration of the moral will, they have no good reason to withhold their admiration from greater, immoral or amoral feats of self-overcoming. If freedom is their god, and freedom is measured by the degree of resistance overcome, then they should admire even

[92] J.-J. Rousseau, *Social Contract*, 3:364; 56.
[93] See H. Barth, *Truth and Ideology*, 171, 173, for a similar argument about Nietzsche and his predecessors.
[94] *Twilight of the Idols*, 6:140; *Portable Nietzsche*, 542. See the similar statement in *The Will to Power*, 404.
[95] *Twilight of the Idols*, 6:140; *Portable Nietzsche*, 542.

more than the moral man the individual who consciously overcomes a strong inclination to act morally. The former, after all,
merely denies his instincts; the latter denies his self-denial.
Nietzsche concludes that if self-overcoming made us human, then
overcoming of self-overcoming will make us superhuman. And
thus his most striking image of the superman is the "Roman Caesar
with the soul of Christ."

Nietzsche is a notorious lover of paradox. But this paradox, the
"Roman Caesar with the soul of Christ," is clearly meant to be
taken seriously. It is Nietzsche's most concise and accurate formula
for the superman. "The highest man would have the greatest multiplicity of drives, in the relatively greatest strength that can be en-
dured."[96] "So far the most powerful men still bowed reverently before the saint as the riddle of self-conquest and deliberate final
renunciation. . . . They sensed in him the superior force that
sought to test itself in such a conquest."[97] Even the Caesars of this
world recognize, Nietzsche suggests, the saint's superior will to
power. But a Caesar with the soul of Christ, a man who could will
the saint's self-denial and then will the denial of his denial, a man
whose love of satisfaction in the world would compel him to strike
at his enemy even while his own Christian compassion urged him
to stay his hand—the tension of his double self-denial would be
truly unprecedented.[98]

Nietzsche, in all likelihood, would have suggested that this interpretation of his superman smells, like his first works, offensively
Hegelian.[99] It is, I admit, somewhat one-sided. It emphasizes the
tension of self-overcoming that goes into the making of the super-

[96] F. Nietzsche, *The Will to Power*, 513, 506.
[97] *Beyond Good and Evil*, 5:71; 65.
[98] Walter Kaufmann's rather squeamish interpretation of this image—he suggests
that the superman stays his hand though he knows he has the power to strike his
enemy—is unacceptable. The self-denial that is required to keep oneself from harm-
ing others would be nothing new. It would not create the unprecedented internal
tension that Nietzsche seeks in the superman. And, indeed, for Kaufmann, the
superman is nothing new. Socrates, Caesar, Napoleon—all the great individuals in
history—were Nietzschean supermen in his account. See W. Kaufmann, *From
Shakespeare to Existentialism*, 300, and *Nietzsche: Philosopher, Psychologist, Anti-
Christ*, 316ff.
[99] *Ecce Homo*, 1:310; 270.

man, rather than the Dionysian affirmation of all things, which is to characterize his existence. In Zarathustra's famous speech "On the Three Metamorphoses," Nietzsche insists that we must not rest content with the "sacred 'No' " of the lion, the "creation of freedom for oneself for new creation." We must go beyond the lion's self-overcoming and regain the "innocence and forgetting," the "sacred 'Yes' " of the child.[100] It is difficult to imagine a Caesar with Christ's soul as an example of childlike innocence. Nietzsche's recommendation of childlike affirmation appears so contrary to notions of inner tension and self-overcoming that some interpreters deny that Nietzsche places any value on struggle and self-overcoming. One "cannot overemphasize," Gilles Deleuze insists, "how foreign struggle, war, rivalry, or even competition are to Nietzsche."[101] One need not have read very much of Nietzsche's works to recognize that this assertion is an exaggeration. Nietzsche, after all, insists that "we are delighted with all who love, as we do, danger, war, and adventures; . . . we think about the necessity for new orders, also for a new slavery—for every strengthening and enhancement of the human type also involves a new kind of enslavement."[102] Nevertheless, one cannot deny that Nietzsche seems to endorse two different ways of being as the most valuable for man: self-overcoming and childlike affirmation.

Nietzsche's longing for both ways of being manifests itself in the two basic images of nobility we find in his later writings. According to the first of these images, the noble individual is one who takes his superior rewards in life for granted and thus enjoys life with a good conscience and looks on nature with trust and gratitude.[103] Such an individual corresponds to the healthy blond beast of the opening essay of the Genealogy of Morals and to the child of Zarathustra's three metamorphoses. But Nietzsche also speaks of the saint's self-sacrifice as the "noblest feeling" of which man has yet

---

[100] Thus Spoke Zarathustra, 4:30-31; Portable Nietzsche, 139.
[101] G. Deleuze, Nietzsche and Philosophy, 82. This interpretation of Nietzsche seems designed to support his claim that there can be "no possible compromise between Hegel and Nietzsche." See D. Breazeale, "The Hegel-Nietzsche Problem," 158-62, for a thorough critique of this position.
[102] The Gay Science, 3:629; 338.
[103] On the Genealogy of Morals, 5:270ff.; 36ff.

been capable. "Noble souls; they do not want anything for nothing, least of all life." They "even rather seek guilt and suffering."[104] From this point of view, "the church is under all circumstances a *nobler* institution than the state," since it "secures the highest rank for the more *spiritual* human beings."[105]

Nietzsche values both types of nobility as worthy of human beings. Indeed, it seems that he hopes childlike affirmation of the world will be the result of the superhuman denial of self-denial that he recommends. The problem with this hope is that without consciousness of internal resistance to be overcome, affirmation of the world is meaningless and without value, while with that consciousness it is the human will to self-overcoming, not the world, that is affirmed. Without the tension and struggle of self-overcoming, the superman is less than human; but without forgetting the sources of these tensions, the superman can never affirm the world.

Wolfgang Müller-Lauter formulates this problem accurately when he suggests that Nietzsche's superman represents the hope for the integration of two mutually exclusive kinds of human greatness. In the first of these, greatness depends on the ability to will the limitations and ignorance necessary for innocent enjoyment of the world; in the second, greatness comes from the ability to take upon oneself the greatest number of contradictions. Strength and wisdom, respectively, are the qualities celebrated in these two images of human greatness.[106] In the first image, the superman is marked by the strength of his will to ignorance. In the second, he is marked by the richness of the contradictory perspectives he lives with; "the wisest man would be the one richest in contradictions, who has, as it were, antennae for all types of men."[107] In other words, the superman of strength is great because he forgets, while the superman of wisdom is great because he remembers everything.

Nietzsche clearly wants both kinds of greatness together; indeed, I suggest, he values each form of greatness only to the extent that

[104] *Beyond Good and Evil,* 5:79; 72.
[105] *The Gay Science,* 3:605; 313.
[106] W. Müller-Lauter, *Philosophie der Gegensätze,* 117ff.
[107] F. Nietzsche, *The Will to Power,* 150.

351

it comes with the other. The superman of wisdom needs the strength of forgetting in order to love the world he knows so well. The superman of strength needs the wisdom that comes from experience of conflicting drives in order to know how and when to test his strength.[108] Without the consciousness of overcoming something, the superhuman life has no value; but without the strength of forgetting, it cannot endure life at all.

As in Nietzsche's early cultural criticism, man's fate rests on the possibility of self-conscious forgetfulness.[109] How can one individual combine such forgetting and remembering in his will? Like Müller-Lauter, I suggest that Nietzsche never answers this question, that he merely points to what man must achieve in order to escape nihilism and rise to new heights.[110] The conscious forgetfulness toward which Nietzsche exhorts us cannot be found in ordinary skills, as some of Nietzsche's readers have maintained. It has been suggested that to play music well, for example, we need to remember harmonic relationships, fingering, and body control, yet we put these aspects of performing out of our mind in order to play with any style or grace.[111] The whole virtue of the self-forgetfulness that Nietzsche praises, however, lies in its being *willed*. We must be conscious of that which we are forgetting as we forget it. We must remember what we are to forget, the valuelessness of the world, if we are to remain human rather than sink back into an animal state.

The ascetic ideal, Nietzsche argues, has devalued the world of becoming for us. It has taught us to treat anything impermanent as valueless. To revalue the world, we must either restore the ascetic ideal, reverse somehow the internalization of our instincts so that we no longer question the value of existence, or find some way to value infinitely what we know to be valueless. The first option is

[108] See W. Müller-Lauter, *Philosophie der Gegensätze*, 122.
[109] T. Strong, in *Nietzsche and the Politics of Transfiguration*, 236-37, also points out these parallels.
[110] W. Müller-Lauter, *Philosophie der Gegensätze*, 132-33.
[111] Musical performance is Bernd Magnus's example of conscious forgetfulness in *Nietzsche's Existential Imperative*, 38. Tracy Strong uses skiing in a similar way to illustrate conscious forgetfulness (T. Strong, *Nietzsche and the Politics of Transfiguration*, 284ff.).

not really open to us, since the commitment to consistency and truth engendered by the ascetic ideal leads us, inevitably, to challenge the veracity of the ideal itself.[112] The second option would lead us back to an animal life of contentment. Only the third option remains open to those who want to preserve and elevate man's humanity. The superman is one who can value infinitely what he knows to be valueless. For Nietzsche, the essential experience that will raise man to new heights is the simultaneous awareness of what man *knows* to be the opposing sides of a contradiction. Nietzsche demands of this higher man a "capacity for the orgiastic or ecstatic unity of opposites."[113]

Nietzsche offers his doctrine of eternal return, at least in part, as a way of resolving the contradictions in the life of the superman; but, in the end, I suggest, it offers instead the most striking illustration of these contradictions. Like Bernd Magnus, I believe that the eternal return is best understood as an "existential imperative," as pointing to a way of "being in the world" we must strive for, rather than as a cosmological doctrine.[114] But I would add, with Müller-Lauter, that he who wills the eternal return has two different ways of "being in the world."[115] Willing the eternal return describes two different states of mind: the joyous affirmation of all life as if it had all the value that we ordinarily ascribe to permanence and the strength of will that constantly recognizes and suppresses knowledge of the world's valuelessness.

"To impose upon becoming the character of being—that is the supreme will to power."[116] Willing the eternal return is the supreme will to power because it is the greatest contradiction that man has yet been asked to bear. We must bestow on becoming the absolute value that the ascetic ideal taught us to bestow on being. We must treat impermanence with the respect with which, up to now, we have treated permanence. Although Zarathustra spends more

[112] See the third essay of *On the Genealogy of Morals*.
[113] P. Heller, *Dialectics and Nihilism: Essays on Lessing, Nietzsche, Mann, and Kafka*, 71-72.
[114] B. Magnus, *Nietzsche's Existential Imperative*, xiii, 34ff.
[115] W. Müller-Lauter, *Philosophie der Gegensätze*, 186ff.
[116] F. Nietzsche, *The Will to Power*, 330.

time bemoaning the eternal reappearance of what is vulgar and contemptible, the truly unbearable burden of the eternal return is its conscious self-contradiction. We must believe that the world has infinite value precisely because it is devalued in our eyes. We must never forget the valuelessness of becoming while celebrating its eternal return as infinitely valuable. Such is the parable that Nietzsche invents as "praise and justification of impermanence."[117]

Whether the doctrine of eternal return represents an "eternalistic countermyth" or "the most scientific hypothesis,"[118] it provides no explanation of how one can simultaneously remember and forget the valuelessness of the world. Nietzsche's analysis of the limitations of modern individuals and institutions teaches him that self-conscious forgetting of the world's valuelessness is our deepest need; but that analysis offers no reason to believe that such a state of mind is a genuine possibility for human beings. In the end, Karl Löwith is right to call the parable of eternal return a *credo quia absurdum est*.[119] We *must* believe in the possibility of such a seemingly contradictory state of mind because only such self-contradiction can save us from our dehumanization.[120] Once again, Nietzsche merely points the way to Rhodes and exhorts us to leap.

The leap Nietzsche asks us to make has some surprising points of resemblance to Kierkegaard's leap of faith. Kierkegaard justifies Christian faith as the "absolute paradox," whose acceptance requires a leap into the absurd.[121] Nietzsche's argument seems especially close to Kierkegaard's portrayal of the leap from infinite resignation to infinite faith in *Fear and Trembling*. The faith of Kierkegaard's knight of resignation is bought at the price of renouncing the world and his hopes for temporal success. His faith in the next world is firm, but he keeps it only by devaluing this world. His resignation seems to be based on something like faith in

[117] *Thus Spoke Zarathustra*, 4:110; *Portable Nietzsche*, 198.
[118] See B. Magnus, *Nietzsche's Existential Imperative*, xiv.
[119] K. Löwith, *Nietzsches Philosophie der Ewigen Wiederkehr des Gleichen*, 77-78.
[120] W. Müller-Lauter, *Philosophie der Gegensätze*, 133.
[121] See S. Kierkegaard, *Philosophical Fragments*, 46-67.

Nietzsche's ascetic ideal. The knight of faith, however, does not despise the goods of this world at all. He has renounced earthly success as his aim and right, but he still believes his renunciation will bring him success, even though every sign points to the contrary. Like Abraham about to sacrifice Isaac, he believes that though he sacrifices everything unto the Lord, even his son, that same son will live and father many sons himself.[122]

Kierkegaard's problem here is strikingly similar to Nietzsche's. How can one love a world that has been devalued by our concept of eternal being? How can we bring value and meaning into that world without giving up our knowledge of its essential meaninglessness? Kierkegaard answers these questions more forthrightly than does Nietzsche, without obscuring the issue with the pretence of a new cosmology. He tells us we must make a leap of faith into the absurd.

Nietzsche too must make a leap into the absurd, for the problem he seeks to resolve cannot be resolved without self-contradiction. We cannot experience the external world of nature as infinitely valuable as long as we think of meaning and value as that which separates man from natural existence. Despite his anti-idealism, Nietzsche continues to view value as arising out man's unique capacities for resistance to the external guidance of nature. The fact that man is nature's "only leap" devalues the rest of natural existence for Nietzsche as surely as human freedom devalues nature for Kant and Hegel. Nietzsche recognizes that the only way to realize man's humanity in the world, so that the world will have the value whose source lies in the human will, is somehow to will forgetfulness of this fact. Thus in the end Nietzsche requires us both to affirm and deny the Kantian dichotomy between human freedom and natural necessity.

Nietzsche never explains what it is that allows man, apart from all other animals, to turn against his own instincts and become such an interesting animal. He disdains such explanations, complaining that they inevitably degenerate into an infinite regress as we discover faculties to explain behaviour and then are compelled to

[122] S. Kierkegaard, *Fear and Trembling.*

search for more faculties to explain the faculties we have discovered.[123]

Nevertheless, given his silence, his celebration of resistance to external forces, and his description of such resistance as the measure of freedom,[124] it is difficult to avoid the conclusion that Nietzsche's description of man's special capacity for internalization is merely another way of describing the freedom of the human mind to resist external determination, which was elaborated by Hegel and Kant. The evidence gathered in this section suggests the plausibility of this conclusion.[125] If we accept this conclusion, then we can agree with Deleuze's assertion that "Nietzsche's relation to Kant is like Marx's relation to Hegel; Nietzsche stands critique on its feet, just as Marx does with dialectic";[126] but only if we add the following gloss. Putting Kantian critique on its feet entangles Nietzsche in the same kind of self-contradiction that entangles Marx in his attempt to turn Hegelian dialectic right side up. Nietzsche must both affirm and deny the dichotomy between human freedom and natural necessity in order to "realize" Kantian critique. In this he stands in exactly the same relation to Kant as Marx stands to Hegel.

Nietzsche's Longing for Great Politics: The "Spiritualization of Cruelty" and the Cruelty of the Spirit

In the preceding section I argued that Nietzsche still expresses in his later works a longing to realize man's humanity in the world, and that the obstacle to that goal remains the spirit of modern culture. Further, I argued that he comes to identify our devaluation of the world, or more precisely, our inability to value man without devaluing the world, as the obstacle to overcoming the dehumanizing spirit of modern culture. Thus I conclude that in longing for the overcoming of nihilism through a transvaluation of values,

---

[123] *Beyond Good and Evil*, 5:24-25; 18.

[124] *Twilight of the Idols*, 4:140; *Portable Nietzsche*, 542.

[125] Of course, given Nietzsche's numerous explicit denials of this conclusion, I cannot go beyond providing evidence that suggests its plausibility.

[126] G. Deleuze, *Nietzsche and Philosophy*, 89.

Nietzsche longs for a total revolution that will take us beyond the spirit of modern culture.

Nietzsche makes it perfectly clear that the transvaluation of values will overthrow the totality of current social relations.

> I know my fate. One day my name will be associated with the memory of something monstrous—a crisis like none on earth that has ever been, the most profound collision of conscience, a decision that was conjured up *against* everything that had until then been believed, demanded, hallowed. I am no man, I am dynamite. . . . I am necessarily also a man of doom. For when truth enters into a fight with the lies of millenia, we shall have upheavals, a convulsion of earthquakes, a moving of mountains and valleys, the like of which has never been dreamed of. The concept of politics will then be raised entirely to that of a war of spirits; all power structures of the old society will have been exploded—all of them rest on lies: there will be wars like none on earth that have ever been. Only beginning with me does the earth see *great politics*.[127]

How can the revaluation of a meaningless world by a single superhuman will, assuming such a revaluation were possible, effect such a total transformation of our culture and institutions? Nietzsche seems to think that the example of the life that wills the eternal return will effect great changes. He also places great hopes on the effects of aesthetic education, an education shaped by the creations of the few superhuman wills. In his early works, Nietzsche limits himself to such Schillerian means of promoting a total cultural revolution. In *Schopenhauer as Educator* he states that he "value[s] a philosopher only insofar as he provides an example. That he can draw whole peoples after him through his example is beyond doubt; Indian history, which is almost the history of Indian philosophy, proves it."[128] And *On the Uses and Disadvantages of History for Life* ends with the hope that a few untimely souls could, through aesthetic education, lead a new generation be-

[127] *Ecce Homo*, 6:365-66; 326-27.
[128] *Schopenhauer as Educator*, 1:350; *Untimely Meditations*, 136-37.

yond the dehumanizing spirit of modern culture.[129] In his later works Nietzsche clings to such hopes, even if he expresses them in a much more provocative way.

> *Genuine philosophers,* however are *commanders and legislators:* they say, "thus shall it be!" They first determine the whither and for what of man, and in so doing have at their disposal the preliminary labor of all philosophical laborers, all who have overcome the past. With a creative hand they reach for the future, and all that is and was becomes a means for them, an instrument, a hammer. Their "knowing" is creating, their creating is lawgiving, their will to truth is—will to power.[130]

But in his later works, Nietzsche begins to express hopes that sociopolitical upheavals might make possible the total revolution he longs for, rather than that revolution merely following from a transvaluation of values. Thus in his later works he sometimes expresses a longing for grand international convulsions, for what he calls great politics, as a means of promoting cultural revolution. For example, in *Beyond Good and Evil* he discusses what needs to be done to secure the Western European nations from "Europe's greatest danger," the Russian empire, but then he adds:

> I do not say this as someone who wants it to happen: the opposite would be rather more after my heart—I mean such an increase in the menace of Russia that Europe would have to decide to become menacing to the same degree, namely, to acquire *one will* by means of a new caste that would rule Europe, a long terrible will of its own that could cast its goals millenia hence—thus the long-drawn-out comedy of its tiny states as well as its tiny dynastic and democratic wills would finally come to an end. The time for petty politics is over: the very next century will bring the fight for world-dominion—the *compulsion* to great politics.[131]

---

[129] *On the Uses of History,* 1:324ff.; *Untimely Meditations,* 116ff.
[130] *Beyond Good and Evil,* 5:145; 136.
[131] Ibid., 5:240; 131.

Nietzsche's prophecies of "wars like none on earth that have ever been" do not lack a sense of dread, for he recognizes full well the tremendous suffering these wars will bring.[132] Still he longs for such wars, since he believes that they will prepare the cultural revolution that will overcome our dehumanization. They will provide the *"compulsion* to great politics," and great politics will provide the compulsion to a total cultural revolution.

Great politics promotes Nietzsche's total revolution in two ways. First, he seems to believe that tremendous international convulsions will provide an opportunity for the establishment of a new ruling caste, a caste that either consists of or is shaped by the philosopher-legislators who transvalue our values. Great politics might give Nietzschean aesthetic educators power to transform man.

> The possibility has been established for the production of . . . a new, tremendous aristocracy, based on the severest self-legislation, in which the will of philosophical men of power and artist-tyrants will be made to endure for millenia—higher kinds of men who, thanks to their superiority in will, knowledge, riches, and influence, employ democratic Europe as their most pliant and supple instrument for getting hold of the destinies of the earth, so as to work as artists upon "man" himself. Enough: the time is coming when politics will have a different meaning.[133]

Second, Nietzsche associates the physical suffering and discipline that these new wars will bring with the spiritual discipline, the self-overcoming, that makes his transvaluation of values possible. The physical suffering imposed on the people by these wars will prepare them for the spiritual discipline required to accept a valueless world as infinitely valuable. For with great politics "the concept of politics will have been raised entirely to that of a war of spirits."[134]

---

[132] But "the revolution, confusion, and distress of peoples is, in my view, inferior to the distress of great individuals during their development" (F. Nietzsche, *The Will to Power*, 506).

[133] Ibid., 504.

[134] *Ecce Homo*, 6:366; 327.

In themselves, political life and activity have no worth for
Nietzsche. The participatory republicanism of the polis inspires in
him, even in his youth, none of the enthusiasm it inspires in Rousseau and the young Hegel. Indeed, he suggests that excessive interest in politics eventually destroyed Athenian culture. To believe in
the total devotion of the individual to the collective purposes of the
state "is to return to stupidity, not paganism."[135] But politics can
become "great" when it contributes to human greatness. And one
way it can do that is to teach us, by example, the need for discipline.
From this point of view, the democratic movements that dominate
modern politics bring about "not merely the decay of political organization, but rather the decay, namely the diminished form, of
man."[136] Through the imposition of physical suffering and discipline, the great politics of ideological war will restore the taste for
spiritual suffering and self-discipline that modern individuals have
lost.

> In order that there may be institutions, there must be a kind of
> will, instinct, or imperative, which is anti-liberal to the point
> of evil: the will to tradition, to authority, to responsibility for
> centuries to come, to the solidarity of chains of generations,
> forward and backward ad infinitum.[137]

> "You shall obey—someone and for a long time: else you will
> perish and lose the last respect for yourself"—this appears to
> me to be the moral imperative of nature which, to be sure is
> neither "categorical" as old Kant would have demanded (hence
> the "else"), nor addressed to the individual (what do individ-
> uals matter to her?), but to peoples, races, ages, classes—but
> above all to the whole animal *"man,"* to men.[138]

The discipline of great politics will help teach us to accept nature's
"moral imperative." Yet nature's imperative has a special meaning
for man. All nature follows this imperative to obey, but only man

[135] *Schopenhauer as Educator*, 1:365; *Untimely Meditations*, 148. See especially
the early essay on "The Greek State," 1:764-77.
[136] *Beyond Good and Evil*, 5:126; 117.
[137] *Twilight of the Idols*, 6:141; *Portable Nietzsche*, 543.
[138] *Beyond Good and Evil*, 5:110; 102.

can do so with an awareness of the arbitrary character of the authority to which he submits. The great politics of war and social convulsion imposes submission to arbitrary authority on those who do not have the strength of will to impose it upon themselves, and in doing so, it saves them from dehumanization.

We must submit to discipline, Nietzsche tells us, lest we "lose the last respect" for ourselves. Whose discipline is irrelevant. The "worst haven" is better than remaining adrift; "we shall find the good harbors later."[139] For what is essential "'on heaven and earth'" is that "there be *obedience* over a long time and in a single direction: given that, something always develops, and has developed, for whose sake it is worth while to live on earth; for example, virtue, art, music, dance, reason, spirituality—."[140]

André Gide later expresses the same idea but makes explicit its shocking implications. It is time, he states, that "we should side with the men who made Socrates drink hemlock." For "man does nothing great without constraint, and those capable of finding this constraint within themselves are very rare." Such is Gide's Nietzschean justification for supporting the Bolsheviks. He is consistent enough to add that "if I approve of Soviet constraint I must also approve of Fascist discipline."[141] Gide's argument follows from genuine Nietzschean premises. If "something always develops" from discipline and constraint, "for whose sake it is worth while to live on earth," and liberal democratic regimes make such constraint impossible for all but the rarest individuals, then our love of man should lead us to embrace those regimes, whatever their character, that offer us discipline. We are fortunate, one could conclude, that the convulsions of the twentieth century have thrown forth new regimes that offer us discipline and cruelty in such generous measure.

I do not mean here to portray Nietzsche as an apologist for Fascist or Bolshevik brutality, let alone to suggest that his ideas, in some way, cause that brutality. Whether Nietzsche would have been attracted or repelled by the particular forms of cruelty devised by twentieth-century dictatorships is not a question we can answer

[139] *On the Uses of History*, 1:324; *Untimely Meditations*, 116.
[140] *Beyond Good and Evil*, 5:109; 101.
[141] Quoted in A. Hamilton, *The Appeal of Fascism*, xxi–xxiii.

with any certainty, despite the claims of his many accusers and defenders. It is clear, however, that on many occasions he expresses a longing for the reimposition of physical discipline and cruelty by a new ruling caste, and that he sometimes expects a cultural revolution to follow from this reimposition of discipline. It is also clear that similar conclusions lead many twentieth-century intellectuals, like Gide, to embrace regimes that would make "Socrates drink hemlock." My aim is to examine and criticize the reasoning that inspires the longing, which Nietzsche shares, for the reimposition of physical discipline and cruelty.

In insisting that given "*obedience* over a long time and in a single direction," something great "always develops," Nietzsche, I suggest, is drawing a fallacious conclusion from his proposition that every culture needs the discipline of a limiting horizon. Since culture requires discipline, discipline will create culture. Nietzsche treats a necessary condition of cultural greatness as its sufficient condition. He could, of course, appeal to historical experience, rather than to the logic of his analysis of culture, to demonstrate his proposition that physical discipline is a sufficient condition for human greatness. But twentieth-century intellectuals possess a wealth of experience of political discipline and cruelty that even Nietzsche never dreams of. And if that experience has taught us nothing else, it has taught us that the only thing that *necessarily* follows from physical discipline and cruelty is physical suffering.

Ironically, it is Nietzsche's love of man that leads him to entertain such unjustified expectations of what we would gain from the reimposition of physical discipline. Existence may be cruel, but at least if we are willing to recognize the need for cruelty, something great will come of our existence. So Nietzsche hopes. Without this faith, Nietzsche would have to admit that the future of man is out of our hands, no matter how strong the will of the few most daring among us. With it, he can point toward actions that will save man from degeneration. Social convulsions will raise us to "great politics" and, consequently, to new heights of human development through the reimposition and affirmation of arbitrary discipline and suffering.

Nietzsche's conceptual confusion about man's humanity, his simultaneous affirmation and denial of the dichotomy between man's humanity and his nature, also contributes to these unjustified hopes. For it leads him to think of the discipline and self-overcoming that characterize cultural greatness as an outgrowth of physical discipline and cruelty. "Almost everything we call 'higher culture' is based on the spiritualization and deepening of *cruelty*: this is my proposition." All of the great achievements of human culture grow out of the cruelty of the spirit, the capacity of the human mind to turn upon itself.

> [E]ven the knowledge-seeker forces his spirit to recognize things against the inclination of the spirit, and often enough against the wishes of his heart—by saying No where he would like to affirm, love, and adore—and thus as an artist and transfigurer of cruelty. Indeed, any sounding of depth and foundation is a kind of violation, a desire to hurt the basic will of the spirit, which unceasingly strives for the apparent and superficial—in all desire to know there is a drop of cruelty.[142]

Human greatness is won only through "the discipline of great suffering." "Do you not know that only *this* discipline has created all enhancements of man so far?"[143] The enhancement of man requires cruelty to oneself—the cruelty of the spirit. This proposition is arguable, but not unreasonable. But what does it mean to say, as Nietzsche does, that psychic self-discipline represents the "spiritualization" of nature's cruelty? Nature's cruelty is physical. "Imagine a being like nature, wasteful beyond measure, indifferent beyond measure, without purpose and consideration, without mercy and justice, fertile and desolate and uncertain at the same time; imagine indifference itself as a power."[144] Every day, nature tears down what it built the day before. It maims without purpose and destroys its greatest achievements. It is capable of producing a Raphael without hands or killing off Mozart at thirty-five. To speak of self-discipline as the "spiritualization" of nature's cruelty is to suggest that spiritual self-discipline arises somehow out of physical

---

[142] *Beyond Good and Evil*, 5:166-67; 158-59.
[143] Ibid., 5:161; 154.
[144] Ibid., 5:21-22; 15.

cruelty. "The spirits increase, virtue grows through a wound." That is "my motto," Nietzsche proclaims.[145]

But the most obvious difference between the physical cruelty of nature and the cruelty of the spirit, in Nietzsche's presentation, is that the latter is *not* purposeless and indifferent to human ends. Even when the cruelty of the spirit demands the affirmation of nature's cruelty, it does so, as does Nietzsche, with a goal in mind: the enhancement of man. This does not make spiritual cruelty any less harsh to man than natural cruelty. Indeed, as Nietzsche well knows, it is often far harsher. But this extenuation does distinguish it from natural cruelty in a way Nietzsche never successfully explains. Once again, Nietzsche seems to both affirm and deny the humanity/nature dichotomy of his idealist predecessors.

Nietzsche's denial that he actually draws this dichotomy between spirit and nature helps him justify his belief that spiritual cruelty, and consequently human greatness, will always grow out of physical discipline and cruelty. This belief, as I have already suggested, develops out of Nietzsche's love of man. It is his respect and, indeed, love for the human spirit that leads him to endorse the reimposition of physical cruelty. Rather than offer an example of the "spiritualization" of physical cruelty, Nietzsche's love of man shows just how cruel the demands of the spirit can be.

[145]*Twilight of the Idols*, 6:58; *Portable Nietzsche*, 465.

CONCLUSION

SINCE THE END of the nineteenth century, longing for the realization of man's humanity has fueled many of the most influential trends in German social criticism—so much so that there are few surer signs that a social critic has been educated in the German/continental philosophic tradition than complaints about dehumanization or demands that our autonomy be embodied in our institutions. The first critiques of the dehumanizing spirit of modern society have been revised, revived, reversed, and demystified by subsequent generations of social critics.

But as diverse and lively as this tradition of social criticism has been, most of its practitioners take for granted the most fundamental propositions upon which it rests: that the failure to realize our humanity in the external world is the source of all our woes, and that the spirit of modern society is the obstacle to the realization of our humanity. Most of the debates within this tradition are about the location of the source of the dehumanizing spirit of modern society and the means of eliminating it. The debate's participants rarely ask how they come to identify the obstacle to a world without social sources of dissatisfaction in this way or whether it makes any sense to do so.

One of the major purposes of this study has been to address these questions. In doing so, it has pursued both historical and critical aims. The historical aim has been to identify and account for two states of mind shared by a large number of European intellectuals since the end of the eighteenth century: a longing to get beyond what is perceived as the dehumanizing spirit of modern society and a longing to eliminate the obstacles to overcoming that spirit— what I call the longing for total revolution. This study also tries to show how conceptual innovations, by suggesting new definitions of the obstacles to our satisfaction in the world, have made these new needs possible. In particular, I have tried to uncover the conceptual innovations that first made possible the identification of the dehumanizing spirit of modern society as the obstacle to a world without social sources of dissatisfaction, to describe the general characteristics of this new state of mind, and to provide evidence that this state of mind is shared by many of the most influential European social critics from Rousseau to Marx to Nietzsche.

My historical investigation of the conceptual sources of this peculiarly modern form of social discontent also supports a critique of the aims of Marx's and Nietzsche's social criticism. It uncovers the two conceptual premises one must hold in order to identify the spirit of modern society as the obstacle to a world without social sources of dissatisfaction, and it shows that Marx and Nietzsche implicitly affirm both. Once these premises are brought to light, we are able to uncover an important self-contradiction in Marx's and Nietzsche's social criticism. In their own ways, both Marx and Nietzsche affirm and deny one of these premises, namely the dichotomy between human freedom and natural necessity.

Although my criticisms focus primarily on Marx's and Nietzsche's arguments, I have tried to suggest that *any* attempt to define the obstacle to the realization of humanity in terms of a particular, historical form of social interaction will eventually fall into something like this self-contradiction. For the premiss that suggests the identification of dehumanization, as I have defined it in this book, as the obstacle to a world without social sources of dissatisfaction—a definition of man's humanity in terms of the individual's ability to resist external conditioning—rules out the realization of our humanity in the external world. Any institution that conditions our behaviour will be dehumanizing, as long as we hold this understanding of man's humanity.

Historicizing the problem of dehumanization, portraying the spirit of modern society, rather than social interaction per se, as the source of dehumanization, seems to allow us to make this immovable obstacle movable. But such a historicization of the obstacle to the realization of man's humanity in the world cannot be maintained without contradiction. If every social phenomenon is always shaped by the spirit of social interaction that informs its epoch or society as a whole, then social phenomena will always be externally conditioned. The only resolution of this contradiction would be to demonstrate that the spirit of society itself represents, in some way, the realization of man's humanity, that the human spirit somehow informs the spirit of social interaction. Hegel explores this possibility more thoroughly than any other thinker. But even he comes to recognize that we cannot separate the forms taken by our social interaction from that which is dehumanizing: the external conditioning of our institutions and needs by the natural contingencies that remain indifferent to human purposes.

The self-contradiction implicit in the project of realizing our humanity in the spirit of social interaction is suggested by Schiller's formulation of that project: to become whole again like nature, but "by means of our reason and freedom." According to Schiller, it is our reason and freedom that separate us from nature, and that lead us to deny that any institution that works through external conditioning of our will embodies our humanity. To ask for reidentification with the external world by means of our reason and freedom is to ask us to make use of faculties defined by their opposition to external conditioning as the means of external conditioning. If we are successful in using these faculties in such a way, we will have "dehumanized" the faculties themselves. If we hold to our understanding of our humanity, then we will fail to realize our freedom in the world. That may be why Schiller ultimately views self-imposed harmony as an ideal, an unreachable model to guide human striving.

In the end, if we view the dependence of institutions on external conditioning as dehumanizing, then we had better become accustomed to living with dehumanization; for dehumanization will exist in every institution and form of social interaction. Marx's and Nietzsche's efforts to locate the particular spheres of social interaction that make modern institutions dehumanizing are, therefore, in vain. No revolution, no matter how it is defined, can take us beyond the dehumanization that they discover in modern individuals and institutions. If we are interested in eliminating some of the sources of dissatisfaction in our interactions with each other, indeed, if we are interested in using Marx's and Nietzsche's insights to do so, then we must develop alternative understandings of the obstacles to our satisfaction. For dehumanization, as they understand it, is an immovable obstacle to the improvement of our world.

My conclusion is that the goal of a total revolution against the dehumanizing spirit of modern society is self-contradictory. By providing a single focus for all of our dissatisfaction with the world, the longing for total revolution raises great hopes for the transfiguration, however defined, of the human condition. By uncovering the self-contradictory nature of such a total revolution, I have tried to uproot the foundations of these hopes.

Does such a conclusion leave us helpless and hopeless in the face of the obstacles to our satisfaction posed by modern institutions? I think not. It renders us passive and hopeless only to the extent that we continue to assume that the modern epoch represents a coherent and consistent whole, integrated by a single spirit of social interaction. This assumption makes social improvement an all-or-nothing venture. Either we uproot the underlying spirit of social interaction or we resign ourselves to the limitations of our institutions and practises. For as long as particular institutions and practises gain their character from the spirit of the whole, efforts to alter their character short of total revolution are bound to fail.

One of the main aims of my deconstruction of the post-Kantian tradition of philosophic social criticism has been to bring to light its uncritical and often unconscious reliance on this assumption. Marx and Nietzsche reject almost everything their predecessors say about the spirit of the modern epoch except that there indeed exists a modern epoch—a single coherent and integrated form of social interaction—standing in our way. Their critiques of modern institutions thus grow out of an assumption about the organization of society, an assumption they share with Hegel.

I have not attempted to demonstrate that this assumption is self-contradictory or indefencible, although I have suggested in Chapters 5 and 7 that it would be difficult to reconcile it with any non-idealist approach to the study of social phenomena. This assumption can help us to construct interesting and original explanations of institutions and behaviour. But however compelling these portraits of modern institutions and behaviour as integrated coherent wholes may be, they represent social constructions of reality. The choice between hopes for a total revolution and hopelessness in the face of the limitations of modern individuals and institutions arises out of a particular way of constructing modern realities, not out of the "realities" themselves. My study of the conceptual premisses of the longing for total revolution suggests that once we bring these premisses to light, we must abandon as a self-contradictory goal total revolution against the dehumanizing spirit of modern society. But once we recognize these premisses as social constructions, rather than as aspects of modern "reality," then the spirit of modern society need no longer pose an immovable obstacle to social change. Partial reform and, indeed, partial revolution regain meaning and importance.

The results of my study of the post-Kantian tradition of philosophic social criticism are thus not entirely negative. Recognition of the futility of total revolution against the spirit of modernity need not lead to helplessness and despair. It can, instead, liberate us to approach our problems in new and creative ways. These approaches may lack the promise of satisfying our age-old longing for a world without social sources of dissatisfaction, but they will have the advantage of not being inherently self-defeating.

BIBLIOGRAPHY

Primary Sources

Aristotle. *Nicomachean Ethics*. Cambridge, Mass.: 1956.
———. *Politics*. Cambridge, Mass.: 1967.
Bakunin, Mikhail. *Selected Writings*. Edited by A. Lehning. London: 1973.
———. *Statism and Anarchy*. New York: 1976.
Burckhardt, Jakob. *Griechische Kulturgeschichte*. 3 Vols. Stuttgart: 1952.
———. *Weltgeschichtliche Betrachtungen*. Bern: 1941.
Cieszkowski, August von. *Prolegomena zur Historiosophie*. Nendeln: 1976 (reprint of 1838 edition).
———. *Selected Writings of August Cieszkowski*. Edited by A. Liebich. Cambridge: 1979.
Constant, Benjamin. *Commentaire sur l'ouvrage de Filangierie*. 2 Vols. Paris: 1822-24.
———. "La Liberté des anciens comparée à celle des modernes." In Constant, *La liberté chez les modernes*. Paris: 1980.
———. *Les "Principes de Politique" de Benjamin Constant*. 2 Vols. Edited by E. Hoffmann. Geneva: 1980.
Engels, Frederick. *Ludwig Feuerbach and the End of Classical German Philosophy*. Moscow: 1957.
Feuerbach, Ludwig. *The Essence of Christianity*. New York: 1957.
———. *The Fiery Brook: Selected Writings of Ludwig Feuerbach*. Edited and translated by Z. Hanfi. Garden City, N.Y.: 1972.
———. *Kleine Schriften*. Frankfurt am Main: 1971.
Fichte, Johann Gottlieb. *Briefwechsel*. 2 Vols. Edited by H. Schultz. Leipzig: 1930.
———. *Schriften zur Revolution*. Edited by B. Willms. Frankfurt: 1967.
———. *The Science of Rights*. New York: 1970.
———. *The Vocation of the Scholar*. In Fichte, *Popular Works*. 2 Vols. London: 1889.
Fustel de Coulanges, N. D. *The Ancient City*. Garden City, N.Y.: 1962.

Goethe, Johann Wolfgang von. *Truth and Poetry: From My Own Life*. 2 Vols. London: 1890.

Hegel, Georg Wilhelm Friedrich. *Aesthetics*. 2 Vols. Translated by T. M. Knox. Oxford: 1979.

————. *Berliner Schriften*. Edited by J. Hoffmeister. Hamburg: 1956.

————. *Briefe von und an Hegel*. 4 Vols. Edited by J. Hoffmeister. Hamburg: 1952-60.

————. *The Difference between the Systems of Fichte and Schelling*. Translated by H. S. Harris and W. Cerf. Albany: 1977.

————. *Dokumente zur Hegels Entwicklung*. Edited by J. Hoffmeister. Stuttgart: 1936.

————. *Early Theological Writings*. Translated by T. M. Knox. Chicago: 1948.

————. *Faith and Knowledge*. Translated by H. S. Harris and W. Cerf. Albany: 1977.

————. *Gesammelte Werke*. Edited by the Rheinische Akademie. Hamburg: 1968-in progress.

————. *Grundlinien der Philosophie des Rechts*. Edited by G. Lasson. Leipzig: 1911.

————. *Hegel and the Human Spirit*. Translated by L. Rauch. Detroit: 1983.

————. *History of Philosophy*. 3 Vols. Translated by E. S. Haldane. New York: 1974.

————. *Lectures on the Philosophy of World History*. Translated by H. Nisbet. Cambridge: 1975.

————. *Logic: Part One of the Encyclopedia of the Philosophical Sciences*. Translated by W. Wallace. Oxford: 1975.

————. *Natural Law*. Translated by T. M. Knox. Philadelphia: 1974.

————. *The Phenomenology of Spirit*. Translated by A. V. Miller. Oxford: 1977.

————. *Philosophy of History*. Translated by J. Sibree. New York: 1956.

————. *Philosophy of Mind: Part Three of the Encyclopedia*. Translated by W. Wallace and A. V. Miller. Oxford: 1976.

————. *Philosophy of Nature*. 3 Vols. Translated by M. J. Petry. New York: 1970.

————. *Philosophy of Religion*. 3 Vols. Translated by E. B. Speirs and J. B. Sanderson. New York: 1974.

————. *Philosophy of Right*. Translated by T. M. Knox. Oxford: 1942.

————. *Science of Logic*. Translated by A. V. Miller. London: 1969.

Hegel, Georg Wilhelm Friedrich. *Theologische Jugendschriften.* Edited by
H. Nohl. Tübingen: 1908.

―――. *Three Essays.* Translated by P. Fuss and J. Dobbins. Notre Dame:
1984.

―――. *Vorlesungen über die Philosophie der Weltgeschichte.* Edited by
G. Lasson. Hamburg: 1976.

―――. *Werke.* 20 Vols. Edited by E. Moldenhauer and K. M. Michel.
Frankfurt: 1970-71.

Heine, Heinrich. *Religion and Philosophy in Germany.* In Heine, *Works.*
20 Vols. London: 1890. Vol. 5.

Herder, Johann Gottfried. *Sämtlichte Werke.* 33 Vols. Edited by B. Su-
phan. Leipzig: 1877-1913.

Herzen, Alexander. *From the Other Shore.* Oxford: 1956.

―――. *Selected Philosophical Works.* Moscow: 1953.

Hess, Moses. "The Recent Philosophers." In L. Stepelevich (ed.), *The
Young Hegelians.* Cambridge: 1983.

Hölderlin, Friedrich. *Hyperion.* Munich: Goldmann, n.d.

―――. *Poems and Fragments: A Bilingual Collection.* Cambridge: 1980.

Humbolt, Wilhelm von. *The Limits of State Action.* Edited by J. W.
Burrow. Cambridge: 1969.

―――. "On the Historian's Task." In L. von Ranke, *The Theory and
Practice of History.* Indianapolis: 1973.

Kant, Immanuel. *Anthropology: From a Pragmatic Point of View.* Car-
bondale, Ill.: 1978.

―――. *Critique of Judgment.* Translated by J. H. Bernard. New York:
1968.

―――. *Critique of Practical Reason.* Translated by L. W. Beck. Indianapolis: 1956.

―――. *Critique of Pure Reason.* Translated by N. K. Smith. New York:
1965.

―――. *Fundamental Principles of the Metaphysics of Morals.* Indianapolis: 1949.

―――. *Metaphysical Elements of Justice.* Indianapolis: 1965.

―――. *On History.* Edited by L. W. Beck. Indianapolis: 1963.

―――. *Philosophic Correspondence.* Edited and translated by
A. Zweig. Chicago: 1967.

―――. *Political Writings.* Edited by H. A. Nisbet. Cambridge: 1970.

―――. *Religion within the Limits of Reason Alone.* Translated by T. M.
Greene and H. H. Hudson. New York: 1960.

―――. *Werke.* 8 Vols. Edited by G. Hartenstein. Berlin: 1867-68. Vol. 8.

Kierkegaard, Søren. *Fear and Trembling.* Princeton: 1968.

————. *Philosophical Fragments.* Princeton: 1969.

Langbehn, Julius. *Rembrandt als Erzieher.* Weimar: 1943.

Lessing, Gotthold Ephraim. "On the Education of the Human Race." In H. Chadwick (ed.), *Lessing's Theological Writings.* Stanford: 1981.

Machiavelli, Niccolò. *The Prince and the Discourses.* New York: 1950.

Mann, Thomas. *Essays of Three Decades.* New York: 1947.

————. "Gedanken im Kriege." In Mann, *Politische Schriften und Reden.* 2 Vols. Hamburg: 1964. 2: 7-19.

Marx, Karl. *Capital, Vol. 1.* Translated by S. Aveling. New York: Modern Library, n.d.

————. *Capital, Vol. 3.* New York: 1967.

————. *Grundrisse.* Translated by M. Nicolaus. New York: 1973.

Marx, Karl & Engels, Frederick. *Collected Works.* New York: 1975-in progress.

————. *The Marx-Engels Reader.* Edited by R. Tucker. New York: 1978.

————. *Selected Correspondence.* New York: 1942.

————. *Werke.* 39 Vols. Berlin: 1953-68.

————. *Werke, Erganzungsbände.* 2 Vols. Berlin: 1968.

Montaigne, Michel de. *Essays.* Translated by D. Frame. Stanford: 1965.

Montesquieu, C. S. de. *Oeuvres Complètes.* 2 Vols. Dijon: 1951.

Nietzsche, Friedrich. *Beyond Good and Evil.* Translated by W. Kaufmann. New York: 1966.

————. *The Birth of Tragedy* and *The Case of Wagner.* Translated by W. Kaufmann. New York: 1967.

————. *The Gay Science.* Translated by W. Kaufmann. New York: 1974.

————. *Briefwechsel.* Berlin: 1975-in progress.

————. *On the Genealogy of Morals* and *Ecce Homo.* Translated by W. Kaufmann. New York: 1969.

————. *Philosophy and Truth: Selections from Nietzsche's Notebooks of the Early 70's.* Edited and translated by D. Breazeale. New York: 1979.

————. *Sämtlichte Werke. Kritische Studienausgabe.* 15 Vols. Edited by G. Colli and M. Montinari. Berlin: 1967-77.

————. *Selected Letters of Friedrich Nietzsche.* Edited and translated by C. Middleton. Chicago: 1969.

————. *Untimely Meditations.* Translated by R. J. Hollingdale. Cambridge: 1983.

————. *The Viking Portable Nietzsche.* (Contains *Thus Spoke Zarathustra, The Antichrist,* and *Twilight of the Idols.*) Edited and translated by W. Kaufmann. New York: 1975.

Nietzsche, Friedrich. *The Will to Power*. Edited and translated by R. J. Hollingdale and W. Kaufman. New York: 1968.

Novalis (Friedrich von Hardenberg). "Christendom or Europe." In H. Reiss (ed.), *The Political Thought of the German Romantics*. Oxford: 1955, pp. 126-41.

Plato. *Republic*. Translated by A. Bloom. New York: 1968.

Plutarch. *The Lives of the Noble Greeks and Romans*. New York: 1953.

————. "Sayings of the Spartans," and "Sayings of Spartan Women." In Plutarch, *Moralia*. 15 Vols. Cambridge, Mass.: 1958. 2:242-424, 454-72.

Robespierre, Maximilien. *Oeuvres*. 10 Vols. Paris: 1967.

Rousseau, Jean-Jacques. *The Confessions of Jean-Jacques Rousseau*. New York: Modern Library, n.d.

————. *Emile*. Translated by A. Bloom. New York: 1979.

————. *First and Second Discourses*. Translated by R. Masters. New York: 1964.

————. *Lettres philosophiques*. Edited by H. Gouhier. Paris: 1974.

————. *Oeuvres Complètes*. 4 Vols. Dijon: 1959-69.

————. *On the Social Contract* and *Discourse on Political Economy*. Translated by J. Masters. New York: 1978.

Ruge, Arnold. *Gesammelte Werke*. 6 Vols. Mannheim: 1846.

Saint Just, L. A. *Oeuvres Choisies*. Paris: 1968.

Schelling, F. *On the Unconditional in Human Knowledge: 4 Early Essays*. Translated by F. Marti. Lewisburg: 1980.

————. *System of Transcendental Idealism*. Translated by P. Heath. Charlottesville, Va.: 1980.

————. *Werke*. 6 Vols. Munich: 1928.

Schiller, Friedrich. *Briefe*. 7 Vols. Edited by F. Jonas. Stuttgart: 1892-96.

————. *Briefwechsel zwischen Schiller und Goethe*. 2 Vols. Jena: 1910.

————. *Briefwechsel zwischen Schiller und Körner*. 4 Vols. Stuttgart: Cotta, n.d.

————. *On Naive and Sentimental Poetry*. Translated by J. Elias. New York: 1966.

————. *On the Aesthetic Education of Man*. English and German facing. Edited and translated by L. A. Willoughby and E. M. Wilkinson. Oxford: 1967.

————. "On the Influence of Woman on the Virtue of Man." In Schiller, *Sämtlichte Werke*. 18 Vols. Leipzig: 1898. 17:69-80.

————. *Werke*. Nationalausgabe. Edited by L. Blumenthal and B. von Wiese. Weimar: 1943-in progress.

Schlegel, Friedrich. *Prosaische Jugendschriften*. 2 Vols. Edited by J. Minor. Vienna: 1906.

Schopenhauer, Arthur. *The World as Will and Representation*. 2 Vols. New York: 1969.

Spengler, Otto. *The Decline of the West*. 2 Vols. New York: 1928.

Strauss, D. F. *The Old Faith and the New: A Confession*. London: 1873.

———. *Streitschriften zur Verteidigung meiner Schriften über der Leben Jesu*. 3 Vols. Tübingen: 1841.

Sturz, H. P. *Denkwürdigkeiten von J. J. Rousseau*. Leipzig: 1779.

Thucydides. *The Peloponnesian War*. Translated by B. Crawley. New York: 1951.

Tocqueville, Alexis de. *The Old Régime and the French Revolution*. Translated by S. Gilbert. Garden City, N.Y.: 1955.

Volney, C. F. de. *Leçons d'histoire*. In Volney, *Oeuvres*. Paris: 1860.

Wagner, Richard. "Art and Revolution." In Wagner, *Prose Works*. 8 Vols. Translated by W. A. Ellis. London: 1895. 1:24-70.

Secondary Sources

Agulhon, Maurice. *Marianne into Battle*. Cambridge: 1981.

Althusser, Louis. *For Marx*. New York: 1970.

———. *Politics and History*. London: 1972.

Andler, Charles. *Nietzsche, sa vie et sa pensée*. 3 Vols. Paris: 1958.

Arendt, Hannah. *The Human Condition*. Garden City, N.Y.: 1958.

———. *On Revolution*. New York: 1965.

Aris, Reinhold. *A History of Political Thought in Germany: 1780-1915*. London: 1936.

Aron, Raymond. *The Opium of the Intellectuals*. New York: 1962.

Avineri, Schlomo. *Hegel's Theory of the Modern State*. Cambridge: 1972.

———. *The Social and Political Thought of Karl Marx*. Cambridge: 1968.

Ayrault, Robert. "Schiller et Montesquieu: Sur la genèse de Don Carlos." *Études Germaniques*. 3 (1948): 233-40.

Bahro, Rudolf. *The Alternative in Eastern Europe*. London: 1978.

Barth, Hans. *Truth and Ideology*. Berkeley: 1970.

Baumler, Alfred. *Nietzsche, der Philosoph und der Politiker*. Leipzig: 1931.

Beck, Lewis White. "Kant and the Right of Revolution." In Beck, *Essays on Kant and Hume*. New Haven: 1978.

Becker, Carl. *The Heavenly City of the 18th Century Philosophers.* New Haven: 1948.

Behler, Ernst. "Nietzsche und die Frühromantische Schule." *Nietzsche Studien.* 8 (1978): 59-87.

Benda, Julien. *The Treason of the Intellectuals.* New York: 1969.

Bennet, Benjamin. "Nietzsche's Idea of Myth: The Birth of Tragedy from the Spirit of 18th Century Aesthetics." *PMLA* 94: 420-33.

Berki, R. N. *Insight and Vision: The Problem of Communism in Marx's Thought.* London: 1983.

Berman, Marshall. *The Politics of Authenticity.* New York: 1972.

Bernstein, Richard. *Beyond Objectivism and Relativism.* Philadelphia: 1983.

Billington, James. *Fire in the Minds of Men: Origins of the Revolutionary Faith.* New York: 1980.

Blumenberg, Hans. *Die Genesis der Kopernikanischen Welt.* Frankfurt: 1975.

———. *The Legitimacy of the Modern Age.* Cambridge, Mass.: 1983.

Borghero, Carlo. "Sparta tra storia e utopia. Il significato e la funzione del mito di Sparta nel pensiero di Jean-Jacques Rousseau." In G. Solinas (ed.), *Saggi sull'illuminismo.* Cagliari: 1973.

Boucher, Michel. *La Révolution vue par les écrivains allemands.* Paris: 1954.

Bracher, Karl Dietrich. "Turn of the Century and Totalitarian Ideology." In *Totalitarian Democracy and After.* Jerusalem: 1984.

Brandes, Georg. *Friedrich Nietzsche.* New York: 1972.

Brazill, William. *The Young Hegelians.* New Haven: 1971.

Breazeale, Daniel. "The Hegel-Nietzsche Problem." *Nietzsche Studien* 4 (1975): 146-64.

Bubner, Rüdiger (ed.), *Das Älteste Systemprogram.* Bonn: 1971.

———. *Theorie und Praxis: Eine Nachhegelsche Abstraktion.* Frankfurt: 1971.

———. "Was ist Kritische Theorie." In Bubner et al., *Hermeneutik und Ideologiekritik.* Frankfurt: 1971.

Buck, Gunther. "Selbsterhaltung und Historizität." In H. Ebeling (ed.), *Subjektivität und Selbsterhaltung.* Frankfurt: 1976.

Burgelin, Pierre. *La philosophie de l'existence de J. J. Rousseau.* Paris: 1973.

Butler, E. M. *The Tyranny of Greece over Germany.* Boston: 1958.

Cassirer, Ernst. *The Philosophy of the Enlightenment.* Princeton: 1951.

————. *The Question of Jean-Jacques Rousseau.* Bloomington, Ind.: 1964.

————. *Rousseau, Kant, and Goethe.* Princeton: 1945.

Castoriades, Cornelius. "From Marx to Aristotle and from Aristotle to Ourselves." In Castoriades, *Crossroads in the Labyrinth.* Cambridge: 1984.

Chapman, John W. *Rousseau: Totalitarian or Liberal.* New York: 1956.

Cobban, Alfred. *In Search of Humanity.* New York: 1960.

————. "The Political Ideas of Robespierre during the Convention" and "The Fundamental Ideas of Robespierre." In Cobban, *Aspects of the French Revolution.* New York: 1968.

————. *Rousseau and the Modern State.* Hamden, Conn.: 1961.

Cohen, Gerald A. *Marx's Theory of History: A Defence.* Princeton: 1978.

Cohn, Norman. *The Pursuit of the Millenium.* Oxford: 1970.

Croce, Benedetto. *What is Living and What is Dead of the Philosophy of Hegel.* London: 1915.

Crocker, Lester. "Rousseau et la voie du totalitarisme." *Annales de la philosophie politique 5: Rousseau et la philosophie politique.* Paris: 1965.

Deleuze, Gilles. *Nietzsche and Philosophy.* New York: 1983.

Derathé, Robert. *Rousseau et la science politique de son temps.* Paris: 1950.

————. "Rousseau et Montesquieu." *Revue internationale de philosophie* 9 (1955): 366-96.

Dicke, Gerd. *Der Identitätsgedanke bei Feuerbach und Marx.* Köln: 1960.

Dilthey, Wilhelm. *Die Jugendgeschichte Hegels und andere Abhändlungen.* Stuttgart: 1959.

Droz, Jacques. *L'Allemagne et la Révolution française.* Paris: 1949.

Ehrard, Jean. *L'idée de la nature en France dans la première moitié du XVIIIème siècle.* 2 Vols. Paris: 1963.

Eliade, Mircea. *Cosmos and History: The Myth of the Eternal Return.* New York: 1959.

Elias, Norbert. *The History of Manners.* 2 Vols. New York: 1982.

Elster, Jon. *Making Sense of Marx.* Cambridge: 1985.

————. *Sour Grapes: Studies in the Subversion of Rationality.* Cambridge: 1983.

————. *Ulysses and the Sirens: Studies in Rationality and Irrationality.* Cambridge: 1979.

Fackenheim, Emil. "On the Actuality of the Rational and the Rationality of the Actual." *Review of Metaphysics.* 76 (1970): 690-98.

————. *The Religious Dimension in Hegel's Thought.* Boston: 1969.

Ferrari, Jean. *Les sources françaises de la philosophie de Kant.* Paris: 1979.

Fester, Richard. *Rousseau und die Deutsche Geschichtsphilosophie.* Stuttgart: 1890.

Fink, Zera. *The Classical Republicans.* Evanston, Ill.: 1962.

Fischer, K. F. "Nazism as a Nietzschean Experiment." *Nietzsche Studien* 6 (1977): 116-22.

Fletcher, D. J. "Montesquieu's Concept of Patriotism." *Studies on Voltaire and the 18th Century* 56 (1976): 541-55.

Fleuret, Colette. *Rousseau et Montaigne.* Paris: 1980.

Fralin, Richard. *Rousseau and Representation.* New York: 1978.

Freier, Hans. *Die Ruckkehr der Götter.* Stuttgart: 1976.

Fuhrmann, Manfred. "Die 'Querelle des Anciens et des Modernes': Der Nationalismus und die Deutsche Klassiker." In R. R. Bolgar (ed.), *The Classical Influence on Western Thought 1650–1870.* Cambridge: 1979.

Furet, François. *Interpreting the French Revolution.* Cambridge: 1983.

Gadamer, Hans Georg. *Truth and Method.* London: 1975.

Gaede, Udo. *Schiller und Nietzsche als Verkünder der Tragischen Kultur.* Berlin: 1908.

Gay, Peter. "Carl Becker's Heavenly City." In R. O. Rockwood (ed.), *Carl Becker's "Heavenly City" Revisited.* Ithaca, N.Y.: 1956.

———. *The Enlightenment: An Interpretation.* 2 Vols. New York: 1968.

Gebhardt, Jurgen. *Politik und Eschatologie: Studien zur Geschichte der Hegelschen Schule 1830-1840.* Munich: 1963.

Glucksmann, Andre. *The Master Thinkers.* New York: 1980.

Goldmann, Lucien. *Immanuel Kant.* London: 1971.

Gooch, George Peabody. *Germany and the French Revolution.* New York: 1966.

Gordon, Fred. "The Contradictory Nature of Feuerbachian Humanism." *Philosophical Forum.* 8 (1978): 31-47.

Gossman, Lionel. "Time and History in Rousseau." *Studies on Voltaire and the 18th Century.* 30 (1964): 311-49.

Gouldner, Alvin. *The Future of the Intellectuals and the Rise of the New Class.* London: 1979.

———. *The Two Marxisms.* London: 1980.

Goyard-Fabre, Simone. *Nietzsche et la question politique.* Paris: 1977.

Graham, Ilse. *Schiller's Drama: Talent and Integrity.* New York: 1974.

Gray, J. Glenn. *Hegel and Greek Thought.* New York: 1968.

Griewank, Karl. *Der Neuzeitliche Revolutionsbegriff.* Frankfurt: 1969.

Guerci, Luciano. *Libertà degli antichi e libertà dei moderni: Sparta, Atene e i "philosophes" nella Francia del settocento.* Naples: 1979.

Gurvitch, Georges. "Kant et Fichte, interprètes de Rousseau." *Revue de Metaphysique et Morale* 76 (1971): 386-405.

Guthke, Karl. "Zur Frühgeschichte der Rousseauismus in Deutschland." *Zeitschrift für Deutschen Philologie* 77 (1958): 384-95.

Habermas, Jürgen. *Theory and Praxis*. Boston: 1978.

———. *The Theory of Communicative Action*. Boston: 1984.

Hamilton, Alisdair. *The Appeal of Fascism*. New York: 1971.

Hammer, Christopher. *Rousseau and Goethe*. Lexington, Ky.: 1973.

Harries, Karsten. "Hegel and the Future of Art." *Review of Metaphysics* 27 (1973-74): 677-97.

Harris, Henry S. *Hegel's Development toward the Sunlight 1770-1801*. Oxford: 1973.

———. *Hegel's Development: Night Thoughts*. Oxford: 1983.

Hartmann, Klaus. *Die Marxsche Theorie*. Berlin: 1970.

Hatfield, Henry. *Aesthetic Paganism in German Literature from Winckelmann to the Death of Goethe*. Cambridge, Mass.: 1964.

Heidegger, Martin. *Nietzsche*. 2 Vols. Pfullingen: 1961.

Hell, Victor. *Schiller*. Paris: 1974.

Heller, Erich. *The Artist's Journey into the Interior and Other Essays*. New York: 1965.

———. *The Disinherited Mind*. New York: 1959.

———. *The Ironic German: A Study of Thomas Mann*. Boston: 1958.

Heller, Peter. *Dialectics and Nihilism: Essays on Lessing, Nietzsche, Mann, and Kafka*. Amherst, Mass.: 1969.

———. "Nietzsche in his Relation to Voltaire and Rousseau." In J. C. O'Flaherty (ed.), *Studies in Nietzsche and the Classical Tradition*. Chapel Hill, N.C.: 1976.

Henrich, Dieter. "Der Begriff der Schönheit in Schillers Aesthetik." *Zeitschrift für Philosophische Forschung* 11 (1957): 527-47.

———. *Hegel im Kontext*. Frankfurt: 1971.

———. "Kunst und Kunstphilosophie der Gegenwart." In W. Iser (ed.), *Immanente Ästhetik*. Munich: 1966.

Hillebrand, Karl. "Einiges über den Verfall der deutschen Sprache und der deutschen Gesinnung." In Hillebrand, *Zeiten, Völker und Menschen*. 7 Vols. Berlin: 1874-75. 2: 291-310.

Hirschman, Albert. *The Passions and the Interests*. Princeton: 1978.

Holmes, Stephen. *Benjamin Constant and the Making of Modern Liberalism*. New Haven: 1984.

Hughes, H. S. *Consciousness and Society: The Reorientation of European Social Thought*. New York: 1958.

Hulliung, Mark. *Montesquieu and the Old Regime*. Berkeley: 1976.

Hunt, Lynn. *Politics, Culture, and Class in the French Revolution*. Berkeley: 1984.

Hunt, Richard N. *Marx and Totalitarian Democracy*. Pittsburgh: 1974.

Janicaud, Dominique. *Hegel et la destin de la Grèce*. Paris: 1975.

Jaspers, Karl. *Nietzsche*. Tuscon: 1965.

———. *Nietzsche und das Christentum*. Munich: 1952.

Jauss, H. R. "Schlegels und Schillers Replik auf die 'Querelle des Anciens et des Modernes.' " In Jauss, *Literaturgeschichte als Provokation*. Frankfurt: 1970.

Kain, Phillip. *Schiller, Hegel, and Marx: State, Society, and the Aesthetic Ideal of Ancient Greece*. Kingston, Ontario: 1982.

Kamenka, Eugene. *The Ethical Foundations of Marxism*. London: 1962.

Kaufmann, Walter. *From Shakespeare to Existentialism*. Garden City, N.Y.: 1971.

———. *Nietzsche: Philosopher, Psychologist, Anti-Christ*. Princeton: 1974.

Kelly, Aileen. *Michael Bakunin: A Study in the Psychology and Politics of Utopianism*. Oxford: 1982.

Kelly, George A. "Borrowings and Uses of History in Rousseau." *Studies in Burke and his Time*. 16 (1974-75): 129-48.

———. *Hegel's Retreat from Eleusis*. Princeton: 1978.

———. *Idealism, Politics, and History*. Cambridge: 1969.

Kojève, Alexandre. *Introduction à la lecture de Hegel*. Paris: 1947.

Kolakowski, Leszek. *Main Currents of Marxism*. 3 Vols. Oxford: 1978.

———. "The Myth of Human Self-Identity." In Kolakowski, *The Socialist Idea: A Reappraisal*. New York: 1974.

———. *Der Revolutionäre Geist*. Stuttgart: 1972.

Koselleck, Reinhart. *Kritik und Krise*. Frankfurt am Main: 1973.

Kramnick, Isaac. *Bolingbroke and his Circle*. Cambridge: 1968.

Kroner, Richard. *Von Kant bis Hegel*. 2 Vols. Tübingen: 1921.

Krummel, R. F. *Nietzsche und der Deutsche Geist*. Berlin: 1974.

Kuhn, Helmut. *Die Vollendung der Klassischen Deutschen Aesthetik durch Hegel*. Berlin: 1931.

Kurz, Gerhard. *Mittelbarkeit und Vereinigung: Zum Verhältnis von Poesie, Reflexion, und Revolution bei Hölderlin*. Stuttgart: 1975.

Lasky, Melvin. *Utopia and Revolution*. Chicago: 1976.

Leduc-Fayette, Denis. *Rousseau et le mythe de l'antiquité*. Paris: 1974.

Leroux, Robert. "Schiller: Theoricien de l'état." *Revue Germanique* (1937): 1-28.

Levi-Malvano, Alberto. *Montesquieu e Machiavelli.* Paris: 1912.

Levin, L. M. *The Political Doctrine of Montesquieu's Spirit of the Laws: Its Classical Background.* New York: 1936.

Levy, Bernard Henri. *Barbarism with a Human Face.* New York: 1979.

Lewy, Gunter. *Religion and Revolution.* New York: 1974.

Liebich, Andre. *Between Ideology and Utopia: The Political Philosophy of August von Cieszkowski.* Dordrecht: 1979.

Liepe, Wolfgang. *Beiträge zur Literaturgeschichte und Geistesgeschichte.* Neumunster: 1964.

Livergood, Norman. *Activity in Marx's Philosophy.* The Hague: 1967.

Lovejoy, Arthur. *The Great Chain of Being.* New York: 1960.

———. "Schiller and the Genesis of German Romanticism." In Lovejoy, *Essays in the History of Ideas.* Baltimore: 1948.

Löwith, Karl. *From Hegel to Nietzsche.* New York: 1964.

———. *Jakob Burckhardt.* Lucern: 1936.

———. *Meaning in History.* Chicago: 1948.

———. *Nietzsches Philosophie der Ewigen Wiederkehr des Gleichen.* Hamburg: 1978.

Lübbe, Hermann. *Die Hegelsche Rechte.* Stuttgart: 1962.

Lukács, Georg. *Beiträge zur Geschichte der Aesthetik.* Berlin: 1954.

———. *Goethe und Seine Zeit.* Bern: 1947.

———. *History and Class Consciousness.* Cambridge, Mass.: 1971.

———. *The Theory of the Novel.* Cambridge, Mass.: 1979.

———. *The Young Hegel.* Cambridge, Mass.: 1976.

Lutz, Hans. *Schillers Anschauungen von Natur und Kultur.* Berlin: 1928.

McDonald, Joan. *Rousseau and the French Revolution.* London: 1965.

Maehl, Heinrich. *Die Idee des Goldenen Zeitalters im Werk des Novalis.* Heidelberg: 1965.

Magnus, Bernd. *Nietzsche's Existential Imperative.* Bloomington, Ind.: 1978.

Malia, Martin. *Alexander Herzen and the Birth of Russian Socialism.* New York: 1962.

Mandelbaum, Maurice. *History, Man, and Reason.* Baltimore: 1979.

Manuel, Frank and Fritzie. *Utopian Thought in the Western World.* Cambridge, Mass.: 1979.

Marcuse, Herbert. *Eros and Civilization.* New York: 1965.

Mareijko, Jan. *Jean-Jacques Rousseau et la dérive totalitaire.* Lausanne: 1984.

Megill, Allen. *Prophets of Extremism: Nietzsche, Heidegger, Foucault, Derrida.* Berkeley: 1985.

Meinecke, Friedrich. *Historism*. London: 1972.
Miller, R. D. *Schiller and the Ideal of Freedom*. Oxford: 1970.
Mornet, Daniel. *Les origines intellectuelles de la Révolution française*. Paris: 1954.
Mosse, George L. *The Crisis of German Ideology*. New York: 1964.
Mounier, Jacques. *La fortune des écrits de J. J. Rousseau dans les pays de la langue allemande*. Paris: 1980.
Müller-Lauter, Wolfgang. *Nietzsche: Seine Philosophie der Gegensätze und die Gegensätze seiner Philosophie*. Berlin: 1971.
Niemeyer, Gunter. *Between Nothingness and Paradise*. Baton Rouge: 1971.
Nisbet, Robert. *The Sociological Tradition*. New York: 1975.
Pangle, Thomas. *Montesquieu's Philosophy of Liberalism*. Chicago: 1974.
Parker, Harold. *The Cult of Antiquity and the French Revolutionaries*. Chicago: 1937.
Pascal, Roy. *The German Sturm und Drang*. Manchester: 1953.
Peperzak, Adrien. *Le jeune Hegel et la vision morale du monde*. The Hague: 1960.
Pire, Georges. "Du bon Plutarque au citoyen de Genève." *Revue de la literature comparée* 32 (1958): 510-47.
Pitkin, Hanna. "Justice: On Relating Private and Public." *Political Theory* 9 (1981): 327-52.
Pocock, J. G. A. *The Machiavellian Moment*. Princeton: 1975.
Pohlenz, Max. *Freedom in Greek Life and Thought*. Dordrecht: 1966.
Popitz, Heinrich. *Der Entfremdte Mensch*. Basel: 1953.
Popper, Karl. *The Open Society and its Enemies*. 2 Vols. New York: 1962.
Rawson, Elizabeth. *The Spartan Tradition in European Thought*. Oxford: 1969.
Regin, Doric. *Freedom and Dignity: The Historical and Political Thought of Schiller*. The Hague: 1965.
Rehm, Walter. *Griechentum und Goethezeit*. Bern: 1952.
Reill, Peter. *The German Enlightenment and the Rise of Historicism*. Berkeley: 1975.
Riedel, Manfred. "Hegels Kritik des Naturrechts." *Hegelstudien* 4 (1967): 177-204.
Rihs, Charles. *Les philosophes utopistes*. Paris: 1970.
Riley, Patrick. *Will and Political Legitimacy*. Cambridge, Mass.: 1982.
Rippere, Vicki. *Schiller and Alienation*. Berne: 1981.
Ritter, Joachim. *Hegel und die Französische Revolution*. Frankfurt: 1965.
Rosen, Zvi. *Bruno Bauer and Karl Marx*. The Hague: 1977.

Rosenkranz, Karl. *Hegels Leben*. Berlin: 1844.

Rosenzweig, Franz. *Hegel und der Staat*. 2 Vols. Berlin: 1920.

―――. *The Star of Redemption*. Boston: 1971.

Röttgers, Kurt. *Kritik und Praxis*. Berlin: 1975.

Rudé, George. *Robespierre: Portrait of a Revolutionary*. London: 1975.

Rusen, Jorn. "Die Vernunft der Kunst." *Philosophisches Jahrbuch* 2 (1973): 241-319.

Sannwald, Rolf. *Marx und die Antike*. Zurich: 1957.

Schacht, Richard. *Nietzsche*. London: 1983.

Schatz, Richard. *Rousseaus Einfluss auf Robespierre*. Leipzig: 1905.

Schmidt, Alfred. *The Concept of Nature in Marx*. London: 1971.

Schwartz, Joel. *The Sexual Politics of Jean-Jacques Rousseau*. Chicago: 1984.

Schwartz, Nancy. "The Distinction between the Private and the Public Life: Marx on the Zoon Politikon." *Political Theory*, 7 (1979): 245-66.

Seigel, Jerrold. *Marx's Fate*. Princeton: 1978.

Shackleton, Robert. *Montesquieu: A Critical Biography*. Oxford: 1961.

―――. "Montesquieu and Machiavelli: A Reappraisal." *Comparative Literature Studies* 1 (1964): 1-13.

Shell, Susan. *The Right of Reason*. Toronto: 1980.

Shklar, Judith. *Freedom and Independence*. Cambridge: 1976.

―――. *Men and Citizens: A Study of Rousseau's Social Theory*. Cambridge: 1969.

―――. "Political Theory of Utopia: From Melancholy to Nostalgia." In F. Manuel, *Utopias and Utopian Thought*. Boston: 1967.

Silverstone, M. J. "Rousseau's Plato." *Studies on Voltaire and the 18th Century*. 16 (1973): 235-49.

Stack, George. *Lange and Nietzsche*. Berlin/New York: 1983.

Starobinski, Jean. *Jean-Jacques Rousseau: La transparence et l'obstacle*. Paris: 1971.

Stern, Fritz. *The Politics of Cultural Despair*. Garden City, N.Y.: 1965.

Stern, J. P. *Ernst Junger: A Writer for our Times*. Cambridge: 1953.

―――. *A Study of Nietzsche*. Cambridge: 1979.

Sternhell, Zeev. *La droite révolutionnaire 1885–1914*. Paris: 1978.

―――. "Fascist Ideology." In W. Laquer (ed.), *Fascism: A Reader's Guide*. Berkeley: 1976.

―――. *Ni droite, ni gauche: L'idéologie fasciste en France*. Paris: 1983.

Strauss, Leo. *Natural Right and History*. Chicago: 1953.

―――. "On the Intention of Rousseau." In M. Cranston (ed.), *Hobbes and Rousseau Studies*. Garden City, N. Y.: 1972.

Strong, Tracy. *Nietzsche and the Politics of Transfiguration*. Berkeley: 1975.

Stuke, Horst. *Die Philosophie der Tat: Studien zur Verwirklichung der Philosophie*. Stuttgart: 1963.

Szondi, Peter. *Poetik und Geschichtsphilosophie I*. Frankfurt: 1974.

Talmon, Jacob L. *The Origins of Totalitarian Democracy*. New York: 1960.

———. *Political Messianism: The Romantic Phase*. New York: 1960.

Taminiaux, Jacques. *La nostalgie de la Grèce à l'aube de l'idéalisme allemand*. Louvain: 1968.

Theunissen, Michael. *Gesellschaft und Geschichte: Zur Kritik der Kritische Theorie*. Berlin: 1969.

———. *Hegels Lehre vom Absolute Geist als Theologisch-Politischer Traktat*. Berlin: 1970.

Thompson, James M. *Robespierre*. 2 Vols. Oxford: 1935.

Toews, John. *Hegelianism*. Cambridge: 1980.

Trahard, Pierre. *La sensibilité révolutionnaire*. Paris: 1936.

Troeltsch, Ernst. *Der Historismus und seine Probleme*. Tübingen: 1922.

Tucker, Robert C. *The Marxian Revolutionary Idea*. New York: 1969.

———. *Philosophy and Myth in Karl Marx*. Cambridge: 1961.

Tuveson, Ernest Lee. *Millenium and Utopia*. New York: 1964.

Vaughan, C. E. *The Political Writings of Rousseau*. 2 Vols. Oxford: 1962.

Venturi, Franco. *Utopia and Reform in the Enlightenment*. Cambridge: 1971.

Vidal-Nacquet, Pierre. "Le mirage grec et la Révolution française." *Esprit* 43 (1975): 825-39.

Voegelin, Eric. *The New Science of Politics*. Chicago: 1969.

———. *Science, Politics and Gnosticism*. Chicago: 1968.

Wartofsky, M. W. *Feuerbach*. Cambridge: 1977.

Wieland, Wolfgang. "Die Anfänge der Philosophie Schellings und die Frage nach der Natur." In M. Riedel (ed.), *Natur und Geschichte*. Stuttgart: 1967.

Wiese, Benno von. *Der Mensch in der Dichtung*. Düsseldorf: 1958.

———. *Schiller*. Stuttgart: 1959.

———. *Zwischen Ütopie und Wirklichkeit*. Düsselfdorf: 1963.

Williams, W. D. *Nietzsche and the French*. Oxford: 1952.

Willms, Bernard. "Introduction." In J. Fichte, *Schriften zur Revolution*. Edited by B. Willms. Frankfurt: 1967.

Wolfe, Bertram. *Marxism: 100 Years in the Life of a Doctrine*. New York: 1965.

Wood, Ellen M. *Mind and Politics*. Berkeley: 1972.

Yack, Bernard. "Community and Conflict in Aristotle's Political Philosophy." *Review of Politics* 47 (1985): 92-112.

————. "The Rationality of Hegel's Concept of Monarchy." *American Political Science Review* 74 (1980): 709-20.

INDEX

Abraham, 355
Adorno, Theodor, 129–130, 132
Aeschylus, 326
Agulhon, Maurice, 83 n. 52
Andler, Charles, 331
Arendt, Hannah, 62 n. 3, 71–72
Aristophanes, 337
Aristotle, 38, 44, 53, 63, 278 n. 65, 293–
   294; and Rousseau, 66–67, 68–72

Bahro, Rudolf, 288 n. 83
Bakunin, Mikhail, 233 n. 11, 239, 242–
   243, 287–288
Bauer, Bruno, 227, 239, 246, 295
Becker, Carl, 11
Beethoven, Ludwig van, 315
Bentham, Jeremy, 326
Berki, R. N., 127 n. 76, 269 n. 44,
   282 n. 70
Bernstein, Richard J., 132 n. 84
Bielinsky, V. G., 233 n. 11
Billington, James, 11, 13, 14
Blumenberg, Hans, 14 n. 18, 16,
   17 n. 27, 24 n. 38
Boucher, Michel, 149 n. 42
Brandes, Georg, 320
Bubner, Rüdiger, 130, 245–246
Burckhardt, Jacob, 336
Burgelin, Pierre, 75 n. 30
Burke, Edmund, 9 n. 8

Caesar, Julius, 349 n. 98
Cassirer, Ernst, 94
Cato the Younger, 44, 67
Charles I, 116
Cieszkowski, August von, 183, 227,
   234–238
Cohen, Gerald, 303
Cohn, Norman, 15
Comte, Auguste, 23

Constant, Benjamin, 36, 39, 50 n. 35,
   78–79, 80

Deleuze, Gilles, 311, 339, 350, 356
Democritus, 308
Descartes, René, 216
Diderot, Denis, 25
Dilthey, Wilhelm, 111
Droz, Jacques, 168 n. 85
Dunn, John, xviii

Ehrard, Jean, 21, 52 n. 41
Elias, Norbert, 93 n. 6
Elster, Jon, 297 n. 106
Engels, Frederick, 221 n. 77, 222,
   238 n. 23, 247–248
Epicurus, 308

Ferrari, Jean, 94 n. 10
Fester, Richard, 159 n. 67
Feuerbach, Ludwig, 227, 239; and the
   concept of nature, 247–250, 261, 292;
   and Hegel, 231–233, 234; and Marx,
   304–307
Fichte, Johann Gottlieb, 28, 90, 98, 100,
   101, 102, 108, 118, 148, 188, 190,
   302; on the Revolution, 109, 114, 117
Fink, Zera, 38 n. 4
Fleuret, Colette, 50 n. 37
Frederick the Great, 116
Freier, Hans, 121
Freud, Sigmund, 346
Furet, François, 112
Fustel de Coulanges, N. D., 79–80

Gay, Peter, 16
Gentz, Friedrich, 9 n. 8
Gibbon, Edward, 46
Gide, André, 361, 362
Gluck, Christoph, 315

Goethe, Johann Wolfgang von, 137, 168, 174, 315; on Rousseau, 90, 92
Gordon, Fred, 250 n. 49
Gouldner, Alvin, 290
Graham, Ilse, 137 n. 12
Griewank, Karl, 9 n. 8, 82 n. 43
Guerci, Luciano, 76 n. 32

Habermas, Jürgen, 130, 131
Hamilton, Alisdair, 361 n. 141
Haydn, Franz Joseph, 315
Hegel, G.W.F., xii, 8, 9, 19, 25, 29, 80, 90, 101, 112, 120, 129, 181, 183, 185–223, 243, 292, 296, 302, 312, 367, 368; and the ancients, 36, 120, 181, 189, 196–197, 200–209, 215, 336, 337; and Cieszkowski, 234–238; and Feuerbach, 227, 231–233, 247–250; and Kant, 97, 100–102, 108, 109, 114, 118, 120, 185–186, 188, 190–195, 198, 212–213, 216, 230, 234, 235; and the "Kantian left," 29, 102, 107, 118, 189–198, 209–210, 216, 219–220, 223, 234; and the left Hegelians, 221–223, 227–250; and Marx, 124, 220–223, 240, 250, 255–256, 259–260, 265–268, 277, 280, 284, 291, 292, 295–296, 302–304, 308; and Montesquieu, 23, 202, 205 n. 46; and Nietzsche, 124, 311, 314, 324, 326, 327, 328–329, 335–341, 355–356, 360; and Rousseau, 90, 97, 120–122, 197; and Schiller, 29, 133–134, 187, 190–191, 193–198, 201, 203, 207, 209, 215, 216, 335
Heidegger, Martin, 8
Heine, Heinrich, 108, 110–111, 114
Heller, Peter, 353 n. 113
Henrich, Dieter, 213, 254
Herder, Johann Gottfried, 22, 91–92, 93, 119 n. 63, 137
Herzen, Alexander, 235, 241–242
Hess, Moses, 182, 227, 235, 239, 242, 243–244, 283
Hillebrand, Karl, 339–340
Hirschman, Albert, 45
Hobbes, Thomas, 36
Hölderlin, Friedrich, 74–75, 85, 90, 93, 100, 108, 109, 118 n. 58, 121, 194, 199, 268, 316

Holmes, Stephen, 79 n. 37
Horkheimer, Max, 129–130, 132
Hugo, Gustav, 256
Hulliung, Mark, 42 n. 15
Humboldt, Wilhelm von, 23, 168, 174, 175–176
Hunt, Lynn, 84 n. 52

Isaac, 355

Jacobi, Friedrich Heinrich, 93
Jesus, 118, 192, 201, 349
Joachim of Fiore, 183
Julian the Apostate, 46

Kant, Immanuel, 5, 28, 30, 89–123, 127, 128, 181, 216, 243, 310, 324; and Hegel, 97, 100–102, 108, 109, 114, 118, 120, 185–186, 188, 190–195, 198, 212–213, 216, 230, 234, 235; and the "Kantian left," 28, 102–123, 230, 242; and Marx, 255–257, 292; and Nietzsche, 311, 317, 322, 327, 334, 348, 355–356; and Rousseau, 20–22, 24, 53 n. 44, 89–98, 120; and Schiller, 28, 98, 101–103, 108, 109, 114, 117, 120, 134–135, 137, 144–147, 151, 156, 159, 162–166, 180, 184, 235, 250
Kaufmann, Walter, 349 n. 98
Kelly, George, 74, 183 n. 123
Kierkegaard, Søren, 354–355
Klopstock, F. G., 148, 149
Kolakowski, Leszek, 17 n. 26, 271–272, 282 n. 70, 295
Körner, Gottfried, 147, 174–175
Koselleck, Reinhart, 82 n. 42
Kroner, Richard, 101 n. 25, 118 n. 58, 133 n. 1
Kurz, Gerhard, 113 n. 46

Lange, Friedrich Albert, 323
Lasky, Melvin, 15 n. 19
Leibniz, G. W., 327
Lenin, V. I., 286
Lessing, G. E., 183–184
Levin, L. M., 41 n. 8
Liepe, Wolfgang, 136 n. 9
Livy, Titus, 78
Louis XIV, 40

Louis XVI, 116
Lovejoy, Arthur, 110 n. 39, 189 n. 6
Löwith, Karl, 17, 183 n. 123, 247 n. 40,
    252, 282 n. 70, 354
Lukács, Georg, 168 n. 86, 288–289,
    302, 307 n. 126
Luther, Martin, 118, 199
Lutz, Hans, 169–170

Mably, Bonnet de, 40
Machiavelli, Niccolò, 35, 36, 44–45, 46
Magnus, Bernd, 352 n. 111, 353,
    354 n. 118
Mandelbaum, Maurice, 22 n. 33
Mann, Thomas, 181–182
Marcuse, Herbert, 8
Marcus Favonius, 67
Marx, Karl, xviii, 3, 6, 8, 9, 10, 19, 22,
    23, 25, 26–27, 29–31, 80, 126, 127,
    128, 129, 131, 181, 182, 187, 188,
    196, 227, 230, 234, 251–309, 310,
    311, 314, 356, 366, 367, 368; and
    Bakunin, 287–288; and Feuerbach,
    261, 292, 304–307; and Hegel, 124,
    220–223, 240, 250, 255–256, 259–
    260, 265–267, 277, 280, 284, 291,
    292, 296, 302–304, 308; and Hess,
    239, 243, 244; and Kant, 255–257,
    292; and Left Hegelianism, 30, 227, 229,
    238 nn. 22, 23, 239, 242–244, 252–
    254, 259, 261–266, 270, 271, 279,
    280, 282–284, 286, 295–296, 308–
    309; and Nietzsche, 124, 312, 314,
    321, 326, 343, 344; and Schiller, 29,
    133, 158–159, 260, 262–263, 282–283
Megill, Allen, 313–314
Meinecke, Friedrich, 73
Meslier, Jean, 15
Montaigne, Michel de, 35, 37, 50
Montesquieu, C. S. de, 23, 35–60, 73,
    77, 84, 202, 205 n. 46; Considera-
    tions, 39, 46–48, 49, 51; and Machia-
    velli, 44–45, 46; and Rousseau, 23,
    28, 35–46, 49–52, 54–60, 73–74, 122;
    Spirit of the Laws, 39–48, 49, 51
More, Thomas, 76
Mozart, Wolfgang Amadeus, 315, 363
Müller-Lauter, Wolfgang, 343 n. 80,
    351, 352, 353

Napoleon, 349
Nicholas I, 233 n. 11
Niemeyer, Gunter, 15 n. 21
Nietzsche, Friedrich, xviii, 3, 6, 8, 19, 22,
    25, 26–27, 29–31, 80, 109, 126, 127,
    181, 182, 187, 188, 200, 208 n. 54,
    310–364, 366, 367, 368; and the an-
    cients, 36, 323–324, 326, 328–329,
    332–334, 336–337, 360; and Hegel,
    124, 250, 311, 314, 324, 326, 327,
    328–329, 335–341, 355–356, 360; and
    Kant, 311, 317, 322, 327, 334, 348,
    355–356; and Marx, 124, 312, 314,
    321, 326, 343, 344; and Rousseau,
    27 n. 42, 311 n. 4, 317, 321, 322,
    347–348, 360; and Schiller, 29, 133,
    312, 317, 324, 328–329, 331–336,
    340–341, 342, 357; and Schopen-
    hauer, 319, 323, 324, 327, 331, 334,
    336, 340, 342
Nisbet, Robert, 12 n. 12
Novalis, 182–183

Ossian, 200

Peperzak, Adrien, 194 n. 21
Pitkin, Hanna, 72 n. 22
Plato, 53; and Hegel, 217–218; and
    Rousseau, 63–66, 70, 76
Plutarch, 44, 51, 56, 63, 67, 76, 77, 134,
    136
Pocock, J.G.A., xviii, 37
Polybius, 38

Ranke, Leopold von, 23
Raphael, 363
Regin, D., 158 n. 65
Reinhold, K. L., 101
Riedel, Manfred, 205
Rihs, Charles, 15
Rippere, Vicky, 158
Robespierre, Maximilien, 4, 83–85, 108
Rosenkranz, Karl, 230 n. 7
Rousseau, Jean-Jacques, xviii, 3, 8, 12,
    19, 25, 26, 27–28, 35–60, 61–85, 89,
    120, 139, 239, 298, 312, 366; and
    Aristotle, 68–70; and Hegel, 90, 97,
    120–122, 197; and Kant, 20–22, 24,
    53 n. 44, 89–98, 120; and the "Kant-
    ian left," 28, 104, 107; and Marx, 70;

Rousseau, Jean-Jacques (*cont.*)
and Montesquieu, 23, 28, 35–46, 49–52, 54–60, 73–74, 77; and Nietzsche, 27 n. 42, 311 n. 4, 317, 321, 322, 347–348, 360; and Plato, 63–66, 70; and Schiller, 90, 93, 98, 120–122, 136–137, 142–143, 144, 154, 161–163, 179; and Sparta, 38, 40, 49, 57, 59–60, 66–67, 74, 76–79, 197
Ruge, Arnold, 220, 227, 239, 242, 246, 262, 263; and Schiller, 240–241

St. Simon, Claude Henri de, 23
Schelling, Friedrich, 9, 28, 101, 108–109, 111–112, 121, 190, 194, 199, 201, 205, 240, 268; on the realization of autonomy, 103–104, 185, 257, 261
Schiller, Friedrich, xii, 8, 9, 10, 19, 28–29, 85, 89, 90, 102, 107–108, 113–114, 120, 122, 123, 124–125, 129, 133–184, 228, 237–238, 241–242, 244, 315, 323, 367; and the ancients, 120–122, 144, 157–160, 178–183, 196–197, 201, 203, 207, 209, 332–333; *Don Carlos*, 137, 138–143, 150, 176; and the French Revolution, 123, 147–154, 283; and Hegel, 29, 133–134, 187, 190–191, 193–198, 201, 203, 207, 209, 215, 216; and Humboldt, 168, 174, 175–176; and Kant, 28, 98, 101, 102–103, 108, 109, 114, 117, 120, 134–135, 137, 144, 145–147, 151, 156, 159, 162–163, 164–165, 166, 180, 184, 235, 250; *Letters on the Aesthetic Education of Man*, 135, 144–177; and Marx, 29, 133, 158–159, 260, 262–263, 282–283; and Nietzsche, 29, 133, 312, 317, 324, 328–329, 331–336, 340–341, 342, 357; *On Naive and Sentimental Poetry*, 177–181; and Rousseau, 90, 93, 98, 120–122, 136–137, 142–143, 144, 154, 161–163, 179
Schlegel, Friedrich, 182 n. 120, 199, 200
Schmidt, Alfred, 294
Schopenhauer, Arthur, 319, 323, 324, 327, 331, 334, 336, 340, 342

Schwartz, Nancy, 294 n. 95
Shakespeare, William, 67 n. 14, 326
Shell, Susan, 96 n. 15
Shklar, Judith, 55 n. 49, 73 n. 23, 76
Silverstone, M. J., 64 n. 5
Skinner, Quentin, xviii, xx
Snell, Reginald, 169 n. 87
Socrates, 207, 208, 330, 334, 336–337, 342, 349 n. 98, 361, 362
Sophocles, 206
Spengler, Otto, 343, 344 n. 81
Stalin, Josef, 288 n. 83
Starobinski, Jean, 57 n. 55, 75 n. 29
Stattler, Benedict, 109 n. 36
Sternhell, Zeev, 5 n. 3
Stirner, Max, 238 n. 23
Storr, G. C., 103
Strauss, D. F., 228, 314–316, 320, 336
Strauss, Leo, 44 n. 19, 57 n. 57
Strong, Tracy, 314 n. 9, 352 n. 111
Stuke, Horst, 220 n. 76, 227 n. 1
Sturz, H. P., 93, 136
Szondi, Peter, 99 n. 21

Talmon, Jacob, xviii–xix, 4 n. 1, 13–14
Themistocles, 270
Theunissen, Michael, 303 n. 118, 304
Thucydides, 66, 67
Tocqueville, Alexis de, 12 n. 13
Toews, John, 228 n. 3, 229, 234 n. 13
Tucker, Robert C., 282 n. 70
Tuveson, Ernest Lee, 15 n. 19

Vaughan, C. E., 62 n. 2
Venturi, Franco, 41 n. 8
Vischer, F. T., 316, 336
Voegelin, Eric, 17 n. 26
Volney, C. F. de, 12, 13, 77–78, 79–80, 91
Voltaire, François Marie, 25, 83

Wagner, Richard, 330, 342
Willoughby, L. A. and Wilkinson, E. M., 169–170, 174 n. 100
Winckelmann, Johann Joachim, 122, 159
Wood, Ellen M., 71 n. 21